Scheduled Castes in the Indian Labour Market

Scheduled Castes in the Indian Labour Market

Employment Discrimination and its Impact on Poverty

SUKHADEO THORAT, S. MADHESWARAN, AND
B. P. VANI

Great Clarendon Street, Oxford, OX2 6DP,
United Kingdom

Oxford University Press is a department of the University of Oxford.
It furthers the University's objective of excellence in research, scholarship,
and education by publishing worldwide. Oxford is a registered trade mark of
Oxford University Press in the UK and in certain other countries

© Sukhadeo Thorat, S. Madheswaran, and B. P. Vani 2023

The moral rights of the authors have been asserted

First Edition published in 2023

Published in the United States of America by Oxford University Press
198 Madison Avenue, New York, NY 10016, United States of America

British Library Cataloguing in Publication Data

Data available

Library of Congress Control Number: 2023931691

ISBN 978–0–19–887225–2

DOI: 10.1093/oso/9780198872252.001.0001

Manu Is Not a Matter of the Past

It might be argued that the inequality prescribed by Manu in his *Smriti* is after all of historical importance. It is past history and cannot be supposed to have any bearing on the present conduct of the Hindu. I am sure nothing can be greater error than this. Manu is not a matter of the past. It is even more than a past of the present. It is a 'living past' and therefore as really present as any present can be.

Dr. B. R. Ambedkar, 1993
Writings and Speeches. Vol. 12

Contents

Foreword

The persistence of inequality across social groups is a global phenomenon, respecting no national boundaries. One of the most enduring and pernicious types of intergroup inequality is caste disparity in India. In this book, the authors provide a landscape view of the contemporary manifestations of inequality, particularly with respect to access to employment and exposure to poverty. For those who want to pretend that caste discrimination is merely an anachronism associated with an earlier India, this volume is a powerful antidote.

This study demonstrates just how extensive and persistent the caste system remains, despite nearly eight decades of Indian affirmative action on behalf of the scheduled castes (or untouchables) at the national level. While the reservation policy has been effective in gaining the scheduled castes access to employment in jobs from which they long had been excluded, the impact has been constrained by its limited application to employment in the civil service or public sector. There is no substantive reservation policy for private sector employment.

Affirmative action's reach in the provision of dalit access to higher education admissions and faculty appointments frequently has been circumvented at the most selective Indian universities. Furthermore, the Indian judicial system has designed a so-called super-speciality category of university programs of study entirely removed from the affirmative action mandate.

The consequence is large and sustained discriminatory deficits in wages and earnings for the scheduled castes. As Thorat, Madheswaran, and Vani show with rigour and detail in the pages of this study, after controlling for the standard array of productivity-linked characteristics, untouchable workers still incurred wage penalties on the order of 20.9 per cent in the public sector in 2017–2018, albeit a decline from the 27.1 per cent penalty they estimate for 2004–2005. Even more striking is the rise in the wage penalty faced by dalits over the 13-year interval from 31.5 per cent to nearly 50 per cent in private sector employment. The rise in the

private sector differential puts a forceful lie to the conventional expectation held by economists that competitive conditions invariably erode
discrimination.

Another claim that emerges from the economists' routine playbook is
the argument that discrimination constitutes a deadweight loss; in principle, the argument goes everyone would be better off if discriminatory
practices somehow evaporated overnight. This position ignores the fact
that when one group suffers from discrimination another benefits—and
may benefit substantially. Thorat, Madheswaran, and Vani estimate the
nepotistic advantage of higher caste status was approximately 35 per cent
in 2004–2005 but increased to about 45 per cent by 2017–2018.

If discrimination only resulted in losses for the marginalized group,
without significant gains for the dominant group, presumably it would
be easy to bring to an end. Otherwise, the dominant group, apparently,
is irrational in maintaining a regime of unfair labour market practices.
However, the evidence in this study shows the large discriminatory wage
penalties confronting the untouchables are matched, at least, by the large
nepotistic wage bonuses received by higher-caste Hindus. Insofar as the
latter are a numerical majority in a country utilizing electoral politics to
arrive at collective decisions, prospects weaken for design and implemen-
tation of major initiatives to eradicate discrimination.

A companion claim often accompanying the deadweight loss view
of the effects of discrimination is the argument that racism or casteism
lowers economic growth.[1] Nonetheless, the presence of a segment of a
population subjected to oppression has not proven inimical to economic
growth. Slavery in the United States arguably was an engine of growth via
the exploitation of enslaved labour in the cotton sector.[2]

Furthermore, even when the oppressed segment of the population
holds a numerical majority, high macroeconomic performance has occurred, perhaps, in part, because of their abuse. For example, apartheid
South Africa achieved the highest levels of per capita income of all the

---

[1] See, e.g., Thomas Piketty, 'How Inequalities in Income and Caste are Holding the Indian
Economy Back', *The Wire*, 22 January 2016 https://thewire.in/economy/how-inequalities-of-inc
ome-and-caste-are-holding-the-indi
[2] Mark Stelzner and Sven Beckert, 'The Contribution of Enslaved Workers to Output and
Growth in the Antebellum United States', Washington Center for Equitable Growth Working
Paper 062421, 2021.

countries across the African continent, a result accomplished by the exploitation of black labour in the mining sector.[3]

Moreover, prior to the pandemic, over the course of the past 30 years, India has experienced rapid economic growth and urban modernization with an ancient structure of caste disparity still in place. Indeed, while real GDP growth was negative during the period of COVID-19 onset, it was back at a roaring 8.8 per cent during fiscal years 2021–2022. In Chapter 5 of this book, the authors argue that one of the factors contributing to India's rapid growth in recent years actually has been repression of wages for the scheduled castes by their forced 'unfavourable inclusion' in employment requiring hard labour and exposure to dangers to health and well-being.

Of course, it is possible, in the absence of the caste system, India's economic growth rate may have been even higher. However, would the hypothetical higher rate of growth more than offset the reduction in nepotistic wages and incomes accruing to the higher castes under the current discriminatory regime?

Caste discrimination, like discrimination in virtually all instances, is a mechanism for redistribution of resources from a subjugated group to a group exercising social dominance.[4] It is crucial to acknowledge this condition. Otherwise, we are left with an unrealistic vision of the obstacles to making a more just and equitable society. The present study compels us to adopt an accurate picture of the impact of caste discrimination in India and its attendant political consequences. This is the definitive study of caste inequality and employment discrimination in India. It is essential reading for anyone concerned about the continuing, devastating economic ramifications of the caste system.

William Darity Jr.
Duke University
Durham, North Carolina

---

[3] Francis Wilson, 'Minerals and Migrants: How the Mining Industry Has Shaped South Africa', *Daedalus*, 130(1) Winter 2001, 99–121.

[4] On the distributional consequences of the caste system, see Charlie Yang, 'Caste and the Indian Economy', *Harvard Economic Review*, August 17, 2020. Yang argues that the structure of the caste system explains 'India's confusing dichotomy of macroeconomic progress and stagnant microeconomic growth.' https://www.economicsreview.org/post/caste-and-the-indian-economy Also see David Mosse, 'Caste and Development: Contemporary Perspectives on a Structure of Discrimination and Adantage', *World Development*, 110, 2018, 422–436.

Preface and Acknowledgements

This book develops an insight into the discriminatory workings of the labour market and its unequal outcomes with respect to employment, wages, and occupations and its impact on the poverty of untouchable wage workers in India. It fosters an understanding of the troubling issue of persistent caste inequality in employment, wages, and occupations between the untouchables and the higher castes in the private and public sectors in India. In the process it identifies the causes of high unemployment and low wages of the untouchable workers and their segregation in low-paid occupations—the economic activities in which they have been traditionally forced to engage in for a long time. It then goes on to estimate the extent to which caste discrimination results in low employment and wages and to which it pushes the untouchable workers into low-paid occupations. It reveals how ancient India is still with us, insofar as we continue to live in the past—the economic behaviour of the higher castes towards the untouchables assumed discriminatory forms in the labour market, despite legal safeguards against economic discrimination and affirmative action policies in the labour market. In the end, it provides convincing empirical evidence on the employment discrimination and wage discrimination and its impact on reduced wage incomes and increased poverty of the untouchable wage workers by a substantial margin. In light of these results, the book suggests policies to provide safeguards against discrimination in employment, wages, and occupations, and also to overcome the effects of discrimination faced by the untouchables in the past. It proposes a reparation policy for redistributive justice, to correct the impact of the denial of rights to own property and to education, and the underpayment for untouchable slave labour in the past. It also proposes appropriate legal safeguards against continuing discrimination in the labour market in the present and also an affirmative action policy for them to get a fair share in employment in the private and public sectors.

We owe gratitude to those who made this book possible. This study was sponsored by Rosa Luxemburg Stiftung (RLS) (www.rosalux.in),

South Asia, New Delhi. It would not have been possible without the generous financial support of RLS. Supporting research on labour issues is one of the prime objectives of RLS. We express our gratitude to the Country Director, Mr. Stefan Mentschel, who extended support to the project from the very beginning. We also thank Mr. Tauqueer Ali Sabri of RLS who extended his cooperation in the course of the work. Initially, the study was based on the employment survey, 2011–12 and by the time the first draft was ready, the employment survey for 2017–18 was out in the public domain. Therefore, we had to redo the whole exercise. It was nice of Mr. Tauqueer Ali Sabri to understand the importance of updating the study and to duly extend his support. The content of the publication is the sole responsibility of the authors and does not necessarily reflect a position of RLS.

We also thank Dr. Vinod Kumar Mishra, who handles administrative issues in the Indian Institute of Dalit Studies on a regular basis and makes the work easy. Our thanks go to the Director of the Indian Institute of Dalit Studies, Dr. Govind C. Pal, for his cooperation. We also thank the assistance provided by the Institute of Social and Economic Change, Bengaluru, where part of the work was done.

The faculties of the Indian Institute of Dalit Studies, Dr. Khalid Khan, Dr. Rajesh Raushan, and Dr. Nitin Tagade also helped whenever their support was required. We also take this opportunity to express our sincere thanks to Dr. Smriti Rekha Singhari, Postdoctoral Fellow at IGIDR, Mumbai; and Dr. Jajati Keshari Parida, Assistant Professor, Central University of Punjab, Bathinda for their technical help in analysing the data.

We thank Professor William A. Darity Jr. for writing the Foreword to the book.

Finally, we thank Oxford University Press, New Delhi for publishing the book with care and on time.

Tables and Illustrations

Tables

Illustrations

Appendix Tables

1

Caste and Unequal Labour Market Outcomes

1.1 Caste and Untouchables' Poverty

It has been 70 years since the discriminatory practice of untouchability was put to an end in India with the enforcement of the Constitution in 1950.[1] However, legal safeguards notwithstanding, the age-old practice continues to rip through the country's social fabric as subtle forms of discrimination in labour market and caste inequality continue to keep the former untouchables (Scheduled Castes) a deprived lot. Despite perceptible progress made by the Scheduled Castes (the official term for the erstwhile untouchables), their class as a whole lags behind the higher castes in all parameters of human development and suffers unacceptable high levels of poverty and deprivation.

The Scheduled Castes (SC) share in the total population of the country is about 16.6 per cent, according to the 2011 census. In 2011–12, the per capita consumption expenditure was ₹2,413 for the higher castes, ₹1,531 for the Other Backward Classes (OBC) and only ₹1,294 for the SC, which is almost half that of the higher castes. Due to low consumption expenditure, the incidence of poverty among the SC at 30 per cent is three-and-half times higher than that of the higher castes, whereas it is 20 per cent for the OBC. The low consumption expenditure also results in high malnutrition and poor health among the SC which is reflected in health indicators, such as high mortality rates and anaemia, among their children and adult population in 2015–16. The average age of death for the SC is 53 years, which is six years less, compared to 59 years for the higher castes and four years less than the national average of 57 years. The mortality

---

[1] Throughout the book, untouchables and Scheduled Castes are used interchangeably.

Scheduled Castes in the Indian Labour Market. Sukhadeo Thorat, S. Madheswaran, and B. P. Vani, Oxford University Press. © Sukhadeo Thorat, S. Madheswaran, and B. P. Vani 2023. DOI: 10.1093/oso/9780198872252.003.0001

rate for the SC children, below five years age, is 60 per thousand population as compared to 37 per thousand population for the higher castes' children and even more than the all-India average of 53 per thousand population. A similar gap persists in the incidence of anaemia among the SC (61 per cent) and higher castes (54 per cent) population. All this shows that SC continue to suffer a high degree of deprivation, both in absolute and relative terms, in comparison with the higher castes.

Researchers who have enquired into the causes of persisting high poverty among the SC have offered various alternative explanations. One line of argument is that the high deprivation of the SC is caused by low access to capital (assets) and education endowments. For instance, in 2013 the share of the SC in the country's wealth was only 7 per cent, much below their population share of 16.6 per cent, while the wealth share of the higher castes was 45 per cent, more than twice their population share of 21 per cent. The average value of wealth across social groups at the all-India level was ₹15 lakh, while it was ₹29 lakh for the higher castes and ₹6 lakh for the SC[2] (AIDIS 2013). The average value of wealth of the SC is almost one-sixth that of the higher castes. In the case of education too, the attainment rate of higher education among the SC is 19 per cent as compared to 38 per cent for the higher castes.

Among other reasons, the persisting discrimination of the centuries-old caste system, which denied them equal access and opportunity to education and capital assets, is presumably the cause for low education, ownership of capital assets, and employment among the SC. The denial of right to property, education, and employment (other than manual wage workers) continues in a significant degree even today through discrimination in the markets and on the market institutions. The past does not remain in the past, but comes alive in the present. The present, in fact, is the living past. The discrimination of the SC, which they faced for a long time in the past and its persistence in modified forms in the present, in access to capital assets, employment and wages in the market remains an important reason for their low income and high poverty. This particularly affects the wage workers who (due to low ownership of capital assets) constitute unusually high proportions among the SC, about 60 per cent of the wage workers. In the labour market, the SC wage workers face

---

[2] All India Debt and Investment Survey, NSS 70th Round, 2013, NSSO, Government of India.

discrimination in occupation, wage employment, and wages with unequal outcomes. Discrimination results in high unemployment and low income among the SC wage workers. The unemployment rate among the SC in 2017–18 was 10.3 per cent as compared to 8.3 per cent for the higher castes and an all-India average of 8.7 per cent. The wages of the SC wage workers are generally low when compared with the higher castes. Besides, the SC wage workers tend to get segregated in low-paid occupations. Thus, high unemployment, low wages, and concentration in low-paid occupations aggravate the poverty of the SC casual wage workers. In 2010–11, about 33.3 per cent non-farm and 42.2 per cent farm rural SC casual wage workers were poor. In urban areas, this rate was 37 per cent for urban casual wage workers. In comparison, poverty was low among the SC regular salaried workers (13.2 per cent in rural and 11.3 per cent in urban areas), although it was high as compared to the regular salaried workers belonging to the higher castes (7.2 per cent in rural and 3.3 per cent in urban areas).

Studies provide empirical evidence on the discrimination faced by the SC labourers in employment and wages. However, some aspects of the labour market discrimination have been studied more than the others. While there is considerable evidence on wage discrimination of the SC regular salaried workers, discrimination in employment and occupation is largely ignored. Still less explored is the estimate of the impact of employment, wage and occupation discrimination on the income and poverty of the SC. Therefore, our knowledge about employment discrimination and its impact on income and poverty of the discriminated groups is limited. Similarly, we have much less idea about the combined impact of discrimination in employment, wages, and occupation on the wage income and poverty or the employment-wages-occupation discrimination as cause of high poverty among the SC wage workers.

Since the principal source of earning of the SC workers continues to be wage work—casual and regular salaried—their earnings depend on how fairly they are treated in the labour market while hiring and awarding wages, including the assignment of occupation. As mentioned earlier, between the casual wage workers and regular salaried workers, the incidence of poverty is much less among regular salaried workers (both SC and higher castes). This indicates the importance of regular salaried work which has both job and social securities for the workers' well-being. Given very high dependence of the SC on the wage labour, regular salaried employment is their ultimate dream for economic mobility. However, their participation in the labour market as regular salaried workers is constrained by discrimination with respect to hiring, wages, and occupation, particularly in the private sector. Therefore, for a better labour market outcome, it is necessary that the SC have non-discriminatory access to regular salaried employment, wage earning, and occupation.

The present study, therefore, focuses on the labour market outcomes for the SC regular salaried workers in the Indian labour market. The SC look forward to a secure regular salaried employment as the main avenue of their poverty reduction and improved well-being. In 2017–18, about 20 per cent of the SC workers had regular salaried employment. The study estimates the income and poverty of these SC regular salaried workers. It tries to capture the link between poverty of regular salaried workers and their employment, wages, and occupation. Thereafter, the study assesses the impact of discrimination in employment, wages, and occupation on the income and poverty of the SC regular salaried workers in 2004–05 and 2017–18 in India. Thus, the study enquires into the linkages of unequal labour market outcome and high poverty among the SC; and in that specifically the role of employment, wage, and occupation discrimination; in the working of labour market for the regular salaried workers. At the centre of the enquiry remains the following questions.

- Are there differences in employment rate, wage rates, and occupation between the SC and the higher castes?
- What is the extent of differences in employment, wages, and occupation between the SC and the higher castes due to differences in endowment factors, such as education and skills?
- What is the extent of inequality in income and poverty between the SC and the higher castes' workers due to discrimination in employment, wages, and occupation?
- How much do the wage income of the SC reduced and the poverty aggravated due to discrimination in employment, wages, and occupation?
- What policies are needed to reduce employment, wages, and occupation discrimination?

These are some of the issues related to caste inequality which have been less explored. Therefore, there is obvious justification for this study. However, before the justification for the study is laid down, we clear the ground by bringing insights into the economic dimensions of the caste system in some detail to explain how discrimination in employment, wages, and occupation is an integral part of caste-economic relations. We also review some earlier studies on this subject, identify the issues for further analysis and lay down the specific objectives of the study.

1.2 Economics of Caste System and Discrimination

The issue of caste-based labour market discrimination needs to be understood from the perspective of the traditional caste system that regulates the higher castes' collective economic behaviour towards the SC in the Indian society, particularly the Hindu society. The answers to some pertinent questions would indeed provide an insight into the issue. What are the economic features of the caste system? How is the labour market discrimination embedded in the economic regulator scheme of the caste system? What are the consequences of caste-based labour market discrimination on employment, occupation, and wages on the SC who face discrimination?

The caste system is the social organization of the Hindu society which regulated the economic and social life of the people in the past (and continues to influence in several covert and overt ways in the present). It laid down normative and legal framework to regulate the economic and social relations in the Hindu society. There are some unique features of the caste system which made it a very distinct economic organization. The system is supposed to be of divine origin and, therefore, a religious and sacred institution. The divine power had also laid down the norms or laws related to economic rights and occupations of each caste in *Manusmriti*,[3] the credit for which goes to the legendary lawgiver Manu. It is supposed to have been written in about 200 BCE. Making the caste system a legal and penal institution in *Manusmriti*, Manu cited the *Purusha Sukta* of *Rig*

---

[3] Manu is not a matter of the past. It is even more than a past of the present. It is a 'living past' and therefore as really present as any present can be (Ambedkar 1993: 719).

Veda to accord divine sanction to it. The constitution of the society pre-scribed by *Purusha Sukta* is known as *chaturvarna*.

> But for the sake of prosperity of the worlds, He (divine power) caused the Brahmins, the Kshatriyas, the Vaishyas, and the Shudras to proceed from His mouth, His arms, His thighs, and His feet.

Quoting the *Rig Veda*, Manu further said:

> Now for the sake of preserving all this creation, the most glorious (being) ordained separate duties for those who sprang from (His) mouth, arms, thigh and feet.
>
> For the Brahmins He ordered teaching, study, sacrifices, and sacri-fices (as priest) for others, also giving and receiving gifts.
>
> Defence of the people, giving (alms), sacrifices and sacrifice, study and absence of attachment to objects of sense, in short for Kshatriyas.
>
> Tending of cattle, giving (alms), sacrifice, study, trade, usury, and also agriculture for Vaishyas.
>
> One duty the Lord assigned to Shudras—service to those (before mentioned) classes without grudging.
>
> (Bühler 1886: 14: 24–25)

Manu also delineated the occupation of each caste and imposed restric-tions and punitive measures for those who transgressed. The occupa-tions bestowed rights and privileges to various castes in a hierarchical or graded order that placed *brahmins* at the top, followed by *kshatriyas*, *vaishyas*, and *shudras*. Manu ordained:

> (Passing) from the Brahmin to the Kshatriya, three acts (incumbent on the former) are forbidden, (viz.) teaching, sacrificing for others.
>
> (Bühler 1886: 419–436)

These restrictions also applied to vaishyas and shudras. Thus, citing the *Purusha Sukta* of the *Rig Veda*, Manu's law endorses the notion of div-ision of occupation (that is right to property and livelihood) and con-verts the scheme of division of work into a scheme of division of workers into fixed and permanent occupational categories (Ambedkar 1987: 31). In other words, the fixing of occupation also means fixing of property rights in agricultural lands, enterprises/businesses, and workers or employees as teachers, military persons, and casual manual wage labour. Caste mobility was restricted as occupational status was hereditary and fixed at birth. Thus, among the occupations the most commendable one is teaching of the Vedas (earmarked for the brahmins), followed by protection of people (for the kshatriyas), trade including agriculture (for the vaishyas), and the most despised was the service of the other three castes, assigned to the shudras. However, Manu made a provision for relaxation of rules related to occupation in situations of distress. It is necessary to understand this point because some of those relaxations subsequently became a regular feature of the caste system. Manu ordained:

But the Brahmin, unable to subsist by his peculiar occupation, may live according to the law applicable to Kshatriya.

If he (Brahmin) cannot maintain by himself, either, he may adopt a Vaishya mode of life, employing himself in agriculture and rearing cattle.

(But brahmin is also allowed to engage in trade with the exception of some commodities.)

A Kshatriya who has fallen in distress may subsist by the mode of life of a Vaishya, but not that of a Brahmin.

A Vaishya, who is unable to subsist by his own duties, may even maintain himself by the Shudra mode of life.

But Shudra, being unable to find service with the twice-born[4], may maintain himself by handicrafts. Let Shudra follow those mechanical occupations and those various practical arts by following which the twice-born are best served.

If Shudra (unable to subsist by serving Brahmins) seeks livelihood, he may serve Kshatriya, or by attending to a wealthy Vaishya.

But let the Shudra serve the Brahmin, for he who is called the servant of Brahmins, thereby get all the ends.

The service of the Brahmins alone is declared an excellent occupation for Shudra, for whatever else beside he may perform will bear him no fruits.

(Bühler 1886: 420–429)

---

[4] Twice-born or *dvija* refers to the Hindu concept wherein a boy is considered born again (second time) on his initiation to the spiritual path after being invested with the sacred thread. The three higher castes that are entitled to thread ceremony are referred to as twice-born.

Thus, a shudra's means of livelihood is derived from his services of the twice-born, three castes above them, as a labourer. Therefore, the shudras were saddled with numerous and varied 'disabilities'. These included obligatory service to the upper castes and physical work as agricultural labourers, artisans, serfs, and even as slaves. They were excluded from the study of the Vedas, that is education, faced inequality before law in matters related to inheritance and criminal offences, lack of access to judicial and high administrative positions, and restrictions on commensality, association, and marriages with superior *varnas* or groups.

1.3   Emergence of Untouchables as the Fifth Caste

The untouchables constituted the fifth caste in the hierarchy of the caste system. As we have seen, all Hindu lawgivers, including Manu, recognized only four castes and there seems to be no mention of the untouchables. This is because, apart from the aforementioned castes, there is reference to another class of people who were not integrated into the caste system based on four varnas. However, *Manusmriti* and other works do recognize the presence of 'outcastes', a social group, outside the fourfold division. For instance, Manu said, 'All those tribes in this world, which are excluded from (the community of) those born from the mouth, the arm, the thighs, and the feet are called *Dasyus*, whether they speak languages of Mlekkas (barbarians) or that of Aryan' (Bühler 1886: 24).

Often, an overlap is seen between the shudra and *ati-shudra* or untouchables in Hindu literature. Therefore, there is a need to bring forth clarity on the status of untouchables. As in our analysis of labour market discrimination, we focus on the inequality in labour market outcomes between the erstwhile untouchables and the higher castes. The question is: While the untouchables are clearly embedded in the caste system as fifth castes, how and when did the untouchables become integrated into the caste system as the fifth caste? Opinions differ on this complex issue. There is a general agreement on two points, namely, the sources or reasons for the emergence of untouchables as the fifth caste, and their social and economic status, even though differences persist on the period of their origin and their inclusion as the fifth caste, below the *Shudras*.[5] There is consensus that the brahmanical idea of 'impurity and pollution' is the initial cause of untouchability (Ambedkar 1948; Jha 1987, 1997, and 2018; Sharma 1958). Several studies have recognized the presence of communities and social groups outside the fourfold division of the caste system, who lived outside the villages as 'outcastes'. It is these groups which were treated as impure and polluting. Later, some subcastes from the shudras (mostly lower artisans, and considered impure) were merged with the untouchable castes (different from the [pure] shudra). They were also treated as outcaste communities, which were considered 'impure and polluting and ati-shudra'. The reasons for this shift are, however, unclear. Jha (1997) observes that by the early medieval period, the untouchables comprised two broad segments: first the backward communities, and a second category of untouchables who included several oppressed artisans (erstwhile shudras). The latter had remained at the level of shudras until the sixth century CE when these subcastes became a part of the untouchable castes (Jha 1997: 27). Thus, the 'inferior outcaste' castes and the (shudra) artisan castes, who were previously looked down as ritually impure, were designated as untouchables. What is important is that with the inclusion of these shudra artisan subcastes in the category of untouchables, many 'disabilities', economic and social, applicable to the shudras in ancient Indian society are now transferred in the principles of untouchability (Yamazaki 1997: 10 and 16). This explains how disabilities imposed on shudras were transmitted and made applicable to untouchables, with the merging of some of the low-caste shudras into the untouchable category. In the process, the (pure) shudra, which was the fourth caste, got elevated as they began to follow agriculture as their main occupation and were freed from many disabilities mentioned in *Manusmriti* (Sharma 1958; Yamazaki 1997: 10, 16).[6]

---

[5] Jha (2018, 23) argued that untouchability emerged in four phases: 'The first phase up to 600 BC provides the Vedic background when the tabooed sections of society appeared first. The second phase extends up to AD 200 when untouchability begins and takes firm and definite shape with respect to a few groups. The third phase up to AD 600 is marked by an intensification of the practice whose numbers record an increase. The ranks of the Untouchables swelled considerably by the accession of several new castes in the fourth and final phase which extends up to AD 1200 and beyond and shows untouchability at its peak.' Ambedkar places the date of the origin of untouchability at around AD 400. We can, therefore, say with some confidence that untouchability had appeared in its full form some time about AD 400 (Ambedkar 1948: 379).

[6] As per *Manusmriti*, in addition to trade, the agriculture was left with vaishyas. However, *Manusmriti* considered agriculture as it says: 'But Brahman or a Kshatriya, living by a Vaishya's

Thus addition of some 'impure' shudra subcastes to outcaste groups signified new social phenomena which distinguished the untouchables from 'pure' shudras.

While attributing the origin of untouchability to the notion of 'impurity and pollution', Ambedkar has drawn a distinction between the 'temporary and permanent notion of impurity and pollution'. In his view, untouchability, that renders communities and social groups untouchable, is a 'permanent and hereditary pollution' based on the birth of an individual into a certain caste. On the other hand, temporary pollution is caused by some events but is considered rectified once the situation that caused the impurity is overturned through purification. This implies that untouchability was caused by 'impurity and pollution of a permanent and hereditary nature', as it was based on birth. Thus, Ambedkar (1948: 259) observed that 'once an untouchable, always an untouchable'. Jha (2018) also agreed with Ambedkar that 'untouchability means permanent and hereditary pollution owing to physical contact with a section of the Indian people' (Jha 1997: 23). Therefore, the disabilities imposed on untouchables are permanent. In this context, Jaiswal (2007) in a foreword to Jha's book (2018), emphasized: 'Ambedkar was right in drawing a clear distinction between the notion of temporary impurity of an individual related to religious or ritualistic beliefs and permanent, hereditary polluting impurity that led to untouchability of a whole community—the latter being a case of socio-political and economic exploitation.'

Untouchability has both social and economic dimensions. In its social dimension, the disabilities refer to the denial of civil rights, while the economic aspect pertains to disabilities related to the denial of economic rights, such as occupational and property rights, and education. The social disabilities imposed on untouchables were most serious in nature. In social spheres, physical contact with such groups was prohibited as it

---

mode of subsistence, shall carefully avoid agriculture, (which cause) injury to many beings and depends on others.' Further, 'Some declared that agriculture is something excellent (but) that means of subsistence is blamed by the virtuous, (for) the wooden (implements) with iron point injures the earth and the (beings) living in the earth' (Bühler 1886: 420–421). Some also refer to the lack of clarity on the occupation of vaishya and shudra. Yamazaki mentioned that 'in India today it is generally understood that Vaishya is the *Verna* of Commerce and that agriculture belongs to the Shudra *Verna*—such a division of labour between Vaishya and Shudra existed as early as the seventh century and continued until the present day' (Yamazaki 1997: 9).

would cause 'pollution' to the higher castes. They cause pollution through proximity, sight, hearing, and speech entailing corresponding atonement. Physical association, commensally and connubial ties, with untouchables were strictly prohibited. Thus, physical contact, interdining and intercaste marriages were proscribed. The prohibition of physical contact and social association resulted in physical segregation and social isolation of these groups. They lived in separate settlements outside the villages which once existed for the outcastes.

The economic dimension of untouchability was equally devastating and harmful for it deprived the untouchables of any economic rights and major occupations. In the early periods (up to 200 CE) untouchables did not have the right to property. The shudras were debarred from higher castes' occupations, such as agriculture, trade and commerce, service as teachers, and as soldiers. Their only job was to serve castes above theirs. The restrictions on property, occupation, and education, as applied to shudras, were transferred to untouchables after some shudra subcastes were merged with untouchables, often called ati-shudra. Due to restriction on their occupations, untouchables performed 'inferior' tasks which, according to the Hindu law, included work at crematoriums, hanging criminals, retrieving bodies of people who committed suicide, whipping adulterous women, defending new settlements in the countryside, sweepers, and refuse collectors. They also continued as hunters, fowlers, and butchers and could own dogs, cats, pigs, and poultry as their property. They wore clothes and ornaments of the dead and executed, and depended on others for food (Jha 1997: 22). In historical time sequence Manu's laws symbolized the ugly face of brahminism; the 'impure' or untouchable castes were required to pursue occupations that were considered lowly. Some were engaged as basket makers, potters, weavers, and barbers (Jha 1997). In the later periods, when untouchables became more integrated in the caste system as the fifth caste, they began to perform agricultural work and some lower-level artisanal activities. However, their involvement in agriculture was forced—mostly as slaves or serf labour which assumed exploitative forms. Therefore, untouchables also became victims of Hindu slavery with its extremely oppressive features. It was governed by the principle of 'graded inequality'. Graded slavery meant it should take place in the natural order of the varna and not in the reverse order, which is to say, a slave should be of a lower varna than his master. So, slavery was provided for the three lower varnas but not for the brahmins. It implies that individuals from shudra and vaishya castes could be slaves to people of the two castes above them. By this rule, untouchables located at the bottom of caste hierarchy were obliged to serve as slaves to all castes above them, particularly the brahmins (Ambedkar 1987: 26). According to Manu:

> A Shudra, whether bought or un-bought, should be reduced to slavery because he is created by God for the service of a Brahmin.
>
> (Bühler 1886: 326)

> A Shudra, though emancipated by his master, is not released from servitude, since that is innate in him, who can set him free from it.
>
> (Bühler 1886: 326)

Thus, a shudra/untouchable was rendered a permanent and hereditary slave or serf. According to further religious sanction to slavery, *Manusmriti* ordained:

> If a Shudra desires to earn a living, he may serve to Kshatriya, or he may seek to earn a living by serving even a wealthy Vaisya. He (Shudra) should serve Brahmins for the sake of heaven or for the sake of both, for when he (Shudra) has the name 'Brahmin' attached to him, he has done all there is to do. The service of a Brahmin alone is declared to be the pre-eminent activity of a Shudra for whatever other work he may do brings him no reward.
>
> (Bühler 1886: 429)

What remuneration is prescribed to a shudra for service to brahmins and castes above them? Dealing with the question on wages to shudras, Manu says:

> They must allot to him (Shudra) out of their own family property a suitable maintenance after considering his ability, his industry and the number of whom he is bound to support.
>
> (Bühler 1886: 429)

And what was the suitable prescribed maintenance? Manu says:

> The remnants of their food (should) be given to him, as well as their old clothes, the refuse of the grains, and their old household furniture.
>
> (Bühler 1886: 429)

Most of the *dharma sutras* also hold this view. *Dharma sutras* were composed between 600–100 BCE and principally four have survived—Vashishta, Gautama, Baudhayana, and Apastamba. Among them, Gautama reiterated what Manu had prescribed:

> Shudras serve the upper castes; seek livelihood from them; use their discarded shoes, umbrellas, clothes, mats, and the like; and eat their leftovers.
>
> (Ambedkar 1987: 430)

Apastamba mentioned:

> There are four classes: Brahmin, Kshatriya, Vaishya and Shudra. Among these, each preceding class is superior by birth to each subsequent. Shudras are to serve the other classes.
>
> (Ambedkar 1979: 24)

Manu also prohibited shudras from accumulating wealth.

> No collection of wealth must be made by a Shudra even though he (is) able to do it, for a Shudra who has acquired wealth gives pain to Brahmins.
>
> (Bühler 1886: 439)

Further, Manu wrote:

> A Brahmin may confidently seize the goods of (his) Shudra (slave), for as that (slave) can have no property, his master may take his possession.
>
> (Bühler 1886: 439)

The existence of slavery goes back to at least 600 BCE (Chanana 1960). It remained in practice for about 2500 years until the British banned it in 1843 (Banaji 1933). As untouchability embeds in itself some features of slavery, the untouchables' conversion into slave castes formalized their enslavement to the higher castes permanently (Ambedkar 1987). Several studies reveal the connection between caste and slavery. Writing about the ancient period (600 BCE–500 CE), Sharma (1958: 280) observed: 'The Shudra was considered identical with slave, although only a section of Shudras may have been legally slaves. The Shudras' servitude assumed different forms, for they served as domestic servants, and slaves, agricultural slaves, hired laborers, and artisans.'

In an in-depth study on slavery in ancient India, Chanana (1960: 116) observes: 'The social and legal restraints on *Shudras* compelling them to do a slave's work, meant a change for the worse for them and could have led at a later stage, to consider all the *Shudras* as slaves of Brahmins.' Lorenzo (1943: 134) observes: '(The) institution of slavery in India, with special reference to agriculture slaves, seems to have been linked with the idea of innate dependence of *Shudras* and their perpetual slavery as one of the axioms of Brahminism because of the *Shudras* being issued from the Almighty's feet denoting service.' A greater insight into the nature of untouchable slavery in southern and other parts of India in the nineteenth century is provided in recent studies concerning the rights of slaves, trade in slaves, their mode of work, wages, and level of living (Law Commission 1840; Saradamoni 1980; Mohan 2015). For example in South India, the Pulayas as an untouchable slave caste did not have the right to property. They could be sold, leased, or mortgaged, like land or cattle (Saradamoni 1980). The 'impure' social status of the untouchables prohibited them from domestic tasks and pushed them into hard work in the fields. The agrarian labour force was drawn largely from the traditional untouchable slave castes, such as Parayas and Pulayas called agrestic slaves or attached to the soil—'soil slave' (Thomas 1999). Thus, the untouchable slaves did not have a life of their own. In its summary, the Law Commission on Slavery (1840: 188) observed the following about the widespread practice of slavery in India:

In the peculiar condition of slavery which prevails on the east and west coasts of southern India, and it would seem more or less elsewhere, whole castes have been regarded as an impure outcaste, subject from remote antiquity to the cultivation of the soil in like manner as pure Hindu castes are bound to particular profession and occupation. The distinction between these outcastes and the pure classes is, in the part of India where it prevails, quite as marked as any that can arise from colour.

Another unique feature of Manu's laws on the caste system is that it laid down the mechanism of social ostracism and a set of penalties for violation of the caste code. Manu provided a set of punishments for those who violated the code, especially shudras. For instance, prohibiting shudras from the study of Vedas, Hindu laws warned of serious penalties for violators. In this context Gautama said:

> If the *Shudra* intentionally listens for committing to memory the Veda, then his ears should be filled with (molten) lead and lac. If he utters the Veda, then his tongue should be cut off, if he has mastered the Veda his body should be cut into pieces.
>
> (Yamazaki 1997: 11–12)

The legal responsibility of enforcing the caste code that included slavery was vested with the state or the king. Manu, thus, ordained:

> The king has been created (as) the protector of the Varnas (castes) and orders, who all according to their rank discharge their several duties. Let the king, after rising early in the morning, worship Brahmins who are well-versed in the threefold sacred science and learned (in polity), follow their advice.
>
> (Bühler 1886: 221)

> The king should carefully compel Vaishyas and Shudras to perform the work (prescribed) for them, for if these two (castes) swerved from their duties, they would throw this (whole) world into confusion.
>
> (Bühler 1886: 327)

1.4 Discrimination as an Integral Part of Caste Labour Relations

Having developed a fair insight into the economic features of the caste system, let us see how labour market discrimination is integral to the economic rules of caste system. The present study is concerned with discrimination in employment, wage occupation, and its impact on the incomes and poverty of the untouchables (Scheduled Castes). The nature of labour market discrimination as governed by rules of caste is unique. The division of people into a fixed occupation, with restrictions on mobility from one caste occupation to another, brings the division of workers in employment corresponding to their caste occupation. The employment of people generally remained confined to caste, without the freedom to take up occupations of other castes. For instance, in the castewise division of labour, teaching and preaching is the domain of brahmins, military the realm of kshatriyas, trade and non-farm production enterprises that of vaishyas, while employment in farming as self-employed workers remains restricted to shudras. Thus, employment gets compartmentalized into caste without freedom of mobility from one economic activity to another. In this sense, discrimination in employment becomes an inherent and integral part of the allocation of work under the legal framework of the caste system. In effect, the restrictions on taking up work in another caste's occupation leads to the development of a segregated labour market on caste lines. Individuals get engaged in their caste occupation without seeking entry to occupations assigned to other castes. In this sense, segmentation means that there exist five occupations as distinct segments in the labour market with barriers on the mobility of workers from one to another segment.

While the division of occupation brings in the division of workers, the situation of untouchables assumes a somewhat different form. Their case involves both segregation (exclusion) and inclusion in employment. Thus employment of SC by higher castes in the labour market is affected by both the processes of exclusion and inclusion. The exclusion of the SC workers is shaped by two opposite processes. First, as mentioned above, the division of work in occupation also brings the division of workers across caste occupations. For instance, an untouchable worker would face denial as an employee in the teaching profession and preaching, as according to the rule of caste it is reserved for the brahmins. Similarly, they could face denial in military earmarked for kshatriyas or in self-employed work in trade and non-farm production reserved for vaishyas, and finally as self-employed farmer which is the occupation of shudras. The SC also face exclusion in some types of works due to their polluting social status. They are excluded in categories of work which involve direct physical contact, domestic work, and tasks related to religious events.

At the same time, as per the rules of caste, an untouchable's main task is to serve the higher castes, particularly the brahmins, as a manual wage labourer. In the event of distress, they could also work for the other three castes. Thus, while they are excluded as a teacher and preacher, soldier, self-employed trader and farmer, they are required to work in all these occupations as wage labourers—tasks that involve hard physical labour. This is obligatory under the Hindu law of caste. Therefore, they seem to be particularly employed in agricultural and allied activities which involve physical labour. Also, they are required to carry out tasks that are considered inferior and polluting, like scavenging and those related to leather (skinning carcasses, tanning, etc.) or minor artisanal work. Thus, the rules regarding the work of the SC are characterized both by exclusion and inclusion, what Sen (2000) has rightly described as 'unfavourable exclusion and unfavourable inclusion'. While they are unfavourably excluded from the work in which the higher castes are engaged as teachers, military personnel or as self-employed farmers or entrepreneurs or traders, at the same time they are unfavourably (often forcefully) included and employed in manual (hard) wage labour required in the occupations of higher castes. As we have discussed earlier, the Hindu law of slavery considered untouchables as slave castes which included them in exploitative labour at very low remuneration.

This shows that under the Hindu laws of caste system, untouchables faced deep widespread discrimination in occupation, employment, and wages. In the present times, despite legal safeguards against discrimination in employment, wages, and occupation, they continue to face differential treatment in the labour market albeit in a modified form. This results in low employment and wages, and in turn low income and high poverty among an overwhelming majority of them. The slavery of untouchables persists in a modern form by way of bonded labour, forced labour, and attached labour (Rudra 1982).

Using official data for recent years, the present study attempts to develop an empirical evidence on prevailing discrimination against the SC in employment, wages, and occupation, and the impact of these on their lower income and enhanced poverty. In the following section, we will review the findings of earlier studies on the persistence of caste-based discrimination in the labour market in India and will identify key issues.

1.5 Earlier Studies on Labour Market Discrimination

The available literature used two types of methods to measure caste discrimination in the labour market—direct and indirect methods (Darity 1995). The direct method to measure discrimination includes audit study and correspondence study, whereas the indirect method to measure discrimination includes different approaches of the decomposition method. Since our study is based on National Sample Survey (NSS) data, it allows us to apply an indirect method. For this reason, we have surveyed literature that uses different approaches of indirect method which apply different decomposition methods to measure the extent of caste discrimination in the Indian labour market, particularly in employment, wages, and occupations.

The indirect method, which attempts to measure discrimination in the labour market outcome, generally explains the earning differentials across social groups using the human capital framework. The decomposition method is applied to partition the gross wage gap into 'explained' and 'unexplained' differences. The explained or endowment difference shows the gross wage gap that is attributed to the differences in endowment of productivity-related characteristics between the two groups. This may reflect pre- or non-market discrimination. The unexplained difference shows the gross wage gap that is attributed to discrimination in the labour market. This shows overt wage discrimination which is usually defined as 'valuation of personal characteristics of workers in the labour market that are unrelated to productivity' (Ehrenberg and Smith 1991: 531).

Several studies have used different approaches of decomposition methods to decompose the caste-based wage gap into two components—an endowment difference and discrimination in the labour market (Lakshmanasamy and Madheswaran 1995; Das and Dutta 2007; Ito 2009; Agrawal 2014; P. Duraisamy and M. Duraisamy 2017). A few studies have examined caste-based inequality in household welfare based on consumption expenditure (Kijima 2006; Azam 2012; Hnatkovska et al. 2012). Besides, the issue of caste-based occupational segregation as a determinant of earning has been analysed in a few studies (Banerjee and Knight 1985; Kijima 2006; Jacob 2006; Madheswaran and Attewell 2007).

Das and Dutta (2007) have explored the wage gaps based on caste in the Indian labour market using NSS data for 2004–05. Their study applies Oaxaca decomposition method and Bourguignon et al. (2007) method for selectivity correction. The findings of the study show that caste is still a determining factor in how individuals are remunerated in the wage labour market. In the regular labour market, the extent of the wage gap between the SC and higher castes workers is substantial at about 0.37 log points of which one-third is attributable to discrimination in the labour market. The wage gap attributable to discrimination in the labour market increased from 35 per cent to 59 per cent after correction for selectivity bias. Similarly, the extent of wage gap between OBC and higher castes workers is about 0.33 log points of which about 40 per cent is attributable to discrimination in the labour market. The percentage contribution of discrimination to the raw wage gap increased from 40 per cent to 56 per cent after correction for selectivity bias. This significant selection effect for SC and OBC regular workers suggests that SC and OBC regular wage employment is more selective in terms of unobservable worker characteristics as compared to higher castes regular wage employment. On the other hand, in the casual labour market the caste-based wage gap is found to be very low, almost entirely accounted for by differences in characteristics. Based on descriptive analysis, the study finds evidence of occupational segregation, i.e. both horizontal segregation (workers are restricted to their occupations) and vertical segregation (within the same employment type, workers from different social groups may be represented differently in the hierarchy of positions).

Also, Agrawal (2014) has analysed wage gap between the SC/Scheduled Tribes (ST) and non-SC/ST using India Human Development Survey data for 2005. The study applies the Blinder-Oaxaca decomposition method. The findings of the study show that the wage gap between SC/

ST and non-SC/ST is higher in the urban sector than in the rural sector. The caste-based wage gap is mostly driven by differences in endowments. The large endowment difference observed across social groups may be the outcome of past discrimination. Keeping in view the limitation associated with mean-based analysis, P. Duraisamy and M. Duraisamy (2017) have measured the wage gap and discrimination against socially-disadvantaged groups across the wage distribution using NSS data for 1983, 1993–94, 2004–05, and 2011–12. Using the Blinder-Oaxaca decomposition method, their study finds that the discrimination component is positive and statistically significant for all social groups irrespective of the study periods, except for the ST. The wage gap attributed to discrimination is found to be higher for OBC than for SC and ST, while the percentage contribution of discrimination to the wage gap between SC and others (including OBC) shows an increasing trend over the years from 1983 to 2011–12. The findings based on quintile regression decomposition analysis show that the wage gap and discrimination against socially disadvantaged groups markedly vary across the entire distribution. The gross wage gap as well as the wage gap due to productive characteristics increases from the bottom to the top of distribution up to the 70th or 80th percentile and thereafter remains stable or declines slightly. However, for ST it declines up to 60th or 70th percentile and then increases. So, the differences in human capital attributes account for a larger part of the wage gap across the wage distribution as compared to the discrimination component for all social groups. The unexplained wage gap is found to be lower at the bottom than at the top of the distribution, except for ST. The study points out that the low-wage earners are mainly low-educated regular contract workers with low bargaining power, while high-wage earners may find it difficult to compete with higher castes workers and, hence, are vulnerable to discriminatory practices.

Our subsequent review focuses on studies that use Brown et al. (1980) decomposition method to decompose the discrimination component further into wage discrimination and occupational discrimination. Banerjee and Knight (1985) have examined the issue of discrimination against SC migrant workers in urban India. The data for their study was collected through a primary survey conducted in Delhi from October 1975 to April 1976. Using Brown et al. decomposition method, the study finds that discrimination accounts for two-thirds of the gross earning difference with wage discrimination being considerably more important than job discrimination. They observe that discrimination against SC is highest in the operative or manual jobs, in which contacts are important for recruitment, and not in white-collar or professional jobs recruitment which involves more formal methods. Job discrimination is the highest, particularly for production occupation, in the formal sector. The reason could be that formal sector jobs are prized jobs and, hence, resistance to hiring SC is a greater number. Besides, non-SC have historically monopolized this sector, while SC have not been able to break their way in. This also reflects the effects of past discrimination in the assignment of workers to occupations which has been carried over to the present.

Madheswaran and Attewell (2007) have examined the caste-based wage gap in the regular urban labour market using NSS data for 1983, 1993–94 and 1999–2000. Their study using different approaches of the decomposition method show that the caste-based wage gap is largely on account of the endowment difference. This study shows the prevalence of pre-market discriminatory practices against the disadvantaged castes concerning education, health, and nutrition. However, the endowment difference has declined over the years. The percentage of the wage gap between SC/ST and higher castes, attributed to discrimination, increased from 13.5 per cent in 1983 to 30.4 per cent in 1993–94. Moreover, the wage gap between OBC and higher castes, attributed to discrimination, was 31.9 per cent in 1999–2000. Using expanded decomposition method, the study finds that occupational discrimination (unequal access to jobs) is more pronounced than wage discrimination (unequal pay in the same job) in the labour market.

Borooah (2010) analysed the different likelihoods that persons from different social groups would *ceteris paribus* attain different degrees of occupational success. The issue here is whether these differences in likelihoods are justified by differences in workers' distribution or whether they are, wholly or in part, due to 'occupational discrimination'. Schmidt and Strauss (1975), Macpherson and Hirsch (1995), and Borooah (2001) are examples of such studies. Borooah (2010) is concerned with both issues— 'earnings discrimination' and 'occupational discrimination'—in the context of the Indian labour market. A major conclusion of his analysis is that it made no difference to the chances of the people in the sample of being in regular salaried wage employment (RSWE) whether their attributes were evaluated using higher castes Hindus or SC coefficients. To put it differently, the results show that there is no discrimination against SC vis-à-vis higher castes Hindu in terms of their presence among those in RSWE. However, compared to the absence of discrimination between higher castes Hindu and SC, in respect of access to RSWE, there is considerable discrimination between men from these groups in respect of remuneration from RSWE. Of the difference of ₹231 between the higher castes Hindu and SC male wage rates in RSWE (₹573 and ₹341, respectively), 62 per cent is due to difference in attributes between males from the two groups and 38 per cent is the result of unexplained difference. This study demonstrates that there is no occupational discrimination among regular male workers but a significant wage difference exists.

Recently, Borooah's (2019) study concludes that the occupational attainment of persons in India is largely a matter of 'what they are', though undeniably, and there is a part which is determined by 'who they are'. Borooah (2019) further notes that the intergroup disparities are factual. They may be due to intergroup disparities in attributes that are necessary for regular employment and the differences that we observe are, therefore, due to the 'unequal treatment of unequals' or, to coin a word, due to 'meritification'. He concludes that men from the higher castes meet with greater success because they are better qualified for regular employment. He also observes that intergroup disparities in employment outcomes regarding 'good' jobs are the 'unequal treatment of equals'. Candidates are rejected because they belong to certain castes or religions even though they may be otherwise qualified to hold on those jobs. In such cases, disparities in employment outcomes can legitimately be regarded as being due to discrimination.

There are some studies which have analysed employment discrimination in the private sector. Some of them have been carried out for both the private and public sectors. These studies provide considerable evidence on caste-related exclusionary and discriminatory practices in the private sector. On the recruitment method, Papola (2007) observes, 'throughout the period of modern industrial development, various modes and mechanisms of employment practised by the private sector amply demonstrate the presence of social exclusion and discrimination'. During the initial period of modern industrial development, the factory enterprise made use of the jobber system. It was replaced in the 1970s by the institution of labour contractor/officer. Both the systems were exclusionary and biased in nature and outcome. The National Employment Service (NES) Scheme, more popular as the Employment Exchange, which followed is considered less inequitable and discriminatory, but its use by industry has declined over time. Between 1949 and 1953, about 50 to 85 per cent vacancies notified by employers were filled by those who had registered with the Employment Exchange. This figure dropped to 65 per cent between 1953 and 1960 and hovered around 60 per cent between 1960 and 1968. During the 1980s, the ratio was steady at about 55 per cent. Studies reveal that private factories and enterprises no longer use NES in any significant way for recruitment. Among the workers surveyed at different centres at different times, jobs were found through the Employment Exchange by only about 2.2 per cent candidates in Pune (1957); 1.87 per cent in Ahmedabad (1971–72); 1.5 per cent in Mumbai (1975–76); and 10.6 per cent in Coimbatore (1986–87). Thus, the only institutional mechanism to ensure a fair and non-discriminatory process of recruitment has not found favour with private employers; instead, they rely on informal (and alternative) channels of recruitment on a large scale. The studies alluded to earlier also highlight the percentages of those who had found jobs through informal and personalized channels. Such persons comprised more than 70 per cent of the working population in Pune (1959); 60 per cent in Mumbai (1976); and an equally high proportion in Ahmedabad (1975), Coimbatore (1986–87), and Surat (1998). Therefore, it is evident that a very high percentage of workers had found jobs through personalized and insider-based recruitment processes. Papola (2007), thus, presumes that these insider groups and persons are socially better endowed. For instance, higher castes or brahmins/ Marathas are over-represented in Pune factories—they account for 50 per cent of the workforce but comprise only 35 per cent of the population. In Coimbatore, 49 per cent of the brahmins held protected jobs as against 23 per cent among OBC and 30 per cent among SC.

There are studies using both direct and indirect methods which have brought to fore the evidence of caste discrimination in the private sector (Madheswaran and Attewell 2007; Thorat and Attewell 2007; Siddique 2008; Banerjee et al. 2009; Deshpande and Newman 2007; Jodhka and Newman 2007). Madheswaran and Attewell (2007) have made the first attempt to analyse the extent of caste discrimination separately for public and private sectors using NSS data for 1993–94 and 1999–2000. Using the Blinder-Oaxaca decomposition method, their study finds that SC/ST workers are discriminated against in both public and private sectors with the discrimination effect being much larger in the private sector. In the public sector, the extent of wage gap attributable to discrimination has been declining over the years. Subsequently, Madheswaran's (2010) is the only study that uses expanded decomposition method to decompose the discrimination component further into wage discrimination and job discrimination. The study finds that in 2004–05, job discrimination against SC is more pronounced than wage discrimination in both the public and private sectors.

The first major correspondence study in India was carried out by Thorat and Attewell (2007) as part of analysing discrimination in hiring practices in the private sector. The study focuses on the highly-educated segment, i.e. university graduates. They sent out identical resumes to private sector firms—both prominent Indian companies and multinational corporations (MNC)—in response to newspaper advertisements during 2005–06. The only difference in the resumes was the easily identifiable names of applicants—Hindu upper caste, Dalit (SC), and Muslims. Using statistical analysis, the study found that caste and religion have a significant effect on job outcome and job applicants with a Dalit or Muslim name, on an average, are less likely to get a positive application outcome as compared to equally-qualified applicants with a higher caste Hindu name. However, if the higher caste applicants lack the required credentials, then the chances of success get considerably reduced. Overall, the study observes that discriminatory processes operate even at the first stage of application processing.

Subsequently, Siddique (2008) conducted an audit study in Chennai to determine the extent of caste-based discrimination in hiring practices in the Indian private sector. The study was carried out over 10 months between March and December 2006. The author sent two resumes, one with a high-caste name and the other with a low-caste name for each job vacancy advertised online. The resumes depicted applicants of approximately the same level of productivity. Using statistical analysis, the study found that on an average a high-caste applicant had to send 6.2 resumes to get one callback, while a low-caste applicant had to send 7.4 resumes to get one callback, a difference of approximately 20 per cent. Being a low-caste applicant reduces the chances of callback more for jobs in front office/administration than it does for jobs in customer services. The study also analysed the variations in callback gaps associated with the recruiter and firm characteristics. It found that the effect of low caste on callback was negative for resumes sent to male and Hindu recruiters, whereas the effect of low-caste on callback was positive for resumes sent to female and non-Hindu recruiters. Besides, low-caste applicants were more actively sought by firms with a larger scale of operations, but not by firms with a smaller scale of operations. The author asserts that at least some of the callback gaps could be due to employer prejudice. This is because the audit study method is unable to distinguish between caste-based discrimination and statistical discrimination explicitly.

Banerjee et al. (2009) have done an audit study on discrimination in hiring practices against lower caste groups in India's new economy sectors—software and call centres. They sent 3,160 fictitious resumes in response to 371 job openings in and around New Delhi advertised in major newspapers and online job sites in 2004. Using statistical analysis, the study found no evidence of discrimination against non-upper caste (SC, ST, and OBC) applicants for software jobs. This finding is contradictory to Thorat and Attewell (2007) study and needs further investigation. However, they observed larger and significant differences between callback rates for upper castes and OBC (and to a lesser extent SC) in call centre jobs. People from lower castes particularly are at a substantial disadvantage when applying for jobs where soft skills are needed. This implies that training and credible skill certification may be crucial to reduce gaps in job opportunities between upper castes and lower castes, such as SC and OBC in the private sector.

Studies have also explored hiring practices which emphasize the role of networks and informal and personalized recruitment, where 'who you know' is often more important than 'what you know'. In a college-to-work study, Deshpande and Newman (2007) have tried to uncover the exact pathways through which discrimination manifests itself. They tracked a group of students from three premier Indian universities in New Delhi for two years to understand what jobs they got, how they got them, and what their interview experiences were. It turned out that employers were extremely conscious of the social identity of the applicant, all the while professing deep allegiance only to 'merit' of the candidate. Similarly, in an employer attitude survey, Jodhka and Newman (2007) found that employers, including MNCs, universally use the language of merit, but managers are blind to the unequal playing field which produces 'merit' and also, the commitment to merit is voiced alongside convictions that merit is distributed by caste and region.

Kijima (2006) has measured the extent of disparities in living standards across caste groups using NSS consumer expenditure survey data for 1983, 1987, 1993, and 1999. Using the Neumark decomposition method, the study finds that about half of the differential in the log consumption expenditure between SC and non-SC/ST is attributable to differences in characteristics. The differences in education and land ownership mostly contribute to such characteristic differences, while differences in returns to education are the major contributor of structural differences. The study also considers the effect of occupational segregation on the disparity in consumption expenditure between SC and non-SC/ST. Kijima observes that the difference in returns within occupations is more pronounced than the difference in returns across occupations. The expenditure gap attributed to the difference in characteristics and returns within occupations has increased. The occupational discrimination accounts for about 37 per cent of the structural difference between SC and non-SC/ST. The extent of occupational discrimination has declined over the years but the total structural difference shows a little change, while two-thirds of the differential in the log consumption expenditure between the ST and the non-SC/ST is due to differences in characteristics. The difference in education and location mostly contribute to such characteristic differences, while differences in returns to location are the major contributor of structural differences.

This review reveals a few aspects concerning the research on caste-based discrimination in the labour market. The first aspect is the relative neglect of studies on discrimination in the labour market. With few exceptions, scholars have not yet recognized the problem of labour market discrimination as a serious issue. The studies, although limited in scope, nevertheless provide useful insights on the nature of discrimination in wage and occupation, particularly in the case of the SC. Generally, the studies show that the contribution of endowment difference to the wage gap is more than that of discrimination in the labour market. The former, in turn, being caused by poor access to education and skill formation of the SC and OBC. Caste discrimination also matters and accounts for about one-third of the differences in wage gap, which is significant. Some studies have also examined the wage gap between the SC and higher castes in the private and public sectors and found higher discrimination in the former as compared to the latter. These studies have also estimated the discrimination in earning for casual wage labour and regular salaried employees separately and found discrimination being higher in the latter. The studies also estimated the wage gap between SC/ST and non-SC/ST in the urban and rural sectors and found the level of discrimination being higher in the urban sector as compared to the rural sector. Most importantly, some have estimated the discrimination by observing differences in the wage gap by earning level. The second important insight relates to evidence that part of the wage gap is due to occupational discrimination. The studies also revealed that discrimination in employment and wages tends to be higher in the private sector than in the public sector. Invariably, most studies have found an increasing trend in wage discrimination.

1.6 Significance of the Study

Notwithstanding these insights from the studies on labour market discrimination, there are significant gaps in research on caste and labour market discrimination. The present study intends to bridge some of these gaps. The gaps relate to the dimensions of labour market discrimination and conceptual issues, specifically in relation to wage, occupation and employment discrimination which are relevant but have suffered relative neglect.

Caste discrimination in employment is one of the most neglected themes in research on labour market discrimination. Surprisingly, employment discrimination which is the main feature of the labour market is governed by the rules of caste, is almost ignored. Perhaps, it is partly due to the neglect in the beginning itself. Becker (1971), who articulated the concept of market discrimination, in the introduction to the second edition of his book *The Economics of Discrimination* acknowledged thus:

> Although the unemployment rate was largely ignored in the first edition, I was aware of this important implication of the analysis and will

include in my suggestion for future research. It would be interesting to determine whether the traditionally greater unemployment of non-White than White is consistent with the analysis presented here. A few calculations that I made indicate that most, but not all, of the high unemployment of non-White results from their concentration in occupations that are prone to unemployment.

(Becker 1971: 4)

Despite this admission by Becker about 15 years after the publication of the first edition in 1957, researchers in India, with some exceptions such as Borooah (2010), followed Becker in 'over-researching' wage discrimination and neglecting the discrimination factor in employment. Some of the later theoretical attempts pointed out the relevance of employment discrimination, particularly of underprivileged sections. For instance, one variant of the imperfect information theory (statistical discrimination theory) indicates that the decision by the employer, based on employer's perception about the educational skill and the productivity of workers, may negatively affect the less privileged workers more than privileged workers as the employer invariably gives preference to workers from the privileged group. The employer perceives them to be holding better education and skills as compared to less privileged workers. Similarly, the theory of discrimination, based on the assumption of the imperfect market situation, implies that subordinate groups, like women or underprivileged groups, whose supply elasticity is low would generally receive low wages from the monopsonistic employers. The monopoly power of monopsonistic employers enables discrimination in hiring and wages of those whose supply elasticity is low. It is necessary to recognize that based on current daily status the unemployment rate of SC has been consistently higher by a margin of three to fourfold than the higher castes. The economic theory of caste tells us that SC had been excluded from better quality work in the occupation of the four castes above them. Their exclusion from most of the work, except the manual casual wage labour, should emerge as an important reason for exceptionally high unemployment rate among them. One of the reasons for lack of studies may be the lack of methods used for the measurement of employment discrimination. Therefore, we attempt to measure and estimate employment discrimination for the SC and higher castes.

The theme of wage discrimination has been researched quite extensively. However, a shortcoming of the existing literature on wages in India is that it primarily concentrates on averages, neglecting the rest of the distribution or earning level, with rare exceptions. Averages may miss important features of the wage structure and it is important to go beyond the averages to present a complete picture. We know that internally, the social groups are not homogeneous—there are significant intra-caste differences. In this respect, averages may hide much more than they reveal. Recent works in other countries using quintile regression technique have shown different effects on the wages of individuals at the top of the wage distribution as compared to individuals at the bottom of the wage distribution. There is also growing evidence from other countries which suggests that, far from being ubiquitous, the growth in wage inequality is increasingly concentrated at the top end of the wage distribution (Lemieux 2007). Given the above, this study will estimate earning functions by social groups across the entire wage distribution using quintile regression and analyse the changes in the contribution of individual characteristics over time. We shall decompose the change in wages in the past two decades into a part that is attributable to endowment difference and another part attributable to unexplained difference (discrimination) across the entire wage distribution.

Yet another issue that has received less attention is the likely impact of occupational segregation on wage earning. The disparities in wages between the SC and higher castes may be partly caused by differential access to better occupation/jobs. Few studies have shown the impact of distribution in occupations and industry as important reasons for unequal pay between SC and the other castes (Blau and Kahn 2000). Therefore, the present study estimates the impact of occupational segregation on wage earning between the SC and higher castes by decomposing the discrimination component further into wage discrimination and job discrimination components by using expanded decomposition method developed by Madheswaran and Attewell (2007).

With the exception of one or two studies (Madheswaran and Attewell 2007), very few have analysed the differences in labour market discrimination between the private and public sectors. It is particularly necessary to know the magnitude of discrimination in the labour market in the private sector. Discrimination in the labour market brings imperfection which affects not only income distribution but also economic growth. It is useful to develop evidence-based affirmative action policies for the discriminated groups in the private sector. Therefore, the present study will estimate caste-based discrimination in the regular salaried labour market in the private as well as public sectors.

An equally important gap is the impact of employment, wage, and occupational discriminations on income loss and the poverty of discriminated groups, such as the SC. All theories of labour market discrimination imply adverse impact on the wages and income of the discriminated groups. Discrimination in hiring results in high unemployment and low wage income among the discriminated workers. Discrimination in occupation invariably pushes workers into low-paying occupations. In effect, the discrimination in employment and wages and concentration in low-paying occupations reduce their income and induce more poverty among the excluded groups. As explained earlier, the theory of statistical discrimination implies that the underprivileged group suffers more from the decision of the employer based on the employer's perception. Similarly, underprivileged workers suffer more from discrimination in a market situation characterized by an imperfection in the labour market due to their low supply elasticity. Unfortunately, the studies on labour market discrimination have nearly bypassed the impact of employment, wages, and occupational discriminations on the income and poverty of discriminated groups, such as SC. The present study will estimate the income loss to the discriminated groups due to discrimination in employment and wages by using the method developed for this purpose.

There are also limitations of the present studies related to methodological issues in the Indian context. One of the methodological issues relates to the categorizing of social groups. The studies which estimate discrimination of the lower castes by the higher castes often grouped SC and ST together as one homogeneous category. It is well known that ST do not constitute a caste category, and their discrimination or exclusion does not originate from the caste system. Therefore, the issue related to labour market discrimination of the SC and the ST needs to be studied separately. Similar problems exist while grouping higher castes. Often, studies group higher castes and OBC together and compare them with the SC. Given significant gaps in the level of development between the higher castes and OBC, it would be appropriate to compare the higher castes with SC by excluding OBC. To capture the impact of caste on labour market outcomes, we have confined our comparison between SC and higher castes (excluding OBC).

As regards data, the study makes use of the NSS data on employment and unemployment for two periods, 2004–05 and 2017–18. The study will empirically analyse the relevant aspects of labour market discrimination in India. It will approach the theme in the following manner.

- Analyse the differences in employment and unemployment rates, wage earning and occupational pattern of the SC and higher castes regular salaried workers at all-India and state levels.
- Identify causes or account for the gap in employment and wage earning between the SC and higher castes in terms of differences in endowment factors and caste discrimination. It will also analyse the influence of occupation on wage earning differences between the SC and higher castes.
- Estimate losses in the earnings of the SC regular salaried workers due to discrimination in employment and wages, and its impact on their poverty.
- Suggest policies that include legal safeguards against discrimination in employment and wages in the private sector and affirmative action policy for improvement in endowments, like education and skills, and reparation policy to improve ownership of capital assets in the form of agricultural land and non-farm enterprises/businesses.

2

Economic Theories of Discrimination

2.1 Introduction

As mentioned in Chapter 1, the central thrust of the study is to develop an insight into the problem of persisting caste inequalities in income and poverty between the lower and higher castes regular salaried workers and to develop an understanding on the impact of labour market discrimination on caste inequality in income and poverty. As a part of this exercise, we estimate the discrimination in employment, wages, and occupation, and assess the impact of discrimination on income and poverty of the Scheduled Castes (SC) regular salaried workers in India. Thus, at the core of this study are these questions: Are there gaps in employment rate, wage rate, and occupation of the SC and the higher castes? To what extent can the differences in employment, wages, and occupation between the SC and the higher castes be attributed to endowment factors, such as education and skill? To what extent do SC face discrimination in employment and wages or both? To what extent does discrimination in employment and wages contribute to lower incomes and increase in poverty of the SC?

Theories of economic discrimination have inquired into these questions and provide possible answers. Theories inquire into sources of discrimination, motives behind discrimination, labour market conditions which make it possible to discriminate, consequences of labour market discrimination on income of the discriminated groups, and policies to overcome discrimination. The insights from the theories would facilitate the interpretation of our empirical results in the later chapters. We, therefore, review the relevant theories of economic discrimination with a focus on the labour market discrimination. In economics, the labour market discrimination assumes a specific meaning. Theoretically, mere observed earning differentials between advantaged and disadvantaged workers cannot be regarded as discrimination in the labour market

Scheduled Castes in the Indian Labour Market. Sukhadeo Thorat, S. Madheswaran, and B. P. Vani, Oxford University Press. © Sukhadeo Thorat, S. Madheswaran, and B. P. Vani 2023.
DOI: 10.1093/oso/9780198872252.003.0002

because earning differentials may be partly due to differences in human capital or productivity between the groups. The notion of discrimination involves an additional concept—that the personal characteristics of the workers which are unrelated to productivity are also valued in the market. These personal characteristics include gender, caste, and religious affiliation (Arrow 1972). In case of wages, for example, discrimination is said to exist when workers do not receive pay or remuneration commensurate with their productivity, i.e. when equal productivity is not rewarded with equal pay.

Labour market discrimination can manifest in different guises. It may assume three forms of discrimination, namely wage discrimination, employment discrimination and occupational or job discrimination. The pay or wage discrimination occurs when an individual is paid less than others working in the same job. In this case, the wage differential between equally capable individuals (say higher castes and SC) in the same job is not based on productivity differences between them; instead, caste identity plays a role in the determination of the employees' wages. Thus, the SC workers are paid less as compared to the higher castes counterparts. In case of employment discrimination in the labour market, an individual is excluded from a job even if s/he has potentially the same level of productivity as those working at a job; s/he may be overqualified in the sense that s/he possesses a higher level of productivity and overall ability as compared to other workers doing the same job. This is primarily discrimination at the entry level in which members of a particular group face discrimination in recruitment and, therefore, cannot access better-paying jobs. In other words, labour market discrimination can occur in hiring when two persons with similar employment experience, education, and training apply for employment, the person from the disadvantaged group faces denial at the time of hiring because of her/his non-economic characteristics. So, unequal access to employment is correlated with certain non-economic (social origins, such as gender, caste, ethnicity and religious background) characteristics of an individual (Thorat and Newman 2010). Occupational or job discrimination occurs when a worker who qualifies for the job is from a disadvantaged group and thus assigned an occupation or job with low earning, thus resulting in occupational segregation. Occupational discrimination occurs when SC workers are excluded from certain high-paid occupations resulting in lower average wages for lower castes and higher pay for higher caste. In summary, the definition of discrimination underlying both the wage rates and employment is the same. This is because it involves an unequal treatment of individuals, who are equally productive (sometimes described as 'of comparable worth'), but differ in their social characteristics, such as race, gender, caste, and religion.

2.2 Neoclassical Theories

Economists have looked into these questions related to labour market discrimination from a varied perspective. However, among them, the neoclassical perspective occupies the main space. Therefore, we first take a look at the views of the neoclassical theories. The neoclassical theory of discrimination is almost entirely a demand-side theory. The supply side of the labour market is effectively neutralized by the assumption that minority and majority groups of workers are equally productive (or have equal productive capacity) and have equal tastes for work. The demand-side may be characterized by a competitive or monopolistic structure.

Becker was probably the first neoclassical economist who attempted to develop insights on sources, motive, consequences, and solutions to the problem of discrimination. Becker argued that employers engage in discrimination against a particular group, such as Blacks or women, in hiring and wages (also include employee and consumer discrimination) because s/he has a taste for discrimination. The motivation for discrimination is influenced by a non-pecuniary variable generally designated as 'taste for discrimination' against a group, and the employer derives utility from discrimination. Thus, for Becker, "taste is the most important immediate cause of actual discrimination" (Becker 1957: 153). Employers with a taste for discrimination against Blacks feel that the real burden is more than the money wage burden. The dissatisfaction or disutility felt by the presence of Blacks in their firm is an additional burden. Therefore, in Becker's view, the employer is willing to forego income or incurs income loss for the utility gains from favouring individuals from a preferred group in hiring or wages, if hired. According to Becker, the taste for discrimination has origins in a set of beliefs or values that are formed without objective consideration of facts. It has its roots in prejudices of the individual. However, how the values/norms or ideas that form prejudice and result in a taste for discrimination is not spelt out. An interesting aspect of Becker's theory is that it recognizes the possibility of 'segregation'. The economic relations between two communities decrease with the increase in discrimination. When the taste for discrimination becomes sufficiently large, each society is in economic isolation and has to get along with its own resources. Since a member of each society works only with each other, complete economic isolation also involves complete economic segregation. As we shall see later, some aspects of economic segregation of the SC bear close similarity with this notion of segregation. To sum, in Becker's views, discrimination has its source in a set of beliefs or values not determined by any objective criteria but by prejudice with a non-pecuniary motive. The employer would be willing to incur income losses to employ individual from preferred groups (like Whites, women, or in India, the higher castes) and avoid individuals from other groups. Becker also indicates the possibility of segregation under the situation of a high degree of discrimination. Becker believes that discrimination would eventually get eliminated if the market acquires competitive nature.

In the early 1970s, Phelps (1972) and Arrow (1973) offered an alternative explanation for labour market discrimination. This approach is designated as 'imperfect information theory' and its variant as 'statistical discrimination theory'. Arrow argued that discrimination is the indirect outcome of the decision of employers about hiring or wages based on her/his perception or belief about the productivity of individuals from different groups. The roots for employers' perceptions, about individuals from two groups, are due to the presence of imperfect information in the labour market and high cost associated with information about the productivity of the individuals. As against the assumption of perfect and costless information, in reality information in the labour market is imperfect and involves high costs. Given imperfect information and high cost of seeking information about the productivity, the decision about hiring or wages are not based on the actual assessment about individual productivity. Instead, employers use alternative methods to judge the productivity of individuals. The employer uses her/his general perception of belief about the productivity of individuals from different groups. The employers, thus, use information on the average productivity of a group, vis-à-vis other groups. For example, the employer may assume that Blacks or SC in India are less productive than Whites or those from higher castes. Thus, the decision of the employer is influenced by the social perception of the relative productivity of the group. In other words, the employer uses group identity (which they can observe) of the employee as a proxy for ability (which they cannot observe) (Deshpande 2011: 39). Since the decisions to hire and wages are based on group affiliation and employer's perception or belief about the average productivity of the group, disregarding the within-group variations in productivity, it may turn out that the individuals with higher productivity (higher than the group average) may get excluded and result in their discrimination in hiring and wages. Thus, unlike Becker's view, the White (or higher castes) employers may discriminate against Black (or lower castes) employees not necessarily because of their desire or taste for discrimination, but the belief that Blacks or lower castes on an average have a low level of skills as compared to Whites or higher castes. In belief theory, the discrimination is not necessarily induced by motive of discrimination, as is the case in taste for discrimination, but discrimination is an indirect outcome of the decision of the employer to maximize the economic gains by depending on self-perception to reduce the information cost or search cost on hiring.

Following Arrow (1971), Phelps (1972) developed a statistical discrimination model which implies that when decisions are based on the employer's perceptions about the productivity of individuals, the ultimate victims of discrimination due to imperfect information are generally the people from the underprivileged groups. The employer's decision is influenced by the perception that, generally, individuals from the privileged groups possess higher education and skill as compared to the individuals from the underprivileged groups. Invariably, the employers take decisions from their past experiences with employees from certain groups as the basis to select individuals, which generally go in favour of the privileged groups. The likelihood of information available to employers on the skill endowment of individual job applicants is relatively sketchy, while information on the average endowment of social groups is (or is believed to be) relatively complete. In the absence of complete information on individual job applicants, unprejudiced employers may give preference in hiring or pay higher wages to members of privileged groups under the assumption that individuals from those groups are better endowed than the individuals from underprivileged groups. Thus, the employers resort to statistical discrimination using past experiences with employees from certain groups as a basis for selecting individuals. In this process, the individuals from lesser privileged groups may get excluded from hiring and productivity-based wages.

So far, we have discussed the different versions of the neoclassical theory of discrimination which assume competitive market conditions. However, there are economists who have raised objections to this competitive framework. Robinson (1965), Thurow (1969), and Madden (1975) are notable among them. One of the earliest theoretical treatments of gender discrimination in non-competitive labour markets was carried out by Robinson (1965). She considers a monopsonistic labour market where male workers and female workers are perfect substitutes in the production process. If the wage elasticity of labour supply is less for women than for men, a profit-maximizing monopsonistic employer would pay lower wages to women. According to Robinson, gender wage differentials are a manifestation of the inefficiency of a non-competitive labour market rather than the cause of inefficiency. Thurow's (1969) analysis of discrimination is also of the market imperfection genre. It is argued that the economic power of discrimination is so pervasive that monopoly gains accrue from the collective practice of discrimination. The author points out that the difference in income distribution between advantaged and disadvantaged groups can be taken as an indicator to measure the extent of economic discrimination. If the distributions are identical, then both consumption and production opportunities are identical, and discrimination does not exist. In support of this argument, Birdsall and Sabot (1991) point out that discrimination arising from inequality can by itself contribute to greater economic inequality between the groups since the effect of discrimination is on the lower-income group which is discriminated against the relatively high-income group. Another variant of the theory of discrimination was developed by Madden (1975). She argues that in order to maximize profit, monopsonist employers discriminate against a group. Madden notes that if the supply of women is inelastic, relative to that of men, then discriminating monopsony power arises from the monopsonist employer power and the prevailing male power in the society. It is to be noted that this lower supply elasticity of female labour supply is on account of lower demand for women with respect to alternative occupations and lower mobility of female workers vis-à-vis male workers.

Another strand of the theory of discrimination was put forth by Akerlof (1976 and 1980). He developed a theory of social custom. According to this theory, discrimination is associated with social prestige and practical benefits for some groups that enjoy the power of influencing which jobs should go to whom and under what conditions. He incorporated social structure into his model to explain the economic phenomenon of income distribution and resource allocation. This theory assumes that utility depends not only on consumption but also on individual's prestige and reputation in society. Hence, a socially conscious individual tends to discriminate against those groups that the prevalent social customs traditionally discriminate against. In support of the argument of Akerlof, Birdsall and Sabot (1991) observe that in low-income societies, social traditions continue to exercise a powerful influence on economic behaviour. Thus, adherence by employers to traditional roles in the labour market while hiring, promoting, and making decisions regarding wages may, therefore, be indistinguishable behaviour from the indulgence of prejudice. It shows revealed preference on the part of the employer in paying higher wages to those belonging to the advantaged groups than to those belonging to the disadvantaged groups, despite workers from the disadvantaged group being more productive. Akerlof's theory of social custom basically discusses caste-based discrimination.

2.3 Discrimination and Segmented Labour Markets

The issue of labour discrimination has also been viewed from the perspective of, what is called, segmented labour market or dual labour market or hierarchical market. Unlike the neoclassical theories which assume single competitive or imperfect competitive markets, the concept of segmented labour market conceives the possibility of dual labour markets. For all the versions of the segmentation theory, the basic idea is as follows: (a) There exists two or more distinct segments in the labour market (called primary and secondary, defined in terms of jobs). (b) Workers compete within each market for jobs. (c) Mobility barriers prohibit the movement of workers from one to another segment (Piore 1970; Doeringer and Piore 1971; Carnoy 1977; Taubman and Wachter 1986). The dual labour market was formally conceived by Piore (1970). The dual labour market model supposes the existence of two distinct sectors of economic activity, usually classified as primary and secondary sectors. The primary sector offers more stable jobs with higher pay, better working conditions and promotional opportunities while the secondary sector is associated with unstable jobs, poor pay, bad working conditions, and few opportunities for advancement (Dickens and Lang 1985; Taubman and Wachter 1986). The central point of the labour market segmentation approach is that segmentation in the labour market does not exist due to skill differentials, but rather institutional rules which substitute for market processes. In a segmented labour market, competitive market forces are replaced by corporate rules. The labour market discrimination in the segmented labour markets is also supposed to occur differently. In this context, Rodgers (1993) makes a clear distinction between labour market discrimination and segmentation. Discrimination arises when some individuals are paid less than others (wage discrimination) or are less likely to be employed (job discrimination) because of factors, such as gender, race, appearance, or other personal characteristics unrelated to their abilities. Segmentation refers to the division of the labour market into separate parts in which the rewards for and conditions of work are different, and between which mobility is limited. The discriminated groups are pushed to the low-wage segments even though they have equal human capital. If there is free mobility across segments, the wage differentials should tend to vanish. But in practice, wage differentials are observed which means that the market is not competitive. Discrimination is usually involved in segmentation since some factors must determine which social groups have access to which labour market segment. On the other hand, discrimination can perfectly exist well without segmentation.

2.4   Identity Theories

From the preceding review, it emerges that economic theories of discrimination invariably look into causes underlying discriminatory behaviour in the labour market. The most probable causes of labour market discrimination identified are the employers' tastes, employers' perception about the productivity of individuals and prevailing social customs, including the prevalence of monopsony in the labour market. The common theme that emerges from the taste, belief (or imperfect information theory) and few variants of the belief theory, including monopsony, is that the labour market recognized social identity of employer and employee impinge on decisions of hiring, wages, and job allocation in the labour market.

In the decade of 2010, the significance of identity in economic decision-making became the central point of discussion in new theoretical formulations about labour market discrimination. Akerlof and Kranton (2010), individually and together in a series of articles, made social identity as the central point of their theoretical formulation related to economic discrimination during 2000–07. This academic effort, through a series of papers on identity and discrimination, ultimately resulted in a book, *Identity Economics*, in 2010 (Akerlof and Kranton 2010). Let us take Akerlof and Kranton theory of discrimination that begins with the recognition of three entities in society, namely social categories, identity, and norms. The theory assumed that there are 'social categories in society' (race, religion, ethnic or social groups, like caste). These social categories have their 'norms'. Norm would determine as to how the individuals from one social category behave towards individuals from other social categories in economic relations in markets. The social categories and their norms constitute the identity of a group. In the authors' view, the decisions of individuals are influenced by self-choices and preferences, but more importantly by norms of the social group to which the individual members belong. In this sense, the economic decision of individuals is socially framed or determined by the groups' norms. The identity norms are brought into the utility function. Thereby, the identity theory incorporates social categories and norms, both being summed up as 'identity' into economic decision by individuals, insofar as the norms influence the economic decision in their engagement in market transactions. To sum up, the theory assumed that—first, there exist social categories; second, there are norms for how someone in those social categories should or should not behave; third, norms affect behaviour. In its application, specifically to race and poverty, the identity theory implies that the behaviour of Whites towards Blacks is determined by group norms that Whites hold towards the Blacks, which perpetuate a distinction of 'us' and 'them'. The Whites think of Blacks as 'them' rather than including them in the category of 'us all'. This division of norms, based on 'us' and 'them', is what authors call 'oppositional identity'. Insofar as norms involve differential treatment, it results in the discrimination of Blacks by Whites in market exchange.

While Akerlof and Kranton were engaged in the discussion on identity between 2000–07, Darity and his colleagues also advanced an idea of identity by putting forward the theory of racial identity norms, almost simultaneously in 2006 (Darity 2007). The main criticism of Darity against neoclassical theories (the taste and imperfect information theories), particularly the identity theory of Akerlof, is that while these theories consider social norms as a source of discrimination in the labour market, which is the case, these theories do not provide insights on how the norms, in the first place, are formed. What causes the emergence of norms, discriminatory or secular? Darity's identity theory (of racial norms) attempts to explain the reasons behind the formation of racial identity norms, which are discriminatory. The racial identity norm theory conceived of three identity norms, namely racial, individualistic, and mixed identity (mix of racial and individual identities). The individual pursues either racial or individualist or mixed strategy in social interaction. The central point of racial identity norms theory is that norms are shaped or formed by the economic motive and the gains which they bring to those who follow these norms. The racial identity norms are formed because these norms yield economic gains to those who practice racial discrimination. In other words, the norms of racial identity emerged primarily because those norms are productive and create wealth and income for those who discriminate in social interactions with the minorities, in this case, Blacks. As long as the racial identity norms yield income gains, the norms will persist. However, people will shift away from racial identity norms to individualistic identity (norms) once the racial identity norms begin to yield less economic returns. The individualistic identity norms yield more gains than racial identity norms. The individualistic identity norms assume a form where race becomes insignificant because it does not yield economic gains as much as the individualistic norms. Finally, the theory also explores the requirements for the existence of a mix of both individualistic and

racialist strategy in social interaction. The mix of individualistic and racial identities depends on the relative economic gains from the mixed
norms. Thus, the productivity or economic gains from identity norms is
the key factor which determines whether people pursue racial, individualistic, or mixed identities. In other words, economic gain is the root of
racial discrimination. A new feature of this theory is that it is dynamic
Insofar as it explains the underlying condition for a change in identity
norms from racial to mix and to individualistic identity in social interaction. The switchover to individualistic identity (away from racial identity) occurs if the gains from racial identity are less and individual merit
is valued more than race. The emergence of mixed identity depends on
the relative economic gains (or productivity) from racial and individualistic identity norms. It is the productivity of norms which decides the
change from one to another. To sum up, the racial identity norms theory
has three messages. First is that the identity norms are influenced (and
formed) by the relative economic gains to the dominant groups in social interactions with subordinate groups. The racial identity norms are
formed because racial discrimination is productive and yields income
to the discriminator. Second, changes from the racial identity norms to
individualistic (where race does not matter) identity norms, through
mixed norms, are influenced by the relative economic gains from those
norms. In other words, the change from racial identity to individualistic identity to mixed identity is conditioned by the 'productivity of the
norms'—the degree of economic gains that the norms would bring to
the parties in the labour market exchange. Thus, by making the identity norms dependent on the productivity of the norms in social interactions, this theory captures the underlying condition for a change
away from racial identity to mixed identity (partially discriminatory
and partially non-discriminatory) and finally to individualistic identity. Thirdly, by proposing interdependence between racial identity and
wealth and income gain from discrimination, it locates the sources of
interracial economic disparities in wealth and income between Whites
and Blacks in racial discrimination. It must be mentioned here that this
theory recognizes the non-pecuniary gains in terms of high social status
associated with racial identity. But they believe that high social status
also becomes a source of additional economic gains (W.A. Darity 2007;
W. Daity Jr 2013).

2.5 Prejudice and Discrimination

Neoclassical theories, namely Taste for discrimination (taste theory henceforth) by Becker, imperfect information by Arrow and its variant, and racial identity theory by Akerlof and Kranton, recognized that prejudice—the cause of discrimination—is embedded in 'individual psychology'. The social psychologists provide insights into the causes of prejudice and motive of discrimination. Allport (1954) treats prejudice primarily as something which is rooted in an individual's psychology. Psychology of prejudice, which produces stereotypical (false) beliefs by the dominant group and results in discriminatory behaviour towards the subordinate group, is a view which is similar to the Taste theory. Blumer (1958) questions Allport's theoretical construct of prejudice as a set of individual feelings and argues that 'race prejudice exists in a sense of group position rather than in a set of individual feelings which members of one racial group have toward members of another racial group' (Blumer 1958: 3). Blumer shifts the focus of the origin of prejudice from individual beliefs to 'attitudes of a group about the relative status and material benefits associated with membership in the group harbouring stereotypical beliefs toward the "other"'. The extent, to which the dominant group perpetuates advantages for their own and disadvantage for subordinate groups, is a key factor for group outcomes' (Blumer 1958: 3–4). In Blumer's notion of prejudice, there are four basic types of feelings or attitudes which always seem to be present in (race) prejudice by the dominant group: 'a feeling of superiority, a feeling that the subordinate race is intrinsically different and alien, a feeling of proprietary claim to certain areas of privilege and advantage, and perhaps the most important, a feeling of fear that the subordinate race harbours designs on the prerogatives of dominant race' (Blumer 1958: 4). Thus, Blumer shifts the axis of prejudice away from individual sentiments towards collective interests to maintain a group interest. The focus is on group position and group efforts (rather than on individual efforts) for material interest and high social status. Prejudice becomes an operative, mobilizing instrument to preserve the advantaged position of the dominant group. There are real (material) interests at stake in the efforts of the dominant group to preserve its privileged position and also the more intangible and psychic benefit of a high-status advantage.

2.6 Summary

Important insights emerge from the review of the theories of economic discrimination in general, and labour market discrimination in particular. Together these theories, although with different viewpoints, bring considerable clarity on the motive, the consequences, and the policies to address labour market discrimination. All the theoretical strands, in one form or another, recognize the presence of social groups or categories in all societies based on race, colour, religion, gender, and ethnic or social origin, like caste. The social categories developed group norms which influence their decisions vis-à-vis other social groups in the labour market, such as in hiring, wages, and allocation of jobs. In this sense, the economic decisions by an employer of one social group in hiring (or wages) of individuals from another group are socially framed or determined. However, these norms which influence a decision about the employment or wages invariably tend to be discriminatory towards other groups. Most theories reflect on the motive behind discrimination, which they believe could be both pecuniary and non-pecuniary. Some theories hold the view more prominently than other and argued about the economic gains being the prime motive behind labour market discrimination. The imperfect information theory argued that the use of social perception to judge the productivity of a group is driven by the motive to minimize the search cost and to maximize the profit. Similarly, the racial identity norms theory argued that the norms are formed to bring economic gains to the employer from discrimination in hiring, wages, or occupation. When the economic gains from racial norms are low, it induce a shift towards individualistic identity norms which respect merit more than race in hiring or wages. We have seen that in Taste, belief, and identity theories, individual prejudice becomes the basis for discrimination. The prejudice, as an individual psychological feeling, produces stereotypical (false) beliefs about others which results in discriminatory behaviour. The alternative view on prejudice shifts the focus from individual psychological feelings to group feelings to constitute prejudice. This prejudice is treated as an amalgam of attitudes of the dominant groups towards subordinate groups developed with the purpose to derive material benefits and high social status. The discriminatory behaviour of the dominant groups towards the subordinate groups thus assumes a functional or instrumental role to accrue material benefit by the dominant groups at the cost of the subordinate groups. The group-based theory shifts the focus from an individual's prejudicial feelings to a group's prejudicial norms for both tangible material gains and high social status through discrimination.

Equally important insights into the theories of discrimination relate to the consequences of discrimination. All theories imply that the labour market discrimination, for whichever reason it is practised, by employers in hiring, wages, and occupation brings losses to the groups which face discrimination in the labour market. Discrimination in hiring results in high unemployment, and discrimination in wage results in low-wage income to workers who face discrimination. Occupational discrimination pushes discriminated workers into low-paying occupations. In effect, the discrimination in employment and wages, and concentration in low-paying occupations reduce income and induce more poverty among the discriminated groups. A variant of the imperfect information theory (statistical discrimination theory) observes that a decision of the employer, based on employer's perception about the education, skill, and productivity of workers, negatively affects the less privileged workers more than the privileged workers, as an employer invariably perceives the latter as being more endowed with education and skill than the former. Similarly, the theory of discrimination, based on the assumption of the monopsonistic market situation, implies that subordinate groups, such as women or underprivileged groups, whose supply elasticity is low would generally receive low wages from the monopsonistic employer than from the firm operating in competitive market. The monopoly power of monopsonistic employer enables discrimination in hiring and wages of those whose supply elasticity is low and who are in desperate need of work due to oversupply.

These theories also have policy implications to overcome labour market discrimination, although the solutions differ. The Taste theory implies that market competitiveness would eliminate those firms which discriminate as against those who do not. The cost, and hence, the price of goods produced by the firms which discriminate, is higher as compared to those employers who employ workers and pay wages governed by productivity. Thus, the employer who discriminates would be outcompeted by the one who does not. However, evidence shows that, in practice, discrimination continues to persist in competitive market situations which calls for other remedies. The imperfect information theory considers lack of information as a reason for discrimination and, therefore, it implies the need for policies to improve the flow of information at relatively low cost. The perfect information would enable the employer to make decisions based on information about the education and skill of individual applicants from a minority group, rather than his perception or belief. The identity theory proposed both affirmative action policy and civil rights movement against the idea which supports discrimination. Given the persistence of discrimination in competitive labour markets, affirmative action policy to ensure fair share to an individual from discriminated groups is considered appropriate. However, the identity theory also asserts that affirmative action alone is not enough, it also requires change in discriminatory norms. Therefore, it proposes a civil rights movement to bring reforms in discriminatory ideas and norms which induce discrimination in society. The outcome of the feministic movements in the USA is cited as an example of the civil rights movement which resulted in several policy decisions in favour of women. The theory of racial identity norm proposed redistribution of wealth through reparation to the discriminated groups who had suffered exclusion from right to property and underpayment to their (slave) labour for a long time. While reparation policy is found appropriate to compensate for exclusion in the 'past' so as to ensure a fair share to the discriminated groups in the 'present', it also proposed legal safeguards and affirmative action policies as safeguards to discrimination in the present.

3

Economic Theories
of Caste Discrimination

3.1 Introduction

A review of the theories of economic discrimination indeed provides useful insights into labour market discrimination, mainly with regard to race and gender in the context of Western society. Against this background, we will now discuss the economic theories of caste discrimination in the Indian context. There are very few attempts to theorize the caste system from the perspective of market discrimination. Among them, the works by George Arthur Akerlof, James Scoville, Deepak Lal, and Bhimrao Ambedkar are important.

3.2 Economic Theories of Caste Discrimination

The formal model of caste equilibrium developed by Akerlof (1976) was probably the first effort that used the neoclassical theoretical framework to analyse the economics of the caste system. The model assumes the caste system's distinct economic features, such as: (a) Society is divided into mutually exclusive groups (called castes). (b) A code of behaviour dictates how members of these castes should behave. The caste rules dictate not only the code of behaviour but also the punishment for infractions, with violators being treated as outcastes. Furthermore, those who fail to treat outcastes in a manner as dictated by the caste code, would be made outcastes. (c) Caste members predict that those who do not follow the caste code would be made outcastes and would receive the treatment of an average outcaste. In the model, all persons of the same caste are predicted to have equal ability. Similarly, under the caste system, the behaviour of

Scheduled Castes in the Indian Labour Market. Sukhadeo Thorat, S. Madheswaran, and B. P. Vani, Oxford University Press. © Sukhadeo Thorat, S. Madheswaran, and B. P. Vani 2023.
DOI: 10.1093/oso/9780198872252.003.0003

one member of society towards another is predicted by their respective caste status. In equilibrium, no employer has an incentive to hire workers from outside their caste. The fear of social and economic exclusion acts as a deterrent for any deviation from the caste rule with regard to employment and occupation. The costs are too high for individuals to break the caste codes. Akerlof writes: 'usually the greatest rewards go to those who do not break social customs. The models of caste explain why economic rewards may follow those who follow prevailing social customs' (Akerlof 1976, 617). With these characteristics, ultimately, the equilibrium arrived in caste economy tend to be suboptimal.

Lal (1988) developed an economic model of the caste system following the Akerlof framework (1976 and 1980). Lal provided an economic rationale for the origin of the caste system in ancient times. He observed: 'given a set of problems that the ancient Indians faced, the political instability, the need for secure labour supply for labour-intensive settled agriculture in the Indo-Gangetic plains, uncertainty concerning outputs, and so forth, the caste system was the second-best optimal response' (Lal 1988, 72). He recognized that the labour market was segmented and therefore imperfectly (though not completely) immobile (Lal 1988, 72). The equilibrium, for obvious reasons, would be suboptimal. The income distribution tends to be generally skewed along caste lines because access to the source of income and economic rewards are determined by economic rules of the caste system. He also observed that a community-based system of enforcement regulates the caste-related privileges using the mechanisms of social ostracism, violence, and economic penalties.

Scoville's (1996, 385–386) theory considers caste as a 'system of human resource allocation as one alternative to reliance on market mechanisms'. While arguing that this is a situation wherein 'strong non-competitive labour market institutions have long prevailed occupations are hereditary, compulsory and endogamous,' Scoville (1991) constructs a *jajamani matrix* to capture some of the reciprocal obligations of the caste system. The use of reciprocity has connotations of fairness or fair exchange. The traditional caste divisions imply a hereditary work allocation, where the specified arrangement of the flow of goods and services between the individuals in the system is called the *jajamani* system. What is intriguing to observers is the degree of stability in caste relationships or the 'absence of institutional change' (Scoville 1996, 390). Scoville identifies three characteristics of the labour market's barriers which ensure that institutional change in the labour market, characterized by caste, is minimal or nil. These characteristics are impermeability (workers cannot easily leave their caste and enter another), inevitability (lack of alternative sources of supply), and permanence (these barriers have a long history and are expected to last into the indefinite future). By highlighting interdependence, Scoville's model takes away the focus from the hierarchal and exploitative nature of the caste system and presents a benign picture that emphasizes nature of caste system as the facilitators of a mutually beneficial division of labour (Deshpande 2011, 49).

3.3 Ambedkar's Perspective on Economic Caste Discrimination

Among Indian thinkers, Ambedkar was a leading scholar who enquired into the economic aspects of the caste system. As early as in 1917, as a PhD scholar at Columbia University (USA), he developed a theory of caste (Ambedkar 1917) followed by writings in the 1930s. In the 1940s, he published two books on castes and untouchability—*Who Were the Shudras?* (1946) and *Who Were the Untouchables?* (1948). But some of his major theoretical writings on caste, also written in the 1940s, were published for the first time after 1979. Other writings of Ambedkar on caste and untouchability are spread all over. These vast writings on the institution of castes and untouchability present his perspective with a common thread running through them. Together, these writings deal with the origin of the caste system, its economic features and motive behind economic discrimination. It may be mentioned that theoretical writings of Ambedkar on economics of caste system appeared before 1950. On the other hand, most of the modern theories of economic discrimination emerged much later. Thereby, Ambedkar did not have the advantage of gathering insights from theories of economic discrimination in general, and that of caste in particular—the former appeared first with Becker's book in 1957 while the latter evolved with the economic theory of caste by Akerlof in 1976.

3.4 Economic Features of Caste System

We will first discuss the views of Ambedkar on issues which are relatively less complex to unfold the features of the caste system, and in subsequent sections switch over to the analysis of a rather complex terrain which involves the sources and motives behind the caste system and discrimination. The aim is to, if not defined, get a better understanding of Ambedkar's perspective on the genesis of caste as an economic system. This would disclose what caste is and how the system works to infer its functions and look into its origins and motives.

Ambedkar classified the features of the caste system into two categories, namely essential principles/features and unique features of the caste system (Ambedkar 2008).[1] Ambedkar recognized some features or principles as essential to the caste system. First, the caste system involves division of the Hindu population into five social groups, called castes. It isolates and segregates the five castes from each other through restrictions on marriages (that is endogamy), interdining, and social relations. In the economic sphere, it fixes the occupation of each caste (or economic and education rights) and makes them hereditary and permanent without freedom for a change. However, the entitlement of occupation or economic rights of each caste is fixed in an unequal and graded manner. It considers the segregation of the Hindu population into five castes with its graded inequalities as an 'ideal norm' to be followed by all. Finally, it converts the norms into laws making the caste system legally binding. Once it is made legal, it also invites penalties for violation of caste rules both by the state as well as by the higher-caste communities. In this sense, the system is foolproof and does not leave scope for assumptions or hypotheses.

---

[1] Ambedkar's writings on the caste system and untouchability are vast. Writings on caste began with a paper in 1917. Some of his main writings on caste appeared in the and late 1940s. Later two main books were published in the late 1940s. Some of his most important unpublished writings on caste were published in 1979 after his death in 1956 by the Maharashtra government. There are also several essays on caste and untouchability. However, the features of the caste system are specially discussed at length in two essays: *Essential Principles of Hindu Social Order* and *Unique Feature of Hindu Social Order Caste*, including an essay *Philosophy of Hinduism* (Ambedkar 1979, 3–129, volume 3) and Chapter 1: The Riddle of the Shudra, and Chapter II: The Brahmanic Theory of the Origin of the Shudra (*Who Were Shudra*, Vol. 7, Dr Babasaheb Ambedkar, Writings and Speeches), including *Caste in India: Their Mechanism, Genesis and Development* (Volume 1, Dr Babasaheb Ambedkar, Writings and Speeches).

Let us discuss each of these features in some detail. Ambedkar's analyses are based on the original Hindu religious texts, particularly the *Vedas* and *Smrutis*. This is necessary for our analysis because the changes in the caste system and their persistence up to the contemporary times can be meaningfully studied with reference to the original codes in Hindu *shastras* only.

The caste system is said to be of divine origin. The reference to the odd origin of the caste system first appeared in an important Hindu religious text, the *Rig Veda*. Ambedkar's quote from *Purusha Sukta* of the *Rig Veda* is as follows:

> For the prosperity of the world He (the creator) from his mouth, arms, thighs and feet created the Brahmin, Kshatriya, Vaishya and Shudra.
>
> (Ambedkar 1987, 112)

However, the divine power not only created four castes but also fixed the occupations (or property rights) of each of the *varna*/caste. Ambedkar quotes:

> To the Brahman, it assigns teaching and preaching of religion, defence to Kshatriya, trade and agriculture to Vaishya and service of these three castes to Shudra.
>
> (Ambedkar 1947, 75)

The occupations of each caste are fixed and made hereditary and permanent by birth in specific castes without the freedom to change them. The assignment and entitlement of the occupation (or property rights) of each caste is governed by the norms or idea of graded inequality. The graded inequality is different from the simple idea of inequality in the sense of either having rights or not having rights as two extremes. Ambedkar defined graded inequality as, 'the four classes are not on horizontal plane, different but equal. They are on a vertical plane. Not only different but unequal in status, one standing above the other. In the scheme of Manu, the Brahmin is placed at the first rank. Below him is the Kshatriya. Below the Kshatriya is the Vaishya. Below Vaishya is the Shudra and below Shudra is the Ati-shudra or the untouchable' (Ambedkar 1987, 197). The gradation is shaped by the entitlement of property rights or occupations and the brahmanical notion of ranks and status of occupation. The brahmins, who are placed at the top of the caste hierarchy, have all the economic privileges and rights, and successively the economic rights get narrower in a graded manner as we move down the caste hierarchy from highest caste (brahmin) to higher caste (kshatriya) to middle caste (vaishya) to lower caste (shudra) and to lowest caste (untouchables). The untouchables, located at the bottom of the caste hierarchy, practically have no property rights except to serve the four castes above them as wage workers. The job of teaching/religious preaching, which is considered a noble profession, is assigned to brahmins; the military, considered second in rank after teaching, to kshatriyas; the trade to vaishyas; agriculture to shudras; and service of the four castes above them through physical labour to the untouchables. Thus, the norms make the principles of economic-graded inequality in entitlement to property rights and occupations, and right to education among the five castes, the foundation of the caste system.

It is important to note that, subsequently, the norms were converted into laws. The credit of converting caste norms into legal code goes to Manu. Manu made the system legal and penal by about 200 BCE (Ambedkar 1947, 9). Once the provisions concerning occupation, education, and other economic rights were made legal, it also made it necessary to codify the punishment for violation of laws. *Manusmriti* provides a set of punishments for violation of caste rules by shudras/untouchables and also for higher castes to be enforced both by the higher-castes community as well as by the State. The Hindu laws made the penalties harsher for shudras/untouchables in all matters. For instance, the study of *Vedas* by the shudras invites serious penalties. Ambedkar quotes *Manusmriti* which says:

> If the Shudra intentionally listens for committing to memory the Veda (Hindu sacred book) then his ears should be filled with (molten) lead and lac. If he utters the Veda, then his tongue should be cut off, if he has mastered the Veda his body should be cut to pieces.
>
> (Ambedkar 1987; Bühler 1886; Law of Manu, 43)

Thus, to summarize, the essential features of the caste system are the division of Hindu population into exclusive and isolated social groups called castes, endogamy, the unequal and graded entitlement of occupations and economic rights to the castes, conversion of norms into laws and making the violation of caste laws subject to punishment, both by state and excommunication or social ostracism by the higher-castes community. These essential features form the foundation of the caste system.

Besides these essential features, Ambedkar also mentioned about the unique features of the caste system. These unique features are as important as the essential features, rather more important than the essential features (Ambedkar 2008, 116–129). What are these unique features? Ambedkar recognized three unique features, namely the supremacy of the brahmin with special privilege and rights, techniques devised for enforcement and preservation of caste system, and to make the caste system a part of the Hindu religion's ideology.

Ambedkar provides evidence on the supremacy of the brahmins, their godly status and also the special privileges enjoyed by them. We present here only a few verses related to the supreme status of the brahmins. Ambedkar quotes:

As Brahmans sprang from the God's mouth, as he was first born, and as he possesses the Vedas, he is by right the lord of the whole creation.

(Ambedkar 1987, 117)

The very birth of a Brahman is an eternal incarnation of the sacred law (Veda) for he is born to (fulfil) the sacred law, and become one with Brahman (God).

(Ambedkar 1987, 117)

A Brahmana coming into existence is born as the highest on earth, the lord of all created beings, for the protection of the treasury of the law (God).

(Ambedkar 1987, 117)

The Brahman is (hereby) declared to be the creator (of the world), punisher, the teacher (and hence) a benefactor (of all created beings) to him let no man say anything unpropitious, nor use any harsh word.

(Ambedkar 1987, 117)

From priority of birth, from the superiority of origin, from a more exact knowledge of scripture, and the distinction in the sacrificial thread, The Brahmin is the lord of all classes.

(Ambedkar 1987, 117)

This shows the godly status of the brahmin in the Hindu social order. We have discussed earlier that the occupation of each caste is fixed and hereditary with restrictions to change. However, the uniqueness is that the brahmins are made an exception to these rules and free from these restrictions. The brahmins could undertake any occupation except that of the shudras. Ambedkar quotes:

Whatever exists in the world is the property of the Brahmana, on account of the excellence of his origin, the Brahmana is indeed entitled to it all. Being a deity, the Brahmana is above law and above the King, Manu directs.

(Ambedkar 1987, 118)

Yet Brahmana, unable to subsist by his duties, may live by the duties of soldier, for that is the next in rank.

(Ambedkar 1987, 120)

If it be asked, how he must live, should be unable to get a subsistence by either of these employment, the answer is, he may persist as a mercantile man applying himself in person to tillage and attendance on cattle.

(Ambedkar 1987, 120)

Ambedkar argued that these privileges of the brahmins are interlinked with denial of rights to the shudras: Manu prohibited the shudras from accumulating wealth.

No collection of wealth must be made by Shudra even though he is able to do it, for Shudra who has acquired wealth gives pain to Brahmans.

(Ambedkar 1987; Buhler 1886; Law of Manu, 439)

He (Shudra) should serve Brahmins for the sake of heaven or for the sake of both, for when he (Shudra) has the name 'Brahmin' attached to him, he has done all there is to do. The service of a Brahmin alone is declared to be the pre-eminent activity of a Südra.

(Ambedkar 1987; Bühler 1886; Law of Manu, 439)

Service to Brahmin alone is declared to be the pre-eminent activity of a Südra, for whatever other work he may do brings him no reward

(Ambedkar 1987; Bühler 1886; Law of Manu, 429)

If a Südra desires to earn a living, he may serve a Kshatriya, or he may seek to earn a living by serving even a wealthy Vaishya. He should serve Brahmins for the sake of heaven or for the sake of both, for when he has the name 'Brahmin' attached to him, he has done all there is to do.

(Ambedkar 1987; Bühler 1886; Law of Manu, 428)

A Brahmin may take possession of goods of a Shudra with perfect peace of mind, for, since nothing at all belong to this Shudra as his own, he is one whose property may be taken away by his master.

(Ambedkar 1946, 50; Bühler 1886; Law of Manu, 417)

The shudras/untouchables were made hereditary slave and serf. The Hindu lawgivers made slavery part of the Hindu law. Manu ordained:

A Shudra, whether bought or un-bought, should be reduced to slavery because he is created by God for the service of a Brahman.

(Ambedkar 1987, 26; Bühler 1886; Law of Manu, 24)

A Shudra, though emancipated by his master, is not released from servitude, since that is innate in him, who can set him free from it.

(Ambedkar 1987, 26; Bühler 1886; Law of Manu, 24)

The remuneration prescribed to the shudra for the service to brahmin and caste above them was pathetically low. In dealing with wages, Ambedkar quotes Manu:

The remnants of their food are given to him, as well as their old clothes, the refuse of the grains, and their old household furniture.

(Ambedkar 1987; Bühler 1886; Law of Manu, 429)

Gautama reiterated what Manu prescribed:

> Shudra serves the upper castes; seek his livelihood from them; use their discarded shoes, umbrellas, clothes, mats, and the like; and eat their leftovers.
>
> (Ambedkar 1987, 430)

Further Manu ordains:

> A Brahmana may confidently seize the goods of (his) shudra (slave), for as that (slave) can have no property, his master may take his possession.
>
> (Ambedkar 1987; Bühler 1886; Law of Manu, 439)

Thus, there is a close connection of disabilities of the shudras/untouchables with the privilege of the brahmins. The privileges and special rights of the brahmin are at the cost of denial of rights to the shudra. The loss of shudra is for the economic gains of the brahmin. The shudra must be ready to sacrifice everything for the sustenance of the life and dignity of Superman (Ambedkar 2008, 123).

The second unique feature of the Hindu social order is the techniques devised for the preservation of the caste system. The technique was to place the responsibility of enforcing the Hindu laws about caste with the highest authority, the State/the King. Manu ordained thus:

> The King has been created (as) the protector of the Varnas (castes) and orders, who all according to their rank, discharge their several duties.
>
> (Ambedkar 1987; Bühler 1886, Law of Manu, 221)

> The King should carefully compel Vaishya and Shudra to perform the work (prescribed) for them, for if these two (castes) swerved from their duties, they would throw this (whole) world into confusion.
>
> (Ambedkar 1987; Bühler 1886; Law of Manu, 327)

As we have discussed earlier, beside the State the higher-caste community itself was required to enforce the caste code with the instruments of social ostracism and excommunication and other punishment in the event of a violation of caste code. The punishments are both for higher castes and untouchables, the latter for violating the caste code and the former for not enforcing the caste code. This mechanism is as powerful as the laws itself. After the removal of caste laws under the new Constitution in 1950, it is this informal mechanism of social ostracism by the higher-caste community which keeps castes alive in their present form.

The third unique feature of the caste system, which Ambedkar particularly mentioned, is the justification of the caste system through religious ideology. The four castes are supposed to be of divine origin. The reference to the divine origin of the caste system, as mentioned earlier, first appeared in the important Hindu religious text, *Purusha Sukta* in the *Rig Veda*. Ambedkar quotes from *Purusha Sukta*:

> The Brahmanas was his mouth, the Rajnya (Kshatriya) was his arms, the being called the Vaishya was the thighs, Shudra sprang from his feet.
>
> (Ambedkar 1990, 22)

All the brahmanical literature repeat the same in one form or another.[2] Ambedkar provides evidence from selected brahmanical texts. Ambedkar invited attention to the provision in Geeta by Lord Krishna, the most respected religious text of the Hindus.

> I have created the arrangement known as chaturverna (that is a fourfold division of society into four castes, Brahman, Kshatriya, Vaishya and Shudra) assigning them different occupation following native capacity. It is I who am the maker of chaturverna.
>
> (Ambedkar 2008, 127)

Even if it may be easier to follow the occupation of another verna, yet to follow the occupation of one's verna is more meritorious, although one may not be able to do it quite efficiently. There is bliss in following the

---

[2] The views of the other Hindu *shastras* on caste (other than Manusmriti) are discussed at length in Chapter II: The Brahmanic Theory of the Origin of the Shudra (*Who Were Shudra*, Vol 7, Dr Babasaheb Ambedkar, Writings and Speeches, Education Department, Government of Maharashtra, 1987) and in Riddle 16: The Four Vernas: Are the Brahmin Sure of Their Origin, (page 189–204) and Appendix I: The Riddle of Varnashram Dharma, (pages 236–261), Dr Babasaheb Ambedkar, Writings and Speeches Vol. 7, The Riddles of Hinduism, Education Department, Government of Maharashtra, 1987.

occupation of one's verna, even if death were to result in performing it, but to follow the occupation of another verna is risky.

(Ambedkar 2008, 80; Geeta III, 35)

In the Geeta, Lord Krishna threatens, Ambedkar quotes:

O Arjuna! Whenever this religion of duties and occupations (that is the religion of Chaturverna) declines, then I myself will come to birth to punish those who are responsible for its downfall and restore it.

(Ambedkar 2008; Geeta IV, 7–8)

These provisions are treated as containing mandatory injunctions from the Creator to the effect that society must be constituted on the basis of four (later five castes) classes mentioned in the *Purusha Sukta*. These provisions contain a divine injunction prescribing a particular form of the constitution of chaturvarna society which moulds the life of the Indo-Aryan community in its early or liquid state. It is this mould which gave the Indo-Aryan community its peculiar shape and structure (Ambedkar 1990, 23). Ambedkar further argued that 'Nowhere has society consecrated its occupation as the way of getting a living. The economic activity has always remained outside the sanctity of religion. The Hindus are the only people in the world whose economic order—the relation of a workman to a workman, is consecrated by religion and made sacred, eternal and inviolate.' Ambedkar goes on to argue that 'this is what has given the Hindu social order its abiding strength to defy the ravages of time and the onslaught of time' (Ambedkar 2008, 128–129). Ambedkar quotes the great Lord Acton 'who says that inequality has grown as a result of historical circumstances; it has never been adopted as a creed. However, for Hinduism, inequality is a religious doctrine adopted and conscientiously preached as sacred dogma. It is an official creed. The inequality for Hindus is a divinely prescribed way of life as a religious doctrine and as a prescribed way of life, it has become incarnated in the Hindu society and is shaped and moulded by it in its thoughts and in its doings' (Ambedkar 2008, 128).

We characterize the essential and unique features of the caste system by reproducing the summary of Ambedkar's perspective in his own words. As early as 1946, Ambedkar wrote:

Though the existence of classes is the de facto condition of every society, nevertheless no society has converted the de factor state of affairs into a de jure connotation of an **ideal society**. The scheme of Purusha Sukta (of Varna/caste system) is the only instance in which the real is elevated to the dignity of an ideal. This is the first unique feature of the scheme set out in Purusha Sukta. Secondly, no community has given the de facto state of class composition a legal effect by accepting it as a de jure connotation of an ideal society—Purusha Sukta is the only instance in which an attempt was made to give reality to the ideal by invoking the sanction of law. Thirdly, no society has accepted that class composition is an ideal one. At most, they have accepted it as being natural. The Purusha Sukta goes further. It not only regards class composition as natural and ideal but also regards it as sacred and divine. No society has an official gradation laid down, fixed and permanent, with an ascending scale of reverence and a descending scale of contempt. The scheme of Purusha Sukta is unique, in as much as it fixes a permanent warrant of precedence among the different classes, which neither time of circumstances can alter. The warrant of precedence is based on the principle of graded inequality among the four classes, whereby it recognises the Brahmin to be above all, the Kshatriya below the Brahmin and above the Vaishya and Shudra, the Vaishya below the Kshatriya but above the Shudra and Shudra below all.

(Ambedkar 1946, 25–26)

Thus, the religious doctrine was constructed to justify inequities so that people obey it as a faith. Insofar as the ideology is concerned, it is a set of ideas and beliefs or an attitude to life that guides behaviour, especially one held by a particular group that influences the way people behave towards others. The ideology was brought into operation to justify economic inequities of the Hindu social order, i.e. the caste system. The persistence of classes in some form in ancient society was a natural thing. But brahmanical scholars attribute meaning to the classes by ranking them into high and low castes, and further made the high caste superior, entitled to special rights and privileges and low caste inferior without any rights, and service to the higher castes as their only occupation. If we look at race, the same route was followed. The race or colour is a fact, but the meaning was attributed to Black and White, treating Whites to be superior and

Blacks as inferior and by virtue of this superiority and inferiority, the former was entitled to economic rights while the latter was denied the same rights. Thus, in both cases of race and caste, racism and casteism, respectively, were developed as an ideological construct with a motive to realize economic gains for Whites and higher castes. However, there is one difference between the two. Presumably, unlike race, an ideal of caste society with its inequalities was regarded as sacred and of divine origin. Ambedkar observed:

> For Hinduism, economic inequality is a religious doctrine adopted and conscientiously preached as sacred dogma. It is an official creed and nobody is ashamed to profess it openly. Inequality for the Hindus is a divinely prescribed way of life as a religious doctrine and, as a prescribed way of life, it has become incarnated in Hindu society and is shaped and moulded in its thoughts and in its doing.
>
> (Ambedkar 2008, 66)

3.5 Sources and Motives of Discrimination

As mentioned earlier, Ambedkar wrote about economics of caste discrimination long before the first systematic theoretical attempt of economic discrimination by Becker in 1957. Hence, Ambedkar did not have the advantage of insights of the modern theories of economic discrimination, although he enquired into similar questions which modern theories of discrimination enquired into. Among other issues, contemporary theories not only enquired into the fact of discrimination but also the sources and motive behind economic discrimination. Neoclassical theories, namely Taste for discrimination, imperfect information theory and its variants, and identity theory, in one form or another, recognized interrelation between economic discrimination and the group norms—norms as a source of discriminatory outcome in labour and other markets—the way individuals from one group behave with the individuals from another group. These theories (Taste, belief, identity, and other variants), as we discussed earlier, also imply that the origin of discriminatory norms is rooted in 'prejudice' which is embedded in the psychology of the 'individual'. The question is: Where does the prejudice originate from? Social psychologists bring insights on this question, namely the sources of prejudice. Allport (1954) treats prejudice primarily as something which is rooted in an individual's psychology. Psychology of prejudice, which produces stereotypical (false) beliefs by the dominant group, results in discriminatory behaviour towards the subordinate group, a view that is similar to the Taste theory. However, Blumer (1958) questions Allport's theoretical construct of prejudice as a set of individual feelings and argues that 'race prejudice exists in a sense of "group position" rather than in a set of individual feelings which members of one racial group have toward members of another racial group' (Blumer 1958, 3). Blumer shifts the locus of the prejudice from individual beliefs to 'attitudes of the group about the "relative status and material benefits" associated with membership in the group harbouring stereotypical beliefs toward the "others". The extent to which the dominant groups perpetuates advantage for their own and disadvantage to the subordinate groups is a key factor for group outcomes' (Blumer 1958, 3–4).

In Blumer's notion of prejudice, four basic types of feelings or attitudes always seem to be present in (race) prejudice by the dominant group: 'A feeling of superiority, a feeling that the subordinate race is intrinsically different and alien, a feeling of proprietary claim to certain areas of privilege and advantage, and perhaps the most important, a feeling of fear that the subordinate race harbours designs on the prerogatives of dominant race' (Blumer 1958, 4). Thus, Blumer shifts the axis of prejudice away from individual sentiments towards collective interests to maintain a relative group interest. The focus is on 'group position' and 'group efforts' for material interest and high social status. Prejudice becomes an operative, mobilizing instrument to preserve the economic and socially privileged position of the dominant group. There are real material interests at stake in the efforts of the dominant group to preserve its privileged position and also the more intangible, and psychic benefit of high status.

Building on Blumer's theory, Darity et al. (2006) in their 'racial identity norm theory' of discrimination, further argued that racial norms in social interaction are formed because the racial norms are productive (or are assets) which bring material gains to the dominant group. The racial norms emerged because they are productive, and they yield economic returns to the discriminators. Racial identity norm theory does not rule out the possibility of high social status as a motive behind discrimination, but in their view, prime motive is economic and the high social status, while cherishing psychological satisfaction, eventually indirectly assists in economic gains.

Two main points emerge quite clearly from Blumer's theory of 'prejudice as group norms or consciousness' and Darity's 'racial identity norm theory'. The first point is that prejudice exists in the sense of 'group consciousness' rather than in a set of individual feelings. The second point is that the motive behind market discrimination by dominant groups against subordinate groups is primarily pecuniary, although they do not rule out the occasional possibility of non-pecuniary motive. In other words, it is the material interest which is the core of motivation for discriminatory behaviour on the part of the dominant group against the subordinate groups.

What is the position of Ambedkar relating to these two important questions, namely the individual or group consciousness aspect of prejudice, and the motive behind the group consciousness and group action? On both the points, namely group character of prejudice and the motive behind prejudice (or caste norms and ideology), Ambedkar's analysis is fairly similar to that of Blumer's and Darity's approaches. More importantly, Ambedkar not only holds similar views but also brings additional insights and advances in the discourse further on these two points. Ambedkar's approach brings new insights from his analysis of the caste system. His analysis of caste system takes the discourse on discrimination beyond assumptions and hypotheses and provides extensive evidence from the normative framework of the caste system. On this point, Ambedkar quotes Oscar Wilde who said 'that to be intelligible is to be found out'. Manu (the principal Hindu lawgiver) is neither afraid nor ashamed of being found out. Indeed, Manu did not leave it to be found out. He expressed his views in resonant and majestic notes 'about the origin of social classes' (Ambedkar 1987, reprint 2014, 72). Ambedkar provides evidence from the Hindus laws on caste prejudice—as it exists in the sense of group position rather than in a set of individual feelings which members of the higher caste hold toward the untouchables caste. Ambedkar, while stating that caste does not recognize an individual, his worth and distinctiveness, goes on to add that:

the Hindu social order does not recognise the individual as a centre of social purpose. For the Hindu social order is based primarily on the class or Verna and not on individuals—the unit of Hindu society is not the individual Brahmin or the individual Kshatriya or the individual Vaishya or the individual Shudra or the individual panchama (Untouchables). The unit of Hindu social order is the class or Verna. In the Hindu social order, there is no room for individual merit and no consideration of individual justice. If an individual has privileges it is not because it is due to him personally. The privilege goes with Verna and if he is found to enjoy it, it is because he belongs to that Verna. Contra wise, if an individual is suffering from a wrong, it is not because he, by his conduct deserves it. The disability is the disability imposed upon the Verna.

(Ambedkar 1987, 99–100)

It is clear from this position of Ambedkar that the caste acquired a group character because the economic and social rights of each caste are defined as group rights based on the caste identity. The actions of the individuals are influenced by a motivation to optimize the material interests of the community. The group interest is central to the action of the individuals as a member of a group.

Ambedkar's view on the motivation behind caste discrimination again is fairly similar to Blumer's and Darity's (Darity 2007) views which emphasize pecuniary motives, although the non-pecuniary motive is not altogether ruled out. The way the economic rights are appropriated by higher castes, the material gains seem to be the main motive (W. Darity Jr 2013). Ambedkar has provided enough evidence on the property rights and special privileges claimed and enjoyed by the brahmin. As we have seen earlier that the privileges of the brahmin are beyond any restriction, everything in the world is supposed to be their property. In this respect, Ambedkar observed:

To a question of what is right and what is good, the answer which the philosophy of Hinduism gives is remarkable. It holds that to be right and good the act must serve the interest of this class of supermen, namely the Brahmins.

(Ambedkar 1987, 72)

The privileged position of the brahmin as a social group of higher caste (as well as the other castes) is quite obvious from the extensive evidence from Manu's laws.

There are two more aspects of Ambedkar's interpretation of the caste system which brings new insights. The first relates to the methods of enforcement of the iniquitous caste laws relating to occupations and property rights, and the second is the inclusion of economic rights and occupation under the domain of the Hindu religion. As we have discussed earlier, beside the state, the enforcement of the caste codes is also made of the obligation of higher-caste community. The instruments of social ostracism and excommunication and other punishments are devised to deal with the violation of the caste code both by higher castes and lower castes. This enforcement mechanism of social ostracism is as powerful as the laws. If the caste discrimination persists in modified forms, despite the provision of equal rights and equal opportunity in India's new Constitution in 1950, it is this informal mechanism of social ostracism by the higher-caste community which has kept the caste system alive in the present.

The second feature is the inclusion of caste inequality as a part of religious doctrine which is adopted and conscientiously preached as sacred dogma. This makes the ideal of inequality as a divinely prescribed way of life a religious doctrine for the Hindus. In Ambedkar's view, 'nowhere has society consecrated its occupation, the ways of getting a living'. The economic activity has always remained outside the sanctity of religion. The Hindus are the only people in the world whose economic order, the relation of a workman to a workman, is consecrated by religion and made sacred, eternal, and inviolate (Ambedkar 2008, 128–129). Thus, the caste inequality receives justification both by laws and religious morality. Ambedkar argued that

> in Hinduism, there is no distinction between legal philosophy and moral philosophy. That is because in Hinduism there is no distinction between the legal and moral, the legal being also moral—The word Dharma in Hinduism has two-fold connotations. It means both law and moral. That is one reason why in the philosophy of Hinduism there can be no distinction between legal and moral philosophy.
>
> (Ambedkar 1987, 81–82)

It is this double binding of law and morality which brings the rigidity in the caste system and makes it the most stubborn institution for change. These are some of the new insights by Ambedkar which enriched the modern discourse on sources and motive of economic discrimination based on evidence from the Indian caste system.

There are other aspects on which Ambedkar has brought new insights. One such feature of the caste system is the 'isolation and exclusiveness' in economic exchange. In Ambedkar's view, the economic isolation and exclusiveness is a unique feature of the caste system which makes caste antisocial and inimical towards one another. Isolation with antisocial attitude continues the separation into privileged and underprivileged (Ambedkar 2008, 113). Antisocial spirit is found wherever one group has 'interest of its own' which shuts it out from full interaction with another group so that its prevailing purpose is the protection of what it has got. The higher caste's primary concern is to protect their interest against other castes, and other castes' interest is to protect their interests against higher castes. The Hindus, therefore, are not merely an assortment of castes but they are so many antagonistic groups each living for themselves and for their own interest, observed Ambedkar (Ambedkar 1946, Third Edition 2016, 52). Becker's theory did recognize the possibility of 'segregation' between Whites and Blacks. Becker observed: 'The economic relations between two communities decrease with an increase in discrimination. When the taste for discrimination becomes sufficiently large, each society will be in economic isolation and would have to get along with its resources. Since members of each society would be working only with each other, complete economic isolation would also involve complete economic segregation' (Becker 1971, 22–24). Some aspects of economic segregation of the untouchables bear close similarity with Becker's notion of segregation, insofar as the untouchables face complete exclusion in some economic relations. However, there are unique differences as well. The exclusion of untouchables is combined with their selective but exploitative inclusion. The untouchables face exclusion from access to employment as an employee in teaching, military, trade and commerce, and farming, the occupations of the four castes. The untouchables also face exclusion in some works due to their polluting social status. They are excluded in categories of work which involved direct physical contact, domestic work, and work related to religious events. But at the same time, the unique feature is that

the untouchables are obliged to work or are forced to work in all these occupations as manual wage workers. Untouchables being considered as a
slave caste, they are forced to involve as slave labour or exploitative labour
at very low wages. Thus, the segregation of untouchables is not only characterized by complete economic disconnect/exclusion in some economic
relations from the higher castes but also selective inclusion in their work,
which Sen (2000) term as 'unfavourable exclusion' and 'unfavourable inclusion' respectively. Ambedkar brought forth the exploitative nature of
labour relation involved in caste labour exchange quite clearly.

The comparison of the other variants of neoclassical theories of castes
with Ambedkar's approach also revealed fresh insights. The theories of
caste discrimination of Akerlof and Lal, generally assumed certain features of caste as given and then go on to argue that the equilibrium of the
caste economy reached under these assumptions, tend to be less than optimal and less efficient. Akerlof also recognized the role of social customs
in economic decision-making and its inefficient economic outcome.[3]
These theories, however, are silent about the formation of caste norms,
ideals, or social customs in the first place and the motive behind their
emergence. There are similar limitations of the theory initially proposed
by Arrow (1971) which attribute the origin of discrimination in hiring
based on social perception or belief about the productivity of social
groups due to imperfect information about the individuals. The imperfect information theory has serious limitations to explain the persistence
of caste discrimination even in a situation of perfect information. The
most typical case is the labour market in rural India. In the Indian rural
labour market, where almost three-fourths of the Scheduled Caste found
that the higher-caste employers not only have complete information
about the productivity of the untouchable wage workers, but also about
their work habits and work ethics due to long association with labour
families staying in the same village for generations. Yet, the untouchable workers, who are as productive as higher-caste workers, may face
discrimination in hiring and wages. Between the higher-caste and lower-
caste wage workers, who are similarly placed in terms of productivity, the

---

[3] Ambedkar also analysed the economic consequences of the caste system on economic efficiency and he considered the economics of the caste system as dysfunctional. However, the
economic analysis of the caste system from the efficiency angle would take us beyond the scope
of the study.

employer may prefer individuals from her/his caste and this may not involve loss to the employer but real psychological satisfaction over her/his efforts in maximizing the economic gains of higher caste community of her/his belonging.

Finally, we look at the implications of Ambedkar's theoretical perspective for the present study which deals with labour market discrimination in employment, wages, and occupation. The occupational discrimination, based on caste, carries a specific meaning which needs to be understood because discrimination in occupation and employment often tend to overlap. The caste system follows the notion of division of labour between the occupations. But it converts the scheme of division of labour or work into a scheme of division of labourers or workers and permanently fixed occupational categories without the possibility of intercaste mobility or division of labour into a division of labourer (Ambedkar 2008, 30). This means that individuals from one caste with a specific caste occupation (or economic activity), such as the shudra whose occupation is agriculture, face restrictions to work in occupations of other castes, such as trade, military, and teaching which are the occupations of vaishya, kshatriya, and the brahmin respectively. The work remains confined to occupation or economic activities assigned to each caste. While this is the case for the division of work for the four castes, the case of untouchables is somewhat complex. While the untouchables are prohibited to engage in the occupations of the four castes above them as self-employed workers and salaried workers, they are permitted (rather forced) to work in all occupations as casual manual wage workers. Further, similar compulsion is imposed on them to get engaged in occupations which are considered impure and polluting, like scavenging or those related to leather or other low artisan goods. Thus, except in employment as casual wage workers in all occupations and polluting occupation, the untouchable workers would face exclusion and discrimination. In the present classification of occupations, those untouchables who are hired may be excluded from work in earlier prohibited occupations/economic activities and instead placed in lower occupations despite their merit. This results in occupation segregation of the untouchables in low-level economic activities.

With respect to employment, Ambedkar considered employment discrimination as an integral part of the regulatory framework of the caste system. The caste rules place restrictions on the employment of individuals beyond her/his caste occupation. The untouchables are pro-hibited from employment in the occupation of the four castes above them, namely teaching/preaching, military, trade, and agriculture. Further, they are also excluded from certain categories of work due to their polluting status, which include domestic duties, work which involves physical contact and those related to religious events. However, they are required to serve (rather forced) as manual wage workers for the castes above them. Besides, the untouchables' engagement as wage workers is coercive—similar to that of slave and serf or bonded and attached labourer. In fact, in Ambedkar's view, the untouchability was more akin to slavery. He observed that:

> with reference to the inner meaning, a slave, as defined by Plato, means a person who accepts from another the purposes which control his conduct. In this sense, a slave is not an end in himself. He is only a means for filling the ends desired by others. Thus understood, the Shudra is a slave. In their economic significance, the rules put an interdict on economic independence.
>
> (Ambedkar 2008, second edition, 40)

However, the interpretation apart, Ambedkar also brought enough evidence from Manu's laws about the practice of Hindu slavery in graded forms by which the untouchables were treated as slaves. Therefore, the untouchables' engagement as wage labour was in the form of slave and serf labour. As slave labour, their wage earning was extremely low and below subsistence level, which means wage discrimination. The legacy of slavery may persist in the form of bonded labour, forced, and attached labour. These insights from Ambedkar's theoretical perspective on caste discrimination in occupation, employment, and wages are useful for the empirical analysis on labour market discrimination undertaken in the present study.

4

Measuring Discrimination and its Impact on Poverty

4.1 Introduction

As mentioned in Chapter 1, the main purpose of the study is to estimate the extent of caste discrimination in employment, wages, and occupation and the impact of discrimination on income and poverty of regular salaried workers. In this chapter, we will outline the methods used to estimate the extent of discrimination in employment, wages, and occupation, and also its impact on reduction in income and increase in poverty. In the end we will also discuss the method of selection of caste groups and the years during which the study was carried out.

4.2 Methods to Measure Wage Discrimination

In the case of wage, the gross wage differential between higher castes and the Scheduled Castes (SC) is decomposed using various decomposition methods available in the reviewed literature. Different approaches have been used to measure wage discrimination. The first approach predicts earnings from the characteristics of all workers including gender/caste/religion dummy as a predictor (a single-equation technique). Unfortunately, this approach yields a biased result because it assumes that the wage structure is the same for both advantaged (say higher castes) and disadvantaged groups (SC). In other words, it assumes the values of coefficients of explanatory variables, such as education and experience, to be the same for both groups (Gunderson 1989; Madheswaran 1996).[1]

---

[1] This approach allows only change in intercept, but not the slope. In order to overcome this problem, we estimate earning function for each group separately.

Scheduled Castes in the Indian Labour Market. Sukhadeo Thorat, S. Madheswaran, and B. P. Vani, Oxford University Press. © Sukhadeo Thorat, S. Madheswaran, and B. P. Vani 2023. DOI: 10.1093/oso/9780198872252.003.0004

The second approach uses 'decomposition method' to partition the observed wage gap between advantaged and disadvantaged groups into two components, such as characteristics effect/endowment difference and coefficients effect/discrimination in the wages. The latter is derived as an unexplained residual and is termed the 'discrimination coefficient'. This method was first developed by Blinder (1973) and Oaxaca (1973) and later extended to incorporate selectivity bias (Reimer 1983, 1985) and to overcome the index number problem (Cotton 1988; Neumark 1988; Oaxaca and Ransom 1994). Further improvement has been made in this method. Due to limitation of mean-based decomposition method, recently, studies have used the quintile regression decomposition method proposed by Machado and Mata (2005) and Melly (2006). This method decomposes the wage gap across the quintiles of the wage distribution. Another version of the decomposition method is the expanded decomposition method developed by Madheswaran and Attewell (2007). This method incorporates the occupational distribution into the wage earnings estimation. The advantage of using this method is that both job discrimination (differential access to certain occupational positions) and wage discrimination (differential earnings within the same job) can be estimated simultaneously.

4.2.1 Blinder-Oaxaca Decomposition Method

The decomposition method enables one to separate the wage differential into differences that can be explained by differences in characteristics and those that cannot be explained by differences in characteristics. The gross wage differential can be defined as:

$$G = \frac{Y_{HC} - Y_{SC}}{Y_{HC}} = \frac{Y_{HC}}{Y_{SC}} - 1 \qquad (1)$$

where Y_{HC} and Y_{SC} represent the wages of higher castes' individuals and SC individuals respectively. In the absence of labour market discrimination, the higher castes and the SC wage differential would reflect pure productivity differences.

$$Q = \frac{Y_{HC}^0}{Y_{SC}^0} - 1 \qquad (2)$$

where the superscript denotes the absence of market discrimination. The **market discrimination coefficient (D)** is then defined as the proportionate difference between G + 1 and Q + 1.

$$D = \frac{\left(\dfrac{Y_{HC}}{Y_{SC}}\right) - \left(\dfrac{Y_{HC}^0}{Y_{SC}^0}\right)}{\left(\dfrac{Y_{HC}^0}{Y_{SC}^0}\right)} \qquad (3)$$

Equations (1)–(3) imply the following logarithmic decomposition of the gross earnings differential

$$\ln(G+1) = \ln(D+1) + \ln(Q+1) \qquad (4)$$

This decomposition can be further applied within the framework of semi-logarithmic earnings equations (Mincer 1974) and estimated via OLS such that:

$$\ln \bar{Y}_{HC} = \sum \hat{\beta}_{HC} \bar{X}_{HC} + \varepsilon_{HC} \qquad \left(\textit{Hindu Higher Caste wage Eqn}\right) \quad (5)$$

$$\ln \bar{Y}_{SC} = \sum \hat{\beta}_{SC} \bar{X}_{SC} + \varepsilon_{SC} \qquad \left(\textit{Scheduled Castes wage Eqn}\right) \qquad (6)$$

where ln $\bar{Y}$ denotes the geometric mean of earnings, $\bar{X}$ the vector of mean values of the regressors, $\hat{\beta}$ the vector of coefficients, and εthe error term with zero mean and constant variance. Within this framework, the gross differential in logarithmic term is given by:

$$\ln(G+1) = \ln\left(\frac{\bar{Y}_{HC}}{\bar{Y}_{SC}}\right) = \ln \bar{Y}_{HC} - \ln \bar{Y}_{SC} = \sum \hat{\beta}_{HC} \bar{X}_{SC} - \sum \hat{\beta}_{SC} \bar{X}_{SC} \quad (7)$$

The Oaxaca decomposition simply shows that Equation (7) can be expanded. In other words, the difference of the coefficients of the two earnings functions is taken as a priori evidence of discrimination. If, for the given endowment, SC individuals are paid according to the higher castes wage structure in the absence of discrimination, then the hypothetical SC earnings function can be given as:

$$ln\bar{Y}_{SC} = \sum \hat{\beta}_{HC}\bar{X}_{SC} \tag{8}$$

Subtracting Equation (8) from Equation (7) we get:

$$ln\bar{Y}_{HC} - ln\bar{Y}_{SC} = \sum \hat{\beta}_{HC}(\bar{X}_{HC} - \bar{X}_{SC}) + \sum \bar{X}_{SC}(\hat{\beta}_{HC} - \hat{\beta}_{SC}) \tag{9}$$

Alternatively, the decomposition can also be done as:

$$ln\bar{Y}_{HC} - ln\bar{Y}_{SC} = \sum \hat{\beta}_{SC}(\bar{X}_{HC} - \bar{X}_{SC}) + \sum \bar{X}_{HC}(\hat{\beta}_{HC} - \hat{\beta}_{SC}) \tag{10}$$

In equations (9) and (10) mentioned above, on the right side, the first term can be interpreted as endowment difference and the second term in these equations has been regarded in the literature as the discrimination component.

Blinder (1973) gave the following interpretation of market discrimination coefficient:

R = Raw Differential = E + C + U

E = Portion of differential attributable to differing endowments

$$E = \sum \hat{\beta}_{HC}(\bar{X}_{HC} - \bar{X}_{SC}) \ or \ \sum \hat{\beta}_{SC}(\bar{X}_{HC} - \bar{X}_{SC}) \tag{11}$$

C = Portion of differential attributable to differing coefficients

$$C = \sum \bar{X}_{SC}(\hat{\beta}_{HC} - \hat{\beta}_{SC}) \ or \ \sum \bar{X}_{HC}(\hat{\beta}_{HC} - \hat{\beta}_{SC}) \tag{12}$$

U = Unexplained portion of the differential or shift coefficient = $(\alpha_{HC} - \alpha_{SC})$

D = Portion of the differential attributable to discrimination = C + U

Studies use either of these alternative decomposition forms (Equation 9 or Equation 10) based on their assumptions about the wage structure that would prevail in the absence of discrimination. Some authors take the averages of the estimates of the two equations (Greenhalgh 1980). This kind of problem is called 'the index number problem'. In the present study, we assume male wage structure as the non-discriminatory wage structure.

The index number problem is further depicted in Figure 4.1. The horizontal axis measures education (schooling in years) which can be considered a typical individual characteristic. The vertical axis measures wages. The lower line represents the earnings function for SC, i.e. it shows that SC wages increase by $\hat{\beta}_{SC}$ (the slope of the line) for an additional year of schooling. The upper line is the earnings function for higher castes and $\hat{\beta}_{HC}$ is the corresponding slope coefficient. Let $\bar{X}_{SC}$ and $\bar{X}_{HC}$ be the average level of schooling attained by higher castes and SC respectively. The way the diagram is drawn suggests that SC have on an average lower wages than higher castes, i.e. $\bar{Y}_{SC} < \bar{Y}_{HC}$. The reasons could be as follows: (1) The SC are less educated $\bar{X}_{SC} < \bar{X}_{HC}$. (2) Their education is rewarded less than men $\hat{\beta}_{SC} < \hat{\beta}_{HC}$. (3) Uneducated SC have been assumed

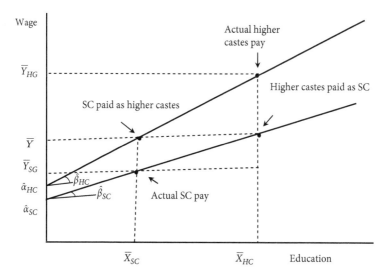

Fig. 4.1 Decomposition of the wage gap between higher castes and Scheduled Castes

to receive a lower wage in the labour market than higher castes (the constant term for women, α_{SC}, is lower than the constant term for men, α_{HC}). Assuming that the difference in educational attainment is the result of SC free choice, one is interested in finding which part of the gross wage gap $(\bar{Y}_{HC}\bar{Y}_{SC})$ is justified, i.e. can be explained by the fact that SC are less qualified than higher castes in the sense that they possess a lower amount of schooling than higher castes (the difference arising from $\bar{X}_{SC} < \bar{X}_{HC}$). If 'no discrimination' is taken to mean that SC should be paid as higher castes $\hat{\beta}_{SC}$ should be equal to $\hat{\beta}_{HC}$ and α_{SC} should be equal to α_{SC}, then SC average pay should increase to $\bar{y}$; hence $\bar{Y}_{SC}\bar{Y}$ is the unjustified part of the wage gap. Alternatively, if 'no discrimination' means that higher castes should be paid as SC $(\hat{\beta}_{HC}$ equal to $\hat{\beta}_{SC}$ and α_{HC} equal to $\alpha_{SC})$, then the unjustified part of the wage gap becomes $\bar{Y}\bar{Y}_{HC}$.

The two decompositions in Figure 4.1 produce dramatically different results. This is purely for expository purposes. In practice, it is not certain if a decomposition based on female means will produce a higher or lower estimate for justified or unjustified discrimination than decomposition based on male means. It all depends on the relative 'flatness' of the two earning functions (i.e. the curvature of the lines around the region of the average SC and higher castes characteristics) which is not captured in the simple linear specification adopted in the figure.

	(Justified)
(Discrimination)	
Decomposition at average SC education $(\bar{X}_{SC})$	$\bar{Y}\bar{Y}_{HC} + \bar{Y}_{SC}\bar{Y}$
Decomposition at average higher castes education $(\bar{X}_{HC})$	$\bar{Y}_{SC}\bar{Y} + \bar{Y}\bar{Y}_{HC}$

For the sake of convenience, our subsequent analysis using Blinder-Oaxaca decomposition method uses the wage structure of the advantaged groups (higher castes) as the non-discriminatory wage structure.

4.2.2 Cotton, Neumark, and Oaxaca and Ransom Decomposition Method

To solve the index number problem, i.e. whether Equation (9) or Equation (10) should be used to calculate the discrimination coefficient,

Cotton (1988), Neumark (1988), and Oaxaca and Ransom (1994) have proposed an alternative decomposition. They have extended the wage discrimination component further. They calculated non-discriminatory or competitive wage structures which can be used to estimate overpayment and underpayment. The latter extension of decomposition allows the sources of discrimination to be developed from the Becker (1971) model of discrimination. In Becker's neoclassical model, individuals, whether they are employers, employees, or consumers, can hold discriminatory 'tastes' against certain people or groups of people.[2] If we discuss this theory in the context of Indian caste system, we can offer the following explanation. Employee discrimination is characterized by overpayment to workers, assumed to be higher castes, since they require a financial compensation to work alongside the SC workers because of their taste for discrimination. Employer nepotism is also characterized by higher castes' workers overpayment, with the non-SC employer gaining a greater non-monetary benefit from employing higher castes rather than SC workers, which increases the demand for higher castes workers. Finally, employer discrimination is inferred when SC workers are underpaid because this compensates the discriminatory employers' taste.

When applied to our scenario, it can be interpreted as implying that discrimination not only lowers the salaries of SC individuals, but also raises the salaries of higher castes individuals. Equations (9) and (10) reveal only the relative pay effects of labour market discrimination and Cotton suggests that they mask overpayment relatively to higher castes' individuals and underpayment to SC individuals as compared to the non-discriminatory wage. Therefore, the discrimination component (unexplained) should comprise two parts—one, representing the amount by which higher castes' characteristics are overcompensated relative to their marginal product and the other representing the amount by which SC characteristics are undercompensated (SC disadvantage, i.e. the cost of belonging to the SC group).

---

[2] Other theories of discrimination developed by Becker include consumer discrimination, government (institutional) discrimination, and market discrimination. Alternative theories of discrimination can be found in Bergmann (1971), Phelps (1972), Roemer (1979), and Lang (1986), with extension of Becker's work found in Goldberg (1982) and Naylor (1994).

The true non-discriminatory wage would lie somewhere between the higher castes and SC wage structure. The Cotton logarithmic wage differential is written as:

$$ln\bar{Y}_{HC} - ln\bar{Y}_{SC} = \sum \beta^*(\bar{X}_{HC} - \bar{X}_{SC}) + \sum \bar{X}_{HC}(\hat{\beta}_{HC} - \beta^*)$$
$$+ \sum \bar{X}_{SC}(\beta^* - \hat{\beta}_{SC}) \tag{13}$$

where β* is the reward structure that would have occurred in the absence of discrimination. The first term on the right side of Equation (13) represents skill differences between the SC and higher castes, while the second term represents the overpayment to higher castes due to favouritism, and the third term represents the underpayment to the SC due to discrimination. The decomposition specified in Equation (13) cannot be made operational without some assumption about the salary structures for the SC and higher castes in the absence of discrimination. The theory of discrimination provides some guidance in the choice of the non-discriminatory wage structure. The assumption is operationalized by weighting the higher castes and SC wage structures by respective proportions of higher castes and SC in the labour force. Thus, the estimator β* used above is defined as:

$$\beta^* = P_{HC}\hat{\beta}_{HC} + P_{SC}\hat{\beta}_{SC} \tag{14}$$

where P_{HC} and P_{SC} are the sample proportions of higher castes and SC populations and $\hat{\beta}$ and $\hat{\beta}$ the higher castes and SC pay structures respectively.

Another versatile representation of non-discriminatory or pooled wage structure is proposed by Neumark (1988), and Oaxaca and Ransom (1994). This can be written as:

$$\beta^* = \Omega\hat{\beta}_{HC} + (1-\Omega)\hat{\beta}_{SC} \tag{15}$$

where Ω is a weighting matrix. 1 is the identity matrix. The weighting matrix is specified by:

$$\Omega = (X'X)^{-1} (X_{HC} X_{HC})$$

where X is the observation matrix for the pooled sample, X_{HC} is the observation matrix for the higher castes sample. The interpretation of Ω as weighting matrix is readily seen by noting that:

$$X'X = X'_{HC}X_{HC} + X'_{SC}X_{SC} \qquad (16)$$

where X_{SC} is the observation matrix of the SC sample, given $\hat{\beta}_{HC}$, $\hat{\beta}_{SC}$ and Equation (15), any assumption about β^* reduces to an assumption about Ω.

4.2.3 Expanded Decomposition to Estimate Wage Discrimination and Occupation Discrimination

Oaxaca (1973), Cotton (1988) and Neumark (1988) methods are criticized on the grounds that they do not distinguish adequately between wage discrimination and job discrimination or even occupational segregation. If the same characteristics that determine wages also determined the choice of occupation, then these methods would be sufficient to calculate the discrimination coefficient. But there are other factors that influence occupational attainment, such as childhood influences, influences due to personal characteristics and some from discriminatory constraints on occupational choice or entry. Persons with similar characteristics, but who have attained different occupational levels, often earn differing wages implying that there are other additional factors that influence occupational attainments.

Brown et al. (1980) incorporate a separate model of occupational attainment into their analysis of wage differentials. Banerjee and Knight (1985) have used this decomposition by introducing a multinomial logit model which could estimate both wage and occupational discrimination for migrant labourers in India, the latter defined as 'unequal pay for workers with same economic characteristics which results from their being employed in different jobs'. In this section, we have combined Oaxaca and

Ransom (1994) and Brown et al. (1980) to form a more refined detailed decomposition analysis of occupational and wage discrimination.

We have seen that the Equation (7) was used following Oaxaca (1973) to estimate the gross logarithmic wage differential between castes. Now, as the concern is to estimate occupational discrimination as well as wage discrimination, the proportion of higher castes (P_{iHC}) and proportion of SC (P_{iSC}) in each occupation i is included in the decomposition. Equation 7 is thus expanded to:

$$ln(G+1) = \sum [P_{isc} ln \bar{Y}_{iHC} - P_{iSC} ln \bar{Y}_{iSC}] \qquad (17)$$

Following Brown et al. (1980), Moll (1992 and 1996), and Banerjee and Knight (1985), this can be further decomposed as:

$$ln(G+1) = \sum [ln \bar{Y}_{iHC} (P_{iHC} - P_{iSC}) + \sum P_{iSC} (ln \bar{Y}_{iHC} - ln \bar{Y}_{iSC})] \qquad (18)$$

The first term on the right represents the wage difference attributable to differences in the occupational distribution and the second term is attributable to the difference between wages within occupations. Each term contains an explained component and an unexplained component. If we define $\hat{P}_{isc}$ as the proportion of SC workers that would be in occupation i if they had the same occupational attainment function as higher castes, then Equation (18) can be further decomposed as:

$$ln(G+1) = \sum [ln \bar{Y}_{iuc} (P_{iHC} - \hat{P}_{isc}) + \sum ln \bar{Y}_{iHC} (\hat{P}_{isc} - P_{isc})$$
$$+ \sum P_{isc} (ln \bar{Y}_{iHC} - ln \bar{Y}_{iSC})] \qquad (19)$$

where the **first term** represents the part of the gross differential attributable to the difference between the observed higher castes occupational distribution and the occupational distribution that SC workers would occupy if they had the higher castes' occupational function. The **second term** is the component of the gross wage differential attributable to occupational differences not explained on the basis of personal characteristics, and may be termed job discrimination. The proportions P_{iHC} and $\hat{P}_{isc}$ are estimated using a multinomial logit model. First, we estimate occupational attainment function for higher castes and then use these estimates to predict the proportion of SC workers that would be in occupation i if they had the same occupational attainment function as higher castes. This predicted probability of SC occupation is used in the further decomposition.

The justification to estimate occupational attainment function is as follows. An individual's occupational attainment is a function of employer's willingness to hire that person and of the individual's desire to work in specific occupations. Willingness of an employer to hire an individual depends on personal qualifications, such as education, training and experience (i.e. human capital). The individual's desire for a particular occupation can be expressed by at least three of the arguments in a utility function. First, utility depends on income which is a function of occupation. Secondly, utility depends on the pure consumption aspects of working, i.e. taste for the work involved. Finally, family size may induce an individual to seek a career that provides stable employment, also a function of occupation. The interactions of these supply and demand factors lead to the individual's employment in a particular occupation. Rather than specifying functional form for the utility function, the human capital production function, and the interactions between them, we specify reduced form probability model. Occupations are indexed by $i(i = 1, 2, ..., N)$. The probability that individual j with a vector of characteristics $Z_j = (1, Z_{2j}, Z_{3j}, ...)$ will be assigned to occupation k is:

$$\breve{P}_{kj} = \frac{\exp(\tilde{\beta}_k Z_j)}{\sum\limits_{i}^{N} \exp(\tilde{\beta}_i Z_j)}$$

where $\tilde{\beta}_i$ is the vector of coefficients corresponding to the ith occupation. Since the probabilities must sum to unity across all occupational groups they are normalized arbitrarily for computational purposes. The **third term** (in Equation 19) represents the within-occupation wage differential. It is this component that is normally decomposed into wage discrimination and caste productivity terms. However, instead of doing this, the term is decomposed into higher castes' overpayment term, the SC underpayment term and within-occupation wage differential explained by certain productivity characteristics. In order to calculate these three terms, the 'pooled' methodology of Oaxaca and Ransom (1994) is used. Equation (20) presents the within-occupation gross caste wage differential, defined as:

$$\sum_i P_{iHC} \ln(G+1) = \sum_i P_{iSC}[\ln \overline{Y}_{iHC} - \ln \overline{Y}_{iSC}] \tag{20}$$

The actual proportion of the SC workers in each occupational group is for simplicity dropped until the final equation is derived. It should be noted that Equation (20) is identical to Equation (7) but for the occupation subscript. Following the methodology of Oaxaca and Ransom (1994), the within-occupation gross wage differential is decomposed into a productivity differential and an unexplained effect which may be attributed to within-occupation wage discrimination. The within-occupation logarithmic productivity differential is defined as: $\sum_i \ln(Q+1)$, where 'Q' is the gross unadjusted productivity differential. In order to calculate the logarithmic term, a non-discriminatory or 'competitive' wage structure is required so that,

$$\sum_i \ln(Q+1) = \ln \overline{Y}^*_{iHC} - \ln \overline{Y}^*_{iSC} \tag{21}$$

where $\ln \overline{Y}^*_{ir}$ is the average non-discriminatory wage structure for caste *r* in occupation *i*. In order to calculate the pooled wage structure, the higher castes and SC logarithmic wage structures are estimated using an earnings function, with the assumption that:

$$\ln \overline{Y}_{ir} = \tilde{\beta}_{ir}(\overline{X}_{ir}) \tag{22}$$

where $\tilde{\beta}_r$ and $\overline{X}_r$ are the vector of coefficients and average productivity characteristics of the different caste workers, estimated by ordinary least squares.[3] The calculation of the non-discriminatory wage structure depends on the weights given to the higher castes and SC wage structures. We have discussed in equations (15) and (16) (Oaxaca and Ransom 1994) about the pooled wage structure. Given the pooled wage structure

---

[3] See Mincer (1974) for a discussion of labour market earning functions.

in Equation (15), within-occupation logarithmic wage discrimination is calculated by subtracting Equation (21) from Equation (20) to give us:

$$\sum_i \ln(D+1) = (\ln \bar{Y}_{iHC} - \ln \bar{Y}^*_{iHC}) + (ln\bar{Y}^*_{iSC} - ln\bar{Y}_{iSC}) \tag{23}$$

The gross wage differential is thus decomposed into a productivity and discriminatory term, meaning that the final within-occupation gross logarithmic wage differential is equivalent to:

$$\sum_i P_{iSC} \ln(G+1) = \sum_i P_{iSC}(ln\bar{Y}^*_{iHC} - ln\bar{Y}^*_{iSC}) \sum_i P_{iSC}(\ln \bar{Y}_{iHC} - \ln \bar{Y}^*_{iHC}) \\ + \sum_i P_{iSC}(ln\bar{Y}^*_{iSC} - ln\bar{Y}_{iSC}) \tag{24}$$

Substituting Equation (24) for the **Third Component** in Equation (19) yields the final decomposition of the gross-logarithmic wage differential.

$$\ln(G+1) = \sum_i ln\bar{Y}_{iHC}(P_{iHC} - \hat{P}_{isc}) + \sum_i ln\bar{Y}_{iHC}(\hat{P}_{iHC} - P_{isc}) \\ + \sum_i P_{iSC}[ln\bar{Y}_{iHC} - ln\bar{Y}_{HC}] + \sum_i P_{iSC}[ln\bar{Y}_{iHC} - ln\bar{Y}^*_{iHC}] \\ + \sum_i P_{iSC}[ln\bar{Y}^*_{iSC} - ln\bar{Y}_{iSC}] \tag{25}$$

Hence, a multinomial logit non-discriminatory model can be calculated which can distinguish between within-occupation SC underpayment, within-occupation higher castes overpayment, and occupational discrimination. Finally, to estimate this model, equations (21) and (13) are substituted into Equation (24) to give final extended decomposition as:

$$\ln(G+1) = \sum_i \tilde{\beta}_{iHC}(\bar{X}_{iHC})(P_{iHC} - \hat{P}_{iSC}) \quad \textit{(Job Explained)} \\ + \sum_i \tilde{\beta}_{iHC}(\bar{X}_{iHC})(\hat{P}_{iSC} - P_{iSC}) \quad \textit{(Job Discrimination)} \\ + \sum_i P_{iSC}(\tilde{\beta}_i)(\bar{X}_{iHC} - \bar{X}_{iSC}) \quad \textit{(Wage Explained)} \\ + \sum_i P_{iSC}(\bar{X}_{iHC})(\tilde{\beta}_{iHC} - \tilde{\beta}^*_i) \quad \textit{(Wage overpayment to HC)} \\ + \sum_i P_{iSC}(\bar{X}_{iSC})(\tilde{\beta}^*_i - \tilde{\beta}_{iSC}) \quad \textit{(Wage underpayment to SC)} \tag{26}$$

Wage overpayment can be interpreted as the benefit of being higher caste in the labour market and underpayment can be interpreted as the cost being SC in the labour market. The wage overpayment and underpayment together give wage discrimination.

4.3 Occupational (Segregation) Dissimilarity Index

The occupation and industry are clearly two distinct points of view from which the economic activity of the population may be regarded. The first is what the individual does, and the second shows the position of the workers in the economic structure of the country. Occupation is the kind of work performed by an individual while industry is the branch of economic activity to which he is connected. Occupational caste segregation is said to exist when SC workers and higher castes workers are differently distributed across occupations regardless of the nature of job allocation. Occupational segregation measures the extent to which higher castes and SC occupy different positions in the division of labour and, as a result, have systematically different opportunities to obtain social and material rewards. Segregation operates both as an intrinsic measure of social inequality and as a precursor to caste differences in the distribution of earnings, opportunities of promotion, workplace authority and other stratification outcomes.

It is usual to compute indices of occupational segregation, and literature is replete with measurements of segregation. No one measure can be considered to be fully satisfactory and appropriate for all times and contexts. In the present study we use the popular Duncan Dissimilarity Index (ID). An underlying assumption is that segregation leads to a different distribution of higher castes and SC across occupations. This measure denotes the share of the employed population that would need to change occupation in order to restore equality in the distribution of higher castes and SC among occupations.

We have used the index of occupational dissimilarity proposed by O. D. Duncan and B. Duncan (1955) in order to provide some objective measure of occupational difference between male and female. The index is defined, in general, as:

$$ID = \frac{1}{2}\sum_{j=1}^{J} |\, P_j^{HC} - P_j^{SC}\,|$$

where P_j^{HC} and P_j^{SC} measure the percentage of higher castes and SC workers in occupational category j. The ID ranges from 0 to 100 with its numerical value indicating the percentage of higher castes, SC or some combination of the two that need to shift occupations so that the two distributions equalize. An ID of 0 means equal occupational representation by social groups, whereas a value of 100 denotes complete caste-based segregation across occupations.

A variant of this index is also calculated on the basis of the predicted SC outcomes or occupational attainment estimated using multinomial logit model regression. This index is given by:

$$ID^* = \frac{1}{2}\sum_{j=1}^{k} |\, P_J^{HC} - \hat{P}_j^{SC}\,|$$

where $\hat{P}_j^{SC}$ denotes the predicted occupational distributions of SC.

4.4 Measuring Employment Discrimination

We will now discuss the method used to estimate the employment discrimination. We disaggregate the differences in probability of access to employment to endowments factors and discrimination faced by the SC in seeking jobs in labour market. There are alternative statistical methods which capture the differences of such types. We used non-linear decomposition method developed by Nielsen (1998) to decompose the caste-based difference in probabilities to get employment into two components, namely endowment difference and discrimination in the labour market. Here, we model the individual's incidence to get employment using a logit model. The model is elaborated as follows.

Let F be the logistic c.d.f., Y the dependent indicator variable, x a row vector of explanatory variables, and N the sample size. Subscripts SC, HC indicates SC and higher castes respectively, whereas subscript i denotes index individuals. The log-likelihood function is:

$$l(\beta, \delta) = \sum_{i=1}^{N_{HC}} \{y_{HCi}lnF[x_{HCi}\beta] + (1 - y_{HCi})ln(1 - F[x_{HCi}\beta])\}$$
$$+ \sum_{i=1}^{N_{SC}} \{y_{SCi}lnF[x_{SCi}(\beta + \delta)] + (1 - y_{SCi})ln(1 - F[x_{SCi}(\beta + \delta)])\}$$

(27)

Maximization of Equation (27) gives $\hat{\beta}$ which is the estimated parameter vector for caste, and $\hat{\delta}$ which should be added for the SC.

The caste-based difference to get employment in a logit model can be estimated by decomposing the difference in log-odds ratios. The log-odds ratios are linear in parameters, and therefore, the Blinder-Oaxaca (1973) decomposition and the extension by Nielsen can be used directly. However, the difference in probabilities is easier to interpret than the difference in log-odds ratios. The first step is to decompose the difference in probabilities into one part which is caused by discrimination (D) and another part which is explained by differences in characteristics (E) between higher castes and SC. The higher castes are used as a standard to define the following probabilities:

$$\overline{P}_{HC} = \sum_{i=1}^{N_{HC}} F[x_{HCi}\hat{\beta}] / N_{HC}$$

$$\overline{P}_{SC} = \sum_{i=1}^{N_{SC}} F[x_{SCi}\hat{\beta}] / N_{SC}$$

$$\overline{P}_{SC}^0 = \sum_{i=1}^{N_{SC}} F[x_{SCi}\hat{\beta}] / N_{SC}$$

where $\overline{P}_{HC}$ and $\overline{P}_{SC}$ are the average probabilities that $Y = 1$ for higher castes and SC respectively, and $\overline{P}_{SC}^0$ is the average probability that $Y = 1$ for SC if they are treated like higher castes. The following identity defines E and D:

$$\overline{P}_{HC} - \overline{P}_{SC} = \left\{ \underbrace{\overline{P}_{HC} - \overline{P}^0_{SC}}_{Endowment\ Difference} \right\} + \left\{ \underbrace{\overline{P}^0_{SC} - \overline{P}_{SC}}_{Discrimination} \right\} \qquad (28)$$

The first component to the right of Equation (28) is the endowment or characteristics effect. It shows the contribution of the covariates to the difference between probability of employment between higher castes and the SC. The second component reflects the coefficients effect or employment discrimination. We estimated logit model separately for the SC and higher castes using the qualitative dependent variable, such as whether the workers have access to regular employment or not. The explanatory variables are age, level of education, marital status, gender, etc. The logit estimates for the SC and higher castes are decomposed using non-linear decomposition method.

4.5 Measuring Impact of Discrimination on Poverty

We will now discuss the method developed to estimate the impact of wage and employment discrimination in income loss and increase in poverty of the discriminated group, i.e. the SC.

4.5.1 Methodology Adopted to Establish Total Wage Loss

Total wage loss is sum of loss due to wage discrimination and loss due to employment discrimination.

4.5.1.1 Wage Earning Loss Due to Wage Discrimination
The following steps are followed to estimate wage income loss due to wage discrimination.

1. Using Oaxaca decomposition method, decompose wage gap between higher castes and SC workers.

2. Predict wage income for the SC if they are paid like higher castes with similar endowment characteristics.
3. Difference between projected wage and actual wage due to discrimination is estimated for SC workers which is the wage loss due to wage discrimination.

4.5.1.2 Wage Earning Loss Due to Employment Discrimination

The following steps are used to estimate the wage loss due to employment discrimination.

1. Using non-linear decomposition method developed by Nielsen (1998), the difference in the probability to get employment is decomposed between the higher castes and SC.
2. Predict probability of employment for the SC, if they were to be treated like higher castes.
3. Those SC who are supposed to be in the labour market, but not available due to discrimination are identified.
4. Estimate their wages based on the wage equation. It is the wage loss due to employment discrimination.

4.5.2 Estimating Poverty Accounting for Wage Loss Due to Wage Discrimination and Employment Discrimination

The following steps are followed to estimate the impact on poverty.

1. The additional wage, due to employment loss and wage loss, is added to the respective monthly household expenditure after converting the same into monthly earning.
2. Compare the new monthly per capita expenditure with Tendulkar's poverty line.
3. Estimate incidence of poverty through head count ratio.

4.6 Sources of Data

The present study has used unit-level data collected by National Sample Survey Organization (NSSO), India. The employment and unemployment surveys (EUS) were conducted during 2004–05 (July 2004 to June 2005, 61st round) and 2017–18 (Periodic Labour Force Survey or PLFS data). The first stage units are the census villages and urban blocks and the second stage comprises the households in these villages and urban blocks. The sample size is very large as it is a nationally representative household survey. In 2004–05, the number of households surveyed was 1,24,680 (79,306 in rural areas and 45,374 in urban areas) and number of persons surveyed was 6,02,833 (3,98,025 in rural areas and 2,04,808 in urban areas). The number of households surveyed during 2017–18 was 1,02,113 (56,108 in rural areas and 46,005 in urban areas) and number of persons surveyed was 4,33,339 (2,46,809 in rural areas and 1,86,530 in urban areas).

The survey provides data related to human capital, demographic, and job characteristics of workers. The human capital characteristics include age and education; demographic characteristics include gender, social group, religion, marital status, location (rural/urban), and region; and data related to job characteristics include industry, occupation, sector, and nature of employment.

The survey divides occupation into nine categories at one digit level, such as: (1) legislators, senior officials, and managers; (2) professionals; (3) technicians and associate professionals; (4) clerks; (5) service workers, shop, and market sales workers; (6) skilled agricultural and fishery workers; (7) craft and related trade workers; (8) plant and machine operators and assemblers; (9) elementary occupations. The skill level assigned to occupation 2 is postgraduate university degree (more than 15 years of formal education); likewise, for occupation 3, it is first university degree (14–15 years of formal education); similarly for occupations 4, 5, 6, 7, and 8 the skill level is secondary education (11–13 years of formal education); and for occupation 9, it is primary education (up to 10 years of formal education and/or informal skills). The concept of skill level has not been applied in the case of legislators, senior officials, and managers as skills to execute task and duties of these occupations vary to such an extent that it would be impossible to link them to any of the four broad skill levels.

In employment and unemployment survey data, the sample of individuals is divided into three mutually exclusive categories based on their status of employment. They are: (i) non-wage earners (i.e. non-participants in the labour market, the self-employed, and the unemployed); (ii) regular wage employment; (iii) casual wage employment.

Regular wage/salaried employees: The regular wage/salaried employees worked in others' farms or non-farm enterprises (both household and non-household) and in return received wages or salary on a regular basis (i.e. not on the basis of daily or periodic renewal of work contract). This category included not only those employees who get timely wages or salary, but also those employees who receive piece wages or salary and paid apprentices, both full time and part-time.

Casual labour: A person who was casually engaged in others' farms or non-farm enterprises (both household and non-household) and in return received wages according to the terms of the daily or periodic work contract was considered a casual labour.

Employment and unemployment in the EUS are measured using alternative concepts called usual principal status (UPS), usual principal and subsidiary status (UPSS), current weekly status (CWS) and current daily status (CDS). The recent PLFS survey has not collected information based on CDS measure. The data on weekly wages and salary earnings of workers are provided based on the CWS of workers. The broadest measure is that of UPSS that is widely used in official documents as well as in most academic studies. We have used the first one as the employment measure, viz. UPSS. It is defined in the EUS as follows: Under this category, all persons who worked for a major part of the year were included as employed under principal status. In addition, those who pursued some economic activity for less than six months, but more than 30 days in the reference year were included as subsidiary workers.

It is important to note what is recorded as wages. This includes not only monetary remuneration received at specified intervals, but also all other monetary and non-monetary benefits arising out of the work excluding overtime payments. The definition adopted in the EUS is worthy of reproduction here.

Wage and salary earnings: Information on wage and salary earnings was collected separately for each of the wage/salaried work recorded for a person in a day, i.e. based on the current daily status of employment. Here, earnings referred to the wage/salary income (and not total earnings taking into consideration of all other activities done) received/receivable for the wage/salaried work done during the reference week by a wage/salaried employee and casual labourer. The wage/salary received or receivable may be in cash or kind or partly in cash and partly in kind. While recording the earnings, the following conventions were used. (i) The wages in kind were evaluated at the current retail price. (ii) Bonus and perquisites, such as free accommodation, reimbursement of expenditure for medical treatment, free telephones, etc., evaluated at the cost of the employer or at retail prices and duly apportioned for the reference week were also included in earnings. (iii) Amount receivable as 'overtime' for the additional work done beyond normal working time was excluded. It may be noted that in the survey, at most two activities could be recorded for a person in a day. Therefore, it is possible that a person might have carried out two or more wage/salaried activities in a day, but only one activity or two activities at the most, depending upon the time spent on those activities, was recorded. In that case, the wage/salary income only from that activity(s) was collected and recorded separately, and not the total income of the person from all the activities done for the entire day.

We have calculated daily wage rate by dividing the total wages and salaries (in cash and in kind) received for the work done in the reference week with total number of days reported working in that week. The wage data used in the study are measured in rupee (₹) terms. The wage distribution is trimmed by 0.1 per cent from the top and bottom tails in order to get rid of outliers and potentially anomalous wages at the extreme ends of the distribution. The nominal daily wages are deflated by 2001 prices using the official state-level monthly consumer price indices of agricultural labour (base year 1960) for rural wages and consumer price indices of industrial workers (base year 1982) for urban wages (Labour Bureau, various years).

Regular salaried workers: Regular salaried workers, both from rural and urban areas, are selected for the purpose of discrimination analysis. We thus exclude the casual wage labourer from analysis. The studies show that the discrimination among regular salaried workers is significantly higher than among casual wage labourers. The regular salaried jobs being more secure and better paying than casual wage labour, the probability of employment discrimination and wage discrimination is higher than that across casual wage labour. Besides, the issues related to affirmative action policy in employment in the private sector become relevant mainly for regular salaried workers both in rural and urban areas.

Caste grouping: While applying the decomposition method, we have taken Hindu higher castes as the advantaged groups and the SC as the disadvantaged groups. There are specific reasons for selecting the SC and higher castes. In theoretical discussion we have noticed some unique features of the caste system. The caste system not only divides the Hindus into four groups, it is also fixed and assigns occupations to each of the four castes, namely brahmin, kshatriya, vaishya, and shudra. But most importantly, these occupations are fixed by birth, without freedom for change. The worker from one caste would face restriction on employment in occupations pursued by other castes. In this sense, discrimination in employment is inbuilt in allocation of work under the rule of caste system. However, the untouchables who are placed at the bottom of the caste hierarchy face restriction in employment and occupation from employers who belong to any of the four castes above them. Thus, the discrimination in employment, occupation and wages is most intense in the case of the SC vis-à-vis the four castes above them. Therefore, the study focuses on the comparison between the SC and the higher castes. Given the limitation of the NSS data, we derive the higher castes by excluding the Other Backward Classes (OBC). Thus, the higher castes are a category which is net of OBC, ST, and SC. In case of the SC, we include Hindu, Sikh, and Buddhist Scheduled Castes.

Estimation of Poverty: In the study, the poverty rates are estimated using the consumption expenditure data from the Employment Survey. Normally the poverty ratios are estimated based on the Consumption Expenditure Survey of the National Sample Survey, which is the appropriate survey. However, since we are using the employment and wage data from the Employment Survey and linking it with poverty, this exercise would be possible provided we use the consumption expenditure data from the same source. Besides, the Consumption Expenditure Survey for 2017–18 is not available as it has been kept on hold. In any case, we are not interested in absolute poverty rate but the relative poverty rate of the SC vis-à-vis the higher castes. Since we used employment data, wage data and poverty rate from the same source, we could estimate the impact of employment discrimination and wage discrimination on the poverty levels of the SC. However, we should be aware about the limitation of poverty estimates derived in the study.

5

Employment and Untouchables

5.1 Introduction

In Chapter 3 we discussed the economic features of the caste system
with respect to occupation and employment. We observed that the caste
system assigns and fixes the occupation of each of the four castes and
places restrictions on mobility of workers for employment from one caste
to another caste's assigned occupation (with the exception of manual
wage labour by the untouchables, which is their assigned occupation).
This ensures that the employment of workers remains confined to castes'
occupation without the freedom to change. Determined by the castewise
division of labour, teaching- and preaching-related works are restricted to
brahmins, military to kshatriyas, trade and commerce and non-farm enterprises to vaishyas, and farming (self-employed farmers) and low-level
artisan activities to shudras, and finally wage labour to the untouchables.
Thus, employment gets segregated across castes without the freedom of
mobility from one to another (caste-based) economic activity. Insofar as
there are restrictions on employment in another caste-defined occupation, irrespective of capability and labour productivity, segregation and
discrimination in employment become internal to the allocation of work
under the legal and normative framework of the caste system. In effect,
the restrictions to take employment in another caste's occupation bring
segregated labour markets on caste lines with people getting engaged
in their own caste's occupations without entry to occupations classified
as belonging to another caste. This translates into a scenario wherein a
worker from the shudra caste is debarred from employment in the occupation of vaishya, i.e. trade and commerce, of kshatriya, i.e. defence, and
of brahmin, i.e. teaching and preaching. Similarly, each caste above the
shudra (namely vaishya and kshatriya) faces restriction on employment
in each of the castes above their own. Also, all castes face restrictions to

Scheduled Castes in the Indian Labour Market. Sukhadeo Thorat, S. Madheswaran, and B. P. Vani,
Oxford University Press. © Sukhadeo Thorat, S. Madheswaran, and B. P. Vani 2023.
DOI: 10.1093/oso/9780198872252.003.0005

obtain employment in the occupation of castes below them. It is in this sense that employment (or occupations) in the caste system is segregated and discriminatory.

However, the untouchables' employment is an exception to this general rule of castewise employment segregation. The employment of untouchables in the labour market is governed by the rules of both exclusion and inclusion from employment in caste occupations. The inclusion of untouchables in employment occurs through hiring as manual wage workers (which is the main occupation of the untouchables) in the occupations of all castes above them. Thus, the untouchables are required to work as manual wage workers which involves physical labour for all the castes. This is obligatory under the Hindu law of caste. Also, the untouchables are assigned, as part of their menial occupations, to carry out work which is considered polluting (e.g. scavenging, and those related to leather or minor artisan production) as per the Hindu notion of purity and impurity. As wage labourers, their work is exploitative in nature characterized by strenuous work coupled with low wages. As discussed earlier, the Hindu law also recognized slavery which considered the untouchables as slave caste, and thus offered them only those jobs which involve exploitative labour at very low remuneration. This is as far as inclusion in employment is concerned.

The untouchables also face exclusion in employment in higher castes' occupations. While they are permitted (rather forced) to work as wage labourers in occupations that involve hard physical labour, they are excluded as employees in the occupations of the four castes above them in other than non-manual wage labour. The exclusion of the untouchable workers in employment operates in two ways: first, the untouchables are excluded in four occupations of the higher castes as self-employed and as (non-manual) regular salaried workers. Thus, untouchables face exclusion from access to non-manual regular salaried work in teaching, military, trade and commerce, and farming. Second, the untouchables are excluded in some works due to their polluting social status. They are excluded in categories of work which involve direct physical touch. They are also excluded from those works which are considered auspicious. Some excluded works include all domestic work, such as cooking, milking cows, and other works like vegetable and fruit processing, work related to religious and cultural events, and in some cases, construction of houses (Thorat 2010; Jodhka and Shah 2010). Thus, the rules regarding the untouchables' work are characterized both by exclusion and inclusion which Sen (2000) rightly described as 'unfavourable exclusion and unfavourable inclusion' (often forced inclusion) respectively. While they are unfavourably excluded as self-employed and employee in teaching, military, farming, entrepreneurship, or trader, they are unfavourably (often forcefully) included and employed in hard manual wage labour often as serf, bonded or slave labour, required in the occupations of higher castes as well as the forced work in activities considered inferior and low by the Hindus.

This analysis of caste system from the point of view of employment indicates that discrimination in occupation, employment and wages is embedded in the economic system based on caste hierarchy in India. This implies that the untouchables face discrimination as self-employed in farming, trade and commerce, on-farm production, and as employees, i.e. regular salaried workers in all occupations (with the exception of manual wage workers). The issue is to what extent the traditional caste restrictions still influence the employment pattern of the untouchables. Recognizing that regular salaried occupations are the most preferred category of jobs in India, we have analysed the employment pattern of the SC and higher castes' regular salaried workers in India and in the states based on the Employment Survey 2004–05 and 2017–18. In employment pattern we examine the labour force participation rate, work participation rate, employment by industry and occupation and other characteristics of regular salaried workers.

5.2 Labour Force and Workforce Participation Rate

Before we discuss the aspects of regular salaried workers, we will look at the labour force participation rate and workforce participation rate or employment rate at the aggregate level and by caste groups. We will then estimate the share of regular salaried workers among the total number of workers. We have considered the definition of labour force as the 'economically active' population which refers to the section of the population that supplies or seeks to supply labour for production of goods and services; and therefore, includes both the 'employed' and 'unemployed' above the age of 15 years.

Table 5.1 Labour force participation rate (LFPR)—UPSS

Social groups	2004–05			2017–18		
	Rural	Urban	Total	Rural	Urban	Total
ST	51.89	40.43	50.89	42.49	36.54	41.82
Hindu SC	44.81	39.75	43.83	37.25	38.56	37.54
Hindu OBC	45.52	40.58	44.50	36.88	38.30	37.25
Hindu higher castes	44.28	37.06	41.42	37.17	36.71	36.97
Muslims	34.76	34.45	34.66	30.68	31.99	31.17
Others	47.37	39.61	44.55	38.19	38.79	38.43
Total	44.62	38.25	43.00	36.99	36.79	36.93

Source: Authors' calculation based on NSS 61st round and PLFS 2017–18 data.

In 2017–18 about 39 per cent of the Indian population was in the labour force or were economically active. The total labour force participation rate (LFPR), considering the usual principal and subsidiary status (UPSS), recorded a decline from 43 per cent in 2004–05 to 37 per cent in 2017–18. The LFPR has also declined for the SC, Other Backward Classes (OBC) and higher castes between 2004–05 and 2017–18. The LFPR rate among the SC (37.54 per cent) is similar to the country's average of 37 per cent and also of other castes, namely OBC (37.25 per cent), and higher castes (37 per cent) (Table 5.1).

The workforce participation rate (WPR) denotes the percentage of workers in the total labour force (Table 5.2). In 2017–18, 35 per cent of

Table 5.2 Workforce participation rate (WPR)—UPSS

WPR	2004–05			2017–18		
	Rural	Urban	Total	Rural	Urban	Total
ST	51.50	39.22	50.42	40.77	34.00	40.01
Hindu SC	44.10	37.69	42.87	35.15	35.16	35.15
Hindu OBC	44.89	39.02	43.67	35.01	35.42	35.12
Hindu higher castes	43.31	35.32	40.14	35.01	34.03	34.59
Muslims	33.92	33.06	33.63	28.69	29.28	28.91
Others	45.30	36.78	42.20	35.86	35.21	35.60
Total	43.88	36.53	42.01	35.02	33.91	34.69

Source: Authors' calculation based on NSS 61st round and PLFS 2017–18 data.

the total labour force (unemployed and employed) was gainfully employed with the WPR of the SC being nearly similar to that of OBC and higher castes (about 35 per cent). Between 2004–05 and 2017–18, the WPR has declined from 42 per cent to 35 per cent at the overall level as well as among the SC, OBC, and higher castes. However, in term of percentage points, the decline is relatively higher among the SC and OBC as compared to higher castes (although lower than Scheduled Tribes or ST).

5.3 Magnitude of Regular Salaried Workers

The NSSO defines regular wage/salaried employees as 'those who worked in either farm or non-farm enterprises (both household and non-household) and in return received salary or wages on a regular basis'. It includes not only those who get timely wages but also those who get piece wage or salary, apprenticeship, full or part-time. Table 5.3 shows the percentage of workers in self-employed, regular salaried, and casual labourer categories. Of the total workers (based on UPSS) in 2017–18, about 23 per cent are regular salaried with the remaining being shared by self-employed (52 per cent) and casual wage labour (25 per cent). As mentioned earlier, traditionally the SC were generally excluded from regular salaried jobs. This is reflected in the lower percentage of SC as regular workers (19.7 per cent) as compared to 32.7 per cent for higher castes, and 21 per cent for OBC (Table 5.3). Inequality in the incidence of regular salaried workers across castes can also be seen by comparing the share of regular salaried workers by social groups and their share in the workforce in 2017–18 (Table 5.4). It is seen that the share of SC regular salaried workers continues to be lower than their share in the workforce. On the other hand, in case of higher castes, the share of regular salaried workers is much higher than their share in the workforce. In 2017–18, the share of the SC among the total regular salaried workers in the country is 16.7 per cent which is lower than their share in workforce (19.4 per cent), while the share of the higher castes regular salaried workers which is 29 per cent exceeds their share in workforce (20.5 per cent). In the case of OBC, the share is close to the workforce share. This shows that although the SC have now

Table 5.3 Share of workers by employment status

	Self-employed	Regular Salaried Workers	Casual Labourers	Total
		2004–05		
ST	53.9	6.7	39.4	100.0
Hindu SC	40.2	12.2	47.6	100.0
Hindu OBC	61.4	12.0	26.6	100.0
Hindu higher castes	63.4	23.7	13.0	100.0
Muslims	61.8	12.6	25.5	100.0
Others	61.4	22.1	16.5	100.0
Total	56.9	14.3	28.9	100.0
		2017–18		
ST	55.9	**12.9**	31.2	100.0
Hindu SC	39.0	**19.7**	41.3	100.0
Hindu OBC	56.3	**21.4**	22.3	100.0
Hindu higher castes	56.1	**32.7**	11.2	100.0
Muslims	52.6	**20.9**	26.4	100.0
Others	48.2	**34.2**	17.6	100.0
Total	52.2	**22.8**	25.0	100.0

Source: Authors' calculation based on NSS 61st round and PLFS 2017–18 data.

gained better access to regular salaried jobs, but still they are in a disadvantaged position as compared to the higher castes (Table 5.4). Due to relatively low proportion in regular salaried jobs, the SC continue to depend on their traditionally assigned job as casual wage workers. Of the total SC workers, about 41.3 per cent are casual wage workers which is four times that of the higher castes (11 per cent). Similarly, the SC face restrictions on being farmers and entrepreneurs/business workers. Although about 39 per cent of the SC are self-employed, the ratio is less than 56.1 per cent for the higher castes and 56.3 per cent for OBC.

Thus, it is evident that although the SC have gained some space in regular salaried work, their participation is low as compared to the higher castes. Also, their share in total regular salaried workers in the country is less than their share in total workers and population in 2017–18.

Table 5.4 Share of regular salaried workers in relation to their share in the workforce

Social Groups	Share in Population	Share in Workforce	Self-employed	Regular Salaried Workers	Casual Labourers
			2004–05		
ST	8.3	10.0	9.5	4.7	13.7
Hindu SC	19.4	19.8	14.0	17.0	32.7
Hindu OBC	35.1	36.5	39.4	30.7	33.7
Hindu higher castes	21.2	20.2	22.5	33.6	9.1
Muslims	12.7	10.2	11.1	9.0	9.0
Others	3.2	3.2	3.5	5.0	1.9
Total	100.0	100.0	100.0	100.0	100.0
			2017–18		
ST	9.2	10.6	11.4	6.0	13.3
Hindu SC	19.1	19.4	14.5	16.7	32.1
Hindu OBC	35.2	35.6	38.4	33.3	31.8
Hindu higher castes	20.6	20.5	22.0	29.4	9.2
Muslims	12.7	10.6	10.7	9.7	11.3
Others	3.2	3.3	3.0	4.9	2.3
Total	100.0	100.0	100.0	100.0	100.0

Source: Authors' calculation based on NSS 61st round and PLFS 2017–18 data.

5.4 Characteristics of Regular Salaried Workers

We have seen that the rule of castes, related to the SC, confined their employment to casual wage workers. The change in rule and provision of equal employment opportunity has brought some improvement in regular salaried jobs for the SC. But their share continues to be low as compared to the higher castes. Therefore, we have a reason to believe that the entry of the SC in regular salaried jobs, particularly in the private sector, may be constrained by traditional restrictions in employment. It may also be due to their low educational attainment (as they were debarred from the right to education). Given the positive correlation between education and employment in regular salaried jobs, the SC engagement in the latter is likely to be low as compared to the higher castes. The low level of education and skill also enviably push the SC to low-paid jobs in some specific industries and occupations as informal workers. The works in the informal sector are generally less protected through job and social securities. Thus, the SC employment in regular salaried jobs is likely to be characterized by high engagement in the informal sector in industries and occupations with low-wage earning and poor job and social securities. What is the empirical evidence?

Given this background, we will examine the employment of the SC by industry and occupation groups. We will also study the interrelation between income, education, and regular salaried employment to see the influence of income and education on the pattern of employment in specific occupations. In the end, we will look at the quality of the regular salaried jobs, in term of their composition in the formal and informal sectors, their share in the private sector and public sector, and the nature of the job and social securities.

5.5 Employment by Industry and Occupation Groups

We will examine the participation of the SC and higher castes by industry and occupation groups of their employment. We will analyse the industry first. At the overall level, a high percentage of regular salaried workers is employed in agriculture (44 per cent) followed by construction (19 per cent), manufacturing and other services (about 10 per cent each), trade, hotel, and restaurant (8 per cent) and transport, storage, and communication (Table 5.5). Clearly, there is a difference between the SC and higher castes. The SC share is relatively high in agriculture and construction. The SC share is particularly high in the construction industry, almost three times higher than the higher castes. But the SC share is low compared to the higher castes in manufacturing, trade, storage and restaurant, and other services, and the gap is particularly high in the last two industry groups. Thus, the share of SC in low-paid agriculture and related activities, and construction is much higher as compared to the higher castes in 2004–05 as well as in 2017–18. But it is particularly low in trade, storage and restaurant, and other services.

Table 5.5 Industrial distribution of regular salaried workers by social groups (UPSS)

	2004–05				2017–18			
	Hindu SC	Hindu OBC	Hindu Higher Castes	Total	Hindu SC	Hindu OBC	Hindu Higher Castes	Total
Agriculture	61.3	62.9	48.3	58.5	44.4	46.8	37.4	44.1
Mining and quarrying	0.7	0.5	0.5	0.6	0.3	0.5	0.2	0.4
Manufacturing	10.3	11.7	12.1	11.7	10.5	12.0	13.4	12.1
Electricity, water, etc.	0.3	0.2	0.4	0.3	0.7	0.6	0.7	0.6
Construction	8.7	4.9	3.2	5.6	19.1	10.5	5.8	11.7
Trade, hotel, and restaurants	6.4	9.0	15.2	10.2	8.4	12.2	15.6	12.0
Transport, storage, and communication	3.8	3.2	4.6	3.8	5.1	5.0	5.8	5.3
Other services	8.5	7.5	15.8	9.3	11.6	12.6	21.1	13.8
Total	100.0	100.0	100.0	100.0	100.0	100.0	100.0	100.0

Source: Authors' calculation based on NSS 61st round and PLFS 2017–18 data.

This shows that the SC are mainly occupied in industrial sectors with low earning.

Higher engagement of the SC in low-paying economic activities is again clear from their employment by occupation groups (Table 5.6). The distribution of workers by caste groups in top eight occupations in regular jobs reveals an interesting pattern (Table 5.6). Clearly, the share of the SC in three occupations, namely legislators, senior officials and managers, and professionals and clerks, is low as compared to the higher castes. The opposite is the case in low-paying occupations where the share of SC is high. In elementary or unskilled occupations, like domestic helpers, cleaners, garbage collectors, etc., the SC workers occupy more positions. This indicates the continuing caste-based occupational segregation of the SC in low-paid occupations. This also means that the share of better occupations, which were prohibited under the rule of caste, continues to be low despite the opening of these occupations to SC. In turn, the SC

Table 5.6 Position of different social groups as per occupation groups in regular labour market (rank and percentage of workers), 2017–18

		NCO 2004 Occupation Groups	Total (%)	Aggregate Percentage			
				Total	Hindu SC	Hindu OBC	Hindu Higher Castes
Legislators, senior officials, and managers	112	Administrative and Executive Officials	1.34	4.91 (8)	2.65 (8)	4.37 (8)	7.93 (8)
	122	Production and Operations Dept. Managers	1.58				
	123	Other Department Managers	1.26				
	130	General Managers	0.73				
Professionals	213	Computing Professionals	1.46	9.49 (5)	5.61 (6)	8.9 (6)	15.2 (1)
	214	Architects, Engineers, and Related Professionals	1.45				
	231	College, University, and Higher Education Training Professionals	0.99				
	232	Secondary Education Teaching Professionals	3.19				
	233	Other Teaching Professionals	1.1				
	241	Business Professionals	1.3				
Technicians and associate professionals	312	Computer Associate Professionals	1.05	8.93 (6)	7.39 (5)	9.15 (5)	9.37 (4)
	331	Middle and Primary Teaching Associate Professionals	4.84				
	332	Pre-primary Teaching Associate Professionals	1.81				
	341	Finance and Sales Associate Professionals	1.23				

Clerks	411	Secretaries and Key Board-operating Clerks	1.09	7.14 (7)	4.79 (7)	7.17 (7)	9.59 (3)
	412	Numerical Clerks	1.43				
	419	Other Office Clerks	3.6				
	421	Cashiers, Tellers, and Related Clerks	1.02				
Service workers and shop and market sales workers	512	Housekeeping and Restaurant Service Workers	3.22	16.63 (1)	17.73 (2)	16.93 (1)	13.86 (2)
	513	Personal Care Workers	1.98				
	514	Other Personal Services Workers	1				
	516	Protective Services Workers	2.33				
	522	Shop Salespersons and Demonstrators	7.18				
	523	Stall and Market Salesperson	0.92				
Craft and related trades' workers	713	Building Finishing and Related Trades Workers	0.83	10.37 (3)	10.99 (3)	10.63 (3)	8.31 (6)
	721	Metal Moulders, Welders, Sheet Metal Workers, Structural Metal Preparers, and Related Trades Workers	1.49				
	723	Machinery Mechanics and Fitters	2.29				
	724	Electrical and Electronic Equipment Mechanics and Fitters	1.68				
	741	Food Processing and Related Trades Workers	0.99				
	743	Textile, Garment, and Related Trades Workers	3.09				

(continued)

Table 5.6 Continued

	NCO 2004 Occupation Groups	Total (%)	Aggregate Percentage			
			Total	Hindu SC	Hindu OBC	Hindu Higher Castes
Plant and machine operators and assemblers	826 Textiles, Fur, and Leather Products Machine Operators	1.12	9.89 (4)	10.44 (4)	10.4 (4)	8.04 (7)
	829 Other Machine-related Assemblers	1.08				
	832 Motor Vehicle Drivers	7.69				
Elementary occupations	913 Domestic and Related Helpers, Cleaners, and Launders	3.48	13.26 (2)	21.59 (1)	12.49 (2)	9.15 (5)
	915 Messengers, Porters, Doorkeepers, and Related Workers	2.15				
	916 Garbage Collectors and Related Labourers	1.38				
	920 Agricultural, Fishery, and Related Labourers	1.5				
	931 Mining and Construction Labourers	0.83				
	932 Manufacturing Labourers	3.92				
	Total	80.62	80.62	81.19	80.04	81.45

Note: Figures in the brackets are ranks.

Source: Authors' calculations based on PLFS 2017–18 data.

continue to be prominently engaged in those occupations which are their traditional occupations. We have a reason to believe that SC probably face restrictions through discrimination in access to occupations where their employment was prohibited under the Hindu laws.

To sum up, a few important conclusions emerged from the discussion regarding the characteristics of the regular salaried workers from the SC and higher castes. About 19 per cent of the SC workers are engaged in regular salaried jobs in the private and public sectors which is lower than higher castes (32 per cent). A high percentage of SC workers are employed in low-paid 'agriculture' and 'construction' industrial sectors both in 2004–05 and 2017–18. Their share in a better industry group is low, such as trade, storage and restaurant, and other services. This shows that the SC are mainly concentrated in an industry group with low earning, like agriculture and construction. This is also the case concerning their employment in occupations. Clearly, the share of SC is low in better occupations, like legislators, senior officials and managers, professionals and clerk as compared to the higher castes, and much high in low-earning occupations. In elementary or unskilled occupations, like domestic helpers, cleaners, garbage collectors, etc., the SC stand in the first position. Thus, although there has been a partial break from the past, the caste-based occupational segregation of the SC in low-paid occupations continue in the present. This also means that the share of better occupations, which were prohibited under the rule of caste, continues to be low despite the equal opportunity to all occupations. In turn, they continued to be prominently engaged in those occupations which are their traditional occupations, namely the wage labourers. We have a reason to believe that the SC probably continue to face restrictions through discrimination in access to occupation where their employment had been restricted in the past for a long time.

5.6 Income and Education Interlinkage

We have discussed earlier that untouchables were prohibited from ownership of capital assets—land and enterprises. Besides, they were also debarred from right to education. The impact of this past legacy is reflected in low ownership of capital assets in the present which in turn results in low income. The low income, in turn, results in low access to higher education and low employability. The low employability or capabilities, in turn, reduces their share in regular salaried jobs in the organized or formal sector and pushes them to work in the informal sector. The analysis of the participation of the SC regular salaried workers by their income and education revealed this interrelation between income, education, and occupations.

The educational distribution of regular salaried workers by caste groups across monthly per capita consumption expenditure quintiles is given in Table 5.7. In 2017–18 the distribution of SC regular salaried workers (in percentage) by income groups indicates their higher concentration in lower quintile and less in the top quintile. Table 5.7 presents the share of the regular salaried workers by consumption expenditure quintile into the bottom 20 per cent and top 20 per cent and in the middle Q2, Q3, and Q4. In the bottom 20 per cent quintile, the share of SC is the highest with 26 per cent and lowest with 11 per cent for the higher castes, followed by 20 per cent for OBC. At the other end, the share of

Table 5.7 Percentage distribution of regular salaried workers by social groups and consumer expenditure class

	2004–05				2017–18			
	Hindu SC	Hindu OBC	Hindu Higher Castes	Total	Hindu SC	Hindu OBC	Hindu Higher Castes	Total
Q1 (Bottom 20%)	27.9 (15.2)	18.8 (9.7)	8.1 (3.9)	20.0 (9.3)	26.3 (13.0)	20.1 (10.7)	11.6 (6.3)	20.0 (10.5)
Q2	24.2 (17.7)	21.6 (14.6)	12.6 (7.6)	20.0 (13.0)	23.9 (21.4)	22.4 (17.0)	18.3 (14.6)	20.0 (17.2)
Q3	20.9 (23.2)	21.5 (18.3)	18.5 (14.1)	20.0 (17.4)	20.8 (17.7)	20.8 (16.9)	19.1 (14.8)	20.0 (16.3)
Q4	16.1 (20.3)	20.9 (25.2)	25.5 (24.9)	20.0 (23.6)	16.7 (22.7)	19.5 (24.6)	23.9 (25.7)	20.0 (24.1)
Q5 (top 20%)	10.9 (23.6)	17.4 (32.2)	35.4 (49.5)	20.0 (36.7)	12.2 (25.1)	17.1 (30.8)	27.1 (38.6)	20.0 (31.9)
Total	100	100	100	100	100	100	100	100

Note: Figures in the bracket are regular salaried workers.

Source: Authors' calculations based on NSS 61st round and PLFS 2017–18 data.

SC in the top 20 per cent quintile is the lowest with 12 per cent as compared to 27 per cent for higher castes, followed by 17 per cent for OBC. Thus, a majority of the SC (50.2 per cent) belongs to the poorest and the poor categories, while 51.1 per cent of the higher castes belongs to rich or richest. Among the OBC, 36.6 per cent belongs to the rich and richest and 42.5 per cent belongs to the poor and poorest classes.

The educational background of the regular salaried workers also revealed a similar pattern (Table 5.8). Of the total SC regular salaried workers, about 63 per cent possessed less than secondary education and the remaining 37 per cent are with more than higher secondary education that includes graduate and above. Of these, about 22 per cent hold graduation and above education. By comparison, about 60 per cent higher castes hold education which is above higher secondary, and among them 42 per cent are with education above graduation. Thus, the share of those with less than secondary education was high among the SC (63 per cent) which is more than the higher castes (40 per cent). Conversely, the share of the regular salaried workers with more than higher secondary, and graduation and above was lower for the SC as compared to the higher castes. This pattern is also true for 2004–05.

The cross-classification of education level by income (monthly per capita consumption expenditure) indicates the expected relationship between the two for the regular salaried workers. In the regular labour market, workers with higher levels of education mostly belong to better economic classes whereas workers with lower levels of education, i.e. up to secondary and higher secondary education, mostly belong to lower quintile households. The proportion of graduates in richer households is much higher than the proportion of graduates in poorer households and this is the case across all social groups. This means that a bulk of the SC regular salaried workers possess a low level of education as compared to the higher castes. The SC with low education also come from the bottom income group. Alternatively, it also means that the regular salaried workers with a higher level of education mostly belong to better economic classes whereas workers with lower levels of education, i.e. up to secondary and higher secondary education, mostly belong to lower quintile households. So the concentration of SC regular salaried workers in low education bracket is due to their higher share in the low-income group. The low income of the SC reduces their access to higher education.

Table 5.8 Percentage distribution of regular salaried workers across educational categories for SC, higher castes, and total—UPSS

	Illiterate	Primary	Middle	Secondary	Higher Secondary	Graduate	Postgraduate	Total
Hindu Scheduled Castes								
2004–05								
Q1 (Bottom 20%)	25.9	16.3	14.0	10.2	5.0	3.0	2.2	14.7
Q2	23.0	22.5	17.9	14.8	10.5	6.6	4.8	17.8
Q3	24.6	25.7	26.3	18.8	21.4	16.7	14.4	23.2
Q4	14.7	19.9	23.5	22.7	22.5	23.8	23.4	20.5
Q5 (Top 20%)	11.8	15.7	18.3	33.4	40.6	49.9	55.2	23.9
Total	100.0	100.0	100.0	100.0	100.0	100.0	100.0	100.0
2017–18								
Q1 (Bottom 20%)	24.0	18.6	16.7	10.3	8.0	3.8	4.6	13.1
Q2	31.6	24.9	24.2	21.9	16.7	11.2	14.8	21.3
Q3	17.1	24.3	16.1	16.3	20.3	16.4	7.6	17.6
Q4	14.5	19.0	23.5	25.2	25.5	26.9	26.2	22.8
Q5 (Top 20%)	12.8	13.2	19.7	26.2	29.6	41.8	46.9	25.3
Total	100.0	100.0	100.0	100.0	100.0	100.0	100.0	100.0
Hindu Higher Castes								
2004–05								
Q1 (Bottom 20%)	13.6	6.6	5.8	4.8	2.4	1.3	0.2	3.8
Q2	20.5	15.2	12.4	8.9	4.5	2.7	2.2	7.6

	Illiterate	Primary	Middle	Secondary	Higher Secondary	Graduate	Postgraduate	Total
Q3	17.3	23.0	21.4	16.2	13.4	7.7	6.7	14.0
Q4	19.7	28.4	30.4	29.6	26.5	21.0	16.1	24.9
Q5 (Top 20%)	28.9	26.7	30.1	40.4	53.3	67.4	74.8	49.7
Total	100.0	100.0	100.0	100.0	100.0	100.0	100.0	100.0

Hindu Scheduled Castes

2017–18

	Illiterate	Primary	Middle	Secondary	Higher Secondary	Graduate	Postgraduate	Total
Q1 (Bottom 20%)	11.9	13.6	12.0	7.5	5.5	2.9	1.7	6.3
Q2	23.2	24.1	23.2	19.7	15.3	8.6	4.6	14.6
Q3	20.2	24.5	22.9	16.0	13.4	12.0	6.5	14.9
Q4	28.4	23.8	25.2	31.1	26.9	24.7	21.6	25.7
Q5 (Top 20%)	16.3	14.0	16.7	25.8	39.0	51.8	65.5	38.5
Total	100.0	100.0	100.0	100.0	100.0	100.0	100.0	100.0

TOTAL

2004–05

	Illiterate	Primary	Middle	Secondary	Higher Secondary	Graduate	Postgraduate	Total
Q1 (Bottom 20%)	23.0	14.1	10.1	6.8	3.4	1.8	0.5	9.0
Q2	22.8	19.6	16.3	12.3	7.3	4.0	3.8	12.9
Q3	21.0	22.9	22.0	17.4	15.6	9.5	7.8	17.4

(continued)

Table 5.8 Continued

	Hindu Scheduled Castes							
	Illiterate	Primary	Middle	Secondary	Higher Secondary	Graduate	Postgraduate	Total
Q4	17.5	23.9	27.1	26.7	25.7	21.9	18.7	23.7
Q5 (Top 20%)	15.7	19.5	24.5	36.9	48.1	62.8	69.2	37.0
Total	100.0	100.0	100.0	100.0	100.0	100.0	100.0	100.0
				2017–18				
Q1 (Bottom 20%)	20.1	17.9	14.6	11.0	8.0	4.4	3.2	10.5
Q2	26.4	24.3	22.9	19.7	15.3	9.3	7.1	17.1
Q3	22.5	21.3	19.4	16.5	15.9	12.7	8.5	16.3
Q4	19.4	22.1	24.1	26.6	25.2	25.1	22.4	24.1
Q5 (Top 20%)	11.6	14.4	19.1	26.2	35.6	48.6	58.8	32.0
Total	100.0	100.0	100.0	100.0	100.0	100.0	100.0	100.0

Source: Authors' calculation based on NSS 61st round and PLFS 2017–18 data.

But ultimately, the source of low income (which reduces access to higher education and jobs in better occupations) is the result of poor owner-ship of income-earning capital assets, like agricultural land and capital in the form of enterprise, trade, and commerce. The ownership of prop-erty rights is low because of denial of the right to property in the past. It is in this sense that the exclusion from the right to property to SC in the past is the cause of lack of ownership of property in the present—the legacy of the past comes alive in the present, presumably due to persisting discrimination.

5.7 Quality of Employment

5.7.1 Formal and Informal Workers

The labour market is not homogeneous with respect to terms and con-ditions of employment, but characterized by duality. The duality in the labour market was defined, in which primary and secondary segments within the labour market is distinguished (Piore 1970). The dual labour market model supposes the existence of two distinct sectors of economic activities usually classified as the formal (organized) and informal (un-organized) sectors. The organized sector offers more stable jobs with higher pay, better working conditions and promotional opportunities while the unorganized sector is associated with unstable jobs, poor pay, bad working conditions and few opportunities for advancement (Dickens and Lang 1985; Taubman and Wachter 1986). Dualism in the Indian economy refers not only to the sector denoting the enterprises but also to employment. Formal employment refers to workers with social se-curity benefits provided by the employer while informal employment re-fers to its absence. Regular wage workers have regular, contractual hired employment, better service conditions, including high wages (Tendulkar 2003: 2). Regular workers are also covered by the labour market regu-lations that confer some measures of employment security and social security benefits. Informal or casual workers, on the other hand, are generally engaged in those economic activities with low wages, unstable employment contracts and little or no social security benefits. The real nature of the employment, thus, is not that people are not 'employed' in some activity but that a large number of those classified as employed are engaged in low quality of employment which does not provide adequate income to keep a family above the poverty line. Therefore, in the discussion on the quality of regular salaried workers, we measure it by taking the percentage of the formal and informal workers, workers with or without a job and social security, and workers in public and private sectors (public sector jobs are supposed to be more secure).

In India, the National Commission for Enterprises in the Unorganised Sector (NCEUS) has discussed extensively the quality of work like employment security, wage rate, working conditions and social security to wage workers (NCEUS 2009). Various studies like Papola (2004, 2011), Chen et al. (2006), Harriss-White (2010), etc., have focused on the quality of employment in India which were exclusively centred on informal economies and informal nature of employment. For the first time, NCEUS (2009) departed from the notion to treat informal employment with informal sector and estimated a sizeable share of informal employment even in the formal sector in the Indian economy. Following NCEUS framework, recent studies show how the share of informal employment in the formal sector has been rising from 41 per cent in 1999–2000 to 48 per cent in 2004–05 and 58 per cent in 2011–12 with the growing contractualization of employment (IHD-ISLE 2014; D'Souza 2010; Goldar and Suresh 2017; Srivastava and Naik 2017). Concerns have been raised for this increase in 'informalisation of employment in the formal sector' (IHD-ISLE 2014). The NSSO defines regular wage/salaried employee as 'those who worked in either farm or non-farm enterprises (both household and non-household) and in return received wages or salary on a regular basis'. It includes not only those who get time wage but also those who get piece wage or salary, apprenticeship, full or part-time. Thus, given its diverse nature which comes from the definition, all regular work cannot be taken as a synonym to decent work.

First, we will explore the quality of jobs by examining the magnitude of the formal and informal workers in 2004–05 and 2017–18. In 2017–18, of the total regular salaried workers, about 22.5 per cent are formal and the remaining 77.5 per cent informal workers (Tables 5.9 and 5.10). This means that much higher percentage of regular salaried workers, as high as 77.5 per

Table 5.9 Percentage of formal and informal workers

| | 2004–05 | | 2017–18 | |
	Formal	Informal	Formal	Informal
Hindu SC	28.8	71.2	21.2	78.8
Hindu OBC	29.4	70.6	20.3	79.7
Hindu higher castes	40.7	59.3	27.9	72.1
Total	**33.0**	**67.0**	**22.5**	**77.5**

Source: Authors' calculation based on NSS 61st round and PLFS 2017–18 data.

cent, are informal workers who are without written contract and social security. The percentage of informal workers is high among the SC (79 per cent) as compared to 72 per cent among the higher castes and 79 per cent for the OBC. This indicates that although the level of informal workers, i.e. those without both job and social securities, is generally high, the SC workers suffered more from high job and social insecurities than higher castes.

Table 5.10 Percentage of formal and informal workers by caste to total regular salaried workers

| Social Groups | Regular Workers | | | |
| | Formal Employment | | Informal Employment | |
	In million	In %	In million	In %
2004–05				
SC (Hindu, Buddhist, and Sikh)	4.2	18.0	6.9	23.1
Hindu OBC	7.6	32.4	12.5	42.0
Hindu higher castes	11.6	49.5	10.4	34.9
Total	**23.4**	**100**	**29.8**	**100**
2017–18				
SC (Hindu, Buddhist, and Sikh)	6.0	17.3	11.7	23.7
Hindu OBC	13.7	39.4	21.6	43.7
Hindu higher castes	15.1	43.3	16.1	32.6
Total	**34.8**	**100**	**49.4**	**100**

Source: Authors' calculation based on NSS 61st round and PLFS 2017–18 data.

5.7.2   Regular Workers without Job and Social Security

In the earlier discussion, the informal workers were defined as those who are both without a job and social security. However, this definition does not give the number of all those without job security as it excludes those without job security and one or more social security protection. It also does not give the total number of workers without social security, as some of those with social security but without job security are excluded. Therefore, to get the percentage of all those without job security and social security, we have estimated the number for these two subsets separately. Tables 5.11 and 5.12 show the percentage of those without job security and the percentage of those without social security separately.

Table 5.11   Share of regular salaried workers without job security, 2017–18

	ST	Hindu SC	Hindu OBC	Hindu Higher Castes	Muslims	Total
No contract	72.3	75.5	75.7	68.4	84.1	73.8
Contract up to 1 year	1.6	4.4	3.9	3.2	2.4	3.6
More than 1 year to 3 years	1.2	2.8	3.0	3.1	2.3	2.9
More than 3 years	24.8	17.3	17.4	25.3	11.2	19.7
No contract or 1 year contract	74.0	79.9	79.6	71.6	86.5	77.4
Total	100	100	100	100	100	100

Source: Authors' calculation based on PLFS 2017–18 data.

Table 5.12   Share of regular salaried non-agricultural workers by type of social security benefit, 2017–18

	ST	Hindu SC	Hindu OBC	Hindu Higher Castes	Muslims	Total
At least one benefit	47.1	32.5	39.9	50.5	22.9	41.3
No benefit	44.5	58.6	52.2	40.0	64.9	49.6
Not known	8.4	8.9	7.9	9.5	12.2	9.1
Total	100	100	100	100	100	100

Source: Authors' calculation based on PLFS 2017–18 data.

The number of those without any job contract security is quite high. In 2017–18, 73.8 per cent of the total wage workers in the non-agriculture sector are without contract. This means that about 26 per cent are on more than a one-year contract. The share of those with a contract of one to three years is 6 per cent and those with more than three years are about 20 per cent. Those working without a contract are the highest among the SC with 75 per cent as compared to the higher castes (68 per cent). Conversely, the percentage of workers who work for more than one year is 25 per cent among the SC as compared to 32 per cent for higher castes.

The percentage of regular salaried workers without any social security is also high (50 per cent). About 41 per cent are with at least one social security. The percentage of workers without any security is high among the SC (58 per cent) which is higher than 40 per cent for the higher castes. Conversely, the lower percentage of SC are with security (32 per cent) as compared to 50 per cent for the higher castes.

Thus, at the all-India level a very high proportion of non-agricultural regular salaried workers are engaged in informal sector. These workers suffer from a high degree of job and social insecurities. The proportion of informal workers is high among the SC as compared to OBC and higher castes. A high proportion of the SC also suffers from job insecurity as most of them are employed without a contract. Similarly, a high proportion of the SC is without any social security, like provident fund, gratuity, and medical insurance.

5.8 Regular Salaried Workers in Private and Public Sectors

After having discussed the features of regular salaried workers at all aggregate level, we will now examine the same for the private and public sectors. Table 5.13 gives the share of regular salaried workers in the private and public sectors. In 2017–18, of the total regular salaried workers, about 54 per cent are in the private sector and the rest 46 per cent in the public sector. The share of SC in the public sector is more that national average as compared to higher castes (49 per cent) and OBC (52 per cent). Conversely, this means that the share of SC is less in private sector

Table 5.13 Distribution of regular salaried workers in private and public sectors

	2004–05			2017–18		
	Public	Private	Total	Public	Private	Total
Hindu SC	74.9	25.2	100.0	58.5	41.5	100.0
Hindu OBC	65.2	34.9	100.0	52.4	47.6	100.0
Hindu higher castes	63.3	36.7	100.0	49.5	50.5	100.0
Total	66.8	33.2	100.0	53.7	46.3	100.0

Source: Authors' calculation based on NSS 61st round and PLFS 2017–18 data.

which is 41 per cent as compared to 50 per cent for higher castes and 47 per cent for OBC. Thus, compared to other groups, the SC share is less in the private sector. Relatively, more share of SC in the public sector is due to the reservation in jobs.

In 2017–18, the level of the formal and informal workers also differs between the private and public sectors. The percentage of the informal sector is high in the private sector than in the public sector which is 40 per cent in the private sector and 26.5 per cent in the public sector. Conversely, the percentage of formal workers is high in public sector (73.5 per cent) than in private sector (60 per cent). This means that compared to public sector a higher proportion of regular salaried workers are informal workers (both without a job and social security in the private sector) (Table 5.14).

In the private sector (where the regular salaried workers are more insecure), the percentage of informal workers is high among the SC regular salaried workers (about 50 per cent) as compared to 34 per cent among the higher castes and 42 per cent among the OBC. Relatively, a high proportion of the SC regular salaried workers are informal workers (both without job and social security) as compared to higher castes.

5.9 Regional Dimensions of Employment

Regular workers: There are statewise disparities in the level of regular salaried workers (Table 5.15). In 11 states the percentage of

Table 5.14 Sectorwise distribution of regular salaried workers by social groups and formal job contract

Social Groups	Public Sector				Private Sector			
	Formal Employment		Informal Employment		Formal Employment		Informal Employment	
	In million	In %	In million	In %	In million	In %	In million	In %
2004–05								
Hindu SC	3.2	84.2	0.6	15.8	0.6	46.2	0.7	53.8
Hindu OBC	4.8	84.2	0.9	15.8	1.6	51.6	1.5	48.4
Hindu higher castes	7.1	89.9	0.8	10.1	3.1	67.4	1.5	32.6
Total	15.1	86.3	2.4	13.7	5.3	58.9	3.7	41.1
2017–18								
Hindu SC	3.4	68.0	1.6	32.0	1.8	50.0	1.8	50.0
Hindu OBC	6.8	72.3	2.6	27.7	4.9	57.6	3.6	42.4
Hindu higher castes	7.0	77.8	2.0	22.2	6.0	65.9	3.1	34.1
Total	17.2	73.5	6.2	26.5	12.7	59.9	8.5	40.1

Source: Authors' calculation based on NSS 61st round and PLFS 2017–18 data.

regular salaried workers is above the national average of 23 per cent. The percentage is relatively high in Delhi (61.6 per cent), Haryana (35 per cent), Kerala, Punjab, and Tamil Nadu where the ratio is about 33 per cent followed by Maharashtra and Uttarakhand with 30 per cent. The percentage of the regular salaried workers is relatively low in Bihar, Chhattisgarh, Himachal Pradesh, Jharkhand, Odisha, Rajasthan, and Uttar Pradesh where the percentage varies between a minimum of 13 and 19 per cent.

In the case of SC, the percentage of regular salaried workers is higher than the all-India average of 19 per cent in 10 states. The percentage is particularly high in Delhi, Gujarat, Haryana, Karnataka, Kerala, Maharashtra, Tamil Nadu, and Uttarakhand. In all these states, except Delhi and Jammu and Kashmir, the percentage of higher castes is higher than the SC by a significant margin.

Formal and informal workers: There are also disparities in the incidence of informal workers across the states in 2017–18 (Table 5.16). At

Table 5.15   Statewise share of regular salaried workers within total workers

| | 2004–05 | | | | 2017–18 | | | |
	Hindu SC	Hindu OBC	Hindu Higher Castes	Total	Hindu SC	Hindu OBC	Hindu Higher Castes	Total
Andhra Pradesh	10.5	12.3	15.5	13.0	19.9	22.4	23.5	**21.8**
Assam	12.2	19.1	17.7	12.1	18.1	34.4	29.4	**25.1**
Bihar	3.1	3.9	9.3	4.2	8.1	13.3	23.3	**13.1**
Chhattisgarh	8.9	7.4	35.2	8.4	16.3	15.4	31.7	**14.1**
Delhi	65.8	59.6	58.6	61.0	69.8	56.8	65.1	**61.6**
Gujarat	20.4	12.3	28.1	17.3	28.7	23.9	38.9	**28.6**
Haryana	16.1	20.1	22.9	20.2	29.9	37.9	39.9	**35.6**
Himachal Pradesh	10.9	10.6	16.6	14.0	17.2	20.3	21.2	**19.5**
Jammu and Kashmir	13.9	14.7	18.0	16.5	27.2	39.2	28.0	**25.1**
Jharkhand	8.6	8.0	28.3	8.5	12.5	14.8	**40.3**	**15.1**
Karnataka	8.4	11.6	18.7	13.1	24.0	23.3	31.7	**25.5**
Kerala	16.0	18.8	31.0	19.2	26.7	30.8	**45.4**	**32.9**
Madhya Pradesh	11.0	8.7	25.4	10.7	12.1	14.2	29.5	**14.3**
Maharashtra	21.6	16.9	25.1	20.7	26.9	22.4	36.6	**28.9**
Odisha	6.7	8.8	19.5	8.7	10.9	17.2	24.6	**15.4**
Punjab	23.2	29.0	40.0	21.7	29.8	41.9	**44.5**	**33.6**
Rajasthan	11.7	7.7	21.5	10.6	18.7	18.1	32.2	**18.7**
Tamil Nadu	17.3	20.6	55.3	21.6	30.6	32.5	56.1	**33.8**
Uttar Pradesh	5.7	7.4	22.8	9.7	11.8	13.4	24.2	**15.0**
Uttarakhand	12.7	12.0	14.9	13.6	28.0	29.8	32.1	**29.6**
West Bengal	11.2	15.1	22.7	15.1	17.4	23.0	30.2	**22.1**
All India	12.2	12.0	23.7	14.3	19.7	21.4	32.7	**22.8**

Source: Authors' calculations based on NSS 61st round and PLFS 2017–18 data.

the overall level, about 78 per cent of the regular salaried workers are informal workers. In six states, the percentage is above the all-India average. In the case of SC, the percentage of informal workers is 79 per cent. In about eight states, the percentage exceeded the all-India average. The incidence of informal workers is particularly high in Karnataka (94 per cent), Gujarat (94.7 per cent), Punjab (85 per cent), and Rajasthan, Delhi, and Tamil Nadu (about 83 per cent). In about 10 states, the disparities between SC and higher castes are much larger. These include Andhra

Table 5.16 Share of formal and informal workers within regular salaried workers, 2017–18

2017–18	Hindu SC		Hindu OBC		Hindu Higher Castes		Total	
	Formal	Informal	Formal	Informal	Formal	Informal	Formal	Informal
Andhra Pradesh	18.2	81.8	21.6	78.4	31.0	69.0	21.7	78.4
Assam	38.9	61.1	30.4	69.6	46.5	53.5	36.7	63.3
Bihar	22.0	78.0	15.0	85.0	33.3	66.7	22.4	77.7
Chhattisgarh	24.7	75.3	19.6	80.4	43.1	56.9	25.1	74.9
Delhi	16.4	83.6	16.6	83.4	34.7	65.3	24.3	75.7
Gujarat	5.4	94.7	11.4	88.6	10.4	89.7	8.7	91.3
Haryana	25.5	74.5	35.8	64.2	43.4	56.7	34.7	65.3
Himachal Pradesh	28.0	72.0	36.7	63.3	35.5	64.5	32.9	67.1
Jammu and Kashmir	28.8	71.2	65.6	34.4	47.1	52.9	46.3	53.7
Jharkhand	19.5	80.5	25.2	74.8	35.5	64.5	25.3	74.7
Karnataka	5.1	94.9	5.0	95.0	6.1	93.9	5.0	95.1
Kerala	20.3	79.8	23.8	76.2	40.8	59.2	27.8	72.2
Madhya Pradesh	28.3	71.7	35.2	64.8	47.4	52.6	38.7	61.3
Maharashtra	21.7	78.3	21.4	78.6	21.2	78.8	20.1	79.9
Odisha	25.7	74.3	26.1	73.9	33.0	67.0	29.7	70.3
Punjab	14.8	85.2	12.8	87.2	18.8	81.2	18.5	81.5
Rajasthan	17.0	83.1	9.6	90.4	13.9	86.1	12.6	87.4

(continued)

Table 5.16 Continued

2017–18	Hindu SC		Hindu OBC		Hindu Higher Castes		Total	
	Formal	Informal	Formal	Informal	Formal	Informal	Formal	Informal
Tamil Nadu	17.1	82.9	16.7	83.3	11.7	88.3	16.1	83.9
Uttar Pradesh	30.8	69.2	23.3	76.7	35.1	64.9	25.3	74.7
Uttarakhand	33.3	66.7	37.6	62.4	37.2	62.8	35.8	64.2
West Bengal	26.6	73.4	31.1	68.9	31.5	68.5	26.4	73.6
All India	20.9	79.1	19.8	80.2	27.7	72.3	22.2	77.8

Source: Authors' calculations based on NSS 61st round and PLFS 2017–18 data.

Pradesh, Assam, Bihar, Delhi, Gujarat, Jammu and Kashmir, Jharkhand, Kerala, and Madhya Pradesh.

Public and private sector workers: We have seen that in 2017–18 at the all-India level about 41 per cent workers belonging to SCs are employed in the private sector and the rest 60 per cent in the public sector. There are statewise variations in the share of SC in the private sector. There are about 13 states where their share is less than the all-India average and these include Uttarakhand, Uttar Pradesh, Odisha, Madhya Pradesh, Kerala, Jharkhand, Jammu and Kashmir, Himachal Pradesh, Chhattisgarh, Bihar, Assam, and Andhra Pradesh. In a few states, the share in the private sector is much higher than all-India average and these include Delhi, Gujarat, Karnataka, Maharashtra, and Tamil Nadu (Table 5.17).

5.10   Summary

This analysis brings out some features of regular salaried workers concerning the magnitude, industry, and occupation of employment, total and private and public sectors in India. In 2017–18, about one-fifth of the total workers are regular salaried workers. The SC also have gained access to the regular salaried jobs but their share is relatively low as compared to the higher castes. Some unique features of SC employment in regular salaried jobs emerged quite clearly which distinguish them from the higher castes. It emerged that a high percentage of SC workers are employed in low-paid occupations, like elementary and similar jobs, which include domestic helpers, cleaners, garbage collectors, etc., a relatively high proportion of them are engaged in agriculture and construction industries. Thus, although there has been a partial break from the restrictions in the past in regular salaried jobs, the occupational segregation of the SC in low-paid work continues in the present. Low level of education, particularly higher education, seems to restrict their access to regular salaried jobs. Low education also affects the type of occupation of their engagement. The SC concentration in elementary occupations with education below the higher secondary level shows the interrelations between low-level jobs and poor education. In the elementary and similar occupations, the SC are mainly employed as informal workers where a high proportion of them remained without a job and social security. This is particularly

Table 5.17 Statewise distribution of public and private sector workers

| | 2004–05 | | | | | | | | 2017–18 | | | | | | | |
| | Hindu SC | | Hindu OBC | | Hindu Higher Castes | | Total | | Hindu SC | | Hindu OBC | | Hindu Higher castes | | Total | |
	Public	Private	Public	Private	Public	Private	Public	Private	Public	Private	Public	Private	Public	Private	Public	Private
Andhra Pradesh	81.4	18.6	70.7	29.3	76.3	23.7	74.7	25.3	68.3	31.7	56.2	43.8	52.8	47.2	58.0	42.1
Assam	94.8	5.2	91.6	8.4	86.7	13.3	91.3	8.7	81.8	18.2	69.9	30.1	71.0	29.0	75.8	24.2
Bihar	97.1	2.9	82.8	17.2	94.8	5.2	89.0	11.0	71.6	28.4	84.5	15.5	84.3	15.7	83.4	16.6
Chhattisgarh	84.1	15.9	83.4	16.6	83.5	16.6	85.7	14.3	84.7	15.3	73.3	26.7	75.8	24.2	79.3	20.8
Delhi	73.0	27.0	57.8	42.2	54.0	46.0	56.5	43.5	34.9	65.1	33.2	66.8	40.1	59.9	35.6	64.4
Gujarat	58.2	41.8	49.1	51.0	42.4	57.7	49.3	50.7	48.5	51.5	39.0	61.0	37.8	62.2	38.5	61.5
Haryana	73.4	26.6	39.6	60.4	39.0	61.0	46.4	53.7	61.8	38.2	42.6	57.4	36.1	63.9	41.3	58.7
Himachal Pradesh	87.9	12.1	94.1	5.9	80.3	19.7	84.1	15.9	76.0	24.0	70.6	29.4	71.6	28.4	72.3	27.7
Jammu and Kashmir	81.9	18.1	92.7	7.3	91.3	8.7	90.5	9.5	86.1	13.9	90.3	9.7	85.1	14.9	90.6	9.4
Jharkhand	78.9	21.1	72.7	27.3	50.3	49.8	63.6	36.4	62.4	37.6	63.5	36.5	52.1	47.9	58.6	41.4
Karnataka	76.1	23.9	69.3	30.7	52.2	47.8	62.6	37.4	48.4	51.6	39.5	60.5	37.1	62.9	39.5	60.5
Kerala	77.5	22.6	66.9	33.2	72.2	27.8	67.2	32.8	62.3	37.7	54.6	45.4	50.7	49.3	52.2	47.8
Madhya Pradesh	52.2	47.8	60.4	39.6	72.1	27.9	63.5	36.5	75.8	24.2	61.8	38.2	67.3	32.7	70.8	29.2

Maharashtra	68.4	31.6	57.8	42.2	44.1	55.9	53.1	46.9	55.0	45.0	52.4	47.6	37.7	62.3	44.1	55.9
Odisha	81.4	18.7	81.0	19.0	85.5	14.5	84.0	16.0	74.3	25.8	69.4	30.6	61.2	38.8	68.3	31.7
Punjab	79.1	20.9	58.0	42.0	76.9	23.1	77.4	22.6	56.5	43.5	41.0	59.0	50.6	49.4	58.3	41.7
Rajasthan	85.8	14.2	82.0	18.0	89.7	10.3	85.7	14.3	70.4	29.6	73.2	26.8	56.5	43.5	68.0	32.0
Tamil Nadu	70.8	29.2	56.8	43.3	50.5	49.5	58.3	41.7	34.8	65.2	34.1	65.9	34.0	66.0	33.8	66.2
Uttar Pradesh	87.2	12.8	71.8	28.2	72.3	27.7	74.0	26.1	71.9	28.1	60.8	39.3	58.2	41.8	62.7	37.4
Uttarakhand	87.0	13.1	85.4	14.6	84.2	15.8	83.5	16.5	66.6	33.4	59.6	40.4	75.6	24.4	68.4	31.6
West Bengal	84.4	15.6	83.6	16.4	74.5	25.5	76.4	23.6	62.0	38.0	75.4	24.6	58.4	41.6	61.5	38.5
All India	74.9	25.2	65.2	34.9	63.3	36.7	66.8	33.2	58.5	41.5	52.4	47.6	49.5	50.5	53.7	46.3

Source: Authors' calculation based on NSS 61st round and PLFS 2017–18 data.

the case in the private sector. The reservation in public sector jobs seems to have improved the participation of the SC in formal and more secure jobs. To what extent the low participation of the SC in regular salaried jobs, particularly in the private sector, is due to differences between them and higher castes in endowment factors, like education, and to what extent due to caste discrimination in hiring are the questions which we will examine in the next chapter.

6

Employment Discrimination and Untouchables

6.1 Introduction

The analysis of regular salaried workers in the preceding chapter brings out the caste-specific characteristics. We found that in 2017–18 about one-fifth of the total workers are regular salaried workers. The Scheduled Castes (SC) also have gained access to the regular salaried jobs but their share is relatively low as compared to the higher castes which indicates a gap in participation in regular salaried jobs in private and public sectors. It is found that a high percentage of the SC workers are employed in low-paid occupations which indicates that despite the improvement, the occupational segregation of the SC in low-paid work continues in the present. Apparently the low level of higher education seems to restrict their access to regular salaried jobs. Further, a high percentage of them are employed as informal workers where they remained without job and social security. This is particularly the case in the private sector. These results on labour market outcomes, regarding the SC, raised important questions. To what extent is the low participation of the SC in regular salaried jobs, particularly in the private sector, due to differences between them and the higher castes in endowment factors like education? And to what extent are the differences due to caste discrimination in hiring? These are important issues which need examination. If the gap in regular salaried employment between the SC and higher castes is to be reduced, it is necessary to identify the causes of low participation of the SC in regular salaried jobs. The discussion in this chapter attempts to find an answer to these questions. We first identify the determinants of employment of regular salaried workers. Then we estimate the extent to which

Scheduled Castes in the Indian Labour Market. Sukhadeo Thorat, S. Madheswaran, and B. P. Vani, Oxford University Press. © Sukhadeo Thorat, S. Madheswaran, and B. P. Vani 2023.
DOI: 10.1093/oso/9780198872252.003.0006

the endowment factors and caste discrimination cause the differences in the probability of employment between the SC and higher castes in India during 2004–05 and 2017–18.

6.2 Determinants of Employment Status

Within the limitations of unit-level data of the workers from the employment survey, we try to identify the determinants of employment status by using the multinomial logit regression model. The dependent variable is employment status (regular, casual, and self-employed), which is polytomous. The multinomial logit model (MLM) has been used to analyse occupational outcomes by, inter alia, Schmidt and Strauss (1975) and Borooah (2001). The basic question that the MLM seeks to answer is: What is the probability that a person with a particular set of characteristics will be found in a specific category of employment status? These answers are obtained by estimating an MLM where the dependent variable Y_i take the values 1, 2 or 3 depending upon whether person i is a regular salaried or wage worker (1); a casual wage worker (2); or a self-employed (own-account worker) (3). In essence, with self-employment ($Y_i = 3$) as the base category, the model consisted of two equations ($Y_i = 1$ and $Y_i = 2$) each of which takes the following form:

$$\log\left[\frac{\Pr(Y_i = j)}{\Pr(Y_i = 3)}\right]$$
$$= f(\text{landholding, social group, education, state}) + \text{error} \tag{1}$$

Two important points are noteworthy from Table 6.1. First, education has a positive impact on the likelihood of joining regular employment more than self-employed and casual labour. Second, the SC workers are more likely to be regular wage earners and casual labourers than self-employed. On the other hand, higher castes' workers are more likely to be self-employed and in regular employment. In all this, higher education, beyond secondary education, matters.

Table 6.1 Determinants of employment status—multinomial logit estimates

	Self-employed		Regular Wage Earners		Casual Labourers	
	Marginal Effect	Z-value	Marginal Effect	Z-value	Marginal Effect	Z-value
Base Other Religion						
ST	−0.0251	−5.0	0.0493	9.9	−0.0243	−8.0
Hindu SC	−0.1579	−32.1	0.0617	12.5	0.0962	24.7
Hindu OBC	0.0033	0.8	−0.0057	−1.4	0.0025	0.9
Hindu higher castes	0.0497	10.9	0.0091	2.1	−0.0588	−21.1
Rural (Base = Urban)	0.1817	60.7	−0.2221	−78.1	0.0404	20.5
Male (Base = Female)	−0.0158	−4.7	−0.0249	−7.8	0.0407	21.2
Married (Base = Not married)	0.0938	23.8	−0.0638	−16.8	−0.0300	−10.8
Age	−0.0113	−15.7	0.0098	14.2	0.0014	3.2
Age^2	0.0002	23.3	−0.0002	−18.4	0.0000	−8.3
Base Below Primary						
Secondary	−0.0386	−10.8	0.1220	34.1	−0.0834	−43.5
Higher secondary	−0.1229	−22.1	0.2439	42.9	−0.1210	−66.3
Diploma	−0.2572	−23.0	0.3814	33.5	−0.1242	−46.4
Graduate and above	−0.2214	−42.7	0.4011	77.4	−0.1797	−106.1
Base Low Industrialized States						
High industrialized states	0.1193	36.0	−0.0418	−13.5	−0.0775	−37.8
Medium industrialized states	0.0847	24.7	−0.0293	−9.2	−0.0554	−27.1
Per capita expenditure	3.52E–06	3.0	3.71E–05	38.8	−4.1E–05	−38.6
Log-likelihood value	−128857.37					
Number of observations	1,50,039					
Wald chi-square	35612.57					
Probability > chi-square	0.000					
Pseudo R2	0.1576					

Source: Authors' calculation based on PLFS 2017–18 data.

6.3 Occupational Attainment by Social Groups

We have observed that the SC generally tend to be concentrated in low-paid occupations. Although these occupational differences between the SC and higher castes, as reported in the last chapter, are well known, re-searchers continue to investigate whether these employment disparities are due to caste/gender differences in occupational choice, differences in characteristics or market distortions, such as occupational segregation. Occupational segregation occurs when workers are excluded from certain jobs and over-represented in others for non-economic reasons, such as caste, gender, etc. Since the early 1960s, researchers have been interested in the measurement and consequences of occupational segregation in the labour market. Recent empirical works have employed discrete-choice and qualitative-response models of occupational attainment to investigate differences in occupational structures across groups of workers. The qualitative-response model of occupational attainment was developed initially to predict the likelihood that workers are employed in a specified occupational category, given their individual traits. The occupational segregation literature has adopted the model to determine whether after controlling for differences in characteristics, such as human capital variables, certain workers face unequal prospects for occupational achievement. This section assesses occupational distribution of the SC and higher castes in the regular salaried jobs in the Indian labour market. The objective is to determine the extent of differences in occupations that are due to discrimination-based segregation or due to other factors, such as differences in human capital characteristics and labour market choices.

Empirical model: Occupational attainment refers to the net outcome of the processes that ultimately determine a worker's occupation. The demand side of occupational labour markets is influenced by employer-established requirements for jobs in terms of training, education, and experience, and by other labour market factors, such as product demand and labour productivity. On the supply side, a worker's background, demographic characteristics, ability, and aptitude influence the occupational choice and placement. Empirical models of occupational attainment are therefore reduced from specifications that attempt to incorporate both supply- and demand-side factors. This analysis uses a well-established occupational attainment model to estimate the statistical link between a worker's characteristics and the likelihood that the SC or higher castes is employed in a given occupation. In our specification, we assume that the probability that a worker is employed in the jth occupation ($j = 1 \ldots J$) can be expressed as the logistic conditional probability function.

$$P_{ij} \mid X_i = \frac{e^{\delta_j X_j}}{\sum_j e^{\delta_j X_j}} \tag{2}$$

where P_{ij} is the expected probability that the ith individual ($i = 1 \ldots N$) is employed in the jth occupation, X_i is a vector of individual characteristics and δ_j is a vector of coefficients to be estimated. The logistic model in (1) can be expressed in linear terms as the log of an odds ratio:

$$\ln\left(\frac{P_{ij}}{P_j}\right) = \hat{\delta}_j X_j \tag{3}$$

Estimating the parameters in δ_j yields an occupational structure in which the net influence on a worker's occupation is expressed as a function of personal characteristics that are statistically linked to occupational attainment.

We can use Equation (4) to investigate whether the SC face different prospects for occupational attainment than their higher castes' counterparts. The initial step in this process is to estimate the parameter coefficients (Equation 4) for higher castes. Next, these estimated coefficients are applied to workers' characteristics from the SC sample. This step yields an estimated probability that the SC are employed in occupations, given that their personal traits are evaluated according to the estimated occupational structure for the higher castes.

$$\hat{P}_{ij}^{HSC} = \frac{e^{\hat{\delta}_j^{HHC} X^{HSC}}}{\sum_j e^{\hat{\delta}_j^{HHC} X^{HSC}}} \tag{4}$$

Equation (4) can be used to derive the expected percentage of the SC in occupation j, assuming that they are assigned to occupations on the basis of their characteristics and qualifications in a fashion similar to the way higher castes are. The expected occupational distribution for the SC can be compared with their actual distribution to determine whether there are noticeable differences.

To compare the actual occupational distribution of higher castes with the actual and expected occupational distributions of the SC, we calculate the following:

(i) the ID for the actual occupational distributions of higher castes and the SC, i.e. $ID = \left(\dfrac{1}{2}\right)\sum_{j=1}^{k} |\, P^{HHC} - P^{HSC}\, |$

(ii) the ID for the actual higher castes' distribution and the expected SC distribution $ID^{*} = \left(\dfrac{1}{2}\right)\sum_{j=1}^{k} |\, \breve{P}^{HSC} - P^{HSC}\, |$

A significant decline in the index from (i) to (ii) suggests that if the characteristics of the SC are evaluated as though they are higher castes, the occupational distribution of the two groups become more similar. This idea supports the notion of discrimination-based occupational segregation against the SC assuming that the higher castes and the SC have similar tastes with respect to occupational choice. The approach assumes implicitly that any remaining disparity in occupational distributions, once the expected SC distribution is determined, results from differences in occupational choice patterns by social groups. Thus, the empirical model used in this chapter is based on the standard neoclassical labour market approach to higher castes and SC discrimination, an approach which asserts that unequal labour market outcomes between the higher castes and the SC are primarily due to social group differences in skills, qualifications, and choice as well as to labour market imperfections, such as discrimination.

We have estimated occupational attainment equations separately for both the SC and the higher castes which are given in Appendix Table 6.1 and Appendix Table 6.2 and the predicted probabilities are presented in Table 6.1. As we have mentioned in the previous paragraphs, we have used the multinomial logit estimates and presented the actual and predicted occupational difference between the higher castes and the SC in Tables 6.2 and 6.3. It compares the actual occupational distribution of the higher castes with the expected occupational distribution of the SC derived from the above equation.

Table 6.2 Comparison of actual and expected occupational distributions for the higher castes and the SC in regular labour market, 2004–05

	Observed Occupational Distribution		Predicted Occupational Distribution		Observed Difference	Explained Difference	Residual Difference
	P_{HHL}	P_{HSC}	$\hat{P}_{HHC}$	$\hat{P}_{HSC}$	$P_{HHC} - P_{HSC}$	$P_{HHC} - \hat{P}_{HSC}$	$\hat{P}_{HSC} - P_{HSC}$
Administrative	0.0695	0.0243	0.0695	0.0377	0.0451	0.0317	0.0134
Professionals	0.3434	0.1917	0.3434	0.206	0.1517	0.1375	0.0142
Clerical	0.1272	0.0917	0.1272	0.0906	0.0354	0.0365	−0.0011
Service	0.0754	0.1102	0.0754	0.1023	−0.0347	−0.0269	−0.0078
Sales	0.0791	0.0615	0.0791	0.1022	0.0176	−0.0231	0.0407
Production	0.2181	0.2558	0.2181	0.3061	−0.0377	−0.088	0.0503
Elementary	0.0873	0.2647	0.0873	0.1551	−0.1774	−0.0678	−0.1097
Dissimilarity index	ID	0.2498					
	ID*	0.1186					

Source: Authors' calculation based on NSS 61st round data.

Table 6.3 Comparison of actual and expected occupational distributions for the higher castes and the SC in regular labour market, 2017–18

	Observed Occupational Distribution		Predicted Occupational Distribution		Observed Difference	Explained Difference	Residual Difference
	P_{HHC}	P_{HSC}	$\hat{P}_{HHC}$	$\hat{P}_{HSC}$	$P_{HHC} - P_{HSC}$	$P_{HHC} - \hat{P}_{HSC}$	$\hat{P}_{HSC} - P_{HSC}$
Administrative	0.0867	0.0313	0.0867	0.0561	0.0554	0.0306	0.0248
Professionals	0.3106	0.2051	0.3106	0.2129	0.1055	0.0977	0.0078
Clerical	0.1057	0.0752	0.1057	0.084	0.0305	0.0218	0.0087
Service	0.088	0.1185	0.088	0.1221	−0.0305	−0.034	0.0036
Sales	0.0924	0.0847	0.0924	0.1058	0.0077	−0.0134	0.0211
Production	0.216	0.2558	0.216	0.2647	−0.0397	−0.0487	0.009
Elementary	0.1005	0.2294	0.1005	0.1544	−0.1288	−0.0539	−0.0749
Dissimilarity index	ID	0.1991					
	ID*	0.0749					

Source: Authors' calculation based on PLFS 2017–18 data.

The dissimilarity index is 24.98 points during 2004–05 and 19.90 points during 2017–18 when the actual occupational distribution for the SC is compared with the actual higher castes' distribution, whereas the dissimilarity index* for 2004–05 is 11.86 points and 7.49 points during 2017–18. In other words, if the SC are assigned to occupations on the basis of their education, experience, and other characteristics according to the higher castes' occupational structure, the caste disparities in occupation persists, although the overall caste disparity in occupations declines by approximately 47 per cent and 37 per cent during 2004–05 and 2017–18 respectively. This shows that unexplained differences in the occupational distributions of the SC and the higher castes persist, and fell albeit slightly from 2004–05 to 2017–18. This result may also imply that the SC continue to face significant obstacles to occupational mobility than their higher castes' counterpart did, even with more education and with the presence of anti-discrimination laws.

6.4 Magnitude of Employment Discrimination

Table 6.4 shows the (decomposition) results where we decompose the gross difference in access to employment (UPSS) between the SC and the higher castes into two parts. One part is attributable to differences in human capital endowment between them, and the other part is attributable to discrimination in the labour market. We found earlier that the gross difference in probabilities of getting employment between the SC and the higher castes was 0.088 in 2004–05 and 0.070 in 2017–18 (Table 6.4).

The decomposition of gross difference in the probability of employment access between the SC and the higher castes shows that discrimination accounted for 74 per cent of the differences in employment in 2004–05. It remained stagnant at 73 per cent in 2017–18 and the remaining 27 per cent is due to endowment differences. Thus, a low probability of employment for the SC as compared to the higher castes is mainly due to discrimination in hiring. Out of the total unexplained differences, 30 per cent is accounted for by the advantage to the higher castes and 44 per cent is accounted for the disadvantage of being the SC in the labour market during 2004–05. In 2017–18, there is a reversal of this

Table 6.4 Employment discrimination in total labour market in India (non-linear decomposition method)—the higher castes vs. SC, 2004–05 and 2017–18

Category	2004–05	2017–18
Raw differentials (probability)	0.088	0,070
Differences in endowments (in %)	26	27
Employment discrimination (in %)	74	73
Advantage to higher castes (benefit of being higher castes in the labour market) (in %)	30	42
Disadvantage to the SC (cost of being SC in the labour market) (in %)	44	31

Source: Authors' calculation based on NSS 61st round and PLFS 2017–18 data.

trend. About 42 per cent of unexplained differences are due to advantage to the higher castes and 21 per cent for the disadvantage of being SC.

The discrimination in the probability of access to employment is much higher in the private sector as compared to the public sector. Employment discrimination accounted for about 53.15 per cent differences in the probability to access job in the private sector which is much higher as compared to 13.99 per cent differences in the public sector (Table 6.5). The results also quantify the caste advantage to the higher castes and disadvantage to the SC in employment in the labour market. Of the total unexplained differences in the private sector, about 34.12 per cent is due

Table 6.5 Employment discrimination against the SC in public and private sectors: Non-linear decomposition results, 2017–18

Category	Public	Private
Differences in endowments (in %)	86.01	46.85
Employment discrimination (in %)	13.99	53.15
Advantage to higher castes (benefit of being higher castes in the labour market) (in %)	5.44	19.03
Disadvantage to SC (cost of being SC in the labour market) (in %)	8.55	34.12

Source: Authors' calculation based on PLFS 2017–18 data.

to the advantage to the higher castes in private employment and 19.03 per cent due to disadvantage for being SC.

6.5 Conclusion and Policy Implications

The results on the differences in the probability of employment among the caste groups have significant policy implications. The results show that the gross difference in probabilities to get employment between the SC and the higher castes was 0.088 in 2004–05 and 0.070 in 2017–18 indicating a lower probability of employment for the SC as compared to the higher castes. The decomposition of this gross difference in probability of access to employment between the SC and the higher castes shows that discrimination accounted for 74 per cent of the differences in employment in 2004–05 and 73 per cent in 2017–18 and the remaining 26 per cent to 27 per cent is due to differences in the endowment. Thus, the low probability of employment for the SC as compared to the higher castes is significant due to caste discrimination in hiring. These findings also indicate the high degree of discrimination faced by the SC in hiring in the labour market. The employment discrimination of the SC is much higher in the private sector as compared to the public sector. Employment discrimination accounted for about 53.15 per cent differences in the probability to access the job in the private sector which is much higher as compared to 14 per cent in the public sector. These results on employment discrimination have policy implications to minimize the gap in the probability of employment of the SC vis-à-vis higher castes. The policy implication is both for the improvement of human resource endowment of the SC as well as for measures to reduce discrimination in employment.

6.5.1 Policy Implications to Enhance Human Endowment

We have seen that endowment factors account for about 27 per cent difference in the probability of employment between the SC and the higher castes. The endowment effect was high with 86 per cent in the public sector and 47 per cent in the private sector. The results related to the determinants of employment status indicate that education, particularly higher education (exceeding beyond higher secondary), is significantly important to improve the share in regular salaried jobs. The probability particularly increases with a diploma and graduate and above education. The high education level of SC women also tends to improve the possibility of employment. The work experience and stay in urban areas are useful to access employment. Thus, higher education, including women's education, work experience, age and stay in urban areas matter for high probability of the SC to get regular salaried jobs. For obvious reason, this calls for strengthening the policy to improve higher education of the SC men and women. At present, the educational attainment of the SC is lower than higher castes. For instance, in 2014–15 the enrolment ratio of higher education of the SC was 20 per cent which is less than half of the higher castes' enrolment ratio (43 per cent). This gap in educational attainment between the SC and higher castes needs to be reduced. Besides, since the work experience is also useful to get initial entry into the jobs, efforts to provide opportunity for work experience in the initial stage or at entry level would be useful for the SC to facilitate higher regular salaried employment. Similarly, efforts are necessary to encourage migration from rural to urban areas. The results imply that these policy initiatives would enhance the probability of the SC male and female in regular salaried employment both in public and private sectors.

6.5.2 Policies to Reduce Discrimination in Employment

The results indicate that although progress in human endowment would improve the probability to get employment, given the fact that almost 74 per cent difference in probability of employment is due to discrimination of an equally qualified SC, the endowment improvement by itself would not bridge the entire gap. This is particularly likely to be the case in the private sector where the probability of access to employment is much higher as compared to the public sector. Employment discrimination accounted for about 53.15 per cent differences in the probability to access jobs in the private sector which is much higher than 14 per cent in the public sector. This would require changes in policies both for the public and the private sectors. In the public sector, policy initiatives are necessary on two fronts. First, the legal safeguards against discrimination in public employment need to be strengthened. Second, we have seen that the discrimination in the public sector is greater in the low-level jobs than at a higher level. Among other reasons, the appointment of low-level jobs on contract basis through private agencies seems to be the main cause as the private agencies are known for discriminatory practices in appointment (Mamgain 2018). Therefore, the appointment on contract basis should be discontinued and if continued, it should be directly done by public sector bodies.

The policy measures for the private sector are on multiple fronts as the difference in probability to get employment between the SC and higher castes due to discrimination is much higher—more than half of the differences in probability of employment are due to discrimination in hiring. The evidence also suggests that unlike the public sector, the discrimination in the private sector is greater in high-grade posts as compared to lower-level jobs. Therefore, adequate legal protection against discrimination in hiring is necessary at that level. At the same time, it would require an affirmative action policy for recruitment to ensure a fair share in private sector jobs to the SC, at least in proportion to their population. The present affirmative action policy adopted by the private sector, which is voluntary and self-regulatory, has a focus on improvement in education level, orientation-cum-training to improve employability to meet the entry-level requirement of the private sector. Thus, the main focus of the private sector affirmative action policy is on endowment enhancement which is necessary. However, it has much less focus on safeguards against discrimination in hiring and hence, lack of reservation in jobs for the SC. The improvement in the endowment would enhance employability but it would be inadequate to provide protection against discrimination in hiring which is high, particularly in high-level jobs. Therefore, it is imperative for the private sector to develop a policy to provide a fair share to the SC at a different level through reservation policy in jobs. We have seen that the SC are particularly under-represented at high-level positions. The private sector has been quite reluctant to adopt the policy of reservation in jobs. The private sector argues that its hiring practices are guided by merit alone and not by the social identity of a person. Our results provide a clear empirical evidence to the contrary. The study came out with clear empirical evidence on high incidence of discrimination in hiring in the private sector, particularly in upper-level jobs, based on the Employment Survey data for 2004–05 and 2017–18. The private sector should recognize the fact that in a severely caste-ridden society like ours, discrimination is deeply embedded in the jobs market.

The empirical result in this chapter also provides evidence on occupation segregation of the SC into certain occupations which are invariably low paid. The tendency on the part of employer is to place the SC workers in elementary occupations, plant and machine operators and assemblers, craft and related trade workers, service workers, and shop and market sales workers. These results, therefore, call for legal safeguards against discrimination in occupation. But it also requires affirmative action policy for the private sector to ensure fair share in occupations where the SC are under-represented due to differential treatment. The theories of market discrimination (discussed in Chapter 3) inform that discrimination in the private sector is driven by prejudices with economic or material motive and, therefore, is difficult to deal with. Discrimination is an action motivated with self-enlightened economic interest. Therefore, since the decision about discrimination in the market is driven by economic motive, it has a tendency to persist for a long time and those who benefit from discrimination try to hold on to it. Therefore, the legal safeguards to the SC thorough anti-discriminatory laws against employment and occupation discrimination as well as affirmative action policy in hiring to ensure a fair share to the SC, at least in proportion to their population, is necessary. At present, there is neither enough legal protection to the SC against differential behaviour in the private market nor proper instruments to ensure fair share to them in regular salaried markets.

Appendix Table 6.1 Multinomial logit estimates of occupational attainment equation for higher castes, 2017–18

	Legislator and senior officers		Professionals		Clerks	
	Coefficients	Marginal Effects	Coefficients	Marginal Effects	Coefficients	Marginal Effects
Age	0.060	0.006	Base Category	0.010	−0.034	0.000
Age²	0.000	0.000		0.000	0.000	0.000
Male	1.567	0.034		−0.339	0.886	−0.004
Married	0.056	0.001		−0.011	−0.218	−0.036
Base: Education up to Primary						
Secondary	−0.456	0.023		0.254	0.233	0.157
Higher secondary	−0.380	0.042		0.352	0.046	0.169
Diploma	−0.552	0.041		0.500	−1.209	−0.018
Graduate and above	−0.155	0.119		0.573	−0.704	0.152
Base: Regular Formal Worker						
Relatively developed states	0.570	0.027		−0.052	0.336	0.020
Less developed states	0.196	0.011		−0.009	0.094	0.008
Constant	−4.287				−0.638	
Log-likelihood	−18230.0					
Number of observations	11,986					
Wald chi-square	4205.5					
Probability > chi-square	0.000					
Pseudo R-sq	0.168					

Source: Authors' calculation based on PLFS 2017–18 unit-level data.

Service and sales workers		Skilled workers		Plant and machine operators		Elementary occupation	
Coefficients	Marginal Effects	Coefficients	Marginal Effects	Coefficients	Marginal Effects	Coefficients	Marginal Effects
−0.067	−0.008	−0.074	−0.004	−0.025	0.001	−0.101	−0.006
0.000	0.000	0.000	0.000	0.000	0.000	0.001	0.000
1.357	0.084	2.290	0.094	3.390	0.121	1.042	0.010
−0.017	−0.013	0.195	0.015	0.400	0.028	0.213	0.015
−1.785	−0.180	−1.962	−0.091	−1.783	−0.065	−2.247	−0.097
−2.971	−0.238	−3.196	−0.111	−3.357	−0.096	−4.041	−0.118
−4.543	−0.245	−3.387	−0.095	−4.238	−0.086	−5.099	−0.097
−4.751	−0.290	−5.388	−0.172	−5.734	−0.166	−6.201	−0.216
0.013	−0.039	0.469	0.030	0.233	0.004	0.276	0.008
−0.079	−0.026	0.129	0.010	0.108	0.006	0.027	−0.001
3.684		2.347		0.515		4.139	

Appendix Table 6.2 Multinomial logit estimates of occupational attainment equation for Scheduled Castes, 2017–18

	Legislator and senior officers		Professionals		Clerks	
	Coefficients	Marginal Effects	Coefficients	Marginal Effects	Coefficients	Marginal Effects
Age	0.0567	0.0004	0.1263	0.0117	0.0610	0.0012
Age^2	−0.0001	0.0000	−0.0012	−0.0001	−0.0002	0.0000
Male	0.5237	0.0077	−1.0706	−0.2337	−0.0117	−0.0113
Married	−0.0621	0.0032	−0.0761	0.0152	−0.4231	−0.0158
Base: Education up to Primary						
Secondary	2.1097	0.0278	2.5992	0.2504	2.6111	0.1165
Higher secondary	3.1390	0.0188	4.3421	0.5037	3.9800	0.1556
Diploma	3.9068	0.0095	5.5023	0.7105	3.8283	0.0173
Graduate and above	5.8463	0.0556	6.6884	0.6458	5.9130	0.1468
Base: Regular Formal Worker						
Relatively developed states	0.0037	0.0028	−0.6179	−0.0688	0.0121	0.0074
Less developed states	0.4123	0.0057	0.1327	−0.0094	0.6812	0.0339
Constant	−7.0050		−5.3204		−5.8585	
Log-likelihood	−9838.1					
Number of observations	6,463					
Wald chi-square	2201.9					
Probability > chi-square	0.000					
Pseudo R-sq	0.1617					

Source: Authors' calculation based on PLFS 2017–18 unit-level data.

Service and sales workers		Skilled workers		Plant and machine operators		Elementary occupation	
Coefficients	Marginal Effects	Coefficients	Marginal Effects	Coefficients	Marginal Effects	Coefficients	Marginal Effects
0.0026	−0.0108	0.0241	−0.0030	0.1215	0.0094	Base	−0.0089
−0.0001	0.0001	−0.0004	0.0000	−0.0017	−0.0001	Category	0.0001
0.0185	−0.0403	1.3671	0.1425	2.4619	0.1700		−0.0349
−0.2945	−0.0297	−0.2593	−0.0120	−0.1811	0.0009		0.0382
0.8147	−0.0709	0.6157	−0.0705	0.4993	−0.0613		−0.1920
1.3571	−0.1863	0.7885	−0.1474	0.6032	−0.1115		−0.2328
0.7960	−0.2660	1.7513	−0.1393	0.9010	−0.1136		−0.2183
2.1494	−0.2223	1.3150	−0.1773	1.0264	−0.1364		−0.3122
−0.2111	−0.0293	0.0387	0.0237	0.2449	0.0424		0.0217
0.1553	−0.0124	0.1176	−0.0136	0.4931	0.0366		−0.0407
−0.4769		−2.0650		−4.9746			

7

Unemployment Discrimination and Untouchables

7.1 Introduction

In the preceding chapter, we have examined the employment status of the Scheduled Castes (SC) and higher castes. It emerged from the analysis that the probability of employment for the SC in regular salaried jobs is low as compared to the higher castes. The difference in the probability of employment between the SC and higher castes is due to both endowment factors (about 26 per cent) and discrimination, but mainly due to discrimination in hiring (about 74 per cent). For obvious reasons, the low probability of employment results in high unemployment for the SC. In this chapter, we will discuss the characteristics of unemployed persons, particularly the youth among the SC and higher castes. We will look into the incidence of unemployment, the duration of unemployment, variations in the unemployment rate by education level and age, and the factors associated with unemployment among individuals with various educational qualifications. In the end, we will study the relative contribution of endowment factors and discrimination in the gap in the unemployment rate between the SC and higher castes during 2004–05 and 2017–18.

7.2 Measures of Unemployment

The measurement of unemployment and its interpretation with the Indian data is somewhat complex. Taking relevant consideration into

Scheduled Castes in the Indian Labour Market. Sukhadeo Thorat, S. Madheswaran, and B. P. Vani,
Oxford University Press. © Sukhadeo Thorat, S. Madheswaran, and B. P. Vani 2023.
DOI: 10.1093/oso/9780198872252.003.0007

account the National Sample Survey (NSS) on employment/unemployment has developed alternative concepts which look at aspects of employment and unemployment. As mentioned in the earlier chapter, the NSS has used four approaches to capture the aspects of employment and unemployment situation in India. These methods are usual principal status (UPS), usual principal and subsidiary status (UPSS), current weekly status (CWS), and current daily status (CDS). Estimates of unemployment rate based on UPS takes the number of employment days out of 365 days in a year. Therefore, it represents open unemployment of the persons. The UPSS takes note of the subsidiary employment of those classified as 'not working' under the UPS criterion and thus UPSS comprises usually the principal plus subsidiary status. It represents the open unemployment. The CWS approach uses seven days preceding the date of the survey as the reference period. A person is considered to be employed if s/he pursues anyone or more gainful activities for at least one hour on any day of the reference week. Thus, the CWS criterion estimates open (seasonal) unemployment in the reference week. The CDS measures employment or unemployment in terms of person-days and represents the extent of underutilization of labour force in terms of person-days. In other words, the CDS estimate is the most inclusive measure of unemployment and visible underemployment, but it does not represent the actual number of persons unemployed in a particular year. The recent employment survey 2017–18 did not use CDS measure and hence, we confine ourselves to UPSS and CWS measure in this chapter. It may be mentioned that UPSS captures open unemployment, while the CWS mainly captures the underemployment.

During 2017–18, the unemployment rates, as both UPSS and CWS show, in urban areas are higher than those in rural areas irrespective of gender. Table 7.1 shows that the female unemployment rate is lower in rural areas whereas the unemployment rate is higher for females in urban areas. The ensuing section will give a clear picture of the unemployment rate by the social groups in India using two rounds of NSS data (2004–05 and 2017–18).

Table 7.1   Unemployment rates (in per cent) according to UPSS and CWS from 1972–73 to 2017–18

	Rural				Urban			
	Male		Female		Male		Female	
Round (Year)	UPSS	CWS	UPSS	CWS	UPSS	CWS	UPSS	CWS
PLFS (2017–18)	5.8	8.8	3.8	7.7	7.1	8.8	10.8	12.8
68th (2011–12)	1.7	3.3	1.7	3.5	3.0	3.8	5.2	6.7
66th (2009–10)	1.6	3.2	1.6	3.7	2.8	3.6	5.7	7.2
61st (2004–05)	1.6	3.8	1.8	4.2	3.8	5.2	6.9	9.0
55th (1999–00)	1.7	3.9	1.0	3.7	4.5	5.6	5.7	7.3
50th (1993–94)	1.4	3.1	0.9	2.9	4.1	5.2	6.1	7.9
43rd (1987–88)	1.8	4.2	2.4	4.4	5.2	6.6	6.2	9.2
38th (1983)	1.4	3.7	0.7	4.3	5.1	6.7	4.9	7.5
32nd (1977–78)	1.3	3.6	2.0	4.1	5.4	7.1	12.4	10.9
27th (1972–73)	1.2	3.0	0.5	5.5	4.8	6.0	6.0	9.2

Source: PLFS report, 2017–18.

7.3   Castewise Disparities in Unemployment Rates

During 2017–18, the overall unemployment rate based on the UPSS is 6.2 per cent. The unemployment rates in urban areas are higher than those in rural areas—5.3 per cent in rural and 7.8 per cent in urban areas. The unemployment rate, based on CWS, is higher than UPSS which is 8.9 per cent. The unemployment rate is higher in urban areas with 9.6 per cent than the rural unemployment rate which is 8.5 per cent.

The unemployment rate varies between caste groups (Table 7.2). In 2017–18, the difference in the unemployment rate based on UPSS between the SC and higher castes is relatively less, the rate being 6.4 per cent for the former and 6.1 per cent for the latter. In rural areas, the unemployment rate is almost similar for the SC and higher castes. In urban areas, however, the unemployment rate of the SC is higher than higher castes—it is 8.8 per

Table 7.2 Unemployment rate by social groups and location

	2004–05				2017–18			
	Hindu SC	Hindu OBC	Hindu Higher Castes	Total	Hindu SC	Hindu OBC	Hindu Higher Castes	Total
RURAL								
UPSS	1.6	1.4	2.2	1.7	5.7	5.1	5.8	5.3
CWS	5.1	3.4	3.6	3.9	10.4	7.6	8.0	8.5
URBAN								
UPSS	5.2	3.9	4.7	4.5	8.8	7.5	7.3	7.8
CWS	7.5	5.4	5.9	6	11.1	9.5	8.7	9.6
TOTAL								
UPSS	2.2	1.9	3.1	2.3	6.4	5.7	6.4	6.1
CWS	5.5	3.8	4.4	4.4	10.5	8.1	8.3	8.9

Source: Authors' calculation based on NSS 61st round and PLFS 2017–18 data.

cent for the SC and 7.8 per cent for higher castes. The disparities between the SC and higher castes emerged more clearly based on the CWS, total as well as rural and urban areas. The result indicates high underemployment of the SC as compared to higher castes. For instance, unemployment in 2017–18 based on CWS rate is 10.5 per cent for the SC as compared to 8.3 per cent for higher castes and 8.1 per cent for Other Backward Classes (OBC). The difference is more in urban areas being 11.1 per cent for the SC, 8.7 per cent for higher castes and 9.5 per cent for OBC. In rural areas the rates are 10.4 per cent for the SC, 8 per cent for higher castes and 7.6 per cent for OBC. Thus, exception apart, the unemployment rate is generally high for the SC than OBC and higher castes.

7.4 Education Level and Unemployment

The unemployment rate during 2017–18 by education also varies between the social groups (Table 7.3 and Figure 7.1). A perusal of the numbers shows that the SC suffer from higher unemployment rate at all the

Table 7.3 Unemployment rate across educational categories

Unemployment rate by level of education	UPSS								CWS							
	2004–05				2017–18				2004–05				2017–18			
	Hindu SC	Hindu OBC	Hindu Higher Castes	Total	Hindu SC	Hindu OBC	Hindu Higher Castes	Total	Hindu SC	Hindu OBC	Hindu Higher castes	Total	Hindu SC	Hindu OBC	Hindu Higher castes	Total
Rural																
Illiterate	0.34	0.23	0.41	0.30	1.38	0.92	0.86	1.15	2.10	1.27	0.86	1.47	5.07	3.17	2.53	3.74
Primary	1.64	1.15	1.30	1.46	4.81	3.78	2.98	4.17	2.61	1.96	1.34	1.95	6.75	3.77	2.78	4.72
Secondary	5.26	3.86	3.89	4.44	7.74	4.82	4.70	5.45	3.04	1.93	1.83	2.31	8.73	5.88	5.14	6.79
Higher secondary	10.50	6.76	5.40	7.72	15.03	11.02	9.94	12.08	7.00	4.45	4.23	5.20	9.40	5.75	5.30	6.40
Graduate and above	12.79	8.73	7.64	9.36	22.39	20.89	17.26	20.17	11.93	8.96	8.17	9.59	19.08	15.84	13.47	15.98
Urban																
Illiterate	1.17	0.59	0.41	0.96	1.66	1.64	2.36	1.72	2.17	1.37	1.20	1.77	3.45	3.51	2.56	3.20
Primary	5.35	2.32	3.78	3.42	6.55	3.38	4.06	4.88	3.11	1.97	2.23	2.06	6.87	3.62	3.95	4.80
Secondary	7.42	5.59	4.36	5.41	7.78	5.43	5.59	6.39	6.06	3.05	4.69	4.24	8.70	5.42	6.26	7.12
Higher secondary	9.82	7.19	5.52	6.98	15.70	10.60	7.98	11.20	8.51	5.54	4.87	5.76	7.64	5.45	5.99	6.57
Graduate and above	14.25	10.41	6.21	8.23	20.33	16.15	10.64	13.88	14.41	10.52	6.38	8.49	17.76	14.27	9.65	12.70
Total																
Illiterate	0.43	0.27	0.41	0.37	1.42	1.02	1.14	1.24	2.11	1.28	0.90	1.50	4.83	3.22	2.54	3.66
Primary	2.45	1.39	1.94	1.90	5.19	3.68	3.35	4.36	2.69	1.96	1.50	1.97	6.77	3.73	3.16	4.74

(continued)

Table 7.3 Continued

Unemployment rate by level of education	UPSS								CWS							
	2004–05				2017–18				2004–05				2017–18			
	Hindu SC	Hindu OBC	Hindu Higher Castes	Total	Hindu SC	Hindu OBC	Hindu Higher Castes	Total	Hindu SC	Hindu OBC	Hindu Higher castes	Total	Hindu SC	Hindu OBC	Hindu Higher castes	Total
Secondary	5.94	4.36	4.08	4.78	7.75	5.00	5.05	5.75	3.68	2.16	2.56	2.74	8.73	5.77	5.53	6.88
Higher secondary	10.29	6.92	5.46	7.39	15.24	10.88	9.02	11.75	7.40	4.76	4.49	5.39	8.93	5.66	5.58	6.45
Graduate and above	13.42	9.57	6.63	8.65	21.51	18.33	12.79	16.50	12.96	9.71	6.95	8.94	18.59	15.14	11.16	14.35

Source: Authors' calculation based on 2004–05 unit-level data and PLFS 2017–18 data.

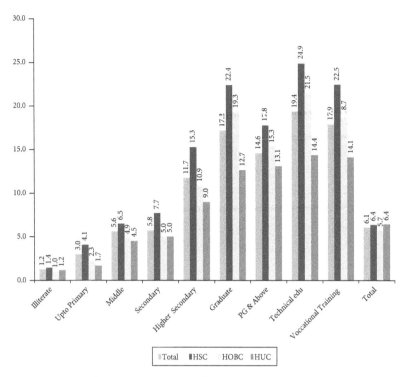

Fig. 7.1 Unemployment rate across educational categories, 2017–18 (UPSS)

Source: Authors' calculation based on PLFS 2017–18 data

levels of education as compared to higher castes and OBC both under UPSS and CWS. The gap is particularly high in the unemployment rate at higher secondary, and graduate and above level. For instance, in 2017–18 for graduate and above, the unemployment based on UPSS is 21.51 per cent for the SC which is much higher as compared to 12.79 per cent for higher castes and 18.33 per cent for OBC. Similarly, at higher secondary level it is 15.24 per cent for the SC, 10.88 per cent for OBC and 9 per cent for higher castes. Similarly, for CWS the unemployment rate for graduate and above is 18.59 per cent for the SC, 15 per cent for OBC and 11.16 per cent for higher castes. For higher secondary, it is 9 per cent for the SC, 6.4 per cent for higher castes and 5.66 per cent for OBC.

The same pattern is observed in urban areas where the gap in the unemployment rate is high at graduate and above, and higher secondary levels. For instance, the unemployment rate based on UPSS is 20.33 per cent for the SC and 16.64 per cent for higher castes. In the higher secondary category, the rate is 15.70 per cent and 8 per cent for the SC and higher castes respectively. A similar pattern is observed for unemployment rate based on CWS. The unemployment rate for graduate and above category is 17.76 per cent and 9.65 per cent for the SC and higher castes respectively. In the case of higher secondary, the unemployment rate is 7.66 per cent for the SC and 6 per cent for higher castes.

Therefore, although unemployment rates, based on both UPSS and CWS, are generally high at all levels of education for the SC, the gap between the SC and higher castes is particularly high for education at higher secondary, and graduate and above levels. This is particularly the case in urban areas. The SC suffer more from both open and under unemployment than any other group in the Hindu society.

7.5 Regional Disparities and Trends in Unemployment Rate

The unemployment rate in India, based on UPSS, has shown a significant increase from 2.3 per cent in 2004–05 to 6.1 per cent in 2017–18. A similar increase is seen in the case of unemployment based on CWS from 4.4 per cent in 2004–05 to 8.9 per cent in 2017–18. This is the first time that an increase of this magnitude has been witnessed in India since the early 1970s. Across all states, except Kerala, the unemployment rate irrespective of UPSS or CWS has shown a sharp increase between 2004–05 and 2017–18. The states with higher increase in unemployment rates between 2004–05 and 2017–18 are Haryana, Madhya Pradesh, Rajasthan, Tamil Nadu, Uttar Pradesh, Jharkhand, and Uttarakhand (Table 7.4).

In 2017–18, unemployment based on UPSS shows interstate disparities (Table 7.5). In 11 major states, the unemployment rates are higher than the national average of 6.1 per cent. The 11 states are Bihar, Odisha, Uttarakhand, Jharkhand, Kerala, Assam, Haryana, Uttar Pradesh, Tamil Nadu, Punjab, and Telangana. The unemployment rate was highest in Kerala with 11.4 per cent followed by Haryana at 8.6 per cent and Assam at 8.1 per cent. On the other hand, the lowest unemployment was in Chhattisgarh at 3.3 per cent followed by Madhya Pradesh at 4.5 per cent and West Bengal at 4.6 per cent.

Table 7.4 Unemployment rate—high and low states based on current weekly status

Groups	States where Hindu SC has high unemployment rates as compared to Hindu higher castes in 2017–18	States where Hindu SC has lower unemployment rates as compared to Hindu higher castes in 2017–18
States where Hindu SC has high unemployment rates as compared to Hindu higher castes in 2004–05	Andhra Pradesh, Gujarat, Haryana, Kerala, Madhya Pradesh, Maharashtra, Uttar Pradesh, Chhattisgarh, Uttarakhand	Himachal Pradesh, Karnataka, Rajasthan, Tamil Nadu
States where Hindu SC has lower unemployment rates as compared to Hindu higher castes in 2004–05	Jammu and Kashmir, Odisha, West Bengal, Delhi, Jharkhand	Assam, Bihar, Punjab

Source: Authors' calculation based on NSS 61st round and PLFS 2017–18 data.

7.6 Youth Unemployment

The emerging feature of Indian demography is the growing youth population. Some considered the growth in youth population as an opportunity for the country as the young labour force provides human resource which is necessary for economic growth. However, a high proportion of youth in India is associated with equally high rate of unemployment and underemployment and this results in the underutilization of human resource. We, therefore, examine the employment and unemployment situation of the youth by caste groups in India during 2004–05 and 2017–18. In the current Youth Policy 2014 document, the youth age group is defined as 15–29 years.

The youth unemployment rate, based on UPSS, has increased from 5.4 per cent in 2004–05 to more than threefold (17.8 per cent) in 2017–18 (Table 7.6). The unemployment rates also varied between the SC and higher castes in 2017–18. The UPSS unemployment rate is 17.9 per cent for the SC, 18.1 per cent for the OBC, and 20.4 per cent for higher castes, with the all-India average being 17.8 per cent. Similar disparities are observed for unemployment based on CWS. The CWS unemployment rate is 22.8 per cent for the SC, 21 per cent for the OBC and 23.3 per cent for

Table 7.5 Statewise unemployment rates by castes in India in 2004–05 and 2017–18

Name of the states	UPSS								CWS							
	2004–05				2017–18				2004–05				2017–18			
	Hindu SC	Hindu OBC	Hindu Higher castes	Total	Hindu SC	Hindu OBC	Hindu Higher castes	Total	Hindu SC	Hindu OBC	Hindu Higher castes	Total	Hindu SC	Hindu OBC	Hindu Higher castes	Total
Andhra Pradesh	1.3*	1.3*	1.5*	1.3*	6	3.7	4.7	4.5	6.1	3.9	3.2	4.1	11.1	6.8	8.3	8.3
Arunachal Pradesh	0	0	1.1	0.9	17.6	4.4	2.7	5.9	0.0	0.0	1.8	1.5	17.8	4.5	2.7	6
Assam	2	1.4	6.1	3	6.9	7	9.3	8.1	4.6	2.8	7.2	4.5	6.7	7.2	9.7	8.5
Bihar	1.3	1.6	4.2	1.9	7.1	7.8	7.9	7.2	5.0	2.7	5.3	3.6	8.9	8.9	9	8.4
Gujarat	1.6	0.6	1.3	1	7.8	3.4	4.5	4.8	3.0	2.0	2.1	2.2	9.5	3.9	5	5.2
Haryana	2.7	1.8	2.7	2.6	7.8	6.7	9.4	8.6	6.5	4.5	3.4	4.6	13.1	7.5	10.9	11.1
Himachal Pradesh	2.7	2.3	1.6	2	4.4	6.9	4.8	5.5	5.5	4.0	3.5	4.0	6.4	9.4	6.8	8.5
Jammu and Kashmir	1.6	6.6	3.1	2.3	4	10.1	4.9	5.3	2.0	7.9	4.2	4.5	8.8	10.6	8.4	9.3
Karnataka	1.4	1.2	1.1	1.2	4.4	4.6	5.8	4.8	3.7	1.8	2.2	2.3	5.8	5.8	6.3	6.2
Kerala	10.4	11.9	12.3	11.9	10.1	11.8	9.5	11.4	18.0	16.1	13.6	16.1	14.9	15.2	12.9	14.7
Madhya Pradesh	0.5	0.8	1.9	0.9	4.9	4.3	6.1	4.5	4.8	3.3	2.7	3.1	11.6	5.9	8.7	8.2
Maharashtra	2.5	1.4	1.6	1.9	8	4	4.8	4.9	7.8	4.8	3.6	5.1	11.2	7	7	7.7
Odisha	6.6	6.8	11.3	6	8.8	7.2	8.5	7.1	9.4	8.4	11.7	8.1	14.8	10.4	10.6	10.6
Punjab	3.2	8.3	5.9	4.2	9.4	9.4	6.4	7.8	6.1	8.5	6.3	5.2	10.3	11.7	6.8	9.4

Rajasthan	1.1	0.9	1.8	1.1	5.2	4.1	7.6	5	6.0	2.4	2.9	3.3	8.5	7.1	12.8	9.4
Tamil Nadu	1.9	1.6	1.2	2	7.8	7.3	8.4	7.6	4.4	3.0	3.0	3.6	12.2	10.4	12.5	11.1
Uttar Pradesh	0.9	0.8	1.7	1.1	6.1	5.8	7.8	6.4	2.9	1.7	2.5	2.5	11.9	9	9.7	10
West Bengal	3	3.7	4.8	3.5	4.1	4.1	5.3	4.6	6.2	5.7	6.5	6.2	8.4	6.1	7	7.5
Delhi	2.9	4.4	4.6	4.6	11	8.9	8.7	9.7	4.2	4.0	5.6	5.3	11.2	10.2	9.2	10.5
Chhattisgarh	0.9	1.1	3.2	0.9	4.5	2.6	3.1	3.3	7.0	6.7	5.2	5.3	9	7.3	4.4	7.8
Jharkhand	2.8	1.8	5.2	2.1	9.9	8.2	7.9	7.7	4.6	4.4	8.0	5.0	15.1	11.3	9.7	11.5
Uttarakhand	1.2	2.8	2.4	2.1	7.7	8.6	7	7.6	4.0	3.2	3.9	3.6	9	8.2	7.8	8.7
Telangana	–	–	–	–	6.9	7	11.2	7.6	–	–	–	–	8	8.1	11.9	8.6
All India	**2.1**	**1.9**	**3.1**	**2.3**	**6.3**	**5.7**	**6.4**	**6.1**	**5.5**	**3.8**	**4.4**	**4.4**	**10.4**	**8.1**	**8.3**	**8.8**

Note: * undivided Andhra Pradesh.

Source: Authors' calculation based on NSS 61st round and PLFS 2017–18 data.

Table 7.6 Youth unemployment rates

| Name of the states | Youth Unemployment Rates UPSS (in %) | | | | | | | | Youth Unemployment Rates CWS (in %) | | | | | | | |
| | 2004–05 | | | | 2017–18 | | | | 2004–05 | | | | 2017–18 | | | |
	Hindu SC	Hindu OBC	Hindu Higher castes	Total	Hindu SC	Hindu OBC	Hindu Higher castes	Total	Hindu SC	Hindu OBC	Hindu Higher castes	Total	Hindu SC	Hindu OBC	Hindu Higher castes	Total
Andhra Pradesh	3.1	3	4.5	3.2	18.1	14.8	20.5	16.1	7.8	5.9	7.4	6.3	22.7	20.9	26.0	21.7
Assam	6.4	3.1	16.9	7.8	21.3	23.1	35.2	27	10.3	7.5	19.6	11.1	20.3	23.3	35.3	27.3
Bihar	3.6	5.3	14	5.4	19.8	25.2	39.4	22.8	7.2	6.7	18.0	7.6	22.9	26.1	42.5	24.6
Gujarat	3	1.4	2.9	2.4	21.1	10.1	12.1	13.3	5.1	3.1	4.6	4.0	21.4	10.3	13.0	13.5
Haryana	6.2	4.3	6.8	6.3	16.4	18.3	23.5	20.7	10.0	8.0	8.5	9.1	20.0	20.3	26.3	24.0
Himachal Pradesh	7.1	5.5	3.7	4.7	11.2	25.4	17.1	18.4	13.1	11.7	8.8	10.1	16.9	31.8	23.4	26.6
Jammu & Kashmir	4.4	22.2	8.8	6	13.7	29.9	14.4	15	4.8	23.7	12.2	8.6	27.6	31.1	27.7	25.3
Karnataka	2.3	2.9	2.8	2.8	14.7	15.3	19	15.8	4.6	3.9	4.9	4.3	15.3	17.5	19.1	17.6
Kerala	24.3	27.9	33.4	28.2	28.5	37	32.4	36.3	31.8	30.7	35.1	32.5	29.6	39.4	37.7	38.9
Madhya Pradesh	1.1	2.2	4.8	2.1	13.3	13.2	14.7	12	5.9	5.9	7.5	5.1	21.0	15.5	21.0	16.8
Maharashtra	6.3	3.5	4	4.7	21.8	13.1	15.7	15	14.8	7.9	7.2	9.1	25.1	16.9	18.1	18.5
Odisha	14.7	14.6	23.3	12.5	28.7	24.7	30.6	23.6	19.3	17.7	26.2	16.6	35.6	29.5	32.1	27.8
Punjab	6.9	17.7	12.8	10	20.6	24	22.3	21.6	11.8	18.1	13.2	11.2	23.2	26.8	22.8	22.8
Rajasthan	2.8	2.2	4.3	2.7	13.9	12.7	25.5	14.3	7.4	4.2	6.1	5.6	16.4	16.5	33.2	20.5
Tamil Nadu	5.9	4	4.2	5.2	24.9	26.2	23.7	25.6	9.5	6.0	7.5	7.6	30.1	28.2	30.1	28.8

Uttar Pradesh	2.3	2.1	4.5	2.7	15.6	15.7	24.7	16.7	5.9	3.5	6.1	4.8	23.6	19.6	27.0	21.3
West Bengal	7	8.8	11.5	7.7	13.1	14.7	15.4	13.2	12.2	11.1	14.2	11.6	18.2	17.3	18.9	17.0
Delhi	5.3	10.7	12.4	10.4	24.5	19.8	22.8	22.2	8.1	9.5	15.1	12.2	23.4	20.5	24.0	23.4
Chhattisgarh	2.5	2.2	7.1	2	11.9	8.1	12.4	10.1	8.7	11.0	8.9	8.5	20.2	17.3	17.1	19.9
Jharkhand	8	5.1	14.8	5.5	26.4	29.7	26.7	20.4	9.8	7.8	20.2	8.5	29.3	34.9	29.4	25.9
Uttarakhand	2.2	6.2	6.6	5.1	26.6	27.1	30.1	27.5	8.2	7.4	11.3	9.1	28.9	25.0	31.4	28.5
Telangana					20.7	22.3	32.5	23.3					27.7	23.5	22.5	23.2
All India	**4.9**	**4.5**	**7.6**	**5.4**	**17.9**	**18.1**	**20.4**	**17.8**	**9.5**	**7.0**	**10.2**	**8.4**	**22.8**	**21.0**	**23.3**	**21.4**

Source: Authors' calculation based on NSS 2004–05 and PLFS 2017–18 data.

the higher castes, the average being 21.4 per cent. While the intercaste differences in CWS unemployment rate are much less, the unemployment rate based on UPSS is slightly high for the higher castes.

Thus, it emerged that in 2017–18 the youth unemployment rate, based on both UPSS and CWS, is much higher (17.8 per cent for UPSS and 21.4 per cent for CWS) than the average unemployment rate for all population, both with respect to UPSS and CWS (6.1 per cent and 8.8 per cent under UPSS and CWS respectively). Second, the youth unemployment rate, both with respect to UPSS and CWS, is much higher than the whole population for SCs, OBCs, and higher caste as well. Third, youth unemployment rate, based on both UPSS and CWS, shows less difference between SCs, OBCs, and higher castes. Fourth, at all-India level, the number of unemployed youth, based on UPSS, has increased at a higher rate of 9.2 per cent annually for the SC than for the higher castes (6.5 per cent).

A wide variation is found across the states in youth unemployment. In 2004–05, unemployment based on UPSS ranged from 2.1 per cent in Madhya Pradesh to 28.2 per cent in Kerala. During 2017–18, it ranged from 10.1 per cent in Chhattisgarh to 36.3 per cent in Kerala. A similar pattern of interstate variation is seen for both the SC and the higher castes. Comparing youth unemployment between the SC and higher castes across states, we see that in the states of Gujarat, Himachal Pradesh, Maharashtra, and Tamil Nadu the SC had higher unemployment rate as compared to higher castes during 2004–05. In the same states, the differences are observed between the SC and higher castes in 2017–18, except Himachal Pradesh.

As far as the change between 2004–05 and 2017–18 is concerned, we notice that all the states have witnessed a drastic increase in youth unemployment, as per UPSS and CWS, across all social groups. During 2004–05, only two states, namely Kerala (24.3 per cent) and Odisha (14.7 per cent) had double-digit unemployment rate for the SC but by 2017–18 all the states had two-digit unemployment rate, and states like Kerala, Odisha, Tamil Nadu, Jharkhand, and Uttarakhand had youth unemployment rate of more than 25 per cent.

At all-India level, the number of unemployed youth, based on UPSS, has increased at a higher rate of 9.2 per cent annually for the SC as compared to higher castes which grew at 6.5 per cent annually (Table 7.7). In 11 states, the percentage increase in the number of unemployed youth has increased at a rate higher than the higher castes during 2004–05 and 2017–18. These states are Andhra Pradesh, Bihar, Gujarat, Maharashtra,

Table 7.7 Number of youths unemployed (in lakh) as per UPSS

| Name of the States | Youth Unemployment (in lakh) as per UPSS | | | | | | | | Annual Growth Rates between 2004–05 and 2017–18 | | | |
| | 2004–05 | | | | 2017–18 | | | | | | | |
	Hindu SC	OBC	Hindu Higher castes	Total	Hindu SC	Hindu OBC	Hindu Higher castes	Total	Hindu SC	Hindu OBC	Hindu Higher castes	Total
Andhra Pradesh	0.87	2.17	1.12	4.74	3.09	4.06	2.22	11.44	10.2	5.0	5.4	7.0
Assam	0.21	0.20	1.32	2.89	0.67	2.33	1.78	8.40	9.3	20.9	2.3	8.6
Bihar	0.77	2.07	0.87	4.23	3.83	9.92	2.95	18.06	13.1	12.8	3.9	11.8
Gujarat	0.39	0.53	0.63	2.29	1.29	3.00	2.32	10.28	9.6	14.2	10.5	12.3
Haryana	0.55	0.44	1.04	2.39	1.67	1.26	3.09	7.51	8.9	8.5	8.7	9.2
Himachal Pradesh	0.25	0.09	0.23	0.59	0.28	0.38	0.70	1.74	1.0	11.3	9.0	8.7
Jammu and Kashmir	0.07	0.07	0.19	0.62	0.13	0.11	0.57	2.13	5.6	3.6	9.0	9.9
Karnataka	0.47	1.02	0.63	2.79	1.97	4.37	3.25	11.84	11.7	11.9	13.4	11.8
Kerala	1.45	4.38	1.70	13.34	0.96	3.76	1.14	10.17	-3.1	-1.2	-3.1	-2.1
Madhya Pradesh	0.18	0.89	0.61	2.22	2.58	4.69	2.09	12.67	22.7	13.6	10.0	14.3
Maharashtra	1.03	1.83	2.11	7.85	2.48	4.51	7.13	18.97	7.0	7.2	5.8	7.0
Odisha	2.00	3.58	2.58	8.73	2.87	3.61	2.31	10.55	2.8	0.1	-0.8	1.5
Punjab	0.41	0.50	0.63	4.11	1.08	0.73	1.02	6.88	7.7	3.0	3.8	4.0
Rajasthan	0.59	0.93	0.57	2.71	2.11	3.84	2.54	11.81	10.3	11.5	12.2	12.0
Tamil Nadu	1.16	2.61	0.06	4.92	5.53	13.31	0.76	22.00	12.8	13.4	21.6	12.2

(continued)

Table 7.7 Continued

| Name of the States | Youth Unemployment (in lakh) as per UPSS | | | | | | | | Annual Growth Rates between 2004–05 and 2017–18 | | | |
| | 2004–05 | | | | 2017–18 | | | | | | | |
	Hindu SC	OBC	Hindu Higher castes	Total	Hindu SC	Hindu OBC	Hindu Higher castes	Total	Hindu SC	Hindu OBC	Hindu Higher castes	Total
Uttar Pradesh	1.34	2.02	1.39	6.07	8.22	13.44	6.96	36.28	15.0	15.7	13.2	14.7
West Bengal	2.24	0.66	4.59	9.50	4.07	0.65	5.26	15.12	4.7	-0.1	1.1	3.6
Delhi	0.27	0.22	0.93	1.89	1.08	0.99	1.91	5.15	11.2	12.1	5.7	8.0
Chhattisgarh	0.17	0.39	0.18	0.84	0.84	1.42	0.22	4.14	13.1	10.4	1.5	13.1
Jharkhand	0.37	0.65	0.44	2.00	1.21	2.55	0.59	6.99	9.7	11.1	2.4	10.1
Uttarakhand	0.07	0.10	0.45	0.69	0.62	0.25	1.10	2.39	18.7	7.3	7.1	10.0
Telangana	0.00	0.00	0.00	0.00	1.79	5.18	1.69	10.73				
All India	15.42	26.15	22.98	88.58	48.69	85.20	52.37	250.63	9.2	9.5	6.5	8.3

Source: Authors' calculation based on NSS 61st round and PLFS 2017–18 data.

Tamil Nadu, Jharkhand, and Uttarakhand (Table 7.7). Mehrotra and Parida (2019) noted that this increase in youth unemployment is due to fall in agricultural employment and they expect this problem to mount further unless non-farm jobs are created. Further, it is noted by the authors that the slow growth of non-farm jobs and rising unemployment have resulted in a massive youth population being 'Not in Labour Force, Education, and Training' (NLET).

7.7 Youth Unemployment by Education Level

The unemployment rate during 2017–18 by education level differs between caste groups (Table 7.8 and Figures 7.2 and 7.3). The UPSS unemployment rate is high among the SC as compared to higher castes at higher education level. Beginning with higher secondary, the unemployment remains high for those with graduate, postgraduate and above, technical education and vocational education (Figure 7.4). In case of unemployment rate based on CWS, it is high for the SC at all levels of education, except medium and secondary levels. Between the SC and higher castes, unemployment is particularly high for graduate, postgraduate and above, technical education and vocational education. Thus, the educated SC youth suffered more from both open and underemployment than higher castes youth. This is particularly the case for education beyond higher secondary and for technical and vocational education categories.

7.8 Not in Employment, Education, and Training

Unemployed or not in employment is an indicator which shows the vulnerability of the youth. However, youth 'Not in employment, education, or training' (NLET) is a relatively new concept which represents the youths' inactivity. NLET is a measure which estimates the share of young people (age 15–29 years) not in employment, education, or training as a percentage of the total number of young people in the corresponding age group. The number is simply the total number of young adults minus the number of youth (between 15 and 29 years of age) in education, training or in jobs. These are the youth who are doing nothing. A high NLET rate as compared

Table 7.8 Youth (age 15 to 29 years) unemployment rate by social groups in India

Unemployment rate by level of education	UPSS								CWS							
	2004–05				2017–18				2004–05				2017–18			
	Hindu SC	Hindu OBC	Hindu Higher castes	Total	Hindu SC	Hindu OBC	Hindu Higher castes	Total	Hindu SC	Hindu OBC	Hindu Higher castes	Total	Hindu SC	Hindu OBC	Hindu Higher castes	Total
Rural Area																
Illiterate	1.1	0.7	1.3	0.9	7.8	7.9	9.4	7.3	5.5	3.3	2.9	4.0	14.9	12.8	10.0	12.1
Up to primary	1.4	2.9	2.9	2.3	10.3	7.3	8.4	8.1	6.5	4.8	3.8	5.1	16.1	10.9	12.1	12.7
Middle	2.4	2.2	2.6	2.3	13.3	12.7	16.6	13.4	8.5	4.5	6.1	6.3	18.6	16.8	20.0	17.9
Secondary	4.4	3.5	3.3	3.5	15.7	12.9	15.8	13.9	12.4	9.2	9.8	10.7	19.3	15.8	19.5	17.3
Higher secondary	8.9	7.8	8.4	8.0	28.0	22.9	23.4	23.8	21.7	14.6	15.4	17.7	32.6	25.8	28.2	27.7
Graduate	16.6	11.2	11.2	12.1	37.9	41.4	35.6	39.1	29.4	21.9	22.8	24.7	41.8	43.0	37.7	41.5
Postgraduate and above	26.4	16.9	21.2	20.2	40.9	38.0	44.8	41.4	33.7	22.3	19.6	24.8	47.8	40.3	46.5	44.2
Technical education	16.5	18.6	18.9	19.1	44.5	45.5	41.3	44.1	27.8	22.0	24.9	24.8	50.6	47.5	43.9	47.5
Vocational training	20.9	19.6	21.9	21.6	40.3	35.9	30.0	35.0	17.6	18.3	29.0	25.7	48.8	35.9	32.4	38.0
Urban Area																
Illiterate	4.1	2.3	0.9	2.2	5.0	7.2	6.5	6.1	6.0	2.0	4.8	3.8	7.2	8.5	7.2	7.4
Up to primary	10.2	3.1	3.3	4.7	10.7	7.9	8.7	9.0	11.7	5.5	6.4	6.8	14.1	10.9	13.6	13.0

Middle	7.4	3.0	5.4	4.8	16.3	13.0	16.2	14.7	17.2	8.3	10.0	11.3	20.3	15.5	18.0	17.5
Secondary	13.4	6.3	8.3	8.4	13.9	15.0	17.6	15.8	15.0	12.4	14.7	13.7	15.7	16.3	19.0	17.2
Higher secondary	13.5	13.1	10.0	11.4	29.3	23.2	22.1	23.8	24.7	18.4	15.1	18.7	31.1	25.5	23.9	25.9
Graduate	15.8	15.7	12.4	13.9	39.5	35.1	28.1	32.5	33.4	26.4	19.2	23.7	39.8	36.9	29.0	33.6
Postgraduate and above	36.2	25.4	19.8	22.8	39.3	33.7	30.0	32.5	45.3	22.8	24.6	26.4	39.5	35.0	30.4	33.2
Technical education	38.5	17.5	22.1	22.7	44.5	45.5	41.3	31.9	29.5	22.9	20.0	23.8	50.6	47.5	43.9	33.7
Vocational training	21.8	17.9	20.1	19.9	31.3	32.6	30.5	31.2	30.9	15.7	26.1	24.6	35.6	36.6	32.1	34.1
Rural + Urban Areas																
Illiterate	1.4	0.9	1.2	1.0	7.3	7.8	8.4	7.1	5.6	3.1	3.3	4.0	13.5	12.0	9.0	11.2
Up to primary	2.9	2.9	3.0	2.7	10.4	7.4	8.5	8.3	7.5	4.9	4.5	5.5	15.6	10.9	12.7	12.8
Middle	3.4	2.4	3.4	2.9	13.9	12.8	16.5	13.7	10.6	5.4	7.3	7.6	19.0	16.5	19.3	17.8
Secondary	6.6	4.2	4.8	4.7	15.2	13.5	16.4	14.4	13.1	10.0	11.4	11.6	18.3	15.9	19.3	17.3
Higher secondary	10.1	9.1	8.9	9.0	28.4	23.0	22.8	23.8	22.5	15.8	15.3	18.1	32.2	25.7	26.4	27.1
Graduate	16.4	12.5	11.7	12.7	38.5	38.4	31.1	35.8	31.1	23.9	20.4	24.1	41.0	40.1	32.5	37.6
Postgraduate and above	30.0	20.7	20.3	21.6	40.3	35.5	35.2	36.2	37.9	22.5	23.0	25.8	44.1	37.3	36.0	37.8
Technical education	23.3	18.1	20.9	21.1	39.8	38.9	32.4	37.3	28.6	22.5	21.5	24.3	45.4	41.4	34.1	39.8
Vocational training	21.4	18.9	20.8	20.7	32.4	32.9	30.7	33.0	24.8	17.0	27.1	25.1	44.1	36.2	32.2	36.0

Source: Authors' calculation based on NSS 61st round and PLFS 2017–18 data.

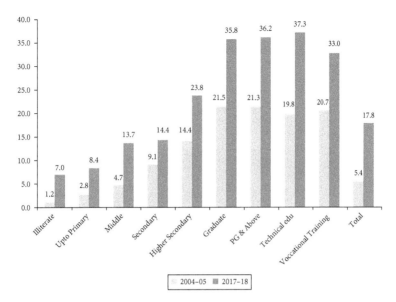

Fig. 7.2 Youth unemployment rates by levels of education, 2004–05 and 2017–18

Source: Authors' calculation based on NSS 61st round and PLFS 2017–18 data

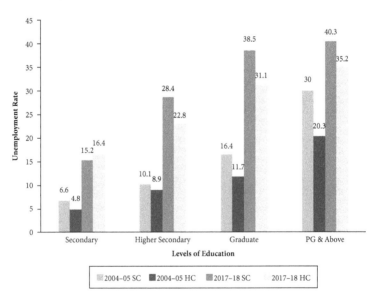

Fig. 7.3 Youth unemployment rates for secondary and above education level, UPSS 2004–05 and 2017–18

Source: Authors' calculation based on NSS 61st round and PLFS 2017–18 data

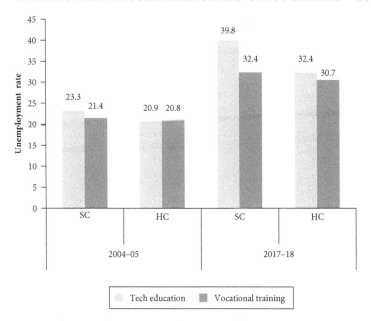

Fig. 7.4 Youth unemployment rates for technical and vocational, UPSS 2004–05 and 2017–18

Source: Authors' calculation based on NSS 61st round and PLFS 2017–18 data

to the youth unemployment rate could mean that a large number of youth are discouraged workers who do not have access to education or training.

As much as 27.2 per cent of India's 423 million youth population are NLET. These are the young adults who are currently isolated from the mainstream and have either given up or do not have access to any opportunities. Thus, over one-third of youth aged 15–29 years in India are not in employment, education, or training.

In the background of NLET, we have estimated NLET for states by social groups. The total NLET population has increased by about 2.5 million per annum between 2004–05 and 2017–18. The NLET population among the SC has increased by 5.25 lakh per annum, whereas the same among the higher castes has increased by 1.77 lakh per annum. During 2017–18, about 19.8 million SC and 17.1 million higher castes' youths declared themselves as NLET (Table 7.9). Further, it is seen that the annual growth rate of NLET youth population is 1.1 per cent for higher castes whereas it is 3.3 per cent for the SC. In most of the states, the SC youth NLET population grew at a higher rate as compared to higher castes (Table 7.10).

Table 7.9 Youth NLET (as per UPSS) in percentage

	Youth NLET (as per UPSS) in Percentage							
	2004–05				2017–18			
States	Hindu SC	Hindu OBC	Hindu Higher Castes	Total	Hindu SC	Hindu OBC	Hindu Higher Castes	Total
Andhra Pradesh	15.2	15.8	23.4	18.4	22.5	21.1	24.1	22.8
Assam	33.9	22.1	21.4	27.5	29.5	27	28.9	30.4
Bihar	35.4	38.6	31.6	38.1	36.6	33.7	24.4	33.4
Gujarat	15.4	20.7	24.4	20.9	27.1	27.4	27	29.3
Haryana	27.1	21.2	20.1	22.3	23.6	28.5	22.2	25.4
Himachal Pradesh	9.9	1.7	7.7	7.5	16.1	4	12.6	12.7
Jammu and Kashmir	18.9	23.1	15.5	17.8	21.7	9.7	11.2	14.9
Karnataka	14.3	21.1	20.7	20.3	27.8	27	20	26.9
Kerala	14.3	14.6	12	19.2	14.9	11.7	12.9	17.6
Madhya Pradesh	22.3	21.9	29.2	22.4	24.5	26.6	24.8	24.9
Maharashtra	24.4	16.9	19.3	19.3	23.5	22.3	20.1	22.5
Odisha	26.6	27.4	31.3	25.6	33.4	31.6	30.2	32.1
Punjab	27.4	22.4	24.3	22	25.3	23.2	21.6	24.8
Rajasthan	22.8	16.9	23	19.1	27.5	25.9	21.3	25.8
Tamil Nadu	20.1	19.7	22.9	20.8	21.3	22	17.2	21.7
Uttar Pradesh	27.8	29.8	27.4	29.9	34.4	30	26.1	32.2
West Bengal	33.1	28.8	28.3	31.2	32.1	27.5	29.2	31.1
Delhi	28.2	27.4	21.8	24	29.3	28.6	24.6	27
Chhattisgarh	16.6	15.6	17.5	14.4	18.7	19.3	18.8	17.9
Jharkhand	33.1	27.5	26.8	25.9	36.2	30.4	20.8	30.2
Uttarakhand	15.9	25.6	10.6	15.2	23.8	22.7	20.5	22.5
Telangana					21.1	23.6	18.9	22.7
All India	**24.9**	**23.2**	**23.7**	**24**	**29.1**	**26.8**	**23.6**	**27.2**

Source: Authors' calculation based on NSS 61st round and PLFS 2017–18 data.

Table 7.10 Number of youth NLET (in lakh) as per UPSS

| States | No of youth remained NLET (as per UPSS) in lakh | | | | | | | | Annual Growth Rates between 2004–05 and 2017–18 | | | |
| | 2004–05 | | | | 2017–18 | | | | | | | |
	Hindu SC	Hindu OBC	Hindu Higher castes	Total	Hindu SC	Hindu OBC	Hindu Higher castes	Total	Hindu SC	Hindu OBC	Hindu Higher castes	Total
Andhra Pradesh	6.1	16.4	10.6	41.7	7.1	12.3	6.5	33.3	1.2	-2.2	-3.7	-1.7
Assam	2.2	2.7	3.3	19.8	2.7	7.1	4.2	25.9	1.6	7.7	1.9	2.1
Bihar	14.2	33.9	6.6	66.5	23.9	55.3	11.2	108.5	4.1	3.8	4.2	3.8
Gujarat	2.6	11.3	10.3	31.6	4.1	18.2	12.7	52.3	3.6	3.7	1.6	4.0
Haryana	4.3	4.1	5.9	15.6	5.6	5.8	8	23.9	2.1	2.7	2.4	3.3
Himachal Pradesh	0.5	0	0.8	1.4	0.93	0.11	1.24	2.7	4.9	0.0	3.4	5.2
Jammu and Kashmir	0.5	0.2	0.6	3.8	0.51	0.08	1.02	5.2	0.2	-6.8	4.2	2.4
Karnataka	4.1	11.7	8.4	32.6	8.8	19.1	8.5	50.4	6.1	3.8	0.1	3.4
Kerala	1.4	3.9	1.1	16.9	0.9	2.7	1.2	13.1	-3.3	-2.8	0.7	-1.9
Madhya Pradesh	5.7	14.9	9.1	38.9	10.9	23.4	9.2	59.2	5.1	3.5	0.1	3.3
Maharashtra	7.2	14.5	17.8	54.8	5.9	20	22.9	71.8	-1.5	2.5	2.0	2.1
Odisha	5.5	11.4	7	28.8	8.3	12.8	7.4	38.4	3.2	0.9	0.4	2.2
Punjab	3	1	2.9	16.5	3.1	1.4	2.7	19.9	0.3	2.6	-0.5	1.5
Rajasthan	7.7	10.9	6.4	31.1	11.3	21.8	6.2	55.6	3.0	5.5	-0.2	4.6
Tamil Nadu	6.5	20.9	0.9	33.3	9.5	25.6	1.1	41.3	3.0	1.6	1.6	1.7

(continued)

Table 7.10 Continued

| States | No of youth remained NLET (as per UPSS) in lakh | | | | | | | | Annual Growth Rates between 2004–05 and 2017–18 | | | |
| | 2004–05 | | | | 2017–18 | | | | | | | |
	Hindu SC	Hindu OBC	Hindu Higher castes	Total	Hindu SC	Hindu OBC	Hindu Higher castes	Total	Hindu SC	Hindu OBC	Hindu Higher castes	Total
Uttar Pradesh	28.1	56.4	22.1	137.6	51.9	75.9	25.9	207.4	4.8	2.3	1.2	3.2
West Bengal	20.2	4.2	23.7	75	24.9	3.9	25.4	87.9	1.6	-0.6	0.5	1.2
Delhi	2.9	1.1	4.3	10	3.6	3.5	5.8	16.2	1.7	9.3	2.3	3.8
Chhattisgarh	1.8	4.1	1.1	9.1	2.8	7.1	1	15.2	3.5	4.3	-0.7	4.0
Jharkhand	3	6.8	2.2	17.2	4.5	9.2	2.1	29.7	3.2	2.4	-0.4	4.3
Uttarakhand	0.8	0.8	1.3	3.7	1.8	0.8	2.9	6.9	6.4	0.0	6.4	4.9
Telangana					3.9	13.7	2.5	25.1				
All India	129.7	233.1	148	694.2	198	342	171	1002.4	3.3	3.0	1.1	2.9

Source: Authors' calculation based on NSS 61st round and PLFS 2017–18 data.

Table 7.12 Continued

	Total		
	3–6 months	7–9 months	10–12 months
Hindu Higher castes			
Illiterate	7.63	8.71	83.66
Below primary	11.79	18.79	69.42
Primary	0.46	2.91	96.63
Middle	4.98	8.55	86.46
Secondary	3.96	6.19	89.85
Higher secondary	1.4	10.06	88.54
Diploma	6.27	1.9	91.83
Graduate	5.61	4.51	89.88
Postgraduate and above	10.52	10.12	79.36
Total	5.04	6.93	88.02

Source: Authors' calculation based on NSS 61st round and PLFS 2017–18 data.

duration of unemployment for unemployed people with different levels of education for caste groups. We also presented the average waiting time of unemployment—the weighted mean of the duration of unemployment for each educational category by caste groups (Figure 7.5). Except for OBC, we found that there is an inverted 'U' curve between levels of education and duration of unemployment. Few features emerged quite clearly. First, there is a positive linear relationship between the proportion of candidates searching for jobs and the duration of unemployment.

This is true across the educational categories and is particularly very obvious around and after secondary education. This means that with a high level of youth seeking jobs, the waiting period also increases. The second observation is that the mean duration of unemployment increases with the levels of education and it peaks around secondary and higher secondary levels of education in all castes groups, except OBC. Again, it tapers down after higher secondary level. Most of the unemployed people fall in long-duration unemployment category (10–12 months).

Figure 7.6 presents the percentage distribution of the duration of unemployment for the unemployed with different levels of education for SC and higher castes. The duration of unemployment is slightly higher for the SC in below primary, middle, higher secondary, graduate, and

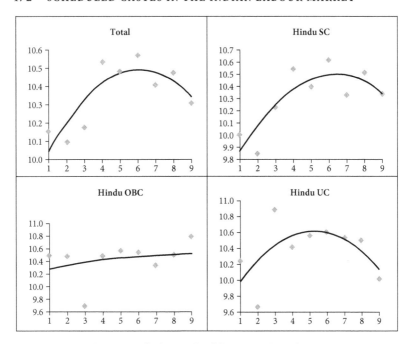

Fig. 7.5 Mean duration of job search of the unemployed, 2004–05
Note: 1-Illeterate; 2-Below Primary; 3-Primary; 4-Middle; 5-Secondary; 6-
Higher secondary; 7-Diploma; 8-Graduate; 9-Postgraduate and above.
Source: Authors' calculation based on NSS 61st round data.

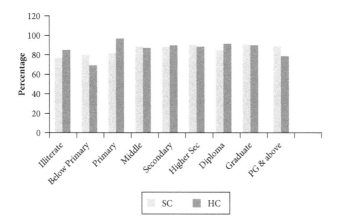

Fig. 7.6 Duration of unemployment for SC and higher castes, 2004–05
Source: Authors' calculation based on NSS 61st round data

postgraduate levels. Thus, in general, there is a tendency for the formation of inverted 'U' curve so far as the duration of unemployment and level of education are concerned. In the literature of the incidence of unemployment in developing countries, it is often argued that there is a high incidence of unemployment among the higher educated manpower group. There are several factors which explain this tendency. Dominantly, there are three main reasons. First, the high incidence of unemployment among the higher educated is attributed to as a case of 'voluntary unemployment' (Harberger 1971; Ghose 2004). Second, this is considered an outcome of 'unrealistic expectation' (Sheers 1971; Islam 1980). Third, it is possible that the duration of unemployment is age-specific (Psacharopoulos 1982; Visaria 1998; Ghose 2004; Mitra and Verick 2013). Finally, some literature indicates that this phenomenon is due to the quality of education, i.e. those who could not excel in academics are likely to remain unemployed (Prasad 1979).

7.10 Determinants of Unemployment

We will now look at the determinants that cause high and low unemployment. Given the broad patterns that we have observed in relation to youth unemployment, a probit regression is attempted to highlight the impact of the variables on the probability of unemployment and these include age, gender, caste, sector and education, marital status, per capita expenditure, etc. The determinants of being unemployed are estimated using non-linear probability regression model. The non-linear model is conceptually preferable when the outcome variable is dichotomous. The dependent variable here is unemployed (CWS) which is equal to 1 and the rest of them are zero in the total labour force. Therefore, we have employed a probit model to study the determinants of unemployment. Since the probability of being unemployed is a binary choice model, and the probability of being unemployed (y) is a function of a vector of explanatory variables (x), it is assumed that there is an underlying response variable y_i.

Where,

$$y_i^* = \beta' x_i + u_i \tag{1}$$

However, in reality, Yi^* is unobservable. Hence, the observable dummy variable is (y).

Where,

$$y = 1 \quad if \ y_i^* > 0 \ (being \ unemployed)$$
$$= 0 \ otherwise \tag{2}$$

From equations (1) and (2), we get

$$Prob(y_i = unemployed) = prob \ (u_i > -\beta'x_i)$$
$$= 1 - F(-\beta'x_i) \tag{3}$$

where F is the cumulative distribution function for u. In this case, the observed values of y are just the realization of a binomial process with probabilities given by Equation (3) and varying from trail-to-trail (depending on x_i). Hence, the likelihood function is:

$$L = \prod_{y=0} F(-\beta'x_i) \prod_{y=1} [1 - F(-\beta'x_i)] \tag{4}$$

where taking the logarithm of L and maximizing with respect to β gives the maximum likelihood estimator of slope coefficient.

Table 7.13 presents the probit results for both 2004–05 and 2017–18. As expected, youth (15–29 years) coefficient is positive and highly significant at 1 per cent level. It implies that there is more likelihood that the youth become unemployed. Gender has a significant impact on the decision to join the labour market as the likelihood of males becoming unemployed is less compared to females. This also confirms the fact that the likelihood of females remaining out of the labour market as well as in education is very high. The available literature shows the increasing participation of females, including youth, in education and an improvement in income levels as the main reasons for the recent decline in the participation of females in the labour market in India (Neff et al. 2012; Rangarajan et al. 2011). Our results, however, partly explain such reasons for lower female participation—being poor, being women and being SC. There are other issues, such as deteriorating working conditions; increasing casualization

Table 7.13 Determinants of unemployment—probit estimates

	2004–05			2017–18		
	Coefficient	Z	P > Z	Coefficient	Z	P > Z
Youth (15 to 29 years) (base: other age groups)	0.518	42.1	0.000	0.724	46.4	0.000
Male (base: female)	−0.281	−22.7	0.000	−0.292	−18.1	0.000
Rural (base: urban)	−0.174	−13.4	0.000	−0.091	−6.1	0.000
Social groups (base: SC)						
Hindu OBC	−0.210	−14.8	0.000	−0.062	−3.7	0.000
Hindu Higher castes	−0.214	−13.1	0.000	−0.106	−5.6	0.000
Education (base: illiterate and up to primary)						
Secondary	0.333	18.9	0.000	0.259	12.1	0.000
Higher secondary	0.473	22.8	0.000	0.492	19.5	0.000
Diploma	0.711	21.9	0.000	0.817	21.5	0.000
Above graduation	0.690	31.9	0.000	0.874	38.0	0.000
Married (base: not married)	−0.522	−43.3	0.000	−0.842	−55.3	0.000
Household size	−0.001	−0.3	0.741	0.029	9.7	0.000
Per capita expenditure	−0.000	−6.0	0.000	−0.000	−11.9	0.000
_cons	−1.187	−38.5	0.000	−1.398	−43.0	0.000
Log-likelihood	−28642.5			−21029.9		
Number of observations	1,67,879			1,09,469		
Wald chi-square	7240.49			11473.73		
Probability > chi-square	0.0000			0.000		
Pseudo R-sq	0.147			0.2784		

Source: Authors' calculation based on NSS 61st round and PLFS 2017–18 data.

of employment; and restrictions on free mobility, safety, and dignity at the workplace. These issues discourage women's participation in work in general and SC women's participation in work in particular. The underlying reasons for the decisions of young females to refrain from taking up work, thus, need further explanations.

Location is another important factor which determines the likelihood of becoming unemployed. Our results show that there is more likelihood of urban workers becoming unemployed. How do education levels determine the probability of becoming unemployed? The likelihood of becoming unemployed is more with a secondary and above level of education which is highly significant and positive. This finding underscores the need to reduce the higher number of dropouts among youths at the primary and middle levels of education. Further, household size is also an important factor in determining unemployment, i.e. larger the household size, higher is the unemployment rate. Stated otherwise, individuals belonging to large household sizes (if some other members are earning) can afford to remain unemployed for a long time searching for a better job.

As discussed earlier, the caste background of people also has a significant influence on their participation in the labour market vis-à-vis their counterparts from other backgrounds despite both groups having similar levels of education, age, gender, and places of residence. This is confirmed by our estimates (Table 7.13). The SC coefficient is positive and highly significant. Regarding the SC, their probability of becoming unemployed is more as compared to their counterparts from the OBC and higher castes. This adversely affects the educational development of the SC youth and consequently their chances of securing high-quality employment.

Finally, after controlling for other factors, the per capita expenditure coefficient is negative and highly significant. The greater the per capita expenditure, the less likely the chance of becoming unemployed. Consumption variable is important in the decision-making process of whether to remain unemployed for some time or not. In order to decide whether to remain unemployed, the question of affordability comes in (Harberger 1971). In general, it can be assumed that a better economic situation can allow one to be unemployed or remain unemployed for a longer period. Rama (2003) has mentioned that in a survey conducted in Sri Lanka, 94 per cent of the unemployed has declared that their main source of income during their job search is family support. Only 1 per cent of the unemployed received any government assistance during their job search. In the Indian context, Ghose (2004) has observed that groups with higher levels of education have higher levels of unemployment. Again, the level of education and level of poverty are inversely related. He argues that unemployed people in India are not poor and poor people in India are not unemployed (Ghose 2004: 5111). This is true among the poor SC workers as they cannot afford to be unemployed and they end up with low-paid jobs and low earnings. This in turn leads to poverty among the SC workers. Thus, individuals with better income could afford to remain unemployed for a medium period.

7.11 Decomposing Unemployment: Endowment Factors and Discrimination

We have seen that the unemployment rate among the SC is usually higher than the higher castes. We will now try to explain the reasons for the gap in unemployment rate between the SC and higher castes in 2017–18. We have used non-linear decomposition method, developed by Nielsen (1998), to decompose the caste-based difference (SC vs. HC) in probabilities of being unemployed into two components, such as endowment difference and discrimination in hiring. Here we model the individual's incidence to get into unemployment using a logit model. The decomposition of gross difference in unemployment rate between the SC and higher castes shows that discrimination accounts for 65 per cent of the differences in unemployment, whereas endowment difference accounts for 35 per cent. Out of the total unexplained difference, 28 per cent is accounted for the advantage of being higher castes and 36 per cent is accounted for the disadvantage of being SC in the labour market (Table 7.14). This result is consonant with the earlier results where 73 per cent of the differences in the probability of employment between the SC and higher castes was due to discrimination in employment and the remaining 27 per cent due to endowment factors, such as lack of education among the SC. In both

Table 7.14 Decomposition of unemployment rate between SC and higher castes, 2017–18

Components	Percentage
Differences in endowments	34.98
Discrimination	65.02
Advantage being Hindu higher castes	28.44
Disadvantage to Hindu SC	36.99

Source: Authors' calculation based on PLFS 2017–18 data.

the exercises, the caste discrimination emerged as a prominent factor in employment-unemployment.

7.12 Summary and Policy Implications

The main purpose in this exercise is to develop insights into the problem of high unemployment among the SC vis-à-vis higher castes, identify the determinants of high unemployment and highlight policy implications of the findings. The castewise analysis of unemployment for 2017–18 gives insights on a number of aspects of unemployment of the SC, including the youth, unemployment by educational level, duration of unemployment, determinants of unemployment, and the role of endowment factors and discrimination in unemployment gap between the SC and higher castes. We summarize the main findings from the results and then indicate the policy implications to reduce unemployment, particularly among the SC.

It emerged that in 2017–18 the unemployment level among the SC is higher than higher castes and OBC. This is the case with respect to open unemployment based on UPSS as well as underemployment captured by CWS. The gap between the unemployment rate of the SC and higher castes, however, is more pronounced in the case of CWS than UPSS. The low gap in open unemployment between the SC and higher castes, based on UPSS, is related to the economic situation of the SC. A majority of the SC being economically weak have less choice to remain unemployed for a long time, so they would resort to any employment irrespective of duration and wage rate. Hence, the gap in the open unemployment between them and higher castes may tend to be low. However, the high unemployment among the SC becomes obvious when measured by CWS in terms of hours of work in a week. Underemployment turns out to be much higher among them as compared to higher castes. This shows that although they appear to be employed, based on annual counting of the number of days, the actual employment in terms of hours in a week turns out to be much less which is reflected in their high underemployment under CWS. The other important finding is unemployment by education. The unemployment rates, based on both UPSS and CWS, are generally high at all levels of education for the SC. However, the gap in the unemployment rate between the SC and higher castes is particularly high for education at higher secondary and graduate and above levels, particularly in urban areas. Among the SC, the youth (15–29 years age group) suffered the most from much higher unemployment as compared to higher castes. The SC youth unemployment rate tends to be higher beyond higher secondary, including technical and vocational education. The number of NLET is also high among the SC as compared to higher castes. It has also increased at a faster rate as compared to higher castes between 2004–05 and 2017–18. This shows a distressful situation among the SC. The duration of the SC unemployed youth tends to be slightly longer for most of the educational levels. In brief, it emerged that the SC not only suffered from high unemployment than higher castes, but their youth particularly those with higher level of education suffered more, including a longer wait for a job.

The study also identified the determinants of high unemployment by taking the age, gender, location (urban or rural), education, marital status, per capita expenditure, and caste as sources of unemployment. It emerged that all factors have a significant impact on the probability of unemployment. As expected, age (15–29 years), which indicates a lack of work experience, matters in high unemployment of the SC. Gender also has a significant impact as the likelihood of females remaining out of the labour market as well as in education is very high. The SC women suffer triple handicap—being poor, being women, and being SC. The location also came out as a significant factor in unemployment. There is more likelihood of urban workers remaining unemployed. The likelihood of becoming unemployed is high with the secondary and above level of education. Further, household size is also an important factor in determining unemployment as a large household tends to induce high unemployment in the family. The per capita consumption expenditure is equally important in the decision-making process of whether to remain unemployed for some time or not. The affordability factor too plays an important role. In general, a better economic situation can permit a person to remain unemployed for a longer period. Therefore, groups with higher levels of education, which also generally happens to be economically better, tend to have higher levels of unemployment. The reverse is true for the less educated and the poor. The SC who are poorer cannot afford to be unemployed and therefore fall back on any job. Finally, the caste background of people also has significant influence which results in high unemployment among the SC as compared to higher castes, despite both groups having similar levels of education, age, gender, and place of residence. The probability of the SC becoming unemployed is more as compared to higher castes and OBC. All these factors cause a gap in the unemployment rate between the SC and the higher castes. The study found that endowment factors and caste discrimination account for 65 per cent and 35 per cent respectively. Thus, the influence of discrimination is larger than that of endowment factors in causing higher unemployment among the SC. The numerical estimation of the impact of caste discrimination on unemployment is the most insightful finding of this study.

These results have useful implications for policies to reduce unemployment. Among the endowment factors, we found that about 35 per cent of the unemployment gap between the SC and higher castes is due to lack of some attributes which reduce employability. The results related to factors associated with high unemployment indicate that the big household size, lack of work experience for the initial entry to jobs, low education level, particularly education beyond higher secondary, low education of SC women, rural location of persons and poor economic situation cause relatively high unemployment among the SC. In the case of higher castes, small family size, more opportunities for work experience, high education level of both males and females, and stay in urban areas are the factors that reduce unemployment. This indicates that, among the factors which could be influenced by policy, education—particularly education beyond higher secondary—is significantly important which would improve the employability of SC. This would also include skill and professional education. Advancement of higher education and skill of SC women would particularly reduce unemployment of SC families. Since work experience is also useful to get initial entry to jobs, schemes, or measures to provide the opportunity for work experience in the initial stage or at entry level for the SC would be necessary. Similarly, policy to encourage migration from rural to urban areas, through positive help, is equally necessary. In all the policy initiatives to enhance the higher education, particularly the professional and skill development of both males and females, measures to provide early work experience and encourage migration from rural to urban areas would improve employment opportunities and reduce unemployment among the SC.

The above-mentioned measures would improve employability and increase the chances of employment in regular salaried jobs. However, since almost 67 per cent gap in the unemployment rate between the SC and higher castes is caused by discrimination, improved employability may not translate into actual employment. This would need extra measures in addition to the one for endowment improvement. This would need legal safeguards which would act as a deterrent on discrimination in hiring of the SC and ensure equal opportunity in employment. Besides, it will also need affirmative action policy through reservation or other ways for the private sector to ensure fair representation of the SC in employment at various levels of jobs in the private sector. The private sector at present has affirmative action policy for improvement of employability but not for job reservations.

8

Wage Inequality and Untouchables

8.1 Introduction

After having analysed the employment pattern and employment discrimination in the regular salaried labour market, we will now examine the caste inequalities and discrimination in wages of regular salaried workers. In the section on economic theories of castes, we recognized that the regulatory and normative framework of the traditional caste system prescribed differential wages for the untouchables and other castes. As per the Hindu laws of wages, the untouchables were supposed to receive a bare minimum wage fixed too low and much below their productivity levels. As slave labourers, the untouchables receive a fraction of the wage received by higher castes' wage workers. The working conditions involve overwork and hugely exploitative forms of work. Thus, the rules regarding wages and terms and conditions of work for the untouchable workers were unequal and discriminatory. The unequal wage earning and wage discrimination for the untouchables was part of the internal regulatory framework of the caste system. We have reason to believe that although the regulatory framework has now changed to a more equalitarian framework, the legacy of the past continues in the present in a modified form. This is obvious from the review of the studies presented in the earlier chapter which establishes that inequality in wages persists between the Scheduled Castes (SC) and higher castes. Therefore, before we undertake the analysis of wage discrimination in the next chapter, we will first discuss the inequalities in wage earning and related aspects of the regular salaried workers for the year 2004–05 and 2017–18.

Scheduled Castes in the Indian Labour Market. Sukhadeo Thorat, S. Madheswaran, and B. P. Vani,
Oxford University Press. © Sukhadeo Thorat, S. Madheswaran, and B. P. Vani 2023.
DOI: 10.1093/oso/9780198872252.003.0008

8.2 Measuring Inequality in Wages

We have used different measures of wage inequality, such as interquantile ratio and Theil decomposition method. The sophisticated Gary Fields' decomposition method is also used to find out the contribution of relative factors to explain wage inequality across social groups.

8.2.1 Interquantile Ratio

Quantile ratio measures the dispersion of wages across the distribution. We have measured wage inequality by taking the percentile ratios of average daily wages at three distinct points of the wage distribution, i.e. top to bottom (90th to 10th percentile ratio), top to middle (90th to 50th percentile ratio), bottom to middle (10th to 50th percentile ratio), and 75th to 25th percentile ratios. The dispersion ratio is easily interpretable and can be interpreted as the wage earning of top as multiple times of the low-wage earners or median-wage earners (50th percentile).

The quantile ratio (QR) is estimated by:

$$\widehat{QR}(P_1, P_2) = \frac{\hat{Q}(P_1)}{Q(P_2)}$$

where $Q(P)$ is the quantile and P_1 and P_2 are the percentiles.

The limitation with this method is that the quantile ratio ignores the information between the two percentiles which are taken into consideration.

8.2.2 Gary Fields' Decomposition: Accounting for Inequality in a Regression Framework

The above-mentioned measures are traditional measures of inequality. Recent studies prefer to use Gary Fields' decomposition method (2002). The merit of this method is that it is independent of the measure of inequality chosen and is based on robust decomposition rules which are derived axiomatically. Here, wage distribution approximates to log normal rather than a normal distribution. The exception of this method is that we can decompose the contribution of various explanatory variables to the level of and change in inequality within a regression framework. We have used the Mincerian semi-logarithmic earning function for this purpose. The dependent variable in the wage equation is the logarithm of real daily wages and explanatory variables include human capital, demographic, and job characteristics of workers like age, age square, levels of education, gender, marital status, sector, occupation, nature of employment, and region. The model is written as:

$$\ln(w_i) = \sum \beta_j Z_{ij} + \varepsilon_i$$

where, $ln(.)$ is the natural log operator, w_i real daily wages, β_j coefficients, and Z_{ij} the explanatory variables ($j = 1 \ldots J$) for individual i (at time t) and ε_i is the random error term.

The Equation (1) can be written as follows:

$$\ln(w_i) = \sum_{j=1}^{J+1} a_j Z_{ij} = a' Z$$

where a = $[\beta_1 \ldots \beta_J, 1]$ and Z = $[Z_1 \ldots Z_J, \varepsilon]$ are vectors of coefficients and explanatory variables respectively. An inequality index I can be defined on the vector of wages (w).

The Gary Fields inequality measure applies Shorrocks' theorem to compute the percentage of inequality that is accounted for by the jth factor. This is as follows:

$$s_j[\ln(w)] = \frac{\text{cov}[a_j Z_j, \ln(w)]}{\sigma^2 \ln(w)} = \frac{a_j \times \sigma(Z_j) \times cor[Z_j, \ln(w)]}{\sigma \ln(w)}$$

where cov[.], cor(.), and σ(.) are the covariance, correlation coefficient, and standard deviation respectively. The inequality index I(w) which is continuous and symmetric (including Gini coefficient and the generalized entropy measures) for which I(ε) = 0 should satisfy the following conditions:

$$\sum_{j=1}^{J+1} s_j[\ln(w) = 1 \quad \text{and} \quad \sum_{j=1}^{J} s_j[\ln(w)] = R^2[\ln(w)]$$

The fraction of inequality explained by the *jth* explanatory factor, $P_j[ln(w)]$, is the following:

$$P_j[\ln(w)] = \frac{s_j[\ln(w)]}{R^2[\ln(w)]}$$

the percentage contributions of factors to the change in inequality between two time periods (0, 1) can be written as follows:

$$I(w)_1 - I(w)_0 = \sum_j [s_{j,1} \times I(w)_1 - s_{j,0} \times I(w)_0]$$

The contribution of *jth* factor to the change in inequality is given by:

$$\Pi_j(I(w)) = \frac{s_{j,1} \times I(w)_1 - s_{j,0} \times I(w)_0}{I(w)_1 - I(w)_0}$$

where $\Pi_j I(w)$ is the fraction of inequality measure $I(w)$ chosen and $\sum_{j=1}^{J+1} \Pi_j I(w) = 1$.

8.2.3 Decomposition of Wage Inequality

In order to understand the contribution of different factors which affect wage inequality, we decompose wage inequality to 'within' and 'between' groups' inequality components by using Theil index. The first task was to decide on the number of categories within the universe of wage workers in the country (Papola and Kannan 2017).

To assess the contribution of different subgroups on inequality, we used Theil index in our analysis. It decomposes overall inequality (I) into within group inequality (I_W) and between group inequality (I_B).

$$I = I_W + I_B$$

To decompose Theil measure of inequality (I), let w be total wage earnings of the total wage workers, w_j the wage earnings of a subgroup, N the total wage worker population, and N_j the population in the subgroup. The Theil index (I) is defined as:

$$I(Theil) = \sum_{i=1}^{N} \frac{w_i}{N\overline{w}} \ln\left(\frac{w_i N}{\overline{w} N}\right) = \sum_{i=1}^{N} \frac{w_i}{W} \ln\left(\frac{w_i N}{W}\right)$$
$$= \sum_j \left(\frac{w_j}{w}\right) I_j + \sum \left(\frac{w_j}{w}\right) \ln\left(\frac{w_j/w}{N_j/N}\right)$$
$$= (I_W) + (I_B)$$

The first component measures within group inequality (I_W) and the second component measures between group inequality (I_B). It can be seen in percentage terms, such as $R_W = (I_W/I) * 100$, which explains the percentage of inequality explained by between group differences and $(100 - R_W)$ as the percentage of inequality explained by within group differences. By increasing the number of mutually exclusive subgroups, one can account for the effect of a wider range of structural factors.

8.3 Wage Inequality by Caste

8.3.1 Wage Inequality and Regular Salaried Workers

We analyse the disparity in earnings between the SC and higher castes' workers for regular salaried workers in the labour market in India. We also analyse caste-based wage differentials by the level of education, industries, and occupations.

Table 8.1 shows the average daily wages and wage ratios of workers across caste groups for regular salaried workers. We see graded inequality in wage earning across the caste groups. For instance, in 2017–18 the average real daily wage was ₹169 at all-India level. The wage of the SC regular salaried workers was ₹142 followed by ₹163 for OBC and ₹202 for higher castes. The wage ratio of the SC to higher castes captured the wage gap between the SC and higher castes. Both in 2004–05 and 2017–18, the SC to higher castes wage ratio is higher, 38.22 per cent in 2004–05 and 30 per cent in 2017–18. Thus, in 2017–18 the wages of the SC were lower by one-third margin. The wage gap, however, has declined from 38.22 per cent in 2004–05 to 29.91 per cent in 2017–18. The wage gap between the SC and the higher castes is found to be higher in urban regular market than in rural areas in both the years. Thus, whether we considered total or rural-urban wage gap,

Table 8.1 Average real daily wage (in ₹) by employment status, location, and social groups, 2004–05 and 2017–18 (at 2001–02 prices)

	2004–05						2017–18					
	SC	Hindu-OBC	Higher castes	Total	(HC-OBC/HC)*100	(HC-SC/HC)*100	SC	Hindu-OBC	Higher castes	Total	(HC-OBC/HC)*100	(HC-SC/HC)*100
Regular Salaried Workers												
Rural	103.87	105.46	156.57	118.32	32.64 (0.47)	33.66 (5.55***)	130.34	144.02	172.25	146.27	16.39 (2.45**)	24.42 (5.99***)
Urban	129.93	136.36	204.76	162.11	33.40 (1.50)	36.55 (16.68***)	153.98	179.68	216.07	186.48	16.84 (6.20***)	28.74 (15.04***)
Total	117.44	122.35	190.08	144.48	35.62 (1.75*)	38.22 (17.87***)	141.82	162.98	202.22	169.15	19.40 (6.08***)	29.91 (16.35***)
Casual Labour												
Rural	45.28	45.13	44.59	45.19	-1.21 (-0.35)	-1.55 (-1.12)	87.04	87.98	84.45	86.30	-4.18 (0.92)	-3.07 (1.76*)
Urban	59.45	63.72	67.16	62.45	5.12 (2.91***)	11.48 (2.48***)	104.09	112.86	97.64	106.72	-15.59 (4.16***)	-6.61 (2.77***)
Total	46.69	47.59	48.70	47.32	2.27 (2.17**)	4.13 (2.52***)	89.16	92.30	87.58	89.58	-5.39 (3.30***)	-1.80 (1.25)

Total Workers

Rural	53.67	58.55	91.17	60.41	35.77 (6.43***)	41.13 (8.96***)	97.34	108.40	132.27	86.28	18.34 (5.89***)	26.41 (9.99***)
Urban	103.21	114.15	188.20	135.64	39.34 (3.68***)	45.16 (24.01***)	137.81	163.33	203.38	106.71	19.69 (8.44***)	32.24 (20.03***)
Total	63.60	74.04	141.55	82.69	47.69 (10.63***)	55.07 (30.45***)	107.45	127.81	172.74	89.57	26.01 (12.58***)	37.80 (28.60***)

Note: t-statistics are given in the parentheses. ***, **, * denote mean of the difference between two groups which is significant at 1 per cent, 5 per cent, and 10 per cent respectively.

Source: Authors' calculation based on NSS 61st round and PLFS 2017–18 data.

everywhere it is characterized by a graded inequality in wage earning. The average wage earning of the SC regular salaried workers is lower than that of OBC and higher castes. The wage of OBC workers is higher than that of SC workers but lower than higher castes' workers. Thus, wages get reduced as we go down the caste hierarchy from higher castes to OBC and further down to the SC who are at the bottom of the caste ladder.

8.3.2   Wage Differentials by Levels of Education

Several studies across various countries as well as in India demonstrate that workers with higher levels of education and skills earn higher wages. The general assumption is that wages rise with higher levels of education. This applies more to regular salaried workers, where educational endowments play a more important role in wage determination than for casual workers. Papola and Kannan (2017) observed that 'In India, those with the highest level of education earn five times more than those with the lowest level of education and this pattern of disparity is prevalent amongst all categories of workers, except for certain categories of casual workers'. The results of the present study are presented in Tables 8.2 and 8.3 which show the difference in average daily wages according to the education level. We find that in 2017–18 the caste-based wage differentials in the regular labour market are the highest at diploma and graduate levels; the wages paid to the SC graduates are about 80 per cent of that of higher castes, while the wages paid to OBC graduates are about 76 per cent of that of higher castes. With minor variations, the trend in 2004–05 is the same. During 2004–05 to 2017–18, the wage gap decreased from 20 per cent to 16 per cent for the graduate and above level of education. However, the wage gap between the SC and higher castes increased for the diploma/certificate from 15.29 per cent in 2004–05 to 23.54 per cent in 2017–18. Similarly, the wage gap increased from 5.69 per cent to 18.32 per cent during the same period for the higher secondary level of education.

What happened to wage inequality within the same educational category? Table 8.4 gives the inequality ratio for wages between the SC and higher castes by 25th, 50th, and 75th percentiles, i.e. wage gap at the bottom, middle, and top percentiles of wage distribution for 2004–05 and 2017–18. Few features emerged from Table 8.4 about inequality in wage across the caste groups. First, without any exception at all levels of education the wages

Table 8.2 Average real daily wage (in ₹) by employment status, levels of education, and social groups, 2004–05 (at 2001–02 prices)

	Hindu SC	Hindu OBC	Hindu Higher castes	Total	(HC-OBC/ HC)*100	(HC-SC/ HC)*100
Regular Salaried workers						
Illiterate	63.90	55.46	71.36	59.47	22.28	10.45
Literate and up to primary	79.29	74.61	90.36	79.75	17.43	12.25
Middle	94.73	90.49	106.22	95.81	14.81	10.82
Secondary and higher secondary	147.77	131.80	156.69	146.31	15.88	5.69
Diploma/Certificate	203.77	189.80	240.55	215.73	21.10	15.29
Graduate and above	237.73	227.05	295.28	265.91	23.11	19.49
Total	117.45	122.34	190.11	144.49	35.65	38.22
Casual Labour						
Illiterate	41.90	40.37	40.51	41.14	0.35	−3.43
Literate and up to primary	51.35	52.05	50.39	51.64	−3.29	−1.91
Middle	54.89	57.95	56.72	57.54	−2.17	3.23
Secondary and higher secondary	52.42	57.96	61.93	57.36	6.41	15.36
Diploma/Certificate	92.83	70.99	63.47	77.74	−11.85	−46.26
Graduate and above	55.41	62.19	65.39	63.85	4.89	15.26
Total	46.69	47.59	48.70	47.32	2.28	4.13
Total Workers						
Illiterate	44.15	42.27	46.01	43.28	8.13	4.04
Literate and up to primary	57.54	57.94	67.25	59.20	13.84	14.44
Middle	67.66	71.78	86.09	73.76	16.62	21.41
Secondary and higher secondary	106.63	110.75	143.91	123.06	23.04	25.91
Diploma/Certificate	186.54	178.72	234.29	204.65	23.72	20.38
Graduate and above	226.93	220.35	293.01	260.87	24.80	22.55
Total	63.60	74.03	141.56	82.69	47.70	55.07

Source: Authors' calculation based on NSS 61st round data.

Table 8.3 Average real daily wage (in ₹) by employment status, levels of education, and social groups, 2017–18 (at 2001–02 Prices)

	Hindu SC	Hindu OBC	Higher castes	Total	(HC-OBC/ HC)*100	(HC-SC/ HC)*100
Regular Salaried workers						
Illiterate	75.12	79.46	80.67	78.96	1.50	6.88
Literate and up to primary	88.42	98.58	100.31	95.08	1.72	11.85
Middle	117.50	112.06	120.82	114.43	7.25	2.75
Secondary and higher secondary	134.97	146.20	165.24	151.06	11.52	18.32
Diploma/Certificate	197.54	188.96	258.36	212.06	26.86	23.54
Graduate and above	235.86	249.71	283.59	264.08	11.95	16.83
Total	141.73	163.01	202.22	169.15	19.39	29.91
Casual Labour						
Illiterate	82.90	81.85	78.03	81.49	−4.90	−6.24
Literate and up to primary	90.30	90.98	86.57	89.83	−5.09	−4.31
Middle	95.48	101.05	93.03	96.99	−8.62	−2.63
Secondary and higher secondary	95.75	102.41	93.10	98.19	−10.00	−2.85
Diploma/Certificate	132.49	122.31	117.00	124.90	−4.54	−13.24
Graduate and above	93.54	98.42	114.49	100.52	14.04	18.30
Total	89.16	92.30	87.58	89.58	−5.39	−1.80
Total Workers						
Illiterate	81.80	81.44	78.69	81.08	−3.49	−3.95
Literate and up to primary	89.85	93.26	93.00	91.38	−0.28	3.39
Middle	103.13	105.97	110.35	104.76	3.97	6.54
Secondary and higher secondary	117.08	130.98	152.99	133.57	14.39	23.47
Diploma/Certificate	185.69	181.73	252.94	203.07	28.15	26.59
Graduate and above	221.98	244.62	281.54	258.31	13.11	21.16
Total	107.45	127.81	172.74	128.23	26.01	37.80

Source: Authors' calculation based on PLFS 2017–18 data.

of the SC are lower than higher castes for 25th, 50th, and 75th percentile of wage earnings. Second, the average wage earning at 75th percentile is higher than 50th and 50th is higher than 25th percentile. Third, this tendency is seen at all levels of education, but more prominently at higher levels of education, namely higher secondary and graduate and above.

Inequality is evident within educational categories. For those who have attained secondary schooling and above, the ratio between wages at 50th percentile and 25th percentile and between 75th percentile and 25th percentile shows a perceptible increase (Table 8.4). The biggest rise has occurred for graduates and above. However, this pattern is not observed for lower educational levels. In 2017–18, only the ratio of wages between 75th percentile and 25th percentile shows some increase for graduates and above. For all other ratios, one can discern a clear decline.

To sum up, the results show that wage gaps are relatively high for higher levels of education, namely secondary/higher secondary, diploma/certificate, and graduate and above; and less for lower level of education

Table 8.4 Caste-based wage differential within educational groups of regular wage workers, 2017–18 (at 2001–02 prices)

Educational Levels	Percentile	Wage Rate			Wage ratio of 25th, 50th, and 75th percentiles		
		Hindu SC	Hindu OBC	Hindu Higher castes	Hindu SC	Hindu OBC	Hindu Higher castes
Illiterate	25th	39.73	40.54	46.64	1.00	1.00	1.00
	50th	65.47	65.40	77.96	1.65	1.61	1.67
	75th	97.68	98.80	111.07	2.46	2.44	2.38
Up to primary	25th	55.91	55.86	64.91	1.00	1.00	1.00
	50th	81.27	83.53	93.29	1.45	1.50	1.44
	75th	117.09	122.59	124.12	2.09	2.19	1.91
Middle	25th	67.36	65.88	74.67	1.00	1.00	1.00
	50th	93.67	95.83	104.61	1.39	1.45	1.40
	75th	134.73	136.22	140.51	2.00	2.07	1.88
Secondary and higher secondary	25th	74.53	78.59	89.40	1.00	1.00	1.00
	50th	106.55	111.75	132.21	1.43	1.42	1.48
	75th	170.28	179.69	222.75	2.28	2.29	2.49
Graduation and above	25th	97.64	109.11	136.64	1.00	1.00	1.00
	50th	176.27	193.08	245.17	1.81	1.77	1.79
	75th	334.13	334.13	389.82	3.42	3.06	2.85
Total	25th	67.36	74.55	89.82	1.00	1.00	1.00
	50th	101.05	113.52	142.24	1.50	1.52	1.58
	75th	170.28	196.14	278.44	2.53	2.63	3.10

Source: Authors' calculation based on PLFS 2017–18 data.

(illiterate, literate, and middle level). Regarding wage level, within the educational group, without any exception at all levels of education, the wages of the SC are lower than higher castes for the low, medium, and high wage earning levels. The wage gap is particularly high in high wage-earning level for graduate and above.

8.3.3 Wage Differentials by Industry Groups

Industrial wage structure by caste groups is shown in Table 8.5. In the regular labour market, the average earnings of the SC are lower than

Table 8.5 Average real daily wage (in ₹) of regular workers by industrial categories and social groups in India, 2017–18 (at 2001–02 prices)

Industry Categories	Rural			Urban		
	Hindu SC	Hindu OBC	Hindu Higher castes	Hindu SC	Hindu OBC	Hindu Higher castes
Agriculture, forestry, and fisheries	74.25	76.67	91.41	126.71	131.59	163.16
Mining and quarrying	142.34	127.96	205.53	314.87	199.43	337.57
Manufacturing 1 (agro-based)	90.91	100.41	115.02	99.68	117.87	137.11
Manufacturing 2 (others)	113.26	121.23	140.95	136.77	159.67	204.64
Electricity, water supply, etc.	149.33	131.95	245.80	199.57	254.04	343.94
Construction	155.69	156.72	184.50	169.18	192.19	232.80
Trade, hotel, and restaurants	77.77	89.80	105.27	105.00	108.66	132.45
Transport, storage, and communication	129.44	136.71	142.86	175.32	223.24	238.68
Financial, business, and professional services	140.91	200.66	209.40	183.66	215.92	259.23
Public administration and other services	167.93	186.77	215.99	191.67	220.84	255.13
Total	126.63	141.40	169.67	148.65	173.63	209.74

Note: As per NIC 2008 classification, manufacturing 1 includes industries with 10–18 codes; manufacturing 2 includes industries with 19–33 codes. Sample of individuals belongs to 15–65 age groups in 18 major states.

Source: Authors' calculation based on NSS 61st round and PLFS 2017–18 data.

OBC and higher castes workers irrespective of location and industrial affiliation. The wage earning of the OBC is higher than the SC but at the same time it is lower than higher caste workers. In the regular rural labour market, SC to higher castes wage differential is the highest in manufacturing, other than agro-based, followed by public administration and other services. Similarly, OBC to higher castes wage differential is the highest in agriculture, forestry, and fisheries followed by manufacturing, other than agro-based. On the other hand, in the regular urban labour market, SC to higher castes wage differentials is the highest in agriculture, forestry, and fisheries followed by mining and quarrying, electricity, water supply-related industries, financial, business, and professional services. Similarly, OBC to higher castes wage differentials is the highest in agriculture, forestry, and fisheries followed by electricity, and water supply-related industries.

8.3.4 Wage Differentials by Occupational Groups

Since wage differentials would invariably exist across different occupations because of the different levels of education and skill endowment required for such jobs, the differences among two groups in the occupational distribution of workers, i.e. between the SC and higher castes, would lead to dissimilarity in mean wages of these two groups. Such differences in occupational pattern may be because of variations in endowment or skill patterns of the two groups of workers, and also because of entry barriers in the job market where some groups are discriminated against even if they have adequate skill (Brown et al. 1980; Miller and Volker 1985; Dolton and Kidd 1994). Apart from such a hierarchical structure, evidence of spatial or interpersonal wage differences even within occupations are also quite substantial in India. A part of such wage differential may be because of endowment gaps, differences in educational attainment and training, among the different competing groups. On the other hand, pure discrimination in terms of lower wage rates paid to certain groups is also common. In this section, we will examine inequalities in occupations and earnings between various subgroups for regular workers and then decompose those gaps into separate components which are explainable through differences in occupational patterns and wage rates, subdivided into a part due to endowment factors, such as education and training, and the other representing discrimination in both employment and wages. To the extent that preferred and generally better-paid occupations or positions are rationed, we would expect differential earnings between otherwise similar workers from different social groups. As expected, in the regular labour market, the average daily earnings of the SC are lower than higher castes and OBC workers and that of OBC are lower than higher castes in almost all occupations (Table 8.6). The wage gap between SC and higher castes is less in clerical, elementary, and production occupations.

Table 8.6 Average real daily wage (in ₹) by employment status, occupational categories, and social groups, 2017–18 (at 2001–02 prices)

	Hindu SC	Hindu OBC	Hindu Higher castes	Total	(HC-OBC/ HC)*100	(HC-SC/ HC)*100
Regular Salaried Workers						
Administrative	275.56	295.12	357.42	322.04	17.43	22.90
Professional	217.11	233.38	263.24	242.51	11.34	17.52
Clerical	201.32	196.85	228.85	210.10	13.98	12.03
Service	121.84	142.19	152.19	140.39	6.57	19.94
Sales	89.35	94.35	111.19	99.11	15.15	19.64
Agriculture and allied occupations	96.42	153.54	181.81	139.86	15.55	46.97
Production	121.65	128.58	142.39	128.19	9.70	14.57
Elementary	89.56	98.94	107.73	95.15	8.16	16.87
Total	141.73	163.01	202.22	169.15	19.39	29.91
Casual Labour						
Administrative	52.95	84.35	71.43	68.48	−18.09	25.87
Professional	107.12	122.61	107.38	113.76	−14.18	0.24
Clerical	69.61	117.46	53.21	98.97	−120.75	−30.82
Service	88.88	103.14	95.66	97.81	−7.82	7.09
Sales	82.87	87.08	83.68	88.14	−4.06	0.97
Agriculture and allied occupations	83.57	79.64	74.35	81.21	−7.11	−12.40
Production	108.30	114.94	102.90	109.20	−11.70	−5.25
Elementary	85.05	84.64	82.07	84.04	−3.13	−3.63
Total	89.23	92.32	87.38	89.61	−5.65	−2.12

Table 8.6 Continued

	Hindu SC	Hindu OBC	Hindu Higher castes	Total	(HC-OBC/ HC)*100	(HC-SC/ HC)*100
			Total Workers			
Administrative	243.52	291.46	346.55	311.23	15.90	29.73
Professional	214.62	231.10	260.37	240.24	11.24	17.57
Clerical	201.06	196.18	228.33	209.43	14.08	11.94
Service	119.87	136.87	147.97	136.34	7.50	18.99
Sales	88.99	93.73	109.73	98.21	14.58	18.90
Agriculture and allied occupations	84.93	103.07	113.40	93.51	9.11	25.11
Production	114.60	122.49	131.87	119.73	7.11	13.10
Elementary	85.66	87.07	90.31	85.88	3.59	5.15
Total	107.91	128.24	173.20	128.82	25.96	37.70

Source: Authors' calculation based on NSS 61st round and PLFS 2017–18 data.

This gives clear evidence of caste-based occupational segregation in the regular labour market. Wage differences between caste groups are mostly due to skewed occupational distribution caused mainly by their lower endowment levels. Thus, the educational development of the SC would enable them to access white-collared occupations and also raise their wage levels.

8.3.5 Regional Variations in Wages

We have seen visible inequalities in wage earnings, in total and by educational levels, between the SC and higher castes at all-India level. We see a significant variation in the wage gap between the SC and higher castes for the regular workers in the states (Table 8.7). In 2004–05, in some states, the wage gap is higher than others. The states which have highest wage gap are Tamil Nadu, Madhya Pradesh, Haryana, and Andhra Pradesh. A similar pattern persists in wage gap 13 years later in 2017–18. Following all-India trend, the wage gap has reduced in all the states, except Himachal Pradesh and Bihar. However, wage gap between SC and higher caste for casual workers both at all-India and state level is negligible (Table 8.8).

Table 8.7 Statewise average real daily wages (in ₹) of regular (rural + urban) workers by caste and overtime (at 2001–02 prices)

States	2004–05						2017–18					
	Hindu SC	Hindu OBC	Hindu Higher castes	Total	(HUC-HOBC)/HUC*100	(HUC-HSC)/HUC*100	Hindu SC	Hindu OBC	Hindu Higher castes	Total	(HUC-HOBC)/HUC*100	(HUC-HSC)/HUC*100
Jammu and Kashmir	157.39	150.37	181	188.47	16.92	13.04	215.78	302.51	246.9	255.96	−22.52	12.60
Himachal Pradesh	166	177.83	207.57	190.87	14.33	20.03	159.91	216.05	219.33	201.39	1.50	27.09
Punjab	151.41	100.66	193.2	158.14	47.90	21.63	169.19	124.56	195.45	168.22	36.27	13.44
Haryana	115.04	114.44	243.35	174.1	52.97	52.73	136.78	186.48	241.42	196.54	22.76	43.34
Rajasthan	111.97	130.38	193.36	144.06	32.57	42.09	149.14	170.7	200.79	170.32	14.99	25.72
Uttar Pradesh	111.54	114.5	177.72	132.72	35.57	37.24	167.6	168.8	224.73	174.09	24.89	25.42
Bihar	151.61	176.91	209.64	174.17	15.61	27.68	163.31	165.87	230.49	180.03	28.04	29.15
Tripura	102.57	110.91	147.23	130.22	24.67	30.33	177.26	188.83	215.27	203.06	12.28	17.66
Assam	130.68	110.25	173.24	145.52	36.36	24.57	159.15	135.54	210.19	169.08	35.52	24.28
West Bengal	114.59	105.04	176.72	143.76	40.56	35.16	104.42	110.44	144.26	120.9	23.44	27.62
Odisha	116	133.21	184.92	146.79	27.96	37.27	139.55	156.91	186.9	162.2	16.05	25.33
Madhya Pradesh	73.79	90.98	182.45	122.53	50.13	59.56	124.56	143.71	216.62	167.98	33.66	42.50
Gujarat	105.97	111.07	168.69	137.41	34.16	37.18	137.52	173.96	193.65	167.18	10.17	28.99
Maharashtra	142.12	150.6	190.08	163.33	20.77	25.23	154.09	168.21	206.13	186.71	18.40	25.25
Andhra Pradesh	87.93	101.1	179.96	119.67	43.82	51.14	132.29	158.69	219.45	164.2	27.69	39.72

Karnataka	109.91	126.9	209.43	155.1	39.41	47.52	130.83	162.31	202	167.85	19.65	35.23
Kerala	103.41	140.5	169.19	144.66	16.96	38.88	131.32	174.36	214.23	177.63	18.61	38.70
Tamil Nadu	87.81	119.73	322.33	131.69	62.85	72.76	122.61	161.78	239.38	157.12	32.42	48.78
All India	117.44	122.35	190.08	144.48	35.63	38.22	141.83	162.98	202.23	169.17	19.41	29.87

Source: Authors' calculation based on NSS 61st round and PLFS 2017–18 data.

Table 8.8 Statewise average real daily wages (in ₹) of casual (rural + urban) workers by caste and overtime (at 2001–02 prices)

States	2004–05						2017–18					
	Hindu SC	Hindu OBC	Higher castes	Total	(HUC-HOBC)/ HUC*100	(HUC-HSC)/ HUC*100	Hindu SC	Hindu OBC	Higher castes	Total	(HUC-HOBC)/ HUC*100	(HUC-HSC)/ HUC*100
Jammu and Kashmir	86.46	90.15	84.66	91.31	-6.48	-2.13	130.97	149.03	137.16	143.69	-8.65	4.51
Himachal Pradesh	78.62	75.75	72.71	75.75	-4.18	-8.13	109.51	106.56	104.27	104.43	-2.20	-5.03
Punjab	67.96	61.59	75.19	68.06	18.09	9.62	102.54	96.07	112.04	103.01	14.25	8.48
Haryana	66.42	68.37	69.07	67.25	1.01	3.84	100.66	106.74	118.23	103.46	9.72	14.86
Rajasthan	58.74	55.92	57.43	54.77	2.63	-2.28	94.53	96.11	102.16	94.77	5.92	7.47
Uttar Pradesh	46.22	48.6	53.31	47.68	8.84	13.30	94.11	95.78	89.81	93.35	-6.65	-4.79
Bihar	38.74	41.34	50.29	40.28	17.80	22.97	103.7	110.07	124.78	108.65	11.79	16.89
Tripura	60.63	57.49	56.1	58.15	-2.48	-8.07	116.26	113.75	109.25	111.91	-4.12	-6.42
Assam	50.92	54.71	58.49	56.08	6.46	12.94	94.52	87.36	104.7	99.2	16.56	9.72
West Bengal	44.35	51.4	49.75	46.12	-3.32	10.85	75.08	88.26	81.09	79.25	-8.84	7.41
Odisha	37.83	37.12	43.29	36.83	14.25	12.61	79.18	83.29	91.66	80.47	9.13	13.62
Madhya Pradesh	36.29	35.05	39.38	36.3	11.00	7.85	76.81	81.41	89.55	76.21	9.09	14.23
Gujarat	42.59	51.16	58.07	47.48	11.90	26.66	76.44	80.59	72.85	76.16	-10.62	-4.93
Maharashtra	37.98	35.74	44.33	38.22	19.38	14.32	66.64	62.94	69.96	64.55	10.03	4.75
Andhra Pradesh	38.75	39.64	42.63	39.84	7.01	9.10	90.21	85.5	96.79	88.09	11.66	6.80
Karnataka	41.87	42.65	37.54	41.34	-13.61	-11.53	77.12	77.98	73.02	78.95	-6.79	-5.61
Kerala	107.64	111.56	99.35	109.97	-12.29	-8.34	163.2	159.12	146.4	159.4	-8.69	-11.48
Tamil Nadu	49.25	53.94	45.68	52.54	-18.08	-7.82	94.9	101.97	83.21	99.98	-22.55	-14.05
All India	46.69	47.59	48.7	47.32	2.28	4.13	89.16	92.3	87.58	89.58	-5.39	-1.80

Source: Authors' calculation based on NSS 61st round and PLFS 2017–18 data.

We have also analysed the trend in interstate disparities in wage gap by using a ratio of the highest to lowest average wages and coefficient of variations. The ratio of highest to lowest wage rate has increased for regular salaried workers between 2004–05 and 2017–18 (Table 8.9). The increase in the ratio of highest to lowest wages for the regular workers is from 1.6 to 2.1. Similarly, the coefficient of variation for regular workers increased from 14.1 per cent to 15.2 per cent. This indicates that interstate disparities in wage earning have worsened during 2004–05 and 2017–18.

Unlike all-India average, the trend differs between caste groups. The interstate disparities in wage rate are measured through a ratio of highest

Table 8.9 Basic indicators of average daily wages between states, 2004–05 and 2017–18 (at 2001–02 prices)

	2004–05				2017–18			
	Hindu SC	Hindu OBC	Hindu Higher Castes	Total	Hindu SC	Hindu OBC	Hindu Higher Castes	Total
Regular Wage/Salaried Workers								
Maximum wage	166.0	177.8	322.3	190.9	215.8	302.5	246.9	256.0
Minimum wage	73.8	91.0	147.2	119.7	104.4	110.4	144.3	120.9
Ratio of max. to min.	2.2	2.0	2.2	1.6	2.1	2.7	1.7	2.1
Average	118.9	125.9	195.0	150.2	148.6	170.5	211.5	177.2
Coefficient of variation in %	21.7	19.9	19.5	14.1	17.1	23.9	11.2	15.2
Casual Labourers								
Maximum wage	107.6	111.6	99.4	110.0	163.2	159.1	146.4	159.4
Minimum wage	36.3	35.1	37.5	36.3	66.6	62.9	70.0	64.6
Ratio of max. to min.	3.0	3.2	2.6	3.0	2.4	2.5	2.1	2.5
Average	55.1	56.2	57.6	56.0	97.0	99.0	100.4	98.1
Coefficient of variation in %	36.0	35.6	29.0	35.9	23.9	24.1	21.7	24.1

Source: Authors' calculation based on NSS 61st round and PLFS 2017–18 data.

to lowest, and coefficient of variation has declined between 2004–05 and 2017–18 in case of SC and higher castes, but interstate disparities increased for the OBC. The ratio of highest to lowest declined marginally from 2.2 to .12 for the SC, the coefficient declined from 21.7 to 17.1. Similarly, the ratio of highest to lowest for higher castes declined from 2.2 to 1.7. Correspondingly, the coefficient of variation declined from 19.5 to 11.2. The trend in disparities in wage rate is, however, different for OBC. The interstate disparities in case of OBC have increased. The ratio of highest to lowest increased from 2 in 2004–05 to 2.7 in 2017–18 and the coefficient of variation from 19.9 to 23.9. Thus, the interstate disparities in wage gap have reduced in case of the SC and higher castes, but has increased in case of OBC.

Statewise examination of wages of regular and casual workers in 2004–05 and 2017–18 shows a diverse picture. However, juxtaposing daily earnings with that of per capita state domestic product indicates a small relationship between the two which contradicts the general belief that developed states with better economic indicators pay higher wages and the results are in line with Papola and Kannan (2017). In 2004–05, only the casual workers indicate a small association between development and daily wages (r = 0.37) and in all other cases the correlation coefficient is negligible.

8.3.6 Wage Gaps in Public and Private Sectors

Tables 8.10 and 8.11 show the average daily wages of regular workers in public and private sectors across caste groups. Few features have emerged from the analysis of the regular salaried workers' participation in public and private labour markets. First, public sector workers earn more as compared to their private sector counterparts. Second, caste-based wage differentials between the SC and higher castes exist in both the public and private sectors. Third, the caste-based wage differentials between the SC and higher castes are more pronounced in the private sector than in the public sector in urban areas, whereas the inequality is relatively low in the public sector. In the regular labour market, there are differences in wage gap over the wage distribution in the public and private sectors. The wage differentials (gap/ratio) between the SC and higher castes in the

Table 8.10 Average real daily wages (in ₹) of regular workers by caste and enterprise type for 2004–05 and 2017–18 (at 2001–02 prices)

Social Groups	2004–05		2017–18	
	Public	Private	Public	Private
Rural				
Hindu SC	174.78	67.82	207.56	99.00
Hindu-OBC	179.30	76.38	225.45	112.94
Hindu higher castes	207.81	127.28	251.91	133.08
(HC-OBC/HC)*100 OBC wage gap	13.72	39.99	10.50	15.13
(HC-SC/HC)*100 SC wage gap	15.9	46.7	17.6	25.6
Urban				
SC	222.95	78.04	261.67	113.93
Hindu-OBC	251.52	95.45	294.25	145.66
Higher castes	308.88	151.63	325.60	180.52
(HC-OBC/HC)*100 OBC wage gap	18.6	37.1	9.6	19.3
(HC-SC/HC)*100 SC wage gap	27.8	48.5	19.6	36.9

Source: Authors' calculation based on NSS 61st round and PLFS 2017–18 data.

public sector are higher at the lower percentiles, i.e. below 50th percentile than at the top percentile of the wage distribution. On the other hand, in the private sector wage differentials between the SC and higher castes are higher at the upper percentiles, i.e. above 50th percentile than at the bottom percentile of the wage distribution. This means that in public jobs the wage differential is relatively high in grades C and D (as compared to grades A and B). Among other reasons, this may be due to the appointment of Grade D jobs by public sector employers on a contract basis through private agencies that are known for low payment of wages and biases in recruitment (Mamgain 2018).

We have seen that the wage gap between the SC and higher castes is high in the private sector as compared to the public sector. However, within the private and public sectors there are differences in wage gap among formal and informal workers. Table 8.11 presents the wage earning by caste groups for formal and informal workers in public and private sectors. Generally, the wage gap between the SC and higher castes is high among informal workers as compared to formal workers both in public

Table 8.11 Average real daily wages (in ₹) in public and private sectors of regular labour market by socio religious groups, 2004–05 and 2017–18 (at 2001–02 prices)

	2004–05				2017–18			
	Public sector		Private sector		Public sector		Private sector	
	Formal workers	Informal workers	Formal workers	Informal workers	Formal workers	Informal workers	Formal workers	Informal workers
ST	269.7	104.3	116.9	64.6	326.1	156.8	156.3	115.9
Hindu SC	225.5	67.2	122.3	65.6	305.7	115.1	178.7	92.4
Hindu_OBC	264.8	91.1	167.5	72.8	337.1	135.8	211.5	111.8
Hindu higher castes	322.7	123.9	229.9	101.8	365.3	143.3	232.7	132.5
Muslims	257.4	75.7	177.9	80.5	314.8	119.4	184.8	104.9
Others religions	333.5	81.8	203.0	92.0	365.9	156.5	226.3	123.4
Person	286.6	98.0	194.6	83.7	344.2	134.6	216.6	115.9
Wage ratio (SC/Higher castes)	0.70	0.54	0.53	0.64	0.84	0.80	0.77	0.70
Wage gap in per cent: (Higher castes-SC/Higher castes)*100	30.1	45.8	46.8	35.6	16.3	19.7	23.2	30.3

Source: Authors' calculation based on NSS 61st round and PLFS 2017–18 data.

and private sectors. In 2017–18, the wage gap ratio in the private sector between the SC and higher castes is 23.2 per cent for formal workers and 30.30 per cent for informal workers. Similarly, the wage gap in public sector for formal workers is 16.3 per cent and that for informal workers is 19.7 per cent. Thus, both in private and public sectors, the wage gap between the SC and higher castes is higher among informal workers than formal workers. The wage gap has declined both in public and private sectors for formal and informal workers during 2004–05 and 2017–18.

8.4 Wage Inequality

So far we have measured the wage gap between the caste groups by taking the average wage of the SC, OBC, and higher castes. The limitation of these exercises is that the averages do not generally estimate the wage gap at different points or range the wage dispersion, such as lower, middle, and top levels. There are methods developed to measure inequality at different points of wage distribution, although there are supporters as well as critics who debate these various methods. However, we focus on one such method. We attempt to capture Indian wage inequality through wage dispersion ratios, between the top, middle, and bottom levels, throughout wage distribution. To measure inequality and highlight the differences in the wage distribution, the ratio of the two extremes—the highest and lowest wages—is used. For instance, the ILO Global Wage Report (ILO 2016) has used this indicator to compare low and high wage earners (P90/P10) as well as to compare the two extremes with the middle wage earners (P50/P10 and P90/P50). It must be mentioned that interdecile ratio method measures the 'within-group inequality' for the SC, OBC, and higher castes but not the inequality between these three groups (or between group inequality). It also identifies the factors which cause within-group inequality for the three groups separately.

It is evident from Tables 8.12 and 8.13 that in 2017–18 inequality between the top and bottom wage earners, i.e. P90/P10 interdecile, the indicator is around 7.50 for regular workers and 3.0 for casual workers for the three caste groups, namely SC, OBC, and higher castes which do not indicate much variation between the three groups. The interdecile ratio decreased for the lower half and the bottom for the social groups.

Table 8.12   Wage inequality among regular workers by social groups (interdecile ratio), 2004–05 and 2017–18

	2004–05			2017–18		
	Hindu SC	Hindu OBC	Hindu Higher Castes	Hindu SC	Hindu OBC	Hindu Higher Castes
p90/p10	11.75	11.04	10.41	7.67	7.23	7.50
p90/p50	3.63	3.67	2.72	3.27	3.12	3.12
p10/p50	0.31	0.33	0.26	0.43	0.43	0.42
p75/p25	4.19	4.21	4.12	2.53	2.63	3.10

Source: Authors' calculation based on NSS 61st round and PLFS 2017–18 data.

Table 8.13   Wage inequality among casual workers by caste and location (interdecile ratio), 2004–05 and 2017–18

	2004–05			2017–18		
	Hindu SC	Hindu OBC	Hindu Higher Castes	Hindu SC	Hindu OBC	Hindu Higher Castes
p90/p10	3.70	4.08	4.03	2.81	3.12	2.87
p90/p50	1.91	2.01	2.00	1.42	1.50	1.45
p10/p50	0.52	0.49	0.50	0.50	0.48	0.50
p75/p25	1.96	2.19	2.02	1.78	1.91	1.88

Source: Authors' calculation based on NSS 61st round and PLFS 2017–18 data.

Using Gary Fields' decomposition method, we have estimated the relative contribution of factors to wage inequality within the group for regular workers. From Table 8.14 it is evident that five factors, namely education, public sector employment, gender, age, and occupation, in that order matters in within-group inequality in average wage earning. This order is equally found in all three caste groups. Education is the most dominant factor which contributes to the level of wage inequality for all social groups. Next is employment in the public sector which ensures a secure income. The age and occupation are the next important contributors to wage inequality. Gender also matters in wage earning to

Table 8.14 Relative factor inequality shares by castes in regular labour market (Gary Fields' decomposition method), 2017–18

	Hindu SC	Share	Hindu OBC	Share	Hindu Higher Castes	Share
Age	0.05	12.50	0.05	11.82	0.04	9.88
Education	0.13	28.98	0.14	33.99	0.15	35.73
Gender	0.08	17.50	0.08	18.50	0.06	14.20
Married	0.002	0.39	0.01	2.35	0.01	3.32
Region	0.003	0.76	0.003	0.69	0.01	1.35
Occupation	0.05	11.71	0.05	11.82	0.07	15.48
Public sector dummy	0.11	24.65	0.09	21.97	0.09	21.08
Residual	0.58		0.59		0.57	
R-squared	0.43		0.41		0.43	
No. of observations	5806		9354		9277	

Source: Authors' calculation based on PLFS 2017–18 data.

create wage inequality. The pattern of relative factor inequality shares remains almost the same for all social groups. However, there are castewise differences in relative contribution in wage inequality. In the case of education, the return seems to be relatively greater for the higher castes followed by OBC and SC. Similarly, occupation also has high significance for the higher castes (given their concentration in superior occupations) followed by SC and OBC. Gender, age, and public employment are more significant for the SC. Among these three, the assured public employment is more important for the SC as compared to OBC and higher castes in wage earning.

The limitation of the Gary Fields decomposition method is that it only focuses on within-group inequality. To overcome this limitation, the Theil index (one of the generalized entropy measures) is used to have a more disaggregated analysis on wage inequality between the advantaged and disadvantaged groups in the labour market. Using this method, we decompose (total) wage inequality into 'within' and 'between' group inequality components to understand the contribution of different factors which affect wage inequality. Following Papola and Kannan (2017), we have formed four groups using some basic characteristics of wage workers (Table 8.15). Papola and Kannan (2017) have decomposed the inequality

Table 8.15 Construction of groups to decompose inequality

Group	Description of specification	No. of workers' groups
Group 1	Location (rural and urban), gender (male and female), and labour status (regular and casual) $(2 \times 2 \times 2)$	8
Group 2	Location, gender, and employment type and education (low education, middle, secondary and graduate and above) $(2 \times 2 \times 2 \times 4)$	32
Group 3	Location, gender, employment type, and social group $(2 \times 2 \times 2 \times 5)$	40
Group 4	Location, gender, employment type, social group, and education $(2 \times 2 \times 2 \times 4 \times 5)$ (large set)	160

Source: Papola and Kannan (2017).

using the Theil index based on four groups. We have taken their estimates for the year 2004–05 and computed and compared it with 2017–18.

It is evident from Table 8.16 that the explanatory power enhanced considerably when introducing both education and caste variables in Group 4. It increases the between-group inequality contribution from 37 per cent to 53 per cent in 2004–05, while it increases the same from 41

Table 8.16 Inequality decomposition (Theil index) for regular labour market

Group specification 1: Location, Gender, and Labour Status		
Description	2004–05	2017–18
Overall wage inequality	0.445	0.548
Within-group inequality	0.296	0.440
Contribution (per cent)	66.46	80.29
Between-group inequality	0.149	0.108
Contribution (per cent)	33.53	19.70
Group specification 2: Location, Gender, Labour Status, and Education		
Description	2004–05	2017–18
Overall wage inequality	0.445	0.532
Within-group inequality	0.215	0.256
Contribution (per cent)	48.38	48.12
Between-group inequality	0.230	0.276
Contribution (per cent)	51.62	51.87

Table 8.16 Continued

Group specification 3: Location, Gender, Labour Status, and Social Group

Description	2004–05	2017–18
Overall wage inequality	0.445	0.498
Within-group inequality	0.277	0.289
Contribution (per cent)	62.25	58.03
Between-group inequality	0.168	0.209
Contribution (per cent)	37.75	41.96

Group specification 4: Location, Gender, Labour Status, Social Group, and Educational Levels

Description	2004–05	2017–18
Overall wage inequality	0.445	0.540
Within-group inequality	0.208	0.238
Contribution (per cent)	46.78	44.00
Between-group inequality	0.237	0.302
Contribution (per cent)	53.22	55.92

Source: 2004–05 estimates from Papola and Kannan (2017), 2017–18 estimates is authors' calculation based on PLFS 2017–18 data.

per cent to 55 per cent in 2017–18. Simultaneously, the between-group inequality contribution to the overall wage inequality is seen increasing between 2004–05 and 2017–18. Therefore, access to education becomes the crucial first factor to reduce wage inequality. The second one, as noted earlier, is access to quality employment. The third factor which influences wage discrimination is caste identity. The caste identity may also indirectly influence access to education due to discrimination. The results imply that caste identity may influence wage inequality directly by wage discrimination and indirectly through limiting access to education.

8.5 Conclusion

In this chapter, we have examined various aspects of wage inequality across caste groups for regular salaried workers. This includes inequality in average wage rate between the SC and higher castes wages rates by educational level, industry, and occupation groups, and in public and private sectors. The wage inequality is measured by using Gary Fields' decomposition ratio and Theil index. The Gary Fields Decomposition estimates the inequalities at lower, middle, and top wage-earning distribution and also locates the factors for within-group inequality. The Theil index measures the 'within-group inequality and between-group inequality' and their determinants.

There are clear disparities in average daily wage earning between the SC and higher castes when the wage inequality is measured by wage ratio of the SC to higher castes regular salaried workers. The wages of SC regular salaried workers are found to be lower than that of higher castes by almost 30 per cent in 2017–18. While this is the status at all levels, the caste differences between the SC and higher castes are more pronounced in urban areas as compared to rural areas. The wage gaps also differ between the SC and higher castes by educational level. The workers with a high level of education fetch higher wages which indicate a positive association between wage level and education level. Caste-based wage differentials in the regular labour market are the highest at diploma and graduate and above levels which indicate the significance of higher and professional education in wage earning.

We have also examined the disparities in wages across industrial and occupation groups. The average wage earnings of SC and OBC workers are lower than those of higher castes workers irrespective of industrial groups. Industry-wise there are variations in wages for regular salaried workers in the rural labour market, the SC to higher castes wage differential is the highest in manufacturing (other than agro-based industries) followed by public administration and other services. In the urban labour market, the SC to higher castes wage differentials is the highest in agriculture, forestry, and fisheries followed by mining and quarrying, electricity, water supply-related industries, financial, and business and professional services. Similarly, in case of occupational groups in the regular labour market, the average daily earnings of the SC and OBC workers are lower than higher castes workers in almost all occupations. The wage gap between the SC and higher castes is less in clerical, elementary, and production occupations. This gives clear evidence that the wage gap is low where the SC are segregated into low-paid occupations.

The wage earning also varies between public and private sectors. It emerged that regular salaried workers in the public sector earn more as compared to their private sector counterparts. The caste-based wage differentials exist in both public and private sectors. The wage gap between the SC and higher castes is more in the private sector as compared to the public sector. In urban areas, the caste-based wage differentials are more pronounced in the private sector than in the rural public sector, whereas the reverse is the case in rural areas. While this is the pattern at overall levels, the wage differentials (gap/ratio) between the SC and higher castes in the public sector is higher at the bottom percentiles, i.e. below 50th percentile than at the top percentiles of wage distribution; whereas in the private sector, wage differentials between the SC and higher castes are higher at the top percentiles, i.e. above 50th percentile than at the bottom percentiles of wage distribution. Within the private and public sectors, the wage gap between the SC and higher castes is higher for informal workers than formal workers.

We have also measured wage inequality through two measures, i.e. Gary Fields' decomposition method and Theil Index. Gary Fields' decomposition method captures wage inequality through wage dispersion ratios between the top, middle, and bottom percentiles and its determinants. The results suggest that wage inequality between the SC and higher castes persist among the regular salaried workers in the top half of the wage distribution. Education turns out to be the most dominant factor which contributes to wage inequality for all social groups. Moreover, factors like public employment, age, and occupation are the next important contributors to wage inequality. Gender plays a significant role in wage inequality. The relative share of these factors is more or less similar for all caste groups. The Theil index is used to get a more disaggregated analysis on wage inequality between the SC and higher castes in labour market. The results based on the Theil index indicate that education and caste identity matter considerably in intercaste inequality in wage earning.

Significant important findings of the analysis are the visible gap in wage earning between the SC and higher castes. Whether we take rural or urban areas, private or public sector, formal or informal workers and occupation there is a clear gap in wage earning between the SC and higher castes. Among many other factors, education, quality of employment and caste identity are the ubiquitous features of caste inequality in wage earning. In the next chapter we will examine as to what extent the wage gap between the SC and higher castes regular salaried workers is due to endowment factors like education, quality of employment and others; and to what extent it is due to caste discrimination in wage earning.

9

Wage and Occupational Discrimination against Untouchables

9.1 Introduction

The discussion in the previous chapter brought out caste inequalities in wage earnings for the recent year. This analysis revealed significant gaps in wage earning between the Scheduled Castes (SC) and higher castes regular salaried workers. The wages of SC regular salaried workers are found to be lower than that of higher castes by almost 30 per cent in 2017–18. The caste-based wage differentials exist both in public and private sectors, but the wage gap between the SC and higher castes is particularly high in the private sector as compared to the public sector. The caste-based wage differentials are more pronounced in the private sector than in the public sector. While this is the pattern at overall levels, the wage differentials (gap/ratio) between the SC and higher castes in the public sector is higher at the lower percentiles, i.e. below 50th percentile, than at the top percentiles of wage distribution. On the other hand, in the private sector wage differentials between the SC and higher castes are higher at the upper percentiles, i.e. above 50th percentile, than at the bottom percentiles of wage distribution. Higher education is found to be an important factor in wage inequality for all caste groups. Employment in the public sector, age and occupation are the next important contributors to wage inequality. Gender too plays a significant role in wage inequality. The Theil index decomposition results indicate that in addition to education and quality of employment, caste identity of a group also matters in inequality in wage earning between the SC and higher castes. This analysis, thus, makes two important points. First, it indicates that there is significant wage inequality between the SC and higher castes. Second, the inequality in wages between the SC and higher castes is partly due to a

Scheduled Castes in the Indian Labour Market. Sukhadeo Thorat, S. Madheswaran, and B. P. Vani,
Oxford University Press. © Sukhadeo Thorat, S. Madheswaran, and B. P. Vani 2023.
DOI: 10.1093/oso/9780198872252.003.0009

number of endowment factors. An equally important finding is about the influence of caste identity in wage inequality between the SC and higher castes. This raises an important question, i.e. to what extent the wage gap between the SC and higher castes is due to endowment factors like education and quality of employment, and to what extent it is due to caste identity of the SC and higher castes.

In this background, we attempt to estimate the relative impact of the endowment factors and caste discrimination in wage earning differences between the SC and higher castes. The wage discrimination is measured using the 'decomposition technique' to partition the observed wage gap between an 'endowment' component and a 'coefficient' component. The latter is derived as an unexplained residual and is termed the 'discrimination coefficient'. As mentioned in the methodology section, this method was first developed by Blinder (1973) and Oaxaca (1973) and later extended to incorporate selectivity bias (Reimer 1983 and 1985) and to overcome the index number problem (Cotton 1988; Neumark 1988; Oaxaca and Ransom 1994). Since the mid 1990s, newer decomposition methods have gone beyond the focus on single summary measures (Cotton and Neumark 1988; Brown et al. 1980). Studies now seek to go beyond the mean and answer questions like—'What happened?' 'Where?'—in the distribution rather than decomposing only differences at the means (Machado and Mata 2005). Additionally, since policies could have different effects at different parts of the wage distribution, this nuanced understanding is needed to assess their impact on wage inequalities. We also used the expanded decomposition method which incorporates the occupational distribution into the earnings estimation. One advantage of using this method is that job/occupational discrimination (differential access to certain occupational positions) and wage discrimination (differential earnings within the same job) can be estimated simultaneously.

9.2 Determinants of Wages

Before we estimate the extent of caste discrimination in the wage gap between the SC and higher castes, we will first identify the determinants of wage earning. Table 9.1 shows the estimates of the wage equations for the SC and higher castes regular salaried workers in the labour market.

Table 9.1 Estimates of augmented earnings equation for higher castes and SC in regular labour market, 2017–18

Variables	Hindu Higher Castes		Hindu SC	
	Coefficient	t-statistic	Coefficient	t-statistic
Age	0.03	7.19	0.04	7.82
Age square	−0.0003	−4.53	−0.0004	−5.16
Primary	0.22	5.72	0.12	3.40
Middle	0.26	8.41	0.29	10.07
Secondary	0.44	13.82	0.34	11.38
Higher secondary	0.56	17.15	0.45	14.34
Diploma	0.88	19.97	0.72	15.59
Graduate and above	1.01	32.91	0.81	25.31
Male	0.44	23.01	0.59	25.27
Married	0.12	6.90	0.02	0.69
Public	0.43	26.70	0.50	24.10
South	0.01	0.72	−0.01	−0.38
East	−0.18	−10.74	−0.12	−5.06
West	0.07	4.50	−0.02	−0.67
Permanent	0.28	14.86	0.27	10.12
Constant	3.02	34.17	2.66	26.66
R-squared	0.41		0.42	
Number of observations	9277		5806	

Note: Dependent variable is the natural logarithm of real daily wage.

Source: Authors' calculation based on PLFS 2017–18 data.

The natural logarithm of real daily wage rate is used as the dependent variable, and age, level of education, gender, marital status, sector, nature of employment, and regions are taken as explanatory variables. The age variable is taken as the proxy for work experience. We find that in the regular labour market both age and education variables are statistically significant. The sign of the coefficients of the age variable is positive and age square is negative. This implies that there is an increment in earnings with age and it starts declining after the retirement age. As expected, for both the SC and higher castes the coefficient is positive. The value of education coefficient is higher for higher castes than SC and the coefficient increases for all levels of education, except for diploma. Gender variable too is found to be significant for both the SC and higher castes, but the value of the male dummy coefficient is higher for the SC than higher castes. This implies that the gender wage gap is higher among the SC than among higher castes. Besides, marriage has a positive and significant effect on earnings of higher castes but not for SC. The coefficient of public sector dummy is positive and significant for both SC and higher castes; the value of the coefficient of public sector dummy is higher for SC than higher castes. This implies that SC regular salaried workers are relatively in a better position in the public sector presumably due to the positive impact of reservation in public sector jobs. Workers who are in permanent job earn more than those employed on contract irrespective of caste groups. Moreover, being in the western region positively affects the earnings of the SC. On the other hand, being in the eastern region negatively affects the earnings of higher castes; while being in the western region positively affects the earnings of higher castes. The wage determinants of workers in public and private sectors are found to be almost similar to the total workers in the regular labour market (Table 9.2). However, the impact on wage earning differs in case of education. While for the public sector the impact is generally high for all levels of education for the SC, it is low for the SC in private sector as compared to higher castes.

These results have important policy implications. It implies that for improvement in wage earning of the SC workers, an improvement in their work experience and in the level and quality of education, particularly higher education, is necessary. The return on higher education for the SC is low in the private sector. Therefore, there is a need to enhance the quality of education of the SC by the private sector through its affirmative action programme for enhancement of employability. Marriage also makes a difference in the earnings. The positive impact of marriage subsumed the impact of education of women. Therefore, the education of women is important for employment. This asks for improvement in the level of education of the SC women. Insofar as the permanent jobs yield a high return, more employment in permanent jobs, rather than temporary jobs, is necessary to improve wage earnings. Given the low earning of the SC workers in the private sector, add-on training would enable them to get better jobs in the private sector. In turn, the private sector should provide training before and/or after the entry into a job through its affirmative action programme for the SC. These are useful

Table 9.2 Estimates of augmented earnings equation for higher castes and SC in public and private sectors of regular urban labour market, 2017–18

	Public Sector				Private Sector			
	Hindu Higher Castes		Hindu SC		Hindu Higher Castes		Hindu SC	
Variables	Coefficient	t-statistic	Coefficient	t-statistic	Coefficient	t-statistic	Coefficient	t-statistic
Age	0.05	4.56	0.04	2.81	0.04	6.87	0.06	7.24
Age square	-0.0003	-2.64	-0.0002	-1.25	-0.0004	-5.86	-0.0007	-6.39
Primary	0.11	1.09	0.16	2.02	0.13	3.10	0.10	2.17
Middle	0.23	2.78	0.22	3.12	0.20	5.20	0.21	5.04
Secondary	0.44	5.95	0.55	8.19	0.35	9.46	0.32	6.88
Higher secondary	0.54	7.27	0.65	9.30	0.50	12.57	0.46	8.79
Diploma	0.74	9.12	0.97	10.88	0.89	16.40	0.75	8.59
Graduation and above	0.85	12.19	0.88	14.88	1.17	35.83	0.51	18.34
Male	0.16	6.04	0.25	5.30	0.47	19.29	0.55	16.62
Married	0.09	2.44	0.00	-0.01	0.15	6.10	0.02	0.51
Permanent	0.82	15.91	0.72	12.02	0.20	9.96	0.15	5.43
South	-0.07	-2.33	-0.14	-3.02	0.08	2.94	0.15	4.51
East	-0.07	-2.53	-0.03	-0.67	-0.14	-5.04	-0.07	-1.70
West	-0.10	-3.07	-0.05	-0.89	0.20	8.84	0.11	2.85
Constant	2.79	13.30	2.74	9.65	2.72	24.96	2.30	15.57
R-squared	0.31		0.47		0.40		0.37	
Number of observations	3,035		1,130		5,367		1,840	

Note: Dependent variable is the natural logarithm of real daily wage.

Source: Authors' calculation based on PLFS 2017–18 data.

policy implications which emerged from the results on determinants of wage earnings of the SC.

9.3 Wage Discrimination: Blinder-Oaxaca Decomposition Results

We will now use the alternative decomposition methods to decompose the wage gap between the SC and higher castes of regular salaried workers into endowment effect and discrimination effect. The relative impact of endowment and discrimination factors is examined for more than one dimension of the SC and higher castes. We have looked at it in three different ways. First, the extent of wage discrimination is analysed at the aggregate level, and then we see the difference in the level of wage discrimination for the individual variable and also for quintile, i.e. lower and upper quintiles of wage distribution. The variation in the level of discrimination between the youth and the old persons for the SC and higher castes is also studied. Second, we repeat this exercise for the private and public sectors to identify the differences between the two. Finally, we examine the occupational discrimination and its linkages with wage discrimination.

We have employed Blinder-Oaxaca decomposition method to decompose the wage gap between the SC and higher castes workers in the regular labour market into endowment and discrimination components. The results show that the wage gap between the SC and higher castes is due to both endowment difference and caste discrimination (Table 9.3). However, the contribution of endowment difference to the raw wage gap between the SC and higher castes workers is larger than that of discrimination. In 2004–05, the endowment factors account for 68 per cent and discrimination accounts for 32 per cent. In 2017–18, the endowment factors account for 54.5 per cent and discrimination accounts for 45.5 per cent. This result is consistent with the Madheswaran and Attewell (2007) study. It is important to note that, in the regular labour market, the raw wage gap has declined from 2005 to 2018 whereas discrimination coefficient has increased (from 32 per cent to 45.5 per cent). It appears (from the above results on determinants) that a relatively higher share of endowment factors, to explain wage gap between the SC and the higher castes, may be due to low access to education which is caused by

Table 9.3 Results of Blinder-Oaxaca decomposition on higher castes and SC in regular labour market, 2017–18 (in percentage)

	2004–05	2017–18
Amount attributable	16.70	−2.0
- due to endowments (E)	27.70	18.4
- due to coefficients (C)	−10.90	−20.5
Shift coefficient (U)	23.90	35.9
Raw differential (R) {E + C + U}	40.70	33.8
Adjusted differential (D) {C + U}	13.00	15.4
Endowments as per cent to total (E/R)	**68.00**	**54.5**
Discrimination as per cent to total (D/R)	**32.00**	**45.5**

Note: A positive number indicates advantage to higher castes.

A negative number indicates advantage to SC.

Source: Authors' calculation based on NSS 61st round and PLFS 2017–18 data.

denial of property rights and right to education to the SC in the past for a long period of time. The consequences of the denial of the right to property in the past result in low ownership of capital assets in the present. The denial of the right to education in the past also results in low education attainment in the present. Poor access to property in the present, in turn, restrains the capacity of the SC youth to access higher education in the present. Thus, past legacy continues to affect the access to property— the income-earning assets and education in the present. This in a way explains the greater impact of endowment factors, like higher education, on the wage gap between the SC and higher castes.

9.4 Relative Contribution of Each Variable

Table 9.4 depicts the relative contribution of each of the variables to the wage gap between the SC and higher castes workers in the regular labour market. It also shows the relative contribution of variables separately to endowment difference and discrimination in the labour market. A positive entry indicates an advantage for the higher castes (and hence a positive contribution to the overall differentials) and a negative entry indicates an advantage for the SC.

Table 9.4 Relative contribution of specific variables to decomposition in regular labour market among the higher castes and SC (Blinder-Oaxaca decomposition method), 2017–18

	Explained Difference (E)	Unexplained Difference (D)	Total Difference (TD)	%E	%D	%TD
Age	0.02	−0.26	−0.24	4.7	−59.6	−54.9
Primary	−0.01	0.00	−0.01	−1.9	0.6	−1.3
Middle	−0.02	0.00	−0.01	−3.8	0.8	−3.0
Secondary	−0.00	0.00	0.00	−0.3	0.6	0.3
Higher secondary	0.00	0.00	0.01	1.1	0.3	1.3
Diploma	0.01	−0.00	0.01	1.4	−0.1	1.4
Graduation and above	0.26	0.04	0.29	68.3	18.1	66.4
Male dummy	0.01	−0.08	−0.07	3.3	−19.4	−16.0
Married	0.00	0.08	0.09	0.8	19.1	19.9
Public sector dummy	−0.01	−0.04	−0.05	−3.1	−9.25	−10.7
Permanent dummy	0.01	0.01	0.02	2.8	1.3	4.1
Region	0.01	−0.01	0.00	1.2	−1.2	0.0
Constant	-	0.41	0.41	-	92.6	92.6
Subtotal	0.29	0.15	0.44	54.5	45.5	100

Note 1: A positive number indicates advantage to higher castes.
A negative number indicates advantage to Scheduled Castes.
Source: Authors' calculation based on PLFS 2017–18 data.

From the total difference it is observed that age, education—from primary to middle—employment in the public sector and gender variables favour the improvement in the wage earning of the SC. However, although these factors matter in wage earning of the SC, low attainment in higher education—graduation and above—less work experience and low education of the SC women restrict to derive higher benefits in wage earning from these endowment factors. The higher castes, on the other hand, have an advantage in education, i.e. secondary and above, marital status, and nature of employment. Therefore, these factors improve their wage earning more as compared to the SC who lag in these endowment factors. This means that a substantial portion of the overall

earnings advantage to higher castes is due to their greater work experience, higher education (i.e. graduation and above), education of women
and type of employment, while deficiency in these factors among the SC
becomes the source of their disadvantage to bring higher wage earning.
In the case of the SC, the discrimination in access to education by males
and females, low work experience and quality employment also reduce
wage earning. Besides, the results show that much of the wage disparity
comes through the constant term which is in favour of higher castes. The
statewise picture also shows that the endowment difference is high in
many states (Table 9.5).

Table 9.5 Statewise results of Blinder-Oaxaca decomposition among higher
castes and SC in regular labour market, 2017–18

States	2004–05		2017–18	
	Endowment Difference (%)	Discrimination (%)	Endowment Difference (%)	Discrimination (%)
Jammu and Kashmir	76.9	23.1	89.0	11.0
Himachal Pradesh	50.0	50.0	50.4	49.6
Punjab	77.9	22.1	18.5	81.5
Haryana	63.5	36.5	40.4	59.6
Rajasthan	65.4	34.6	73.0	27.0
Uttar Pradesh	63.5	36.5	73.3	26.7
Bihar	67.9	32.1	80.0	20.0
Tripura	83.0	17.0	85.0	15.0
Assam	80.1	19.9	57.5	42.5
West Bengal	74.3	25.7	52.5	47.5
Odisha	68.3	31.7	58.5	41.5
Madhya Pradesh	67.7	32.3	62.5	37.5
Gujarat	69.3	30.7	60.0	40.0
Maharashtra	60.5	39.5	37.9	62.1
Andhra Pradesh	73.8	26.2	28.9	71.1
Karnataka	83.2	16.8	45.4	54.6
Kerala	80.2	19.8	68.0	32.0
Tamil Nadu	80.4	19.6	52.6	47.4
India	68.0	32.0	54.48	45.52

Source: Author's calculation based on NSS 61st round and PLFS 2017–18 data.

9.5 Reimer, Cotton, Neumark, Oaxaca, and Ransom Decomposition Results

The decomposition of the wage gap between the SC and higher castes has also been pursued using Reimer (1983 and 1985), Cotton (1988), Neumark (1988), and Oaxaca and Ransom (1994) approaches to obtain the least objectionable results. For this, we have calculated standard errors of each estimate. It is observed that the Oaxaca and Ransom method has the smallest standard error and should probably be preferred. When this method is used, the discrimination coefficient is somewhat smaller in magnitude but there is still substantial evidence of discrimination against the SC in the labour market. The results obtained using different approaches of decomposition method are given in Tables 9.6 and 9.7.

Using the Oaxaca and Ransom decomposition method, we find that in the regular labour market the human capital difference between the SC and higher castes contributes much to the earning differential between

Table 9.6 Reimer-Cotton-Neumark-Oaxaca and Ransom approaches among higher castes and SC in regular urban labour market, 2004–05

Components	Reimer/ Cotton (w = 0.5)	Neumark/ Oaxaca and Ransom (w = omega)	Oaxaca-Blinder Using Higher Castes means as weight (w = 1)	Oaxaca-Blinder Using SC means as weight (w = 0)
Raw wage differential	0.44 (0.0196)			
Endowment difference (per cent)	60.5 (0.0152)	67.1 (0.0153)	65.3 (0.0154)	55.7 (0.0167)
Discrimination (per cent)	39.5 (0.0143)	32.9 (0.0125)	34.7 (0.0146)	44.3 (0.0158)
Overpayment to higher castes (per cent)	22.1 (0.0079)	8.6 (0.0033)	–	–
Underpayment to SC (per cent)	17.4 (0.0073)	24.3 (0.0093)	–	–

Note: (1) Unexplained component = overpayment component + underpayment component

(2) Figures in parentheses indicate standard errors.

Source: Authors' calculation based on NSS 61st round data.

Table 9.7 Reimer-Cotton-Neumark-Oaxaca and Ransom approaches among higher castes and SC in regular labour market, 2017–18

Components	Reimer/ Cotton (w = 0.5)	Neumark/ Oaxaca and Ransom (w = omega)	Oaxaca-Blinder Using Higher Castes Means as Weight (w = 1)	Oaxaca-Blinder Using SC means as weight (w ¬ 0)
Raw wage differential	0.34 (0.0130)			
Endowment difference (per cent)	49.83 (0.0091)	57.24 (0.0092)	54.48 (0.0096)	45.18 (0.0102)
Discrimination (per cent)	50.17 (0.0107)	42.76 (0.0094)	45.52 (0.0111)	54.82 (0.0116)
Overpayment to higher castes (per cent)	27.41 (0.0058)	16.46 (0.0037)	-	-
Underpayment to SC (per cent)	22.76 (0.0055)	26.30 (0.0059)	-	-

Note: (1) Unexplained component = overpayment component + underpayment component

(2) Figures in parentheses indicate standard errors.

Source: Computed from unit-level data of NSSO, (2017–-18) Round.

them. In 2004–05, the SC and higher castes wage difference due to endowment is 67.1 per cent (Table 9.6) (the corresponding figure is 57.24 per cent in 2017–18). Alternatively, the contribution of discrimination to raw wage differentials between the SC and higher castes is 32.9 per cent in 2004–05 and 42.76 per cent in 2017–18. Thus, between 2004–05 and 2017–18 the share of discrimination component has increased with a corresponding decline in the share of endowment factors. Thus, during this period discrimination in wage earning has been on the rise.

We have further decomposed the discrimination component into overpayment to higher castes and underpayment to the SC in the regular salaried labour market. We find that the overpayment or treatment advantage to the higher castes (benefit of being higher castes in the labour market) is 8.6 per cent in 2004–05 and 16.46 per cent in 2017–18. The higher castes' advantage has increased between 2004–05 and 2017–18. This is the difference between the current wages of the higher castes and what they would otherwise receive in the absence of discrimination. It also reflects nepotism towards the higher castes and the advantage of being higher castes. On the other hand, the underpayment or treatment disadvantage to the SC (cost of being SC in the labour market) is 24.3 per cent in 2004–05 and 26.30 per cent in 2017–18.

This is the difference in the current wages of the SC and the wage they would otherwise receive in the absence of discrimination. The disadvantage of the SC has marginally increased. This form of decomposition procedure yields more accurate estimates of the wage differential because it models the true state of differential treatment by estimating the 'cost' to the group discriminated against as well as the 'benefits' accruing to the advantaged group. Overall, we find that the cost of being SC in the labour market is very high. They are hugely underpaid in the labour market. We also find that in the regular urban labour market, the contribution of endowment difference to the raw wage gap between the SC and others is declining over the years from 2004–05 to 2017–18. But at the same time, the share of discrimination to wage differences between the SC and higher castes has increased. During the same period, the wage discrimination has risen. This result revealed the caste advantage of being higher castes and caste disadvantage or cost of being SC in wage earning. The advantage to the higher castes comes at the cost of the disadvantage to the SC.

9.6 Decomposition by Quantiles

So far, we have analysed the wage gap between the SC and higher castes using mean-based decomposition methods. Due to limitation of the mean-based analysis, as discussed in the methodology section, we have used quantile regression decomposition method (Machada and Mata 2005) to decompose the caste-based wage gap at different quintiles of the wage distribution of regular urban workers. From Table 9.8 and Figure 9.1, it is evident that in the regular labour market the extent of caste-based wage gap as well as discrimination coefficients vary significantly across the quintiles of wage distribution. Generally, the wage gap attributable to discrimination is higher at top quintiles than at the bottom quintiles of the wage distribution. The wage gap attributable to discrimination at top quintiles has also increased over the years from 2004–05 to 2017–18. For instance, in 2017–18, the discrimination coefficient has increased from 53.86 per cent in 10th quantile to 56.80 per cent in 25th quantile,

Table 9.8 Decomposition results across quantiles in regular labour market among higher castes and SC, 2004–05 and 2017–18

Components	10th	25th	50th	75th	90th	OLS
2004–05						
Raw wage differentials	0.45	0.44	0.46	0.36	0.32	0.41
Characteristics (endowment difference)	0.29 (65.92)	0.26 (58.91)	0.25 (54.48)	0.22 (61.5)	0.19 (60.46)	0.28 (67.98)
Coefficients (discrimination)	0.15 (34.08)	0.18 (41.09)	0.21 (45.52)	0.14 (38.4)	0.13 (39.54)	0.13 (32.02)
2017–18						
Raw wage differentials	0.33	0.30	0.35	0.39	0.32	0.34
Characteristics (endowment difference)	0.15 (46.14)	0.13 (43.20)	0.13 (38.09)	0.14 (36.8)	0.14 (42.86)	0.18 (54.48)
Coefficients (discrimination)	0.18 (53.86)	0.17 (56.80)	0.22 (61.91)	0.24 (63.1)	0.18 (57.14)	0.15 (45.52)

Note: Figures in parentheses indicate percentage share.

Source: Authors' calculation based on NSS 61st round and PLFS 2017–18 data.

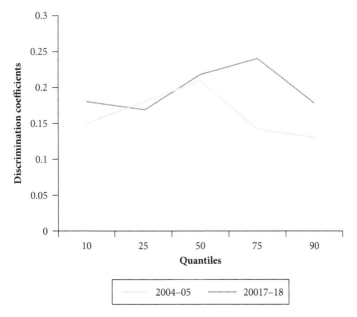

Fig. 9.1 Quantilewise discrimination coefficients in regular labour market among higher castes and SC, 2004–05 and 2017–18

Source: Authors' calculation based on NSS 61st round and PLFS 2017–18 data

62 per cent in 50th quantile, and 63.17 per cent in 75th. It has then declined marginally to 57 per cent in the 90th quantile (which is higher than both 10th and 25th quantiles). We may recall that in the analysis on the wage gap in the preceding chapter we found that the wage gap between the SC and higher castes is greater in the upper quantile as compared to the lower quantile in the private sector. This probably shows the association between the high wage gap at the upper quantile and high discrimination in wage at the upper quantile.

9.7   Wage Differential by Younger and Older Cohorts

We have so far seen the wage differences due to endowment and discrimination at an overall level and by quantile irrespective of the age of the workers. Since young cohorts are the ones who look for jobs in the early stage of their career, we look at the differences by age, namely young cohorts, i.e. population aged between 18–40 years, and not so young or middle-aged cohorts, i.e. population aged between 41–65 years. We have used the Oaxaca-Blinder decomposition method to decompose the wage gap between the SC and higher castes workers into endowment component and discrimination component in the regular labour market for young and the middle-aged workers (Table 9.9). Do young SC face more or less discrimination than middle-aged SC persons? We find that for both young and middle-aged cohorts the contribution of endowment difference to wage gap between the SC and higher castes workers is larger than discrimination. However, there is a difference in the relative contribution of endowment factors and discrimination in the wage gaps in 2004–05 and 2017–18. In 2017–18, the endowment accounts for about 61 per cent in wage difference for young cohort and 71 per cent for middle-aged cohort which mean the endowment contributes more in wage difference in case of middle-aged SC workers. This indicates the deficiencies in endowment, like education and skill, among the middle-aged SC workers as compared to young SC workers. In other words, the young SC workers are better endowed than the middle-aged workers from their castes. However, the young SC workers suffer more from wage discrimination

Table 9.9   Results of Blinder-Oaxaca decomposition among young and old cohorts of regular workers between SC and higher castes for 1983, 1994, 2004, and 2018

Components	1983	1994	2005	2018
Young Cohort: 18–40 Years				
Raw wage differentials	0.27	0.21	0.42	0.40
Explained (endowment)	0.24	0.13	0.23	0.24
Unexplained (discrimination)	0.03	0.08	0.19	0.16
Endowment difference (per cent)	90.21	61.17	53.96	60.99
Discrimination (per cent)	9.79	38.83	46.04	39.01
Old Cohort: 41–65 Years				
Raw wage differentials	0.37	0.32	0.42	0.42
Explained (endowment)	0.37	0.27	0.36	0.30
Unexplained (discrimination)	0.003	0.05	0.06	0.12
Endowment difference (per cent)	99.17	83.61	85.34	71.12
Discrimination (per cent)	0.83	16.39	14.66	28.88

Source: Authors' calculation based on different rounds of NSS data.

than the middle-aged SC workers. In 2017–18, in the case of young SC workers, about 39 per cent of wage differences between young SC and higher castes workers are contributed by discrimination coefficient, while the share of discrimination coefficient for middle-aged SC workers is 29 per cent (this finding is consistent with Arabsheibani et al. 2012). The similar difference between the young and middle-aged SC workers are observed in 2004–05. This indicates that the young SC workers face greater discrimination in wages than middle-aged SC workers. There is an equally interesting feature of the change between 2004–05 and 2017–18. The positive thing is that the share of discrimination coefficient in the case of young SC workers has been reduced between 2004–05 and 2017–18. Conversely, it means that the share of endowment coefficient has increased during the same period. This also means that the SC youth have been facing difficulties in access to higher education, particularly professional education in the 2010s. This may be due to less access to SC youth in private professional higher education institutions which are less affordable to them given the high fee structure in self-financing professional education institutions. The self-financed private education has expanded at a rapid pace in the 2000s. The share of private state/central universities in 2017–18 is close to 40 per cent and that of colleges/institutions is 64 per cent.

We have also estimated the extent of caste-based wage gap as well as discrimination across the quantiles for young and the middle-aged regular workers (Table 9.10). For the young cohort, the wage gaps, attributable to discrimination, is higher at the upper wage quantiles as compared to bottom wage quantiles. This is reflected in the increase in discrimination coefficient from 10th to 90th quantile. For instance, in 2017–18 the discrimination coefficient increased from 36.6 per cent for 10th quantile to 39.7 per cent for 25th quantile, 47 per cent for 50th quantile, 58.7 per cent for 75th quantile, and 65 per cent for 90th quantile. This shows a systematic increase in wage discrimination for the young SC cohort along the quantile scale. The discrimination coefficient is as high as 65 per cent in 90th quantile of wage. In the case of middle-aged SC workers, the relationship between the discrimination coefficient and quantile scale is less systematic, although the discrimination coefficient for middle-aged group is less than young SC workers.

Another feature is that during 2004–05 to 2017–18, the contribution of discrimination to the wage gap (between SC and higher castes) has increased over the years for upper wage quantiles, such as 75th and 90th quantiles. Using Arulampalam et al. (2007) criteria, we find that there exists a 'glass ceiling effect' particularly for workers who belong to young SC cohorts as the 90th percentile wage gap is higher than the estimated wage gaps in other parts of the wage distribution. The glass ceiling effect primarily reflects the fact that the SC and higher castes have different jobs or there exists occupational segregation in the labour market.

These results have policy implications which indicate that efforts are necessary to address the high level of discrimination faced by the SC youth, particularly at the upper end of the wage distribution. Further, given the rise in the share of endowments difference (in wage difference between the SC and higher castes) for SC youth between 2004–05 and 2017–18, there is also a need for policy to enhance endowments through better access to professional education to SC youth which has been reduced due to unaffordable privatization of professional education in the country.

Table 9.10 Decomposition results across quantiles among young and old cohorts of regular workers between SC and higher castes, 2004–05 and 2017–18

Components	2004–05						2017–18					
	10th	25th	50th	75th	90th	OLS	10th	25th	50th	75th	90th	OLS
					Young Cohort: 18–40 Years							
Raw wage differentials	0.41	0.38	0.42	0.46	0.44	0.42	0.31	0.31	0.39	0.49	0.49	0.40
Characteristics effect (endowment difference)	0.23 (56.9)	0.20 (53.3)	0.20 (47.9)	0.21 (46.4)	0.19 (44.3)	0.23 (54.0)	0.20 (63.4)	0.19 (60.3)	0.21 (52.6)	0.20 (41.3)	0.17 (35.1)	0.24 (61.0)
Coefficients (discrimination)	0.18 (43.1)	0.18 (46.7)	0.22 (52.1)	0.24 (53.6)	0.24 (55.7)	0.19 (46.0)	0.12 (36.6)	0.13 (39.7)	0.18 (47.4)	0.29 (58.7)	0.32 (64.9)	0.16 (39.0)
					Old Cohort: 41–65 Years							
Raw wage differentials	0.48	0.53	0.42	0.37	0.32	0.42	0.46	0.53	0.46	0.34	0.26	0.42
Characteristics effect (endowment difference)	0.37 (77.3)	0.34 (63.9)	0.28 (67.3)	0.23 (62.3)	0.14 (41.8)	0.36 (85.3)	0.30 (65.0)	0.27 (51.4)	0.24 (52.4)	0.18 (51.6)	0.16 (59.6)	0.30 (71.1)
Coefficients (discrimination)	0.11 (22.7)	0.19 (36.1)	0.14 (32.7)	0.14 (37.7)	0.19 (58.2)	0.06 (14.7)	0.16 (35.0)	0.26 (48.6)	0.22 (47.6)	0.17 (48.4)	0.11 (40.4)	0.12 (28.9)

Note: The percentage share of raw wage differentials is given in parenthesis.

Source: Authors' calculation based on NSS 61st round and PLFS 2017–18 data.

9.8 Evidence of Caste Discrimination in the Public and Private Sectors

So far we have examined the situation at the aggregate level combining the private and public sectors, we will now look at the difference between the workers in the public and private sectors. We have discussed earlier that caste-based wage gap is high in the private sector than in the public sector. Using Oaxaca-Blinder decomposition method, it is evident that wage gap, attributed to discrimination against the SC, is higher in the private sector than in the public sector (Table 9.11). In 2004–05, about 31.50 per cent wage gap is due to caste discrimination and the rest 68.5 per cent is due to endowment differences between the SC and higher castes workers. In 2017–18, the discrimination and endowment account for about 48.50 per cent and 51.5 per cent of the wage gap between the SC and higher castes in the private sector respectively. Thus, not only the discrimination coefficient is high for the SC in the private sector but it has also increased. Between 2004–05 and 2017–18, there has been an increase in the discrimination component and a corresponding decline in the endowment component. Unlike the private sector, the extent of wage discrimination of the SC has declined in the public sector. In 2004–05, the endowment factor accounts for about 73 per cent and caste discrimination 27 per cent in the public sector. In 2004–05, the share of endowment has increased to 79 per cent with a corresponding decline in the share of discrimination to 21 per cent. It is a good sign that discrimination in wages in the public

Table 9.11 Blinder-Oaxaca decomposition results for regular labour market in public and private sectors among higher castes and SC, 2004–05 and 2017–18

Components	2004–05		2017–18	
	Public Sector	Private Sector	Public Sector	Private Sector
Raw wage differentials	0.34	0.49	0.30	0.37
Endowment difference (per cent)	72.90	68.50	79.1	51.5
Discrimination (per cent)	27.10	31.50	20.9	48.5

Source: Authors' calculation based on NSS 61st round and PLFS 2017–18 data.

sector is not only low but it has also declined. However, this also indicates that the public sector which should be completely free from discrimination is not altogether free from wage discrimination, and this is a matter of concern. But the greater concern is the evidence of the presence of high wage discrimination in the private sector although the private sector denies such discrimination. Claims made by the private sector that it only respects merit and discrimination does not figure in its decision-making about wage determination are not borne out by empirical facts. We have also seen in the earlier chapter that the discrimination in the probability of access to employment is much higher in the private sector as compared to the public sector. Employment discrimination accounts for about 53.15 per cent of the differences in the probability to access jobs in the private sector which is much higher as compared to 13.99 per cent differences in the public sector. Thus, the SC regular salaried workers suffer high employment and wage discrimination in the private sector as compared to the public sector.

In brief, we find that discrimination in wages against the SC is higher in the private sector as compared to the public sector. The magnitude of wage discrimination in the public sector has declined between 2004–05 and 2017–18, while it has increased in the private sector. It must be mentioned that quite a significant part of the difference in wage earning between the SC and higher castes is due to endowment factors, such as education, skills, education of women and experience of wage workers. The results indicate that policy measures are needed on both fronts, i.e. measures to enhance the endowment to improve the capabilities of the SC workers and also to reduce wage discrimination.

9.8.1 Wage Overpayment and Underpayment in Public and Private Sectors

From the analysis it is evident that human capital difference between the SC and higher castes contributes much to the earning differential between them. In 2017–18, the wage differences between the SC and higher castes due to endowment factors (education and skill) are 79 per cent in the public sector and 51.50 per cent in the private sector. In turn, the contribution of discrimination to raw wage differentials between the SC and higher castes is 27 per cent in the public sector and 48.50 per cent in the private sector. In this scenario, we have further decomposed the discrimination component into overpayment to higher castes and underpayment to the SC in the labour market. It is evident that in 2017–18, the overpayment or treatment advantage to the higher castes (i.e. benefit of being higher castes in the labour market) is 11.00 per cent in the public sector and 17.36 per cent in the private sector. This is the difference between the current wages of the higher castes and what they would otherwise receive in the absence of discrimination. Thus, an advantage to the higher castes and disadvantage to the SC is high in the private sector as compared to the public sector. As mentioned earlier, it reflects nepotism towards the higher castes. On the other hand, the underpayment or treatment disadvantage to the SC (i.e. cost of being SC in the labour market) is 16.46 per cent in the public sector and 28.46 per cent in the private sector. This is the difference in the current SC wage and the wage they would otherwise receive in the absence of discrimination (Table 9.12). This form of decomposition procedure yields more accurate estimates of the wage differential because it models the true state of differential treatment by estimating the 'cost' to the group discriminated against as well as the 'benefits' accruing to the advantaged group. Overall, it is evident that the cost of being SC in the labour market is very high in the private sector as compared to the public sector. The SC regular salaried workers are hugely underpaid in the labour market in the private sector.

9.8.2   Discrimination at Different Points of Wage Distribution in Public and Private Sectors

In aggregate level analysis (i.e. public and private sectors combined), it is evident that generally the wage gap attributable to discrimination is higher at top quantiles as compared to bottom quantiles of the wage distribution. The question is: Does this pattern varies between the public and private sector? Do the SC workers face a 'glass ceiling effect' or a 'sticky floor effect'? To test the phenomenon of glass ceiling effect and sticky floor effect in the labour market, the criteria given by Arulampalam et al. (2007) is used. The glass ceiling effect is said to exist if the 90th percentile

Table 9.12 Reimer-Cotton-Neumark-Oaxaca and Ransom approaches among higher castes and SC in regular labour market, 2017–18

Components	Reimers/ Cotton (w = 0.5)	Neumark/ Oaxaca and Ransom (w = omega)	Oaxaca-Blinder Using Higher Castes Means as Weight (w = 1)	Oaxaca-Blinder Using SC Means as Weight (w = 0)
		Public Sector		
Raw wage differential		0.30 (0.0256)		
Endowment difference (per cent)	70.97 (0.0169)	72.63 (0.0167)	73.09 (0.0179)	68.85 (0.0189)
Discrimination (per cent)	29.03 (0.0216)	27.37 (0.0195)	26.91 (0.0227)	31.15 (0.0229)
Overpayment to higher castes (per cent)	15.58 (0.0114)	10.91 (0.0080)	–	–
Underpayment to SC (per cent)	13.45 (0.0113)	16.46 (0.0120)	–	–
		Private Sector		
Raw wage differential		0.37 (0.0129)		
Endowment difference (per cent)	44.33 (0.0084)	54.18 (0.0088)	51.54 (0.0096)	37.13 (0.0095)
Discrimination (per cent)	55.67 (0.0115)	45.82 (0.0101)	48.46 (0.0121)	62.87 (0.0127)
Overpayment to higher castes (per cent)	31.44 (0.0063)	17.36 (0.0040)	–	–
Underpayment to SC (per cent)	24.23 (0.0060)	28.46 (0.0065)	–	–

Note: (1) Unexplained component = overpayment component + underpayment component

(2) Figures in parentheses indicate standard errors.

Source: Computed from unit-level PLFS (2017–18) data.

wage gap is higher than the estimated wage gaps in other parts of the wage distribution by at least two percentage points. The sticky floor effect is said to exist if the 10th percentile wage gap is higher than the 25th percentile wage gap by at least two percentage points.

It was found earlier that irrespective of the wage quantiles, there is clear empirical evidence which indicates that the wage gap, attributable to discrimination, is higher in the private sector than in the public sector. Besides, the wage gap at the 10th percentile is higher than at the 25th percentile in the public sector. This gives evidence of the sticky floor effect in the public sector. On the other hand, in the private sector the wage gap at 90th percentile is higher than the estimated wage gaps in other parts of the wage distribution. This gives evidence of the glass ceiling effect in the private sector.

The unexplained part (wage discrimination) of the wage gap is shown in Table 9.13 and Figure 9.2. It is lower within the public sector organizations than within the private sector, except in lower-wage distribution. Indeed, the public sector is always below the private sector across the entire wage distribution. The wage discrimination or unexplained part of the wage gap decreases within the public sector when we move along the wage distribution. This means that in the public sector the wage discrimination is relatively high in low-level jobs with low wage earning (grades C and D) as compared to high-level jobs (grades A and B). Among other reasons, this may be due to the appointment of Grade D jobs on contract basis and through private agencies, which are involved in discrimination. On the other hand, in the private sector, the wage discrimination is relatively high in high-grade posts and lower in low-grade jobs.

Table 9.13 Decomposition results across quantiles among higher castes and SC in regular labour market, 2017–18

Components	10th	25th	50th	75th	90th	OLS
	Public Sector					
Raw wage differentials	0.38	0.40	0.34	0.24	0.16	0.30
Characteristics (endowment difference)	0.23 (61.66)	0.23 (56.75)	0.20 (58.29)	0.16 (66.45)	0.14 (86.33)	0.22 (73.09)
Coefficients (discrimination)	0.14 (38.34)	0.17 (43.25)	0.14 (41.71)	0.08 (33.55)	0.02 (13.67)	0.08 (26.91)
	Private Sector					
Raw wage differentials	0.33	0.29	0.31	0.42	0.57	0.37
Characteristics (endowment difference)	0.12 (36.28)	0.11 (37.78)	0.10 (33.71)	0.14 (32.12)	0.18 (32.13)	0.19 (51.54)
Coefficients (discrimination)	0.21 (63.72)	0.18 (62.22)	0.20 (66.29)	0.29 (67.88)	0.39 (67.87)	0.18 (48.46)

Note: Figures in parentheses indicate percentage share.

Source: Computed from unit-level PLFS (2017–18) data.

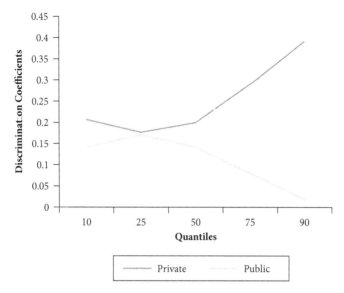

Fig. 9.2 Discrimination coefficient by public and private sectors in regular labour market among higher castes and SC, 2017–18
Source: Authors' calculation based on PLFS 2017–18 data

Thus, irrespective of the wage quintiles, there is clear empirical evidence which indicates that the wage gap attributable to discrimination is higher in the private sector than in the public sector. The unexplained part or discrimination in the wage gap decreases within the public sector when we move up along the wage distribution, indicating higher discrimination in low-grade jobs as compared to high-grade jobs. In the private sector, it is just the opposite where wage discrimination is relatively high in high-grade jobs and low in low-grade jobs.

9.9 Wage and Occupational Discrimination Linkages

We will now look at wage discrimination and its linkages with occupations. We will look into two aspects of wage and occupational linkages. The exercise assumed that the SC invariably face restrictions on the choice of occupations and as a result they get segregated into the low-paid occupations, in which they were traditionally engaged. It is assumed that the segregation in low-paid occupations affects their wage level. Therefore, in effect, part of the wage gaps between the SC and higher castes and wage discrimination are due to the concentration of the SC in low-paid occupations. We, therefore, estimate the impact of occupational segregation on the wage gaps and wage discrimination between the SC and higher castes. We also separately estimate the occupational discrimination during 2004–05 and 2017–18.

To estimate the impact of occupation on wage gap and discrimination, we use a specific method. In this method, we estimate two different model specifications. In the first specification, we exclude occupation dummies (Model 1). Conversely, in the second specification, we account for the potential effects of occupation dummies on wages (Model 2). This is because the comparison of the estimated wage gaps between the SC and higher castes between models 1 and 2 allow us to distinguish the magnitude of the glass ceiling effect from the 'pure' wage discrimination (Etienne and Narcy 2010). From the earlier pooled quantile regression results, Madheswaran (2010) found that in both public and private sectors of the regular labour market, controlling for occupation substantially reduces the wage gap throughout the wage distribution. This implies that the SC workers in both public and private sectors are victims of not only 'pure' wage discrimination but also of occupational segregation. To illustrate this phenomenon further, we compare the estimated wage gap between the SC and higher castes on account of differences in returns to characteristics (discrimination) between Model 1 and Model 2 within the public and private sectors of the regular labour market.

The results are reported in Tables 9.14 and 9.15. Using Model 1 specification, we find that in the public sector the wage gap between the SC and higher castes, attributed to discrimination, is higher at the bottom quantiles than at the top quantiles. But after controlling for occupation, there is a substantial reduction in discrimination coefficients in the public sector, particularly at the bottom wage quantiles (Figure 9.3). This reflects caste-based occupational segregation in the public sector, particularly among workers who are at the bottom wage quantiles. On the other hand, in the private sector, the curve of Model 1 is above the curve of Model 2 at top quantiles of wage distribution (Figure 9.4). This reflects caste-based occupational segregation in the private sector, particularly among workers

Table 9.14 Sectorwise decomposition results across quantiles among higher castes and SC, 2017–18 (Model 1: Excluding occupation in regular labour market)

Components	10th	25th	50th	75th	90th	OLS
Public						
Raw wage differentials	0.40	0.40	0.32	0.24	0.16	0.30
Characteristics (endowment difference)	0.27 (68.0)	0.26 (65.9)	0.22 (67.6)	0.18 (73.5)	0.13 (83.6)	0.20 (66.8)
Coefficients (discrimination)	0.13 (32.0)	0.14 (34.1)	0.10 (32.4)	0.06 (26.5)	0.03 (16.4)	0.10 (33.2)
Private						
Raw wage differentials	0.35	0.30	0.30	0.41	0.54	0.37
Characteristics (endowment difference)	0.16 (46.8)	0.14 (45.1)	0.12 (39.1)	0.14 (35.0)	0.20 (37.0)	0.20 (55.1)
Coefficients (discrimination)	0.19 (53.2)	0.17 (54.9)	0.18 (60.9)	0.27 (65.0)	0.34 (63.0)	0.16 (44.9)

Note: Figures in parentheses indicate percentage share.

Source: Computed from unit-level PLFS (2017–18) data.

Table 9.15 Sectorwise decomposition results across quantiles among higher castes and SC, 2017–18 (Model 2: Including occupation in regular urban labour market)

Components	10th	25th	50th	75th	90th	OLS
Public						
Raw wage differentials	0.40	0.40	0.32	0.24	0.16	0.37
Characteristics (endowment difference)	0.31 (77.7)	0.29 (72.1)	0.23 (71.9)	0.18 (76.3)	0.13 (83.3)	0.22 (60.0)
Coefficients (discrimination)	0.09 (22.3)	0.11 (27.9)	0.09 (28.1)	0.06 (23.7)	0.03 (16.7)	0.15 (40.0)
Private						
Raw wage differentials	0.35	0.30	0.30	0.41	0.53	0.37
Characteristics (endowment difference)	0.18 (50.8)	0.15 (49.4)	0.13 (42.9)	0.16 (39.4)	0.22 (42.2)	0.22 (60.0)
Coefficients (discrimination)	0.17 (49.2)	0.15 (50.6)	0.17 (57.1)	0.25 (60.6)	0.30 (57.8)	0.15 (40.0)

Note: The percentage share of raw wage difference is given in parentheses.

Source: Computed from unit-level PLFS (2017–18) data.

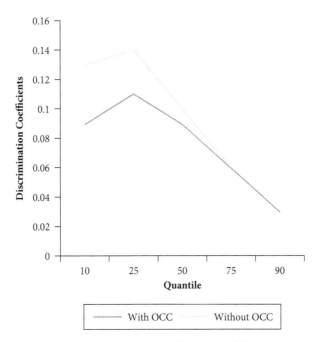

Fig. 9.3 Caste-based discrimination coefficient in public sector
Source: Authors' calculation based on PLFS 2017–18 data

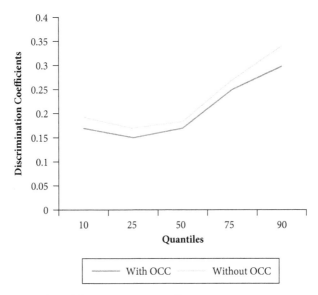

Fig. 9.4 Caste-based discrimination coefficient in private sector
Source: Authors' calculation based on PLFS 2017–18 data

who are in top wage quantiles. It is to be noted that the caste-based wage gap, as well as discrimination, are lower in the public sector than in the private sector irrespective of wage quantiles.

Thus, we find that in both public and private sectors of the regular labour market, controlling for occupation substantially reduces the wage gap throughout wage distribution. This implies that SC workers in both public and private sectors are victims of not only 'pure' wage discrimination but also of occupational segregation.

9.10   Wage and Occupational Discrimination: Expanded Decomposition Results

From the above discussion, it is evident that with the inclusion of occupation variable in the earnings equation, the final calculation of the discrimination coefficient has reduced substantially in both public and private sectors of the regular labour market. The wage gap at the mean, attributable to discrimination, has reduced by 10 per cent in the public sector and by 4.7 per cent in the private sector. Besides, the wage gap, attributable to discrimination, has reduced at the bottom wage quintiles in the public sector and top wage quantiles in the private sector. This implies that discrimination against the SC partially operates through occupational segregation in the low-paid occupations which reduces the wage on account of being engaged in these occupations on a significant scale.

In case of occupation, it is evident that in 2017–18 the SC workers share in middle- and low-level occupations is high (70.56 per cent) as compared to the higher castes (47.23 per cent). The share is particularly high in elementary occupations followed by service workers, shop and market sale workers, craft and related trade workers, plant and machinery operators, assemblers and the elementary occupation. Conversely, the SC share in better-quality occupations is low (29.43 per cent) as compared to higher castes (52.77 per cent). The better-quality occupations include the legislature, senior officials and managers, professionals, technicians and associated professionals, and clerks (Table 9.16). Since a high percentage of SC workers are employed in low-quality occupations, their wage earnings are low.

Table 9.16 Occupational pattern of regular workers, 2017–18 (in per cent)

Occupation	SC	OBC	Higher Castes	Total	Gap in SC and Higher Castes in Occupation
Legislators, senior officials, and managers	3.58	6.16	10.26	7.08	6.67
Professionals	8.08	12.71	17.8	13.7	9.73
Technicians and associated professionals	10.69	13.39	13.66	13.01	2.97
Clerks	6.62	8.23	10.84	8.7	4.22
Service workers and shop and market sales workers	19.52	17.47	16.8	17.59	−2.72
Skilled agricultural and fishery workers	0.46	0.34	0.21	0.38	−0.25
Craft and related trade workers	13.86	16.28	10.01	13.96	−3.85
Plant and machinery operators and assemblers	11.52	12.25	10.61	11.6	−0.91
Elementary Occupation	25.66	13.16	9.81	13.99	−15.86
Total	100	100	100	100	

Source: Authors' calculation based on PLFS 2017–18 data.

Therefore, in the Indian context, we argue that both glass ceiling and glass walls are likely to be in evidence which indicate vertical segregation (within the same employment type, workers from different social groups may be represented differently in the hierarchy of positions) and horizontal segregation (workers restricted to their occupations as they face restrictions in movement across occupations) respectively. In both cases, the upward movement of the SC workers in an occupational category and movement across caste-based occupation may be hampered by institutional barriers and social attitudes. From the distribution of occupation, it is apparent that the SC individuals are concentrated in low-paid occupations. The hierarchical nature of the caste system, combined with low endowments of human and physical capital, implies that a far larger proportion of the SC workers have no option but to engage in low-paid jobs in informal work in the formal sectors.

Using Employment Survey data at the state level, we examined employment segregation by occupations using 1-digit occupation codes for regular workers between the SC and higher castes (Table 9.17). Duncan

Table 9.17 Occupational segregation index between SC and higher castes for regular workers, 2017–18

States	Duncan Segregation Index	Rank
Jammu and Kashmir	0.281	8
Himachal Pradesh	0.275	9
Punjab	0.260	13
Uttarakhand	0.212	15
Haryana	0.365	2
Rajasthan	0.273	10
Uttar Pradesh	0.262	12
Bihar	0.297	7
Assam	0.236	14
West Bengal	0.193	17
Jharkhand	0.376	1
Odisha	0.166	19
Chhattisgarh	0.267	11
Madhya Pradesh	0.318	6
Gujarat	0.165	20
Maharashtra	0.173	18
Andhra Pradesh	0.211	16
Karnataka	0.324	5
Kerala	0.332	4
Tamil Nadu	0.355	3
All India	0.219	
Coefficient of variation (in per cent)	24.68	

Source: Authors' calculation based on PLFS 2017–18 data.

index is calculated for each state to assess the extent of segregation by occupations. The Duncan index is a description of the percentage of workers who would need to switch jobs to obtain an equal distribution of higher castes and SC in each job type. The Duncan index that is closer to zero indicates a more similar distribution of SC and higher castes across employment categories. Occupational segregation is more in advanced states. States with high Duncan index are Jharkhand, Haryana, Tamil Nadu, Kerala, and Karnataka. We have also examined which occupations are dominated by SC and higher castes. Figure 9.5 arranges each occupation

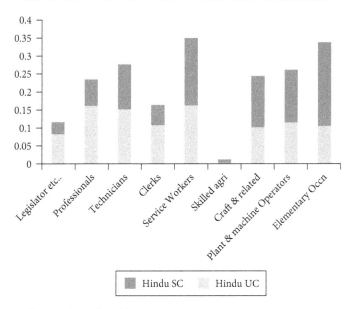

Fig. 9.5 Proportion of social groups across occupations
Source: Authors' calculation based on PLFS 2017–18 data

in order of the proportion of SC and higher castes workers. The occupations dominated by higher castes include legislators, senior officials and
managers, professionals, technicians and associated professionals, and
clerks. The occupational groups dominated by SC are elementary occupations, plant and machine operators, assemblers, craft and related trade
workers, service workers, and shop and market sales workers.

Most studies on occupational segregation measure overall or aggregate segregation. Overall segregation involves simultaneous comparisons
among all subgroups across occupations. Therefore, measures of overall
segregation consider all the subgroups jointly. For instance, in the case
of occupational segregation by gender, the distribution of male workers
across occupations is usually compared with that of female workers. On
the other hand, local segregation measures the segregation of a particular
demographic group (target group) and compares the distribution of the
target group with the distribution of total employment. The measures of
local segregation permit the possibility to determine the contribution
of each group to overall segregation and therefore allow in-depth analysis of segregation. A recent study by Alonso-Villar and Del Río (2010)

Table 9.18 Overall segregation by social groups

Overall Segregation	Rural			Urban		
	Ip	M	G	Ip	M	G
Overall social group segregation	0.13	0.06	0.16	0.15	0.08	0.20
Contribution to Overall Segregation:						
Scheduled Tribes' (ST) contribution	0.16	0.19	0.15	0.05	0.08	0.05
SC contribution	0.38	0.43	0.36	0.39	0.45	0.32
OBC contribution	0.15	0.07	0.18	0.24	0.16	0.26
Higher castes contribution	0.32	0.32	0.31	0.23	0.34	0.29

Source: Authors' calculation from NSS 61st round data.

proposed a theoretical framework to study local segregation. Local segregation measures are related to the overall measures—aggregating them using the population weights of the mutually-exclusive subgroups adds up to the overall segregation. One can also rank the subgroups according to their segregation level using local segregation measures.

We will now analyse segregation among the social groups. Table 9.18 shows measures of overall segregation. If the contribution of each social group to overall segregation (according to the M index) is calculated, it is found that the SC and higher castes contribute most to overall segregation in both the sectors. Especially, the SC face more occupational segregation as compared to other social groups. The occupational segregation is mostly crowded into low-paid jobs for the SC whereas segregation for higher castes is mainly in the high-paid jobs. All the local indices are also higher for the SC (Table 9.19). It is evident that the level of segregation is higher in the urban sector as compared to the rural sector in all social groups. Using local measures of segregation, it is found that OBC have the lowest level of segregation in both the sectors, whereas the SC have the highest level of segregation in both the rural and urban sectors as compared to other groups.

We have mentioned earlier that due to the inclusion of occupation variable in the earnings equation, the final calculation of the discrimination coefficient is reduced substantially, i.e. the wage gap attributable to discrimination is reduced by 7.2 per cent (Madheswaran and Singhari 2016). This implies that discrimination against the SC partially operates through occupational segregation. To substantiate this evidence, we

Table 9.19 Local segregation by social groups

Social Groups	Emp. Share	D^8	G^8	$GE^8_{0.1}$	$GE^8_{0.5}$	GE^8_1	GE^8_2
Rural							
ST	0.13	0.16	0.19	0.12	0.10	0.09	0.07
SC	0.22	0.23	0.26	0.12	0.12	0.12	0.12
OBC	0.43	0.05	0.07	0.01	0.01	0.01	0.01
Higher castes	0.23	0.18	0.22	0.09	0.09	0.08	0.08
Urban							
ST	0.03	0.27	0.36	0.26	0.22	0.21	0.24
SC	0.15	0.25	0.34	0.21	0.19	0.20	0.25
OBC	0.40	0.09	0.14	0.04	0.03	0.03	0.03
Higher castes	0.42	0.16	0.21	0.08	0.08	0.07	0.07

Source: Authors' calculation from NSS 61st round data.

have measured the extent of occupational segregation using combined O.D. Duncan and B. Duncan (1955) index. The results given in Table 9.20 show that in 2017–18, the degree of dissimilarity is 22 per cent for regular workers. It suggests that 22 per cent of either or a combination of both the higher castes and the SC workers would have to shift to obtain equal representation across occupational categories.

The above findings motivate us to measure the extent of caste-based wage gap that is attributable to differential access to occupations in the labour market. We incorporate occupational attainment in the decomposition, estimate job discrimination against the SC in the labour market, and compare the actual and predicted occupational distributions of the SC and higher castes in the regular labour market.

The occupational attainment equation is estimated using the multinomial logit model regression. The occupational attainment result is used to obtain the predicted occupational distribution for the SC $(\hat{P}_{sc})$. For higher castes, this estimation procedure yields a predicted distribution identical to their actual sample distribution, i.e. $\hat{P}_{fc} = P_{fc}$. The difference in the predicted distribution $(P^{fc} - \hat{P}^{sc})$ is the 'explained' component due to differences in characteristics. The residual difference $(\hat{P}^{sc} - P^{sc})$ is the 'unexplained' component due to differential access to occupations.

Table 9.20 Full decomposition of gross earnings difference between higher castes and SC in regular labour market, 2017–18

	Observed Occupational Distribution		Predicted Occupational Distribution		Observed Difference	Explained Difference	Residual Difference
	P_{fc}	P_{sc}	$\hat{P}_{fc}$	$\hat{P}_{sc}$	$P_{fc} - P_{sc}$	$P_{fc} - \hat{P}_{sc}$	$\hat{P}_{sc} - P_{sc}$
	(1)	(2)	(3)	(4)	(5)	(6)	(7)
Administrative and professionals	0.3949	0.2471	0.3949	0.2673	0.1478	0.1276	0.0202
Clerical	0.1077	0.0731	0.1077	0.0803	0.0346	0.0274	0.0072
Service and sales	0.1778	0.1934	0.1778	0.2259	-0.0156	-0.0481	0.0324
Production	0.2190	0.2796	0.2190	0.2781	-0.0605	-0.0591	-0.0014
Elementary	0.1006	0.2068	0.1006	0.1484	-0.1062	-0.0478	-0.0584

	$G = \ln \bar{Y}_{fc} - \ln \bar{Y}_{SC}$	$E = \hat{\beta}_{fc}(\bar{x}_{fc} - \bar{x}_{sc})$	$D = \bar{x}_{sc}(\hat{\beta}_{fc} - \hat{\beta}_{sc})$	$P_{sc} \times E(WE)$	$P_{sc} \times D(WD)$	$(P_{fc} - \hat{P}_{sc}) \times \ln \bar{Y}_{fc}(JE)$	$(\hat{P}_{sc} - P_{sc}) \times \ln \bar{Y}_{fc}(JD)$
	(8)	(9)	(10)	(11)	(12)	(13)	(14)
Administrative and professionals	0.3080	0.1592	0.1488	0.0393	0.0368	0.6833	0.1083
Clerical	0.1118	0.0620	0.0498	0.0045	0.0036	0.1434	0.0377
Service and sales	0.2298	0.1265	0.1033	0.0245	0.0200	-0.2258	0.1524
Production	0.1854	0.0717	0.1137	0.0200	0.0318	-0.2850	0.1069
Elementary	0.1820	0.1243	0.0577	0.0257	0.0119	-0.2165	-0.2647
Dissimilarity index ID		0.2276					
ID*		0.2115					

Source: Authors' calculation based on PLFS 2017–18 data.

The expanded decomposition results in Table 9.20 show that in the regular labour market, the occupational/job discrimination is more highly pronounced than wage discrimination. The important message from Table 9.20 is that, particularly in administrative, professionals, sales, and production occupations, the extent of job discrimination against the SC is higher than wage discrimination; whereas in clerical and elementary occupation the extent of job discrimination is lower. This implies that job discrimination against the SC is high in white-collar jobs. This finding is contradictory to the Banerjee and Knight (1985) study which shows that the extent of job discrimination is less in white-collar jobs.

Thus, we find that in the regular labour market, discrimination accounts for a substantial part of the gross earnings differential between the SC and higher castes with occupational discrimination (inequality in access to certain occupations) being considerably more important than wage discrimination (unequal pay within a given occupation, given one's educational and skill levels).

9.11   Conclusion and Policy Implications

The study came with several new conclusions on wage discrimination with respect to the SC. We summarize the findings on wage and occupational discriminations and indicate policy implications to reduce the wage gap and wage discrimination. There are clear disparities in the average daily wages measured by wage ratios of the SC and higher castes regular salaried workers. The wages of the SC regular salaried workers are found to be lower than that of higher castes by almost 30 per cent in 2017–18. Besides, the wage gap increased from 15 per cent in 2004–05 to 19 per cent in 2017–18.

In a separate exercise on determinants of wage, the study found that age (or work experience), education level, particularly attainment in higher education, marriage, permanent job, type of employment and the caste of regular salaried workers determine their wage earning. Higher castes have an edge in some of these factors, such as work experience, higher education, particularly women's education, and type of employment. The deficiencies in these endowment factors among the SC reduce their wage earning. Besides, the caste identity also matters in wage earning insofar as the earning of the SC tends to be low as compared to higher castes regular salaried workers.

In the rest of the sections, we summarize the findings on the relative role of endowment factors and caste discrimination in wage gaps. This exercise has shown insightful results on the relative contribution of endowment factors and caste discrimination in wage differences during 2004–05 and 2017–18 which have important policy implications.

9.11.1 Summary

The results (based on the method with least standard error, namely Oaxaca and Ransom method) show that in the regular salaried labour market, for the wage difference between the SC and higher castes, both endowments factors and caste discrimination matter. The contribution of endowment difference to gross wage differential between the SC and higher castes in 2017–18 is 57 per cent and caste discrimination is 43 per cent. As we see, the contribution of endowment factors is more than caste discrimination. However, although the endowment difference is higher than discrimination, the contribution of discrimination to wage differential is also substantial (43 per cent). Results, based on the Oaxaca and Ransom decomposition method, indicate that among endowment factors, the human capital difference between the SC and higher castes contributes much to the earning differential between them. The caste-based wage difference due to education and skill is 67.1 per cent in 2004–05 and 57.24 per cent in 2017–18. Thus, the endowment factors favourable for the higher castes are education, particularly higher education (graduate and above), marital status, and nature of employment. For obvious reasons, education also determines the type of employment. Women's education also matters. Conversely, less access to education, including access to education of SC women, and quality of employment remain disadvantages for the SC. The disadvantage, with respect to endowment factors of the SC (education and employment), is partly due to exclusion of the SC from right to education and employment (except casual wage labour) for a long time in the past. This results in a deficiency in ownership of physical and human resources and better employment in the present. It is also due to pre-market discrimination in non-market institutions, like educational institutions. This happens due to the failure of the government to correct the deficiencies through redistributive policies to increase the ownership of capital assets and education. So exclusion in ownership of capital assets, education, and employment in the past continues in the present as the legacy of the caste system.

The results of the decomposition of the discrimination component into overpayment to higher castes and underpayment to SC in the labour market show the magnitude of the advantage of discrimination to the higher castes and disadvantage to the SC. The results reveal that the overpayment or treatment advantage to higher castes (benefit of being higher castes in the labour market) is 8.6 per cent in 2004–05 and 16.46 per cent in 2017–18. This is the difference between the current wages of higher castes and what they would otherwise receive in the absence of discrimination. It also reflects nepotism towards the higher castes. On the other hand, the underpayment or treatment disadvantage to SC (cost of being SC in the labour market) is 24.3 per cent in 2004–05 and 26.30 per cent in 2017–18. This is the difference in the current SC wage and the wage they would otherwise receive in the absence of discrimination. This form of decomposition procedure yields more accurate estimates of the wage differential because it models the true state of differential treatment by estimating the 'cost' to the group discriminated against the 'benefits' accruing to the advantaged group. Overall, we find that the cost of being SC in the labour market is very high. They are hugely underpaid in the labour market.

The results also show that the young SC workers face greater discrimination in wages than middle-aged SC workers. The young particularly face high discrimination at the upper hierarchy of jobs compared to the low-level jobs.

The results also show differences in wage discrimination in the public and private sectors. The caste-based wage gap is found to be higher in the private sector than in the public sector. Also, the discrimination against the SC is higher in the private sector than in the public sector. There are differences in the wage gap and discrimination in the public and private sectors across the wage distribution. The wage gap at the 10th percentile is higher than at the 25th percentile in the public sector. This gives evidence of the sticky floor effect in the public sector which means that upward mobility in job hierarchy is marked with difficulties due to discrimination of the SC in wage earning. In the private sector, on the other hand, the wage gap at 90th percentile is higher than the estimated wage gaps in other parts of the wage distribution. This gives evidence of the glass ceiling effect in the private sector which indicates the constraints in terms of the upper limit of the SC in moving to better-earning occupation. This shows that discrimination or the wage gap decreases within the public sector when we move up along the wage distribution. This means that the discrimination is high at a lower level of distribution than at the upper level. The opposite is true for private sector where the wage gap and discrimination are less at the lower end of wage earning than at the upper level. Irrespective of the methodology used, there is clear empirical evidence to show high degree of wage discrimination against the SC in the private sector, particularly in posts with higher-level of earning.

There is also evidence on occupational segregation for regular salaried workers between the SC and higher castes. In a separate exercise, each occupation is arranged in order of the proportion of higher castes and SC workers to know which occupations are dominated by the higher castes and SC. The results revealed that the occupations dominated by the higher castes include legislators, senior officials and manager, professionals, technicians and associated professionals, and clerks. The occupational groups dominated by the SC are elementary occupations, plant and machine operators and assemblers, craft and related trade workers, service workers, and shop and market sales workers. These findings proved useful to further measure the extent of the caste-based wage gap attributable to differences in occupations. The occupational attainment is incorporated in the decomposition to estimate job discrimination against the SC in the labour market, and to compare the actual and predicted occupational distributions of SC and higher castes in the regular labour market. It is found that occupational discrimination accounts for a substantial part of the gross earning differential between the SC and higher castes, with occupational discrimination (inequality in access to certain occupations) being highly pronounced than wage discrimination (unequal pay within a given occupation, given one's educational and skill levels).

9.11.2 Policy Implications

It emerged that the disparities in wage earning between the SC and higher castes are both due to differences in possession of endowment by them and also due to caste discrimination in wage earning and occupations faced by the SC. Therefore, the results have implications for policies both to improve the access of the SC to endowment factors and the measures to reduce caste discrimination.

9.11.2.1 Policy Implications to Enhance Endowment and Reduce Discrimination

It is seen that endowment factors account for about 57 per cent of the difference in the wage gap between the SC and higher castes. The endowment factors that cause wage gap, which is favourable for higher castes, include education, particularly higher education (graduate and above), women's education and nature of employment. Conversely, less access to education, including access to education of the SC women, and better employment remain as disadvantages for the SC. The disadvantages of the SC in endowment factors are due to the influence of denial of the right to education to them (including women from this group) and better employment in the past for a very long time. At the same time, it is also the result of the failure of redistributive policies to correct the wrong done in the past, to improve the ownership of capital assets, education level and better employment of the SC in the present (other than casual wage workers where SC are over-represented). The data on ownership of capital assets show that of the total wealth in the country in 2013, the share of SC was only 6.5 per cent which is much less than their population share of 16 per cent; while the share of the higher castes in total wealth, which is 35.8 per cent, exceeds their population share by a high margin. This is reflected in the lower share of self-employed (farmers and entrepreneurs) among the SC and regular salaried compared to a higher caste and overdependence on casual wage labour. Similarly, the wide gap continues between the SC and higher castes in education. For instance, in 2014–15 the enrolment ratio in higher education for the SC is 20 per cent which is two times lower than higher castes (43 per cent). This will require reforms in the present policies to increase the enrolment rate of the SC in higher education to bridge the wage gap between them and the higher castes.

The increase in the enrolment rate in higher education and skill, particularly professional education, will improve the employability of the SC and help them to enhance their share in the formal regular salaried jobs.

The results, related to caste discrimination in wage earning, also have important implications for policies to reduce discrimination. The decomposition of the discrimination component into the underpayment or treatment disadvantage to the SC (cost of being SC in the labour market) is 24.3 per cent in 2004–05 and 26.30 per cent in 2017–18. This is the difference in the current SC wage and the wage they would otherwise receive in the absence of discrimination. The underpayment is particularly high in higher-level jobs in the private sector. The present affirmative action policy of the private sectors should incorporate safeguards against the wage discrimination of the SC in higher-level positions.

In the public sector, wage discrimination is lower than the private sector. Nevertheless, public sector is not free from discrimination. Unlike the private sector, the wage gap due to caste discrimination is high at lower level of earning, i.e. lower-grade jobs that include grades C and D. Besides, it is observed that upward movement in the same occupation/job is sticky and therefore marked with difficulties for the SC. It seems that discrimination of the SC in low-level jobs in the public sector (i.e. grades C and D) may be due the recruitment of grades C and D posts on a contract basis by the government and public undertakings through private recruitment agencies. The private agencies are well known for underpayment of wages to workers employed on a contract basis. The SC particularly are the victims of such discriminatory practices. This would need corrective measures to overcome discriminatory practices. The recruitment of lower-category jobs in the public sector should be made more transparent and monitored by the public sector employer.

The study also brings out evidence on occupational segregation of the SC regular salaried workers. The discrimination in occupation pushes the SC into low-earning occupations that include elementary occupations, plant and machine operators and assemblers, craft and trade-related workers, service workers, and shop and market sales workers. The concentration of SC in these low-paying occupations further widens the wage gap. An estimate of wage gaps in decomposition exercise after exclusion of occupation reduces the wage gap significantly. This indicates that a sizable portion of the wage gap between the SC and higher castes is due to occupational discrimination (inequality in access to certain occupations) and relatively less due to 'pure' wage discrimination. These would need measures to reduce the restrictions faced by the SC workers in the allocation of jobs by employers.

The theories of discrimination tell us that labour market discrimination in the private sector is driven by prejudices with economic or material motive and therefore is difficult to deal with. There is self-enlightened economic interest behind wage discrimination. Therefore, it would require legal safeguards to protect the SC regular salaried workers. This could be done by enacting anti-discriminatory laws against wage discrimination by the government for the SC workers working in both the private and public sectors. At present, there is not enough legal protection for the SC against underpayment of wages due to caste prejudice in the private and public sectors or discrimination in assigning low-level occupations. This empirical evidence suggests the need for legal safeguards for the SC regular salaried workers against caste discrimination.

10

Employment, Wage Discrimination, and its Impact on Poverty

10.1 Introduction

The analysis of discrimination against the Scheduled Castes (SC) in the preceding chapters revealed its persistence against them in employment, wages, and occupations. In 2017–18, about 58 per cent of the differences in the probability of employment of regular salaried workers between the SC and higher castes are on account of discrimination in hiring. Similarly, about 35 per cent differences in the wages between the SC and higher castes wage workers are due to wage discrimination. Any discrimination in the labour market, either in employment, wages, and occupation, would exert a negative impact on the earning of the wage workers. Discrimination in employment would result in high unemployment and low income. Similarly, wage discrimination would bring a reduction in wage earning. The occupational discrimination would push the SC workers to low-earning occupations. Together, the high unemployment, low wages, and concentration in low-earning occupations would eventually result in low income and high poverty among the SC affected by discrimination. However, while this fact looks quite obvious, actual estimates of the impact of employment and wage discrimination on income and poverty are scarce. To develop an evidence-based policy against employment and wage discrimination, it is necessary that the magnitude of fall in earning and rise in poverty due to employment and wage discriminations are known. Therefore, in this chapter we estimate the losses in income and the resultant increase in poverty among the SC on account of discrimination in employment and wages using 2004–05 and 2017–18 Employment and Unemployment Survey data. As mentioned earlier, the analysis is confined to regular salaried workers. Before we estimate the

Scheduled Castes in the Indian Labour Market. Sukhadeo Thorat, S. Madheswaran, and B. P. Vani,
Oxford University Press. © Sukhadeo Thorat, S. Madheswaran, and B. P. Vani 2023.
DOI: 10.1093/oso/9780198872252.003.0010

impact of employment and wage discrimination on the poverty of the SC, we look into the characteristics of the poor from regular salaried workers.

We have discussed earlier that in 2004–05 the regular salaried workers constituted about 14 per cent of the total workers, their share increased to about 22 per cent in 2017–18. Thus, within 13 years, the share of regular salaried workers increased by about eight percentage points. The size of regular salaried workers, however, varies between the SC, Other Backward Classes (OBC) and higher castes. In 2017–18, the percentage of regular salaried workers among the SC was low at 19.7 per cent as compared to 21 per cent for OBC and 32.7 per cent for higher castes. Thus, the share of SC regular salaried workers is less by 13 per cent points as compared to higher castes. Between 2004–05 and 2017–18, the share of regular salaried workers has increased for all three groups. In terms of percentage points, the increase has been a little less for the SC (7.5 percentage points) as compared to higher castes (about 9 percentage points) (Table 10.1). This means

Table 10.1   Share of workers across employment categories, 2004–05 and 2017–18

	Self-employed	Regular Wage/ Salaried	Casual Labourers	Total
		2004–05		
Scheduled Tribes (ST)	53.8 (9.5)	6.7 (4.7)	39.4 (13.7)	100.0 (10.0)
Hindu SC	40.2 (14.0)	12.2 (17.0)	47.6 (32.7)	100.0 (19.8)
Hindu OBC	61.4 (39.4)	11.9 (30.7)	26.6 (33.7)	100.0 (36.5)
Hindu higher castes	63.4 (22.53)	23.7 (33.6)	12.9 (9.1)	100.0 (20.2)
Muslims	61.8 (11.1)	12.6 (9.0)	25.5 (9.0)	100.0 (10.2)
Others	61.4 (3.5)	22.1 (5.0)	16.5 (1.9)	100.0 (3.2)
Total	56.9 (100.0)	14.3 (100.0)	28.9 (100.0)	100.0 (100.0)
		2017–18		
ST	55.9 (11.4)	12.9 (6.0)	31.2 (13.3)	100.0 (10.6)
Hindu SC	39.0 (14.5)	19.7 (16.7)	41.3(32.1)	100.0 (19.4)
Hindu OBC	56.3 (38.4)	21.4 (33.3)	22.3 (31.8)	100.0 (35.6)
Hindu higher castes	56.1 (22.0)	32.7 (29.4)	11.2 (9.2)	100.0 (20.5)
Muslims	52.6 (10.7)	20.9 (9.7)	26.4 (11.3)	100.0 (10.6)
Others	48.2 (3.0)	34.2 (4.9)	17.6 (2.3)	100.0 (3.3)
Total	52.2 (100.0)	22.8 (100.0)	24.9 (100.0)	100.0 (100.0)

Source: Authors' calculation based on NSS 61st round and PLFS 2017–18 data.

that not only the percentage of the regular salaried workers (to their total workers) is less among the SC as compared to OBC and higher castes, but the increase in 2004–05 and 2017–18 has also been slow for the SC.

10.2 Characteristics of Poor Regular Salaried Workers

To get the background of the poor for impact analysis, we look into the characteristics of the poor. This includes the analysis of differences between the SC and higher castes in per capita consumption expenditure, poverty by employment categories, by industry groups, occupation types and educational levels. We also undertake the analysis of the determinants of poverty.

The consumption expenditure of SC workers in 2017–18 is ₹1,674 which is lower than ₹1,952 for OBC and ₹2,712 for higher castes, while the all-India average is ₹2,017. Between 2004–05 and 2017–18, the overall consumption expenditure has increased, including the three caste groups (Appendix Table 10.1 and Appendix Table 10.2).

The disparities between the caste groups in per capita consumption expenditure are reflected in the variations in poverty level. Table 10.2 present the poverty of regular salaried workers for 2004–05 and 2017–18. In 2004–05, about 19 per cent of the regular salaried workers are poor. The poverty is relatively high among the SC (30.7 per cent) as compared to 9.1 per cent for higher castes and 19.4 per cent for the OBC. Although the poverty of OBC is lower than SC, it is more than the higher castes. The same pattern is observed in 2017–18. In 2017–18 at all-India level, about 17.5 per cent of the regular salaried workers are poor. The incidence of poverty is 22.8 per cent among the SC which is higher than 18.0 per cent for OBC and 10.2 per cent for higher castes. Thus, compared to higher castes the poverty of SC regular salaried workers is more than double. The important feature that emerged from the analysis is about the graded inequality in the incidence of poverty across caste groups. The poverty is lowest among the higher castes. As compared to higher castes, the level of poverty is more among OBC which further increases among the SC (Appendix Table 10.3). More or less the same trend is found in all states. However, the gap in the incidence of poverty among the SC and higher castes is particularly high

Table 10.2 Poverty across social groups (in per cent)

	2004–05			2017–18		
	Self-employed					
	Rural	Urban	Total	Rural	Urban	Total
ST	55.0	52.4	58.7	54.0	36.0	53.2
Hindu SC	46.0	47.3	51.2	39.7	29.6	38.0
Hindu OBC	34.8	33.4	37.6	34.7	20.8	32.2
Hindu higher castes	22.2	13.2	20.2	27.1	12.0	22.6
Muslims	41.4	46.2	45.1	30.4	32.8	31.2
Others	12.1	6.8	14.3	17.1	10.1	15.0
Total	35.9	30.1	38.9	35.8	21.1	32.7
	Regular Wage Earner					
ST	34.1	22.2	29.4	31.5	17.4	26.3
Hindu SC	34.0	28.1	30.7	25.4	20.4	22.8
Hindu OBC	22.7	16.8	19.4	24.5	12.7	18.0
Hindu higher castes	12.5	7.7	9.1	15.6	8.0	10.2
Muslims	22.9	35.3	31.2	25.4	27.8	26.8
Others	11.1	6.4	8.2	17.0	6.7	10.6
Total	22.6	16.5	18.8	23.2	13.6	17.5
	Casual labour					
ST	68.9	71.4	69.0	58.5	55.7	58.3
Hindu SC	60.5	62.5	60.7	47.3	43.4	46.8
Hindu OBC	53.2	47.8	52.6	42.1	35.4	40.9
Hindu higher castes	42.0	39.9	41.6	35.5	29.1	33.8
Muslims	56.8	60.3	57.5	36.9	48.2	40.0
Others	35.8	32.3	35.2	33.0	23.4	30.7
Total	57.0	53.5	56.6	45.1	39.5	44.1

Source: Authors' calculation based on NSS 61st round and PLFS 2017–18 data.

in Andhra Pradesh, Chhattisgarh, Haryana, Karnataka, Kerala, Madhya Pradesh, Punjab, and Tamil Nadu (Table 10.3).

We will now look at the incidence of poverty among the regular salaried workers by type of industry and occupation. Table 10.4 shows the percentage of workers in different industry groups for the regular salaried workers among the SC, OBC, and higher castes. It emerged that the

Table 10.3 Statewise incidence of poverty among regular workers

	2004–05				2017–18			
	Hindu SC	Hindu OBC	Hindu Higher Castes	Total	Hindu SC	Hindu OBC	Hindu Higher Castes	Total
Andhra Pradesh	30.4	18.5	6.3	18.8	15.3	12.3	3.1	11.8
Assam	37.7	36.2	16.6	25.0	19.6	13.1	9.0	12.3
Bihar	54.0	33.7	10.9	32.8	26.3	38.0	21.4	33.0
Chhattisgarh	16.0	25.9	8.8	19.8	41.9	33.7	16.9	32.6
Delhi	18.3	6.5	5.9	10.4	15.2	19.9	8.2	12.1
Gujarat	27.3	18.3	4.2	16.2	39.0	12.3	7.6	17.6
Haryana	32.5	18.5	6.4	15.0	38.1	27.7	14.4	25.0
Himachal Pradesh	11.9	6.2	8.3	8.3	20.4	24.3	12.2	16.5
Jammu and Kashmir	5.2	1.8	8.6	8.3	5.8	0.0	6.9	12.8
Jharkhand	18.7	18.8	16.8	19.0	17.1	17.8	9.5	16.8
Karnataka	26.8	15.1	9.3	14.9	29.6	20.8	11.2	20.2
Kerala	23.5	11.3	6.0	11.5	25.8	16.3	7.8	15.6
Madhya Pradesh	51.4	33.6	9.4	28.5	27.0	22.6	5.8	19.2
Maharashtra	32.5	18.4	11.8	20.1	20.3	22.7	10.8	16.0
Odisha	44.9	31.1	17.8	28.4	22.6	19.7	14.7	19.0
Punjab	25.7	12.6	8.2	14.8	23.4	10.3	9.3	13.6
Rajasthan	40.9	17.1	6.8	20.8	24.9	17.5	12.9	20.0
Tamil Nadu	24.4	15.3	2.9	16.4	16.2	5.9	1.3	8.0
Uttar Pradesh	42.4	24.1	11.6	24.6	26.2	29.3	11.1	26.1
Uttarakhand	25.1	18.6	8.6	15.3	11.9	12.4	10.7	14.3
West Bengal	23.4	19.4	8.9	18.2	20.4	20.6	11.2	18.4
Total	30.7	19.4	9.1	18.8	22.8	18.0	10.3	17.5

Source: Authors' calculation based on NSS 61st round and PLFS 2017–18 data.

SC regular salaried workers are mainly concentrated in a few industry groups. These groups include other services (40 per cent), manufacturing (20 per cent), and trade and transport (12–13 per cent). Together, these four groups of industries account for about 85 per cent of the total SC regular salaried workers. In the industry group, other services, where a higher percentage of SC are employed (40 per cent), nearly 22 per cent of them are poor. This is higher than OBC and higher castes. For instance, about 16 per cent of OBC and 10 per cent of higher castes are poor in this

Table 10.4 Percentage of poor among regular salaried workers across industry classification, 2017–18

Industry Classification	Hindu SC		Hindu OBC		Hindu Higher castes		Total	
	% of population	% of poor	% of population	% of poor	% of population	% of poor	% of population	% of poor
Agriculture	2.0	35.6	2.7	18.7	1.2	9.1	2.4	30.1
Mining and quarrying	0.7	16.4	1.4	14.2	0.5	3.6	0.9	12.9
Manufacturing	**20.9**	26.3	22.8	16.7	22.3	12.8	22.0	18.7
Electricity and water supply	2.7	24.8	2.2	16.2	1.8	4.7	2.0	17.5
Construction	4.0	18.3	2.6	20.4	2.7	6.6	2.8	17.0
Trade	**13.0**	22.3	14.3	25.2	13.7	13.7	13.9	22.7
Transport	**12.2**	22.0	13.9	21.1	12.6	9.9	13.2	18.1
Accommodation and food service	4.0	11.1	5.4	7.9	9.2	4.1	6.0	6.3
Other service	**40.4**	22.2	34.8	16.2	36.0	9.8	36.8	15.8
Total	100.0	22.8	100.0	18.0	100.0	10.3	100.0	17.5

Source: Authors' calculation based on PLFS 2017–18 data.

industry group. In the manufacturing industry too the poverty level of the SC (26.3 per cent) is higher than OBC and higher castes regular salaried workers, viz. 13 per cent and 17 per cent respectively. Also, in trade and transport industries the incidence of poor is high among the SC. For instance, in trade, about 22 per cent of the SC are poor as compared to 13 per cent of the higher castes. Similarly, in the transport industry, about 22 per cent of the SC are poor which is higher than 10 per cent of the higher castes. In case of OBC, although the percentage of poor regular salaried workers is lower than SC, it is always more than higher castes which indicates a graded hierarchy in the poverty level. In all other groups of industries, namely agriculture, mining and quarrying, electricity and water supply, construction, and accommodation and food services, where the share of SC regular workers is low (which vary from less than 1 per cent to 4 per cent), with some exceptions, the SC are also poorer than higher castes and OBC. Thus, the industry groups where the engagement of SC is high as well as those where their participation is low, their poverty is higher than higher castes and OBC. The poverty level among OBC is lower than SC, but tends to be higher than higher castes.

The incidence of poverty by occupational groups also reveals a similar pattern of graded inequality (Table 10.5). The participation of the SC is high in some occupations where the earnings are relatively low. These five occupational groups together account for about 83 per cent of the total SC regular salaried workers. These include elementary occupations, service workers and shop and market sale workers, craft and related trade workers, plant and machine operators and assemblers, and technicians and associate professionals. The low-earning capacity of these occupations is reflected in high percentage of poor among the SC regular salaried workers. The elementary occupations are the one where the engagement of the SC is the highest (23 per cent). The percentage of poor in this occupation among the SC workers is also high (32.6 per cent), which is much higher than the higher castes (19 per cent). The percentage of poor among OBC in this group is 22.9 per cent which is slightly higher than the higher castes. Among craft and related trade workers, and plant and machine operators and assemblers, where the share of SC is about 14 per cent, 24 per cent of them are poor which is higher than 13–16 per cent for higher castes. The percentage of poor among OBC in this group is similar to that of the SC. In the remaining occupations which are relatively better in terms of earnings, namely legislature, senior officials and managers, clerks, skilled agricultural and fishery workers, the share of SC is relatively low (the percentage vary between 1 and 7 per cent) and the percentage of poor in all these occupations is high for the SC as compared to higher castes. The percentage of poor among OBC in these occupations is also higher than higher castes but almost on a par with the SC.

Thus, it emerged that the SC regular salaried workers are mainly concentrated in low-paying occupations, which include elementary occupations, service workers and shop and market sale workers, craft and related trade workers, plant and machine operators and assemblers, and technicians and associate professionals. Their share is relatively low as compared to higher castes in better occupations, which include the legislature, senior officials and managers, clerks, skilled agricultural and fishery workers. However, in all occupations, the percentage of poor is high among the SC than higher castes. The percentage of poor among the SC is particularly high in low-level occupations.

Table 10.5 Percentage of poor among regular salaried workers across occupational categories, 2017–18

Occupational Classification	Hindu SC		Hindu OBC		Hindu Higher Castes		Total	
	% of population	% of poor	% of population	% of poor	% of population	% of poor	% of population	% of poor
Legislators, senior officials, and managers	3.2	6.7	4.7	6.8	8.5	1.5	5.4	4.7
Professionals	7.5	12.3	11.2	7.9	16.1	3.8	12.0	7.3
Technicians and associate professionals	12.4	14.4	14.6	10.5	15.3	6.3	14.5	10.4
Clerks	5.7	11.9	8.5	16.7	10.8	8.4	8.3	12.2
Service workers and shop and market sales workers	18.7	24.4	17.4	23.7	16.3	14.4	17.2	22.4
Skilled agricultural and fishery workers	0.8	14.3	1.1	21.4	0.5	9.0	0.9	25.5
Craft and related trade workers	14.1	24.6	14.1	19.8	10.3	13.3	13.3	20.8
Plant and machine operators and assemblers	14.6	24.1	14.6	24.1	11.7	16.1	13.8	22.7
Elementary occupations	23.1	32.6	14.0	22.9	10.6	18.9	14.7	26.6
Total	100.0	22.8	100.0	18.0	100.0	10.3	100.0	17.5

Source: Authors' calculation based on PLFS 2017–18 data.

The percentage of poor among regular salaried workers by education level indicates that it is highest among illiterates and individuals with education level up to primary irrespective of the social groups (Table 10.6). Generally, the percentage of poor declined from lower education level to a higher level. Irrespective of the level of education, the percentage of poor is highest among the SC under every educational category. It is surprising to see that the percentage of poor is quite high among the SC who has postgraduate and above level of education. Surprisingly, this is true for both the years for the SC, which needs explanation. The high level of unemployment among the

Table 10.6 Percentage of poor among regular wage earners across educational categories

	ST	Hindu SC	Hindu OBC	Hindu Higher Castes	Muslims	Others	Total
				2004–05			
Illiterate	53.8	47.3	36.8	27.7	51.4	17.4	41.5
Primary	39.7	36.1	28.4	17.7	36.1	22.2	29.3
Middle	23.3	30.6	22.4	14.4	32.6	12.3	22.6
Secondary	15.5	23.2	16.0	11.7	26.1	5.6	15.7
Higher secondary + Diploma	11.1	12.5	8.9	4.9	13.3	5.8	7.8
Graduate	9.1	7.9	5.1	2.8	10.5	0.9	4.3
Postgraduate and above	0.7	10.3	4.0	1.5	3.5	0.2	2.7
Total	29.4	30.7	19.4	9.1	31.2	8.2	18.8
				2017–18			
Illiterate	41.2	35.8	25.1	17.8	38.0	27.5	31.0
Primary	42.5	32.7	22.3	18.4	38.2	19.2	27.5
Middle	30.9	26.7	24.0	18.6	26.9	18.1	23.8
Secondary	21.5	18.6	24.1	14.1	26.2	14.4	19.9
Higher Secondary + Diploma	21.0	15.8	17.7	9.5	21.0	9.7	14.9
Graduate	14.2	10.9	8.5	5.2	12.3	3.7	7.7
Postgraduate and above	7.3	11.2	6.8	2.5	8.0	1.7	5.2
Total	26.3	22.8	18.0	10.3	26.8	10.6	17.5

Source: Authors' calculation based on NSS 61st round and PLFS 2017–18 data.

SC educated youth may be one of the reasons. For instance, the unemployment among the SC (based on current weekly status) in 2017–18 is 19 per cent as compared to 11 per cent among the higher castes. Unemployment among the SC graduate and above is 41 to 44 per cent as compared to 32 to 36 per cent among the higher castes. Thus, generally, the percentage of poor tends to be high among the less literate SC and it gets reduced with improvement in education level up to graduate, after which it shows a rising trend for postgraduate and above. In the case of higher castes and OBC, a negative association exists between education and poverty at all levels of education.

The discussion on castewise poverty revealed some features which are relevant for our discussion on the impact of discrimination in employment and wages on poverty. It emerged that, both in 2004–05 and 2017–18, the incidence of poverty among the SC is significantly higher than higher castes and OBC. Without any exception, the poverty of the SC is also high by a significant margin in all the states. In all group of industries, SC workers are poorer than higher castes and OBC. The SC are mainly concentrated in low-paying occupations, that include elementary occupations, service workers and shop and market sale workers, craft and related trade workers, plant and machine operators and assemblers, and technicians and associate professionals. On the other hand, their participation is relatively low in better occupations, which include the legislature, senior officials and managers, clerks, skilled agricultural and fishery workers. In all occupations, however, the SC are poorer than higher castes. The poverty levels tend to be high among the less literate SC, and it reduces with improvement in education level, but as seen, the poverty picks up for graduate and postgraduate levels, possibly due to very high unemployment rate among them. The negative association between education and poverty is true both for higher castes and OBC at all levels of education.

10.3 Determinants of Poverty

The above descriptive analysis indicates that type of industry, occupation, and education level matter in the incidence of poverty among the SC and higher castes. To get some insight into the causes of poverty among poor regular salaried workers at the individual level, a logit model is estimated using the unit-level NSS data. The results are presented in Table 10.7.

Table 10.7 Determinants of poverty among regular salaried workers, 2004–05 and 2017–18

	2004–05			2017–18		
	Coefficients	Z	Prob > Z	Coefficients	Z	Prob > Z
Base: Hindu SC						
Hindu higher castes	−0.8771	−20.59	0.0000	−0.4654	−9.97	0.0000
Hindu OBC	−0.1843	−4.91	0.0000	−0.1362	−3.24	0.0010
Base: Urban						
Rural	−0.3766	−11.35	0.0000	0.3490	9.65	0.0000
Base: Age ≠ 15–29 years						
Youth	0.0509	1.45	0.1460	0.0888	2.35	0.0190
Base: Education up to primary						
Secondary	−0.8359	−18.73	0.0000	−0.3724	−8.45	0.0000
Higher secondary	−1.2987	−22.38	0.0000	−0.7226	−12.49	0.0000
Diploma	−2.0190	−18.34	0.0000	−1.4904	−12.06	0.0000
Graduate and above	−2.2288	−37.53	0.0000	−1.4360	−25.60	0.0000
Base: Least developed states						
Relatively developed states	−0.3893	−10.06	0.0000	−0.2559	−6.09	0.0000
Less developed states	−0.2960	−7.39	0.0000	−0.3112	−7.10	0.0000
No. of dependents	0.2361	33.97	0.0000	0.3224	37.73	0.0000
Base: Regular formal workers						
Regular informal workers	0.8189	21.86	0.0000	0.8236	16.98	0.0000
Constant	−1.2717	−23.11	0.0000	−3.0129	−37.28	0.0000
Log-likelihood	−13176.7			−11423.6		
Number of observations	32,428			30,924		
Wald chi-square	4534.27			3157.2		
Probability > chi-square	0.0000			0.0000		
Pseudo R-square	0.2022			0.1514		

Source: Authors' calculation based on NSS 61st round and PLFS 2017–18 data.

Let the dependent variable y take the value one if ith worker in a regular job is poor, and value zero if the worker in a regular job is not poor. In this model, the natural logarithm of odds of the regular worker being poor is a function of k explanatory variables represented as follows.

$$\ln \frac{\Pr\,(y_i = 1)}{1 - \Pr\,(y_i - 1)} = \sum \beta_k x_k$$

The explanatory variables are social group, location (rural/urban), age, education, number of dependents, having social security benefits or not and located in a relatively developed state or not.

It emerged that individual regular salaried worker who belongs to OBC and higher castes is less likely to be in poverty as compared to SC. During the period 2004–05, regular workers residing in rural areas are less likely to be poor as compared to those residing in urban areas. However, the sign changed to positive during 2017–18 which indicates that regular workers residing in rural areas are less likely to be poor than the workers residing in urban areas. Coefficient, corresponding to youth, is positive in both the years but significant only during 2017–18 which indicates that compared to workers aged above 30 years, the regular workers who are in their youth are more likely to be poor. This is expected because at the beginning of the career wages are low, and during the initial years most of them are employed on contractual employment with low wages/salary.

Education also makes a difference to the poverty level as it improves the employability of an individual and the income. Illiterate and literate up to primary level is considered as the base category. All the other educational categories processed negative and significant signs which indicate that workers in regular jobs with education above the primary level are less likely to be poor as compared to those who have less than primary education.

The level of economic development of a region plays an important role in the well-being of the workers residing there. Developed regions provide greater job opportunities and higher wages. To know the relationship between the development of a region and poverty, the states are divided into relatively developed, less developed and least developed based on the Multidimensional Development Index developed by Raghuram Ranjan Committee.

As per the Committee, Haryana, Uttarakhand, Maharashtra, Punjab, Tamil Nadu, Kerala, and Goa are relatively developed states; West Bengal, Andhra Pradesh, Jammu and Kashmir, Mizoram, Gujarat, Tripura, Karnataka, Sikkim, and Himachal Pradesh are less developed states; and Odisha, Bihar, Madhya Pradesh, Chhattisgarh, Jharkhand, Arunachal Pradesh, Assam, Meghalaya, Uttar Pradesh, and Rajasthan are least developed states. Results indicate a negative significant coefficient for relatively developed and less developed states which implies that regular workers belonging to developed states are less likely to be poor as compared to the least developed states. The number of dependents also emerged as an important indicator to determine the poverty of regular salaried workers. With more dependents, it is likely that the households would be more prone to high poverty. Further, job and social security also make a difference. The regular workers, without any job contract and social security benefits, are more likely to be poor as compared to regular formal workers with a job and social security.

10.4 Impact of Discrimination on Poverty

Analysis of determinants of poverty revealed that the location of an individual, namely whether s/he is from a rural or urban area, and an economically developed or less developed region, makes a difference to the income and poverty. Apart from location, age, education, number of dependents, job, and social security also matter for income and poverty. However, the most important result is that the caste status of an individual makes a significant difference in the impact of these variables. This means that an individual who possesses similar endowments in terms of age, education, number of dependents, job, and social security, would make a difference to the wage income because of her/his caste.

The econometric exercise related to employment and wage discrimination reveals that even if the SC workers possess similar endowments in terms of age, education, number of dependents, job, and social security, yet their probability of employment is less as compared to equally-placed higher castes individuals. The equally endowed SC workers are also likely to earn lower wages as compared to their higher castes counterparts. Similarly, the SC workers with similar endowments often find them in low-paying occupations. In other words, the SC workers face discrimination while seeking employment despite all personal attributes being equal to that of higher castes workers. We have seen that about 58 per cent of the differences in probability of employment of regular salaried workers between the SC and higher castes are due to discrimination in hiring. Similarly, about 35 per cent differences in the wages received by the SC and higher castes wage workers are due to wage discrimination. The equally-qualified SC workers also tend to be pushed into low-earning occupations. These discriminations in the labour market, either in employment or wage or occupation, have a direct negative impact on the earning of the regular salaried wage workers. Discrimination in employment results in high unemployment/underemployment and low income. Similarly, wage discrimination brings a reduction in wage earning. The occupational discrimination pushes the SC workers to elementary occupations with low earnings. Together, the high unemployment and low wage earning result in low income and induce high poverty among the SC. Although this is evident from our study as well as others' studies, the exact impact of employment and wage discrimination on wage earning and poverty is something which remains unknown. To develop an evidence-based policy against employment and wage discrimination, it is necessary that the magnitude of fall in earning and rise in poverty due to employment and wage discrimination be estimated. Therefore, in this chapter, we will estimate the losses in income and the resultant increase in poverty among the SC regular salaried workers on account of discrimination in employment and wages by higher castes using 2004–05 and 2017–18 Employment and Unemployment Survey data.

10.4.1 Methodology Used to Measure Total Wage Earning Loss

Within the limitation of the data from the Employment and Unemployment Survey on employment and wages, we have developed a method to estimate the wage income loss due to employment and wage discrimination. The methodology is discussed below.

10.4.1.1 Wage Loss Due to Employment Discrimination

The wage loss due to employment discrimination is estimated using the following methods.

1. Non-linear decomposition method developed by Nielsen (1998). The difference in probability to get employment is decomposed between the SC and higher castes regular salaried wage workers.
2. Predict probability for the SC regular salaried workers is considered if they are treated like higher castes.
3. Those SC regular salaried workers who are supposed to be in the labour market, but are not due to discrimination are identified.
4. The wage of the SC regular salaried workers based on the wage equation is estimated. It is the wage loss due to employment discrimination.

10.4.1.2 Wage Loss Due to Wage Discrimination

The wage loss due to wage discrimination is estimated using the following methods.

1. Oaxaca decomposition method to decompose the wage gap between the SC and higher castes regular salaried workers.
2. Predict wage income for the SC regular salaried workers if they are paid like higher castes with similar endowment characteristics.
3. Difference between projected wage and actual wage due to wage discrimination is estimated for the SC and higher castes regular salaried workers. This difference is the wage loss due to wage discrimination.

10.4.1.3 Estimation of Poverty Accounting for Wage Loss Due to Employment Discrimination and Wage Discrimination

The poverty caused as a result of wage loss due to employment discrimination and wage discrimination is estimated using the following methods.

1. This additional wage, due to employment loss and wage loss, is added to the respective household monthly expenditure after converting into monthly earning.

2. Compare the new monthly per capita expenditure with Tendulkar's poverty line.
3. Estimate the incidence of poverty, i.e. headcount ratio.

10.5 Discussion of Results

Oaxaca decomposition and Nielsen's non-linear employment decomposition analyses are carried out both at the state level and all-India level. To mention the results briefly, the decomposition of gross difference in employment rate between the SC and higher castes shows that discrimination accounts for about 58 per cent of the difference in employment and 35 per cent of the difference in wages. A wide variation is also seen across states and most of the developed states have shown less discrimination.

Table 10.8 presents the poverty estimates for regular salaried workers belonging to the SC and higher castes for two scenarios: (i) without accounting for discrimination and (ii) after accounting for discrimination.

After accounting for the wage loss and employment loss due to discrimination in their total expenditure, the incidence of poverty declined by 7.1 percentage points during 2004–05 and 9.2 percentage points during 2017–18 for the SC regular salaried workers. These figures imply that nearly 0.79 million SC regular salaried workers would have been out of poverty in the absence of discrimination during 2004–05, while 1.6 million SC regular salaried workers would have been out of poverty during 2017–18.

At the state level, it is evident that the incidence of poverty is high among regular salaried workers in Bihar, Uttar Pradesh, Odisha, Rajasthan, Madhya Pradesh in both the years (Table 10.9 and Table 10.10). These states have not only witnessed high poverty but have also shown a high decline in poverty after accounting for the discrimination in their monthly expenditure.

The results imply that among various other measures to reduce poverty, elimination of employment discrimination and wage discrimination of regular salaried workers would reduce the number of poor by nearly 40 per cent. These new findings of this study are useful to develop strategy to reduce poverty among the SC workers in India. Thus, poverty would decline substantially if workers were not subjected to discrimination.

Table 10.8 Impact of discrimination on incidence of poverty at all-India level

	Hindu SC		Hindu OBC		Hindu Higher Castes	
	With Discrimination	Without Discrimination	With Discrimination	Without Discrimination	With Discrimination	Without Discrimination
2004–05						
Percentage of poor	30.74	23.64	19.43	13.83	9.07	9.07
Number of regular salaried workers (in million)	11.08		20.06		21.95	
Number of poor regular salaried workers (in million)	3.41	2.62	3.90	2.78	1.99	1.99
Difference (in million)	0.79		1.12		0.00	
2017–18						
Percentage of poor	22.76	13.56	17.97	11.27	10.25	10.25
Number of regular salaried workers (in million)	17.42		34.67		30.63	
Number of poor regular salaried workers (in million)	3.96	2.36	6.23	3.91	3.14	3.14
Difference (in million)	1.60		2.32		0.00	

Source: Authors' calculation based on NSS 61st round and PLFS 2017–18 data.

Table 10.9 Impact of discrimination on incidence of poverty at state level, 2004–05

2004–05 States	Hindu SC		Hindu OBC		Hindu Higher Castes
	With Discrimination	Without Discrimination	With Discrimination	Without Discrimination	
Andhra Pradesh	30.42	25.36	18.48	14.92	6.31
Bihar	53.97	46.97	33.70	28.20	10.85
Chhattisgarh	16.03	10.03	25.86	21.36	8.76
Haryana	32.53	28.03	18.49	15.49	6.43
Himachal Pradesh	11.92	5.72	6.24	1.54	8.27
Jharkhand	18.67	14.37	18.80	16.00	16.84
Karnataka	26.80	21.50	15.14	11.34	9.27
Kerala	23.53	21.03	11.29	10.29	5.98
Madhya Pradesh	51.41	44.61	33.63	28.33	9.41
Maharashtra	32.48	24.38	18.35	11.75	11.75
Odisha	44.86	37.36	31.11	25.11	17.79
Punjab	25.69	20.39	12.63	8.83	8.15
Rajasthan	40.90	35.60	17.13	13.33	6.84
Tamil Nadu	24.40	13.60	15.34	6.04	2.88
Uttar Pradesh	42.36	32.76	24.10	16.00	11.59
Uttarakhand	25.06	19.46	18.57	14.47	8.59
West Bengal	23.40	15.90	19.35	13.35	8.92
All India	30.74	23.64	19.43	13.83	9.07

Source: Authors' calculation based on NSS 61st round data.

Table 10.10 Impact of discrimination on incidence of poverty at state level, 2017–18

2017–18	Hindu SC		Hindu Higher Castes
	With Discrimination	Without Discrimination	
Andhra Pradesh	15.33	9.78	3.12
Bihar	26.33	18.6	21.43
Chhattisgarh	41.86	30.8	16.94
Haryana	38.14	31.6	14.42
Himachal Pradesh	20.36	15.2	12.22
Jharkhand	17.12	11.8	9.47
Karnataka	29.58	20.68	11.21
Kerala	25.79	20.45	7.81
Madhya Pradesh	27.02	18.62	5.77
Maharashtra	20.29	14.68	10.77
Odisha	22.58	12.65	14.71
Punjab	23.4	10.5	9.32
Rajasthan	24.88	18.6	12.85
Tamil Nadu	16.22	10.56	1.31
Uttar Pradesh	26.15	14.65	11.07
Uttarakhand	11.93	8.69	10.71
West Bengal	20.4	12.35	11.23
All India	22.76	13.56	10.25

Source: Authors' calculation based on PLFS 2017–18 data.

10.6 Conclusion

The present study is probably the first which has estimated the impact of employment and wage discrimination on the income and poverty of the SC. The results are new and profound in terms of their relevance. Insofar as the results have disclosed the role of discrimination behind the persistently high poverty among the SC as compared to similarly placed workers from the higher castes. Estimates of the impact of labour market discrimination on the income and poverty of the SC provide the magnitude of their income loss and the extent to which it pushes them into chronic poverty. It has profound policy implications. It implies that the elimination of discrimination in employment and wages would reduce their poverty by a significant margin. It is evident that after accounting for the wage loss and employment loss due to discrimination in their total expenditure, the in-cidence of poverty declined by 7.1 percentage points during 2004–05 and 9.2 percentage points during 2017–18 for the SC. These figures imply that nearly 0.79 million SC regular salaried workers would have been out of poverty in the absence of discrimination during 2004–05, while 1.6 mil-lion SC regular salaried workers would have been out of poverty during 2017–18. The implications are that the elimination of the SC poverty would not only require improvement in the endowment factors, particularly the ownership of agricultural land and capital, and access to higher education but also ways and means to reduce discrimination in the labour market in employment and wages. These policy measures would include legal safe-guards against discrimination in employment and wages in the market, and affirmative action to ensure fair share to the SC workers in employ-ment in regular salaried jobs and their wages, particularly in the private sector where the magnitude of employment and wage discrimination is high, without which they would face under-representation in the regular salaried jobs and also receive wages lower than their productivity.

Appendix Table 10.1 Monthly per capita expenditure across social groups (at 2017–18 prices)

	2004–05	2017–18	Change in ₹	Annual % Change	Ratio with Hindu SC
			Rural		
Hindu SC	1225.8	1388.5	162.7	0.96	1.00
Hindu OBC	1405.9	1516.4	110.5	0.58	1.15
Hindu higher castes	1824.3	1794.6	-29.7	-0.13	1.49
Total	1435.1	1524.1	89.0	0.46	
			Urban		
Hindu SC	1846.0	2256.6	410.5	1.56	1.00
Hindu OBC	2229.3	2780.0	550.7	1.71	1.21
Hindu higher castes	3514.3	3673.1	158.8	0.34	1.90
Total	2610.1	2909.0	298.9	0.84	
			Total		
Hindu SC	1345.2	1579.2	234.0	1.24	1.00
Hindu OBC	1576.3	1844.7	268.4	1.22	1.17
Hindu higher castes	2494.6	2607.6	113.0	0.34	1.85
Total	1734.4	1930.0	195.6	0.83	

Source: Authors' calculation based on NSS 61st round and PLFS 2017–18 data.

Appendix Table 10.2 Monthly per capita expenditure across employment categories

	Hindu SC	Hindu OBC	Hindu Higher Castes	Total	Hindu OBC/ Hindu SC	Hindu Higher castes/ Hindu SC
2004–05 (at 2017–18 prices)						
Rural						
Self-employed	1336.6	1504.3	1845.6	1551.6	1.13	1.38
Regular wage earner	1726.1	2019.2	2747.7	2153.3	1.17	1.59
Casual labour	1168.0	1251.9	1388.2	1210.3	1.07	1.19
Total	1274.5	1465.6	1864.9	1482.1	1.15	1.46
Urban						
Self-employed	1766.4	2093.8	3379.4	2513.5	1.19	1.91
Regular wage earner	2328.4	2799.9	4121.0	3270.7	1.20	1.77
Casual labour	1455.4	1648.4	1832.8	1587.6	1.13	1.26
Total	1908.5	2269.5	3635.2	2673.5	1.19	1.90
Total						
Self-employed	1396.4	1587.3	2225.1	1721.7	1.14	1.59
Regular wage earner	2061.4	2451.6	3727.5	2840.1	1.19	1.81
Casual labour	1195.4	1299.8	1468.0	1253.9	1.09	1.23
Total	1381.8	1614.2	2482.7	1746.0	1.17	1.80

	Hindu SC	Hindu OBC	Hindu Higher castes	Total	Hindu OBC/ Hindu SC	Hindu Higher castes/ Hindu SC
2017–18(PLFS)						
Rural						
Self-employed	1455.0	1552.4	1775.0	1563.2	1.07	1.22
Regular wage earner	2028.0	2086.5	2443.2	2177.7	1.03	1.20
Casual labour	1350.1	1467.5	1549.0	1380.4	1.09	1.15
Total	1474.7	1600.3	1855.3	1590.8	1.09	1.26
Urban						
Self-employed	2147.8	2671.3	3568.5	2847.5	1.24	1.66
Regular wage earner	2837.1	3503.9	4307.5	3642.5	1.23	1.52

(continued)

Appendix Table 10.2 Continued

	2004–05 (at 2017–18 prices)					
	Hindu SC	Hindu OBC	Hindu Higher Castes	Total	Hindu OBC/ Hindu SC	Hindu Higher castes/ Hindu SC
Casual labour	1756.7	2015.2	2114.1	1889.6	1.15	1.20
Total	2381.9	2944.7	3867.6	3080.7	1.24	1.62
	Total					
Self-employed	1569.5	1756.1	2307.2	1833.1	1.12	1.47
Regular wage earner	2454.7	2872.5	3754.5	3041.7	1.17	1.53
Casual labour	1400.7	1568.3	1696.9	1466.3	1.12	1.21
Total	1674.0	1952.5	2712.2	2017.6	1.17	1.62

	Annual Change between 2004–05 to 2017–18			
	Hindu SC	Hindu OBC	Hindu Higher castes	Total
	Rural			
Self-employed	0.66	0.24	-0.30	0.06
Regular wage earner	1.25	0.25	-0.90	0.09
Casual labour	1.12	1.23	0.85	1.02
Total	1.13	0.68	-0.04	0.55
	Urban			
Self-employed	1.51	1.89	0.42	0.96
Regular wage earner	1.53	1.74	0.34	0.83
Casual labour	1.46	1.56	1.10	1.35
Total	1.72	**2.02**	**0.48**	**1.10**
	Total			
Self-employed	0.90	0.78	0.28	0.48
Regular wage earner	1.35	1.23	0.06	0.53
Casual labour	1.23	1.45	1.12	1.21
Total	1.49	1.47	0.68	1.12

Source: Authors' calculation based on NSS 61st round and PLFS 2017–18 data.

Appendix Table 10.3 Incidence of poverty across social groups (percentage share to total)

| | RURAL | | | | | | |
| | 2004–05 | | | 2017–18 | | | Change in HCR (Percentage Points) |
	HCR	% Share in Total population	Contribution to Total Poverty	HCR	% Share in Total population	Contribution to Total Poverty	
ST	59.7	12.0	17.1	53.4	13.5	19.6	6.3
Hindu SC	52.7	21.1	26.6	41.5	21.2	23.9	11.2
Hindu OBC	39.3	38.3	35.9	35.2	36.8	35.2	4.1
Hindu higher castes	24.4	16.9	9.8	26.3	16.5	11.8	–1.9
Muslims	44.9	8.9	9.5	31.7	9.3	8.0	13.2
Others	16.7	2.8	1.1	20.6	2.8	1.5	–3.9
Total	41.9	100.0	100.0	36.8	100.0	100.0	5.1
URBAN							
ST	45.7	3.1	5.0	31.5	3.6	5.5	14.2
Hindu SC	43.7	15.1	23.4	28.5	14.9	20.9	15.2
Hindu OBC	29.9	30.5	32.4	19.4	32.5	31.2	10.5
Hindu higher castes	12.3	31.8	13.9	11.0	30.5	16.6	1.3
Muslims	45.5	14.8	23.9	34.1	14.0	23.5	11.4
Others	8.9	4.6	1.5	9.7	4.6	2.2	–0.7
Total	28.2	100.0	100.0	20.2	100.0	100.0	8.0

(continued)

Appendix Table 10.3 Continued

| | 2004–05 | | | 2017–18 (RURAL) | | | |
| | TOTAL | | | | | | |
	HCR	% Share in Total population	Contribution to Total Poverty	HCR	% Share in Total population	Contribution to Total Poverty	Change in HCR (Percentage Points)
ST	58.7	10.0	15.1	51.3	10.6	17.0	7.4
Hindu SC	51.2	19.8	26.1	38.7	19.4	23.4	12.5
Hindu OBC	37.6	36.5	35.3	31.1	35.6	34.5	6.5
Hindu higher castes	20.2	20.2	10.5	19.8	20.5	12.7	0.4
Muslims	45.1	10.2	11.8	32.6	10.6	10.8	12.5
Others	14.3	3.2	1.2	16.2	3.3	1.7	-2.0
Total	38.9	100.0	100.0	32.1	100.0	100.0	6.8

Source: Authors' calculation based on NSS 61st round and PLFS 2017–18 data.

11

Untouchables' Poverty

Sources and Remedies

11.1 Untouchables' Poverty

The present study has tried to develop an insight into the continuing problem of high poverty among the ex-untouchables (Scheduled Castes), its sources and the possible solution to bridge the gaps between them and others. The study began with the assumption that high poverty among the Scheduled Castes (SC) regular salaried workers is linked with the institution of caste and untouchability. The traditional rules and norms of the caste system related to employment, wages, and occupations are discriminatory to the SC, insofar they are barred from employment in the occupations of the higher castes, except the manual labour. Over a period of time the traditional regulatory framework was gradually eroded and completely overturned by the new Constitution in 1950. However, despite the provision in the Constitution and the laws, contrary to traditional regulatory caste laws, the discrimination that involves differential treatment to the SC in the labour market persists with unequal labour market outcome in employment, wages, and occupations. The legacy of the past exclusion in occupations and hiring, including the wages, continue in the 'present'—the past does not remain in the past, but comes alive in the present—the present in fact is the living past. Hence, the discrimination of the SC in the labour market remains an issue of great concern.

Economic analysis of the caste system implies that labour market discrimination in India is in fact deeply embedded in caste relations and remains integral to the governing (economic) rules of the caste system. In the traditional regulatory framework of the caste system, the occupation of each caste is fixed by birth. The employment of people remained confined to their caste without the freedom to take up occupations of

Scheduled Castes in the Indian Labour Market. Sukhadeo Thorat, S. Madheswaran, and B. P. Vani,
Oxford University Press. © Sukhadeo Thorat, S. Madheswaran, and B. P. Vani 2023.
DOI: 10.1093/oso/9780198872252.003.0011

other castes. For instance, in the castewise division of labour, teaching and preaching are the domains of the Brahmins, military the realm of the kshatriyas, trade and non-farm production enterprises, trade and business that of the vaishyas, while employment in farming as a self-employed worker remains restricted to the shudras. The untouchables' only work is to serve the four castes above them as wage labourer, mostly as slave, bonded, and attached labour. Thus, employment naturally remains segregated into caste without the freedom of mobility from one economic activity to another. In this sense, discrimination in employment becomes an integral part of the allocation of work under the legal framework of the caste system. In effect, the restrictions on taking up the work of another caste bring segmentation in the labour market on caste lines; individuals get engaged in their own caste occupation without entry to occupations assigned to other castes. In this sense, segmentation exists in five caste occupations in the labour market with barriers on the mobility of workers from one to another.

While the division of occupation brings the division of workers for all castes, the situation of untouchables assumes a somewhat different form. They face both exclusion and inclusion in employment. The employment of untouchables by higher castes in the labour market is affected by dual process of exclusion and inclusion. The untouchable workers would face exclusion in employment in teaching and preaching works reserved for the Brahmins. Similarly, they would face denial in work in military earmarked for the kshatriyas, or in self-employed/wage workers in trade and non-farm production reserved for the vaishyas, and finally, as self-employed farmer/wage workers which is the occupation of the shudras. The untouchables also face exclusion in some works due to their polluting social status. They are excluded in categories of work which involve direct physical contact, domestic work, and tasks related to religious events.

However, while the untouchables are excluded as teachers and preachers, soldiers and workers in military, workers in trade and commerce, and self-employed/wage workers in farming, they are included for work as manual labourers and tasks that involve hard physical work. The work that involves physical labour is obligatory under the Hindu law of caste. Therefore, they are particularly engaged in agricultural and allied activities which involve physical labour. Also, they are required to carry out tasks that are considered inferior and polluting, like scavenging, those related to leather (skinning carcasses, tanning, etc.) and minor artisan work. Thus, the norms and rules of the caste system regarding the work for the untouchables involve both exclusion and inclusion, what Sen (2000) has rightly described as 'unfavourable exclusion' and 'unfavourable inclusion'. While they are unfavourably excluded from the (better) work in which the higher castes are engaged as teachers, military personnel, or as self-employed/wage workers in farming or non-farm production enterprises, or trade, at the same time, they are unfavourably (often forcefully) included and employed in manual wage labour required in the occupations of all four castes above them. Their involvement as manual wage labour often assumes the form of attached, bonded, and slave labour with very low remuneration.

This is the traditional regulatory framework of the caste system which has been there since Manu first framed the systematic rules in about 200 BCE. This regulatory framework has now been replaced by the new Constitution in 1950. The Constitution accepted the principle of equality and non-discrimination in employment. It also guarantees equality in right to property and education. The question is: Do the SC enjoy equal opportunity and non-discriminatory access in labour market in practice? Is de jure also de facto? Or is it that the legacy of the past continues in the present in new forms? We have seen that despite the provision in the Constitution and the laws contrary to traditional codes of the caste system, the caste discrimination persists in the labour market in new forms. The legacy of past discrimination in hiring, wages, and occupations continues in the present.

The present study has enquired into these questions of discrimination in labour market with respect to hiring, wages, and occupations. It generated empirical evidence on the practice of discrimination in employment, wages, and occupations, and its impact on income and poverty of the SC regular salaried workers in India based on the National Sample Survey data for the year 2004–05 and 2017–18. First, it analysed the caste inequality in employment and unemployment, in wage earning and the occupations between the SC and the higher castes regular salaried workers at the national and state levels. Second, it looked into the sources of caste inequality in employment, occupations, and wage earning between the SC and the higher castes in terms of differences in endowment factors and caste discrimination in employment, wages, and occupations. Third, it estimated losses in the wage income of the SC regular salaried workers due to discrimination in employment and wages. Finally, it estimated the increase in the poverty of the SC regular salaried workers due to fall in wage income (in term of consumption expenditure) on account of discrimination in employment and wages. In conclusion the study proposed policies to overcome discrimination in employment and wages and its negative impact.

We summarize the findings of the study with respect to:

(a) Caste inequality in income and poverty.
(b) Inequality in employment and unemployment, wage earning, and occupations.
(c) Magnitude of discrimination in employment and unemployment, wages, and occupations.
(d) Impact of employment and wage discrimination on income and poverty of the SC.
(e) Indicate the policy implications of the findings to reduce employment and wage discrimination to improve income and reduce poverty.

11.2 Caste Inequality in Wage Income and Poverty

11.2.1 Wage Income and Poverty

The regular salaried workers form the focus group which constitutes about one-fifth of the total workers in the country in 2017–18. The percentage of regular salaried workers among SC is about 20 per cent. It emerged that the wage earning of the SC regular salaried workers is lower than the higher castes workers. This affects the consumption expenditure of the SC regular salaried workers. The consumption expenditure of the SC is ₹1,674 which is lower than ₹1,952 for the Other Backward Classes (OBC) and ₹2,712 for the higher castes, while the all-India average is ₹2,017. The consumption expenditure of the SC is 61 per cent of the higher castes and 85 per cent of the OBC.

The caste disparities in per capita consumption expenditure also result in gap in poverty of these three castes. In 2011–12 (the latest year for which the poverty data is available), the incidence of poverty among the SC is significantly higher than the higher castes and OBC. At the national level, about 17 per cent of the regular salaried workers are poor. But the incidence of poverty among the SC regular salaried workers is about 23 per cent which is higher than the all-India average and higher castes (10 per cent) and OBC (18 per cent). Thus, there is graded inequality both in per capita consumption expenditure and poverty. The per capita consumption expenditure is highest for the higher castes and considerably reduces as we go lower in the caste hierarchy. The opposite is the case for poverty—it increases as we move down in the caste hierarchy from higher castes to middle castes, the OBC, and to the SC.

11.2.2 Inequality in Employment and Wages

The labour market outcomes in terms of employment, wages, and occupations are unequal between the SC and the higher castes. In case of occupations, it emerged that a high percentage of SC workers are employed in low-paid elementary and unskilled occupations. A relatively high proportion of the SC workers are engaged in agriculture and construction industry. Thus, although there has been a break from the restrictions on occupations, the traditional occupational segregation or concentration of the SC in low-paid work continues in the present.

Coming to employment, the probability of employment is low for the SC as compared to the higher castes. The gross difference in probabilities of getting employment between the SC and the higher castes is 0.088 in 2004–05 and 0.070 in 2017–18, indicating a lower probability of employment for the SC as compared to the higher castes. Low probability of employment results in a high unemployment rate among the SC. In 2017–18, the unemployment (based on current weekly status) rate was 10.5 per cent for the SC which is higher than 8.3 per cent for the higher castes and 8.1 per cent for the OBC. The inter-caste differences are greater in urban areas (11.1 per cent for the SC, 8.7 for the higher castes and 9.5 per cent for the OBC). In rural areas too, the rates are 10.4 per cent for the SC, 8 per cent for the higher castes and 7.6 per cent for the OBC. Thus, without exception, the SC suffers more from unemployment than the higher castes.

Unemployment is generally high at all levels of education among the SC. However, the gap between the SC and the higher castes is particularly high for levels beyond higher secondary and graduate. Among the SC, the youth in the age group of 15–29 years suffered the most from unemployment as compared to their higher caste counterparts.

On the basis of the category of employment, the SCs are concentrated in agriculture and construction industry. Their share in the construction industry is almost three times higher than that of the higher castes. The reverse is the case in manufacturing, trade, storage, restaurant, and other services. Thus, the shares of the SC in low-paid 'agriculture and related activities', and 'construction' are much higher as compared to the higher castes. Higher engagement of the SC in low-paying economic activities is also visible in their higher employment in some occupations. Clearly, the share of SC in three occupations, namely, legislators, senior officials and managers, professionals and clerks, is low; but it is high in low-paying jobs, such as elementary or unskilled occupations, domestic helpers, cleaners, garbage collectors, etc. It, thus, appears that the SC presumably continues to face restrictions in occupations which were prohibited to them in the past.

The wage earning of the SC regular salaried workers is found to be lower than that of the higher castes by almost 30 per cent. The wages of the SC are found to be lower in almost all occupations. Wage earning also varies between the public and the private sectors. The wage gap between the SC and the higher castes is more in the private sector as compared to the public sector. This is particularly the case in the urban private sector. While this is the pattern at the aggregate level, the wage gap between the SC and the higher castes varies across the wage distribution, i.e. between the lower and upper quintiles. In the public sector, the wage gap between the SC and the higher castes is higher at the bottom percentiles, i.e. below 50th percentile, than at the upper percentiles of the wage distribution. On the other hand, in the private sector, the wage gap between the SC and the higher castes are higher at the upper percentiles, i.e. above 50th percentile, than at the bottom percentiles of the wage distribution. Thus, the caste inequalities between the SC and the higher castes in employment/unemployment, occupations, and wages continue to persist despite the guarantee of equal opportunity in the Constitution.

11.3 Caste Discrimination: Employment, Wages, and Occupations

The study also explored the sources of inequality between the SC and the higher castes in employment/unemployment and wages, as attributable to differences in endowment factors and discrimination in employment, wages, and occupations.

11.3.1 Employment Discrimination

The gross difference in probabilities of securing employment between the SC and the higher castes was 0.088 in 2004–05 and 0.070 in 2017–18 indicating a lower probability, albeit with a narrow gap, for the SC as compared to the higher castes. The gap in the probability of getting employment among the SC and the higher castes was partly due to differences in endowment factors (such as ownership of capital assets and higher education) and partly due to discrimination in employment. The decomposition of gross difference in probability of access to employment between the SC and the higher castes shows that discrimination accounted for about 74 per cent of the differences in employment in 2004–05 and 73 per cent in 2017–18 and the remaining 26–27 per cent was due to differences in endowment factors. Thus, the low probability of employment for the SC as compared to the higher castes is mainly caused by caste discrimination in hiring.

The Intensity of discrimination is greater in the private sector as compared to the public sector. In the private sector, employment discrimination accounted for about 53.15 per cent of the differences in the probability of access to employment which is much higher as compared to 14 per cent in the public sector. Conversely, the results on unemployment confirmed these findings. Discrimination accounts for about 65 per cent differences in the unemployment rate between the SC and the higher castes and endowment factors account for about 35 per cent. Thus, in employment the discrimination matters more than the endowment factors in causing high degree of unemployment among the SC.

11.3.2 Wage Discrimination

In case of wage discrimination, however, the endowment factors had a relatively greater impact than discrimination in explaining the wage gap between the SC and the higher castes. About 57 per cent of the wage gap between the SC and the higher castes was due to the endowment differences, with the rest being attributable to caste discrimination. Among the endowment factors, the differences in education, particularly higher education, between the SC and the higher castes contribute greatly to the earning gap between these two groups. The wage gap between the SC and the higher castes due to education and skill was 67.1 per cent in 2004–05 and 57.24 per cent during 2017–18. The higher castes have an edge in higher education (graduate and above) as compared to the SC. The other factors include marital status and nature of employment. Women's education also matter. Conversely, low access to education, including access to education of SC women, and quality of employment remain a disadvantage for the SC workers. This implies that the exclusion of the SC from access to education, employment (other than casual wage labour), and capital assets for a long time in the past seems to continue in the present as a legacy of the caste system in new forms. The discrimination in the 'present' remains an important factor in the wage gap between the SC and the higher castes.

The results of the decomposition of the discrimination component into overpayment to the higher castes and underpayment to the SC in the labour market imply the advantage of discrimination to the higher castes and the disadvantage to the SC. The results revealed that overpayment or treatment advantage to the higher castes (benefit of being higher castes in the labour market) was 8.6 per cent in 2004–05 and 16.46 per cent in 2017–18. This reflects the difference in the current wages of the higher castes which they would receive in the absence of discrimination. It also reflects nepotism towards the higher castes. On the other hand, the underpayment or treatment disadvantage to the SC (cost of being SC in the labour market) was 24.3 per cent in 2004–05 and 26.30 per cent in 2017–18. This measure depicts the difference in the current wage of the SC and the wage which they would receive in the absence of discrimination. This shows the 'cost' to the discriminated group against the 'benefits' accruing to the advantaged group. Overall, we find that the cost of being SC in the labour market is very high. They are hugely underpaid in the labour market.

The results also revealed differences in wage discrimination in the public and private sectors. The caste-based wage gap is higher in the private sector than in the public sector. Irrespective of the wage quintiles, the wage gap attributable to discrimination is high in the private sector than in the public sector. Within the private sector, however, the wage gap at high percentile level (i.e. 90th percentile) is higher than the estimated wage gaps in other parts of the wage distribution. This gives evidence of the 'glass ceiling effect' in the private sector which means that the SC employees face caste-related constraints in moving to higher positions. They seem to face a 'ceiling' in the upper mobility in the hierarchy of jobs in the private sector, despite qualification similar to the higher castes employees.

In the public sector, the wage discrimination is lower than in the private sector (except at the lower levels of wage distribution). Indeed, wage gap and level of discrimination in the public sector is consistently below the private sector across the entire range of wage distribution. However, unlike private sector, the wage gap attributable to discrimination decreases in the public sector as we move up along the wage distribution. This means that discrimination is high at a lower level of wage distribution than at the upper level. The opposite is true for the private sector. The wage gap attributable to discrimination is lower at the lower end of wage earning than at the upper end of wage earning. Thus, irrespective of the methodology used, the empirical evidence clearly exhibits high degree of discrimination against the SC in the private sector, particularly in positions with higher levels of earnings.

11.4 Occupation Segregation

The results show that in the regular salaried labour market, occupation discrimination accounts for a substantial part of the gross earnings differential between the SC and the higher castes, with occupational discrimination (inequality in access to certain occupations) being highly pronounced than wage discrimination (unequal pay within a given occupation, given one's educational and skill levels). Within the SC the younger cohorts faced higher degree of discrimination in allocation of type of jobs or work than the older cohorts.

11.5 Impact of Discrimination on Untouchables' Poverty

The findings related to combine impact of employment and wage discrimination (including occupation discrimination) on the poverty of the SC regular salaried workers are quite telling, insofar as they disclose the sources of persistently high poverty among the SC when compared to similarly placed workers from the higher castes. By estimating the impact of labour market discrimination on the income and poverty of the SC regular salaried workers in numerical terms, it approximates the magnitude of the income loss of the SC regular salaried workers and its contribution in pushing such workers into poverty. This also discloses the reasons as to why the SCs are caught in a chronic poverty trap.

We saw that after accounting for the wage loss and employment loss due to discrimination in their total consumption expenditure, the incidence of poverty declined by 7.1 percentage points during 2004–05 and 9.2 percentage points during 2017–18 for the SC. These imply that nearly 0.79 million SC regular salaried wage workers would be out of poverty in the absence of caste discrimination during 2004–05. During 2017–18, 1.6 million SC regular salaried wage workers would have been out of poverty in the absence of caste discrimination. These are extremely profound results as these provide creditable empirical evidence on the poverty-enhancing effects of discrimination of the SC in employment, wages, and occupations in labour market—a link between unequal outcome of labour market due to discrimination and chronic poverty of the SC in India is indeed real.

11.6 Remedies: Theories and Practices

11.6.1 Lessons from Theories

The economic theories which we reviewed earlier enquire into the motive behind labour market discrimination in employment and wages, and the policies to overcome the labour market discrimination in employment and wages. Theories of labour market discrimination also suggest alternative policies to overcome discrimination.

The Theory of Discrimination, based on 'Taste for Discrimination', suggests market competitiveness as a solution to overcome labour market discrimination. This is because it sees imperfections in the labour market as an enabling factor for employers to discriminate in hiring and wages. It believes that a competitive market on its own would eliminate those firms which indulge in hiring and wage discriminations as against those who do not. The cost and, hence, the price of goods produced by the firms/employers engaged in discrimination would be high as compared to those employers who employ workers and pay wages based on productivity of the workers. Thus, the employer who discriminates would be outcompeted by the ones who do not discriminate. However, in practice, discrimination continues to persist in a competitive market as well. This traditional view, that discrimination may not persist in the face of market competition, is difficult to sustain because there is negligible empirical evidence that discrimination invariably falls under the pressure of market forces. Darity (2005) observed: '... a review of the available time-series evidence across a handful of market-based economies, for which estimates are available, did not identify a pattern of declining discrimination'.

The Imperfect Information Theory considers the lack of information as the reason for discrimination. Therefore, this theory implies the policy to improve the flow of full information at a relatively low cost. The perfect information would enable the employer to make decisions on the basis of information about the education, skills, and productivity of individual applicants from the minority group, rather than perception or belief of the employer about their productivity. The Identity Theory of Discrimination proposed both Affirmative Action Policy and as well as change in norms through the civil rights movement. Given the persistence of discrimination even in the competitive labour market, affirmative Action to ensure fair share to an individual from discriminated groups is considered necessary. At the same time, Identity Theory believes that affirmative action alone is not enough. It also requires changes in the discriminatory group norms in society. Therefore, it proposed efforts to bring changes in ideas and norms that are supportive of discrimination. The outcome of the feminist movement in the United States is cited as an example which resulted in several positive decisions in favour of women.

The Racial Identity Norms Theory by Darity (Darity et al. 2006; Darity and Mullen 2020), on the other hand, proposed redistribution of wealth through reparation to the discriminated communities which suffered due to exclusion from right to property and underpayment to the slave labour for a long time. While reparation policy is found appropriate to compensate for exclusion in the 'past', but with the persistence of discrimination in the 'present', the Racial Identity Norms Theory also favoured legal safeguards and affirmative Action to ensure fair share, particularly in wealth, employment, and education institution.

In the Indian context, Ambedkar was singularly instrumental in developing policies for the empowerment of the untouchables. This was made possible due to his continuous efforts from 1919 to 1950 which came in three stages. In the first stage, the SCs were given representation through nomination in the State Assembly in Bombay Presidency. In the second stage, in 1931 political representation was given to the SC through the Poona Pact in the central and state legislatures. In the third stage, in 1944 the SCs were provided with reservation in government jobs and were also given fund for higher education (in the form of overseas scholarship and scholarship for college and university students). Also, in this stage, in 1950 finally a provision was made in the Indian constitution for the representation of the SC in government jobs, academic institutions, legislatures and other public spheres, such as housing. This provision is popularly called the 'Reservation Policy'. A careful look at the evolution of these efforts during 1919–50 indicates that policies proposed by Ambedkar were in the nature of both Affirmative action policies and Reparation for redistributive justice (that is compensation for denial of right to property, education, and civil rights in the past). Ambedkar in his memorandum in 1919, 1929, 1930, and 1944 has consistently proposed policies for the SC with four elements. These four elements include: (a) equal civil rights to all (b) legal safeguards against denial of civil and other rights due caste- and untouchability-based discrimination; (c) representation for fair share of the SC in legislature, government jobs, and academic institutions as safeguards against discrimination; and (d) measures for economic and educational empowerment through distribution of agricultural land, non-farm enterprises/businesses, and education development funds (Thorat and Kumar 2008).

The provision of equality and equal opportunity in 1935 Act or Constitution and later in the Indian Constitution in 1950 guarantee equal fundamental rights and the citizenship rights to the SC. The enactment of

Untouchability Offence Act, 1955 (renamed as Protection of Civil Rights Act in 1979) and Prevention of Atrocities Act, 1989 provide the legal safeguards against discrimination which also include legal safeguards against employment and wage discrimination. The provision of representation of the SC in the legislature in 1931 through Poona Pact, which become part of the British Indian Constitution in 1935, and provision in legislation, government jobs and academic institutions in the Indian Constitution in 1950 were designed to give fair share to the SC. The legal safeguards through anti-discrimination laws and the Reservation policy thus are a set of measures developed and accepted to provide safeguards against discrimination of untouchables in the 'present' and ensure representation in the ratio of their population.

There are other measures proposed by Ambedkar which are in the mode of 'Reparation or Compensation' for the denial of property rights, agricultural land, non-farm enterprises, education' and civil rights in the past for centuries. Ambedkar believed that the Reservation policy was necessary as safeguards against intense discrimination and anti-social attitude towards untouchables in the 'present' but it is inadequate to deal with the loss property and education rights in the 'past' for a long time which resulted in high landlessness, illiteracy, and deficiency in ownership of capital assets, such as land and enterprises. Therefore, allocation of land to the SC (through distribution of cultivable waste land or nationalization of land), measures for improvement in ownership of enterprises/businesses and fund for education development were conceive as a one-time measure to compensate for the losses and harms caused to untouchables (Ambedkar 1944). As we can see, these are in the nature of reparation and compensation for denial of property rights, right to education, and civil rights.

Similar to the Identity Theory of Discrimination by Akerlof and Kantom, Ambedkar also advocated policies by the government and civil society to reform the old ideas and norms which are supportive of the caste system. In Ambedkar's view, although discrimination is forbidden in laws, it remains in practice, as the behaviour of higher castes continues to be influenced by the ideology of castes which survive in the form of norms, customs, and social and cultural practices. Ambedkar argued that these ideas have their foundation in the Hindu religious philosophy, which make the task of reforming the caste system more difficult as religious belief is more difficult to bring in line with the provision of laws. In addressing the questions 'How to bring about the reforms of Hindu social order?' and 'How to abolish caste?', Ambedkar observed:

> Caste may be bad. Caste may lead to conduct so gross as to be called man's inhumanity to man. All the same, it must be recognized that the Hindu observed the caste not because they are inhuman or wrong-headed. They observed because they are deeply religious. People are not wrong in observing caste. In my view what is wrong is their religion which has inculcated this notion of caste. If this is correct, then obviously the enemy, you must grapple with, is not the people who observed caste. The real remedy is to destroy the belief in the sanity of the *shastras*. How do you expect to succeed, if you allow the *shastra* to continue to mould the belief and opinions of the people?
>
> (Ambedkar 1936, 68)

It is this religious faith which makes the reform of caste more difficult and stubborn for positive change. But what is important is the motive behind this religious idea of caste which makes the elimination of discrimination still more difficult. What purpose does it serve: economic or social or both? Ambedkar pondered over the motive behind the regulatory system of caste. He observed:

> An anti-social sprit is found wherever one group has 'interest of its own' which shut it out from full interaction with other group, so that its prevailing purpose is protection of what it has got. This anti-social sprit, this spirit of protecting its own interests is as much a marked feature of different castes in their isolation from one another as it is of nations in their isolation. The brahmin's primary concern is to protect 'his interest' against those of non-brahmins and the non-brahmins primary concern is to protect their interests against those of the brahmins. The Hindus, therefore, are not merely an assortment of castes but they are so many warring groups each living for itself.
>
> (Ambedkar 1936, 52)

What does the self-interest involve? From the references to the castes in Chapter 2 it is obvious that the 'self-interest' is primarily economic or material and also high social status, so the rights to property, quality employment, and education are reserved for the higher castes but at the cost of denial to the untouchables. The discrimination in labour market in employment, occupations, and wages is an instrument which is used to preserve and protect the economic rights against the untouchables. Labour market discrimination is thus a social instrument used in the market to preserve and protect the old economic privilege in occupations, employment, and education of the higher castes by denying the same to the untouchables through exchanges in the labour markets.

11.6.2 International Experiences on Policies

The policies implied by theories have indeed formed the justification for the policies framed by the government of various countries for the development of the discriminated groups, racial, ethnic, religious, gender, etc. Governments have employed a combination of reparation policy, policy of legal safeguard and Affirmation Action policy in their specific contexts. The experiences of a few countries provide an idea about the nature of policies adopted to address the specific problems of the discriminated communities, these include the United States, Northern Ireland, South Africa, Malaysia, China, Japan, Brazil, some Latin American countries, India, Pakistan, and Nepal, to name just a few. These policies broadly fall into five categories. First is the provision of equality before law, equal opportunity, and non-discrimination for all in their constitutions. Second, countries have also enacted special laws against discrimination so that the discriminated people could seek justice in court in the event of discrimination. The Protection of Civil Rights Act 1955 (formerly known as the Untouchability Offence Act) in India, Equal Opportunity Act and/or Equal Employment Opportunity Act in the United States and Northern Ireland are some of the examples of legal safeguards to the discriminated communities. The third policy relates to reparation or compensation for denial of economic rights and underpayment to slave labour for a long time (De Greiff 2008). In the United States, for example, emancipation from slavery of the Blacks brought the promise of allocation of 45 million acres of land to the ex-slaves under the terms of General Sherman's Special Field Orders, the first Freedman's Bureau Act and the Southern

Homestead Act. But, that promise went unfulfilled as President Andrew Johnson and his allies abrogated the policy of radical racial land redistribution (W.A. Darity 2005; Randall 2000; W.A. Darity Jr and Muller 2020). In 1970, Malaysia developed a comprehensive Reparation policy that include measures for distribution of agricultural land, ownership of capital by specifying a 30 per cent quota in the equity capital (shares) in domestic and foreign companies, and a fund for education development of the Malays which is a majority but discriminated community (Omar 2003). South Africa developed a Reparation policy of Black Economic Empowerment (Turok 2008; Juta's Statutes Editors 2010) based on the recommendations of the Reparation Commission, which include distribution of land, development of enterprises and education for the majority Black community. In Japan a reparation mechanism was developed under the name of 'Special Measures' to enhance the ownership of enterprises by the Burakumin community, and a fund for their educational development. The Reparation policy also include development of Burakumin settlements with all necessary infrastructure, including housing. In the United States American-Japanese were compensated for taking over of their properties during the Second World War. The Jews were also compensated by Germany for the loss of Jewish property. Other examples of Reparation policies in other countries have been discussed in detail by Pablo De Greiff in his book *The Handbook of Reparation* (2008).

The fourth category of policy used by some countries is to ensure a fair share to discriminated communities in business, employment, public housing, education, and legislature as safeguards against discrimination in the 'present'. Reparation policy, mentioned above, is an appropriate measure to compensate the groups which suffered from denial of the right to property and education, and underpayment to the slave labour for the injustices of the 'past'. But Reparation policy has its limitations in providing safeguards against discrimination in the 'present' as discrimination of the minorities continues to persist in one form or another. Therefore, Reparation policy is often supplemented by policies which ensure a fair share to the discriminated communities in employment, education, business, and legislature. The policies are variously referred to as Equal Opportunity Policies, Equal Employment Opportunity Policies, Special Measures, Reservation Policy, Positive Action Policy or Inclusive or Wider Participation Policy. The methods to ensure a fair share for discriminated or excluded communities also differ across countries. In most countries, fair representation is generally defined in terms of population share of discriminated communities. In some countries, specific quotas in proportion to population are fixed while, in others, a general benchmark is used. In the fifth category, the policy to change the persisting ideas, norms, and customs that are supportive of discrimination is selectively used by some countries. Various methods are used to educate and sensitize people on the issues of inequality and discrimination. Citizenship education in higher education institutions in the United States and in a few other countries is an example of such policy. In India, Ministry of Social Justice and Empowerment under the Government of India as well as the State Social Justice and Empowerment under the state governments deal with the SC also undertake various programmes to sensitize and educate the people on the ills of untouchability and caste discrimination through various programmes.

11.7 Policies Implied by the Results

Having the background of the preceding results, we now reflect on policies for the empowerment of the SC to bridge the gap in employment, occupations, and wages between them and others in India. In order to suggest policies based on the findings, we reiterate points related to the sources of disparities in employment, wages, and occupations between the SC and the higher castes. As we have seen, both the endowment factors and caste discrimination matter in low probability of employment of the SC, their low wages, and their higher concentration in low-paid jobs. The empirical results show that the probability of the SC getting employment is low partly due to differences in endowment factors and partly due to discrimination. About 26 per cent of the differences in employment in 2004–05 and 27 per cent in 2017–18 were due to endowment factors, while the remaining 73–74 per cent difference was due to caste discrimination. Endowment and discrimination factors accounted for about 47 per cent and 53.15 per cent respectively in differences in employment between the SC and the higher castes in the private sector. The share of discrimination in the private sector was much higher when compared to 14 per cent in the public sector. The results on unemployment confirmed these results. Discrimination accounted for about 65 per cent differences in the unemployment rate between the SC and the higher castes, while endowment factors contributed about 35 per cent. In the case of wages, the share of endowment factors was higher, with 57 per cent, as compared to 43 per cent due to caste discrimination. The SC also faces discrimination in allocation of work through placement in low-paid occupation which adds to the earning differential between the SC and the higher castes. Thus, caste discrimination plays a major role than endowment factors in employment; but in wages, endowment factors matter more than discrimination. Besides, in the private sector, in employment and wage gap, caste discrimination matters more than endowment factors. The opposite is the case in the public sector. These results have policy implications to reduce the gap in employment and wages between the SC and the higher castes. It requires policies both to enhance endowment of the SC workers as well as measures to ensure their fair share in employment and wages in the labour market by providing safeguards against discrimination. In the next section, we discuss the nature of policies for the enhancement of endowment factors among the SC and the policies to provide safeguards against discrimination and to secure fair share.

11.8 Reparation Policy: For Improvement in Endowment

From the results it emerged that some endowment factors reduce the probability of employment of the SC. The exercise on determinants of employment points towards the factors of age, gender, sector (rural or urban), education, marital status, and per capita consumption expenditure. Among these factors, higher education (beyond higher secondary, graduate and above) is crucial to improve the probability of employment, the probability being particularly high among those with diploma and graduate and above degree. The higher education level of SC women also improves the possibility of quality employment. Work experience also helps, so does residence in urban areas. Thus, higher education of both SC men and women, work experience, quality of employment and stay in urban areas improve the probability of the SC to secure employment.

The higher education also matters in the wage differences between the SC and the higher castes. The education and skill accounted for about 67 per cent in 2004–05 and 57.24 per cent in 2017–18 in wage differences between the SC and the higher castes. The marital status and nature of employment also matter. For obvious reasons, education also determines the quality of employment and helps the SC to get into better occupation. This shows that poor achievement in higher education and skills, particularly of women, reduces the wage earning of the SC workers as compared to the higher castes workers whose education level is relatively better.

It must be mentioned at this stage that low access to higher education among the SC is due to their low income, i.e. there is a positive relationship between education attainment rate and per capita income. In turn, the wage income of the SC is low because of low ownership of income-earning capital assets. Official data provide evidence on poor ownership of property. The data on ownership of capital assets shows that in 2013 the share of the SC in the total wealth of the country was only 7.4 per cent which was much lower than their population share of 17 per cent, while the share of the higher castes in the total wealth of the country was 45 per cent which exceeded their population share by a substantial margin. The average asset per household was ₹6.2 lakh for the SC and ₹29 lakh for the higher castes. Thus, the average wealth of the SC per household was five times lower as compared to the higher castes' households. Similarly, a wide gap persisted between the SC and the higher castes in educational attainment. For instance, in 2014, the enrolment ratio of the SC in higher education was 20 per cent which was less than half as compared to 43 per cent for the higher castes. The quality of employment of the SC regular salaried workers was also poor. The percentage share of the SC formal workers in their total regular salaried workers was 21 per cent as compared to 27 per cent for the higher castes. The share of those covered by job and social security was also low among the SC. Thus, the SC fell way behind the higher castes with respect to endowment factors, namely ownership of capital assets, higher education, and quality employment.

Why do the SCs trail behind the higher castes on these three endowment factors despite policies for improvement in ownership of capital assets and education? We know that, as per the law of Manu, the untouchables were prohibited from the right to property, right to education and jobs (except casual manual wage labour). The untouchables were

assigned work as casual labourers for the caste above them, and were prohibited from getting employment in the occupations of the four castes
above them. It is useful to reiterate the provision in the Hindu laws with
regard to the denial of right to property, education, employment, and
wages of the untouchables.

> One duty the Lord assigned to Shudra—service to those classes without
> grudging.
>
> The service of the Brahmanas alone is declared an excellent occupa-
> tion for Shudra for whatever else besides he may perform will bear him
> no fruits.
>
> (Bühler 1886, Law of Manu, Chapter X, 80–123, 420–429)

The Hindu laws prohibited the shudras to accumulate wealth.

> No collection of wealth must be made by a Shudra even though
> he be able to do it, for shudra who has acquired wealth gives pain to
> Brahmans.
>
> (Bühler 1886, Law of Manu, 129, 439)

There are restrictions on education under the Hindu law.

> Let the three twice-born castes (that is Brahmana, Kshatriya, and
> Vaishya), discharge (prescribed) duties, study (the Veda) but among
> them, the Brahmana (alone) shall teach it, not the other two, that is and
> established rules.
>
> (Bühler 1886, Law of Manu, 401)

The provision with respect to wages in the Hindu laws is as under:

> "They must allot to him (shudra) out of their own family property a
> suitable maintenance after considering his ability, his industry and the
> number of whom he is bound to support.
>
> (Bühler 1886, Law of Manu 124, p. 429)

But prescribed maintenance was too low and undignified? Manu
prescribed:

The remnants of their food be given to him, as well as their old cloths, the refuse of the grains, and their old household furniture.

(Bühler 1886, Law of Manu, 125, p. 429)

In fact, the untouchables were required to work as slaves. The untouchables were considered as slave caste.

The Hindu law in *Manusmriti* says:

A Shudra, whether bought or un-bought, should be reduced to slavery because he is created by God for the service of a Brahman.

(Bühler 1886, Law of Manu, p. 24)

Thus, the disadvantage of the SC with respect to these three endowment factors, namely capital earning assets or property, employment and education, is on account of their exclusion from right to property, education and employment for a long time in the past. The Manu's laws continued till the later part of the nineteenth century when the British partially opened up the right to property, enterprises, employment and education for the untouchables (Galanter 1963; McCormack 1966). Thus, the lack of ownership of property rights, low educational attainment, and quality employment are the legacy of the past which persists in the present. This also indicates the failure of the government to undertake polices to correct the past so as to improve the ownership of agricultural land and enterprises, and education among the untouchables. Thus, in order to bring the SC on a par with the higher castes with regards to property, higher education, and employment, 'reparation or compensation' is the appropriate remedy which the Indian State should used.

All this goes to show that there is an obvious case for reparation for massive material losses and the social, personal, and psychological harm caused to the untouchables since 200 BCE. The enrichment of the higher castes has come at the cost of the impoverishment of the untouchables through underpayment for slave labour, and denial of rights to property and education. In fact, we have reason to believe that bulk of the wealth accumulated by the higher castes was through under payment to the untouchable manual wage labour, including slave labour. The higher castes are more educated and, thus, a greater number of them are employed in government and private sector jobs (other than causal manual labour) because education was confined to them at the cost of denial of access to education to the untouchables. Also, the concentration of wealth or property with the higher castes, in land and enterprises, came at the cost of denial of the same to the untouchables. The gains of the higher castes were at the cost of the loss to the untouchables. Therefore, there are legal and moral justifications that the higher castes pay back the lost wealth to the untouchables. The present generations of high castes are the beneficiaries of the accumulated wealth and human resources which are carried forward through intergenerational transmission of property, education, status of authority and power, therefore they cannot say that they are not responsible (or not beneficiaries) for denial by their forefathers in the long distance past. The redistribution of property, i.e. agricultural land and non-farm enterprises would bridge the gap in ownership of property by the SC and the higher castes. The development of education through education funds, with scholarship, hostel, and financial support would improve the enrolment attainment rate among the SC. The improvement in education would enhance employability and their share in regular salaried jobs, along with an increase in wages. So, reparation policy is essential for the improvement in endowment so as to reduce gaps in employment, wages, and occupations between the SC and the higher castes. The present policies of land distribution, entrepreneurship development and higher education have limited success. It is only the Reparation Policy which involves allocation of agricultural land, measures to improve ownership of enterprises and measures to enhance education which in turn would enable the development of the SC and reduce the inter caste differences in human development.

11.9 Affirmative Action Policies and Legal Safeguards

It emerged from the results that beside the lack of endowments due to exclusion of rights in the past (such as land, enterprise, and education), the discrimination in the present is also a source of low employment and wages of the SC regular salaried workers and their concentration in low-paid occupations. In 2017–18, about 73 per cent gap in employment and about 43 per cent gap in wages between the SC and the higher castes were caused by caste discrimination. This implies that even if the SC are brought on a par with the higher castes in terms of endowment factors, such as higher education, through reparation, which is in any case necessary as a first step, nevertheless it would not be enough. Due to the persistence of discrimination in employment and wages, the equally qualified SC would face low access to employment and better wages. Therefore, there is obvious need to ensure that equally qualified SC would get an equal opportunity in employment and wages which are on a par with the higher castes workers. Thus, although improvement in endowment factors, like higher education of the SC, would enhance their employability, it may not ensure equal opportunity in employment and wages due to discrimination of the SC in employment, wages, and occupations in the present.

This necessitates reforms in the present Reservation Policy related to employment, wages, and occupations. Analysis of determinants of employment/unemployment indicates that the caste background of individuals count in hiring and wages. The coefficient of the SC is positive and significant and, therefore, the probability of being unemployed is greater as compared to their higher castes counterparts. Discrimination is higher in the private sector as compared to the public sector. This would require changes in the present Reservation policies and legal provisions both for the public and the private sectors.

This also demands clearly defined legal safeguards against discrimination in spheres wherein the possibility of discrimination in employment, wages, and occupations is high. Although the Protection of Civil Rights Act, 1955 and Atrocity Act, 1989 currently provide protection against economic discrimination, they do not cover all economic spheres wherein the probability of discrimination is high.

Our results also show that in the public sector discrimination is high at lower-level posts than at the high-level posts, presumably due to recruitments by the government through private agencies, with the latter resorting to discriminatory practices (Mamgain and Tiwari 2017). Therefore, it is in the interest of the SC that recruitments on contract basis is minimized. Also, recruitment on contract basis should be made transparent through direct monitoring by the public sector bodies with a provision of reservation in jobs on contract of various durations.

The safeguards against discrimination in employment in the private sector are equally necessary, given that more than half of the differences in the probability of employment in private sector is caused by discrimination in hiring. The discrimination in the private sector is particularly high in high-level posts than those at the low level. Therefore, adequate legal safeguards against discrimination in hiring are necessary to prevent under-representation at high-level posts in the private sector. This also implies that given the creditable empirical evidence of discrimination in hiring by the private sector, Affirmative Action policy in employment is necessary for private sector to ensure fair share to the SC particularly at high-level positions. The present Affirmative Action policy in the private sector (which is voluntary and self-regulatory) is more focused on the improvement in the employability of the SC through educational schemes, such as scholarship, orientation-cum-training and less on hiring. But capability enhancement alone is not enough as it may not ensure entry of potentially capable SC in jobs due to the presence of discrimination in hiring. Therefore, it is imperative for the private sector to develop a robust policy to provide a fair share to the SC in employment at different levels, particularly in positions where the SC are under-represented. The private sector in India has resisted the policy of reservation in jobs quite consistently, thereby displaying its reluctance to accept affirmative action in hiring. The private sector entities argue that their recruitment practices are guided by merit alone and not by the social identity of the applicants. Our results provide empirical evidence to the contrary. The results, based on analysis of Employment Survey data for 2004–05 and 2017–18, reveal clear empirical evidence on discrimination in hiring in the private sector. The private sector should recognize the fact that in a severely caste-ridden society like ours, discrimination is deeply embedded in its economic governance through markets and non-market institutions.

The empirical results of this study also provide evidence on segregation of the SC in low-paid occupations. There is tendency on the part of employers to place the SC workers, who are as qualified as the higher castes workers, in low-paid elementary jobs. This would require Affirmative Action policies for the private sector to ensure a fair share to the SC in better occupations where they are under-represented.

Thus, the proposed policy would require both legal safeguards to the SC through anti-discriminatory laws in employment and measures to give fair share to the SC in employment. At present, there is neither enough legal protection to the SC against differential behaviour in hiring in private sector nor proper policy to ensure their fair share in regular salaried jobs.

Similar reforms are necessary to reduce discrimination of the SC in wages. The underpayment to the SC regular salaried workers is particularly pronounced in high-grade posts in the private sector. In the public sector, wage discrimination is less but it is not altogether free from discrimination. Unlike the private sector, the wage discrimination is higher in lower-grade posts which mostly include D and C grades in the public sector. Besides, the upward movement in the same job is sticky and marked with difficulties for the SC. It appears that discrimination of the SC in wages in low-level posts in the public sector may be due to recruitment in D and C grades posts on a contract basis by the government through private recruitment agencies. Corrective measures would be required to overcome the discrimination in wages of low-level employees recruited through private agencies for the public sector. Presently, there are not enough legal safeguards for the SC against underpayment of wages due to caste prejudice in the public and private sectors.

All this goes to show that necessary policy changes are required to provide policy safeguards against discrimination in employment and wages through reforms in policies. Dual policies would be necessary, i.e. policies for improvements in endowment, particularly in ownership of capital assets, land, and non-farm enterprises and higher education through Reparation policy. Higher education has emerged as an important determinant of regular salaried employment both in public and private sectors. An improvement in education is dependent on income, which in turn, depends on the ownership of capital assets, such as land. The Reparation policy should include steps to improve ownership of capital assets to enable high education attainment among the SC and thereby enhance their employability. However, although the enhancement of employability is essential as the first step, it is not enough due to persistence of discrimination in hiring. Therefore, in addition to Reparation policy, Affirmative Action policies are required to ensure fair share to the SC in employment, occupations, and wages.

The elimination of discrimination in employment and wages would have an added poverty-reducing impact among the SC regular salaried workers. The finding conclusively proved that after accounting for wage and employment loss due to discrimination in total consumption expenditure, the incidence of poverty declined by 9.2 percentage points during 2017–18 for the SC. In absolute terms, about 1.6 million poor SC regular salaried workers would have moved out of poverty due to elimination of discrimination in employment and wages in 2017–18. Therefore, to reduce poverty, elimination of labour market discrimination is necessary.

References

Agrawal, T. 2014. 'Gender and Caste-based Wage Discrimination in India: Some Recent Evidence.' *Journal of Labour Market Research* 47: 329–340.

Ahmed, T. 2016. 'Labour Market Outcome for Formal Vocational Education and Training in India: Safety Net and Beyond.' *IIMB Management Review* 28, 2: 98–110.

Akerlof, G.A. 1976. 'The Economics of Caste and of the Rat Race and Other Woeful Tales.' *Quarterly Journal of Economics* 90, 4: 599–617.

Akerlof, G.A. 1980. 'The Theory of Social Customs, of which Unemployment may be One Consequence.' *Quarterly Journal of Economics* 94, 4: 749–775.

Akerlof, G.A., and R. Kranton. 2010. 'Identity Economics.' *The Economists' Voice* 7, 2: 1–3.

All India Debt and Investment Survey. 2013. National Sample Survey, India.

Allport, G.W. 1954. *The Nature of Prejudice*. Cambridge, MA: Addison-Wesley Pub. Co.

Alonso-Villar, O., and C. Del Río. 2010. 'Segregation of Female and Male Workers in Spain: Occupations and Industries.' *Hacienda Pública Española* 194, 3: 91–121.

Ambedkar, B.R. 1917. 'Castes in India: Their Genesis, Mechanism, and Development.' The Essential Writings of B.R. Ambedkar, 263–305.

Ambedkar, B.R. 1936. 'Speech Prepared for 1936 Annual Conference of the Jat-Pat-Todak Mandal of Lahore.' Published in Selected Works of Dr. B.R. Ambedkar, WordPress.

Ambedkar, B.R. 1944. *Annihilation of Caste with a Reply to Mahatma Gandhi: Writings and Speeches*, Vol. 1. Department of Education, Government of Maharashtra, Mumbai.

Ambedkar, B.R. 1946. *Who Were the Sudras?* Bombay: Thacker & Co.

Ambedkar, B.R. 1947. *States and Minorities (Memorandum on the Safeguards for Scheduled Castes)*. Government of Maharashtra, Mumbai.

Ambedkar, B.R. 1948. *Untouchables: Who Were They and Why They Became Untouchables*. New Delhi: Amrit Book Company.

Ambedkar, B.R. 1979. 'Caste in India: Their Mechanism, Genesis and Development.' In *Dr Babasaheb Ambedkar: Writings and Speeches*, edited by Department of Education, Government of Maharashtra, Mumbai.

Ambedkar, B.R. 1987. 'Philosophy of Hinduism.' In *Dr Babasaheb Ambedkar: Writings and Speeches*, 3, edited by Department of Education, Government of Maharashtra, Mumbai.

Ambedkar, B.R. 1990. *Dr Babasaheb Ambedkar: Writings and Speeches*. Vol. 3. Government of Maharashtra, Mumbai.

Ambedkar, B.R. 1993. *Dr Babasaheb Ambedkar: Writings and Speeches*. Vol. 12. Government of Maharashtra, Mumbai.

Ambedkar, B.R. 2008. *Dr. Babasaheb Ambedkar: Writings and Speeches*, 3: 3–129. Government of Maharashtra, Mumbai.

Arabsheibani, G., P. Gupta, and T. Mishra. 2012. *Youth, Endogenous Discrimination and Development Conundrum in India*. http://conference.iza.org/conference_files/worldb2012/gupta_p8290.pdf (accessed 19 June 2020).

Arrow, K.J. 1971. *Some Models of Racial Discrimination in the Labor Market.* Santa Monica, CA: Rand Corp.

Arrow, K.J. 1972. 'Models of Job Discrimination.' In *Racial Discrimination in Economic Life*, edited by A.H. Pascall. Lexington, MA: D.C. Heath.

Arrow, K.J. 1973. 'The Theory of Discrimination.' In *Discrimination in Labour Markets*, edited by O. Ashenfelter and A. Rees, 3–33. Princeton, NJ: Princeton University Press.

Arulampalam, W., A.L. Booth, and M.L. Bryan. 2007. 'Is There a Glass Ceiling Over Europe? Exploring the Gender Pay Gap Across the Wages Distribution.' *Industrial and Labour Relations Review* 60, 2: 163–186.

Azam, M. 2012. 'A Distributional Analysis of Social Group Inequality in Rural India.' *Journal of International Development* 24: 415–432. DOI: 10.1002/jid.1706

Banaji, D.R. 1933. *Slavery in India.* 2nd edition. Bombay: D.B. Taraporevala Sons & Co.

Banerjee A., M. Bertrand, S. Datta, and S. Mullainathan. 2009. 'Labour Market Discrimination in Delhi: Evidence from a Field Experiment.' *Journal of Comparative Economics* 37, 1: 14–27.

Banerjee, B., and J.B. Knight. 1985. 'Caste Discrimination in the Indian Urban Labour Market.' *Journal of Development Economics* 17, 3: 277–307.

Becker, G.S. 1957. *The Economics of Discrimination.* 1st edition. Chicago: University of Chicago Press.

Becker, G.S. 1971. *The Economics of Discrimination.* 2nd edition. Chicago: University of Chicago Press.

Bergmann, B.R. 1971. 'The Effect on White Incomes of Discrimination in Employment.' *Journal of Political Economy* 79, 2: 294–313.

Birdsall, N., and R. Sabot. 1991. *Unfair Advantage: Labour Market Discrimination in Developing Countries.* Washington, DC: The World Bank.

Blau, F.D., and L.M. Kahn. 2000. 'Gender Differences in Pay.' *Journal of Economic Perspectives* 14, 4: 75–99.

Blaug, M., R. Layard, and M. Woodhall. 1969. *The Causes of Graduate Unemployment in India.* London: Allen Lane and Penguin Press.

Blinder, A.S. 1973. 'Wage Discrimination: Reduced Form and Structural Estimates.' *Journal of Human Resources* 8, 4: 436–455.

Blumer, H.G. 1958. 'Race Prejudice as a Sense of Group Position.' *Pacific Sociological Review* 1, 1 (Spring): 3–7.

Borooah, V.K. 2001. 'The Measurement of Employment Inequality between Population Subgroups.' *Labour* 15: 169–189.

Borooah, V.K. 2010. 'On the Risk Associated with Belonging to Disadvantaged Groups: A Bayesian Analysis with an Application to Labour Market Outcomes in India.' In *Handbook of Muslims in India*, edited by R. Basant and A. Shariff, 199–220. Oxford: Oxford University Press.

Borooah, V.K. 2019. 'Caste, Gender, and Occupational Outcomes.' In *Disparity and Discrimination in Labour Market Outcomes in India*, 97–131. Cham: Palgrave Macmillan.

Bourguignon, F., M. Fournier, and M. Gurgand. 2007. 'Selection Bias Corrections Based on the Multinomial Logit Model: Monte-Carlo Comparisons.' *Journal of Economic Surveys* 21, 1: 174–205.

Brown, R.S., M. Moon, and B.S. Zoloth. 1980. 'Incorporating Occupational Attainment in Studies of Male/Female Earnings Differentials.' *Journal of Human Resources* 15, 1: 3–28.

Bühler, G. 1886. 'The Laws of Manu.' In *The Sacred Books of the East*, edited by F. Max Muller. Oxford: Clarendon Press.

Carnoy, M. 1977. 'Segmented Labour Markets: A Review of Theoretical and Empirical Literature and Its Implications for Educational Planning.' Working paper, International Institute of Educational Planning.

Chanana, D.R. 1960. *Slavery in Ancient India*. New Delhi: People's Publishing House.

Chen, S.H., C.C. Yang, J.Y. Shiau, and H.H. Wang. 2006. 'The Development of an Employee Satisfaction Model for Higher Education.' *The TQM Magazine* 18, 5: 484–500.

Cotton, J. 1988. 'On the Decomposition of Wage Differentials.' *The Review of Economics and Statistics* 70, 2: 236–243.

Darity, W.A. 1995. *Economics and Discrimination*. Northampton, MA: Edward Elgar Publishing.

Darity, W.A. 2005. 'Stratification Economics: The Role of Intergroup Inequality.' *Journal of Economics and Finance* 29, 2: 144.

Darity, W.A. 2007. *Economic Inequality and the African Diaspora*. Ann Arbor, MI: ProQuest-CSA LLC. http://gateway.proquest.com/openurl?res_dat=xri:bsc&url_ver=Z39.88-2004&rft_dat=xri:bsc:ft:essay:28DARI_intro.

Darity Jr, W.A. 2013. 'Confronting Those Affirmative Action Grumbles.' In *Capitalism on Trial*, edited by J. Wicks-Lim and R. Pollin, chapter 14; 215. Northampton, MA: Edward Elgar Publishing.

Darity Jr, W.A., P.L. Mason, and J.B. Stewart. 2006. 'The Economics of Identity: The Origin and Persistence of Racial Identity Norms.' *Journal of Economic Behavior & Organization* 60, 3: 283–305.

Darity Jr, W.A., and A.K. Mullen. 2020. *From Here to Equality: Reparations for Black Americans in the Twenty-First Century*. Chapel Hill, NC: UNC Press Books.

Das, M.B., and P.V. Dutta. 2007. 'Does Caste Matter for Wages in the India Labour Market?' Working paper. Social Development and Human Development Unit. Washington, DC: World Bank.

De Greiff, P. 2008. *The Handbook of Reparations*. Oxford: Oxford University Press.

Deshpande, A. 2011. *The Grammar of Caste: Economic Discrimination in Contemporary India*. New Delhi: Oxford University Press.

Deshpande, A., and K. Newman. 2007. 'Where the Path Leads: The Role of Caste in Post-University Employment Expectations.' *Economic and Political Weekly* 42, 41: 4133–4140.

Dickens, W.T., and K. Lang. 1985. 'A Test of Dual Labour Market Theory.' *The American Economic Review* 75, 4: 792–805.

Doeringer, P.B., and M.J. Piore. 1971. *Internal Labor Markets and Manpower Analysis*. Lexington, MA: M.E. Sharpe.

Dolton, P.J., and M.P. Kidd. 1994. 'Occupational Access and Wage Discrimination.' *Oxford Bulletin of Economics and Statistics* 56, 4: 457–474.

D'Souza, E. 2010. 'The Employment Effects of Labour Legislation in India: A Critical Essay.' *Industrial Relations Journal* 41, 2: 122–135.

Duncan, O.D., and B. Duncan. 1955. 'A Methodological Analysis of Segregation Indices.' *American Sociological Review* 20, 2: 210–217.

Duraisamy, P., and M. Duraisamy. 2017. 'Social Identity and Wage Discrimination in the Indian Labour Market.' *Economic and Political Weekly* 52, 4: 51–60.

Ehrenberg, R., and R. Smith. 1991. *Modern Labour Economics: Theory and Public Policy*, 4th Edition. New York: HarperCollins.

Etienne, J.M., and M. Narcy. 2010. 'Gender Wage Differentials in the French Nonprofit and For-profit Sectors: Evidence from Quantile Regression.' *Annals of Economics and Statistics* 99, 100: 67–90.

Fields, G.S. 2002. *Accounting for Income Inequality and Its Change: A New Method with Application to the Distribution of Earnings in the United States.* Retrieved [6/19/20] from Cornell University, ILR school site: http://digitalcommons.ilr.cornell.edu/articles/265/

Galanter, M. 1963. 'Law and Caste in Modern India.' *Asian Survey* 3, 11: 544–559.

Ghose, A. K. 2004. 'The Employment Challenge in India.' *Economic and Political Weekly* 39, 48: 5106–5116.

Goldar, B., and R. Suresh. 2017. 'Contract Labour in Organized Manufacturing in India.' In *Labour and Development—Essays in Honour of Professor TS Papola*, edited by K.P. Kannan, R.P. Mamgain, and P. Rustagi, 357–386. New Delhi: Academic Foundation.

Goldberg, Matthew S. 1982. 'Discrimination, Nepotism, and Long-run Wage Differentials.' *Quarterly Journal of Economics* 97, 2: 307–319.

Greenhalgh, C. 1980. 'Male-Female Differentials in Great Britain: Is Marriage an Equal Opportunity?' *Economics Journal* 90, 360: 751–775.

Gunderson, M. 1989. 'Male-Female Wage Differentials and Policy Responses.' *Journal of Economic Literature* 27, 1: 46–72.

Harberger A.C. 1971. 'On Measuring the Social Opportunity Cost of Labour.' *International Labour Review* 103: 559–579.

Harriss-White, B. 2010. 'Work and Wellbeing in Informal Economies: The Regulative Roles of Institutions of Identity and the State.' *World Development* 38, 2: 170–183.

Hnatkovska, V., A. Lahiri, and S. Paul. 2012. 'Castes and Labor Mobility.' *American Economic Journal: Applied Economics* 4, 2: 274–307.

IHD-ISLE. 2014. *India Labour and Employment Report, 2014: Workers in the Era of Globalisation.* Institute for Human Development & Indian Society of Labour Economics. New Delhi: Academic Foundation.

ILO. 2016. *Global Wage Report 2016–17, Wage Inequality in the Work Place.* Geneva: ILO.

Islam, R. 1980. 'Graduate Unemployment in Bangladesh: A Preliminary Analysis.' *The Bangladesh Development Studies* 8: 47–74.

Ito, T. 2009. 'Caste Discrimination and Transaction Costs in the Labor Market: Evidence from Rural North India.' *Journal of Development Economics* 88, 2: 292–300.

Jacob, M. 2006. 'Changes in the Wage Gap of Gender and Caste Groups in India.' Published Ph.D. thesis, University of Maryland, United States.

Jaiswal, S. 2007. 'General President's Address: Caste, Gender and Ideology in the Making of India.' *Proceedings of the Indian History Congress*, 68, 1: 1–35. Indian History Congress.

Jha, V. 1987. 'The Concept of Penance in the Bhagvadgita.' In *Proceedings of the Indian History Congress* 48: 91–94.

Jha, V. 1997. 'Caste, Untouchability and Social Justice, Early North India Perspective.' *Social Scientist* 25, 11/12: 19–30.

Jha, V. 2018. *Candala: Untouchability and Caste in Early India*. Delhi: Primus Books.

Jodkha, S., and K. Newman. 2007. 'Meritocracy, Productivity and the Hidden Language of Caste.' Paper presented at the *National Conference on Social Exclusion and Inclusive Policies*, organised by Indian Institute of Dalit Studies (IIDS), 26–27 October, New Delhi.

Jodhka, S., and G. Shah. 2010. 'Comparative Contexts of Discrimination: Caste and Untouchability in South Asia.' *Economic and Political Weekly* 45, 48: 99–106.

Juta's Statutes Editors. 2010. Broad-Based Black Economic Empowerment Act 53 of 2003 & Related Material. Kenwyn, South Africa: Juta & Company Ltd.

Kijima, Y. 2006. 'Caste and Tribe Inequality: Evidence from India, 1983–1999.' *Economic Development and Cultural Change* 54, 2: 369–404.

Lakshmanasamy, T., and S. Madheswaran. 1995. 'Discrimination by Community: Evidence from Indian Scientific and Technical Labor Market.' *Indian Journal of Social Sciences* 8: 59–77.

Lal, D. 1988. *Hindu Equilibrium: Cultural Stability and Economic Stagnation* Vol. I. Oxford: Clarendon Press.

Lang, K. 1986. 'A Language Theory of Discrimination.' *The Quarterly Journal of Economics* 101, 2: 363–382.

Law Commission. 1840. *Lex Loci (Role and Authority of English law in India)* (31 October 1840).

Lemieux, 2007. 'The Changing Nature of Wage Inequality' WP 13523, NBER, Massachusetts Avenue Cambridge, MA 02138.

Lorenzo A.M. 1943. *Agricultural Labour Conditions in North India*. Bombay: New Book Company.

Machado, J.A.F., and J. Mata. 2005. 'Counterfactual Decomposition of Changes in Wage Distributions using Quantile Regression.' *Journal of Applied Econometrics* 20, 4: 445–465.

Macpherson, D.A., and B.T. Hirsch. 1995. 'Wages and Gender Composition: Why Do Women's Jobs Pay Less?' *Journal of Labor Research* 13: 426–471.

Madden, J.F. 1975. *The Economics of Sex Discrimination*. Lexington, MA: D.C Health and Co.

Madheswaran, S. 2010. 'Caste Discrimination in the Urban Labour Market: Methodological Developments and Empirical Evidence—India.' Project report submitted to Institute for International and Regional Studies, Princeton University, USA and Indian Institute of Dalit Studies, New Delhi.

Madheswaran, S. 1996. 'Econometric Analyses of Labour Market for Scientists in India.' Unpublished Ph.D. Thesis, University of Madras, Madras.

Madheswaran, S., and P. Attewell. 2007. 'Caste Discrimination in the Indian Urban Labour Market: Evidence from the National Sample Survey.' *Economic and Political Weekly* 42, 41: 4146–4153.

Madheswaran, S., and S. Singhari. 2016. 'Social Exclusion and Caste Discrimination in Public and Private Sectors in India: A Decomposition Analysis.' *The Indian Journal of Labour Economics* 59, 2: 175–201.

Mamgain, R.P. 2018. 'New Forms of Recruitment Processes and Discrimination in Urban Labour Market in India.' *Journal of Social Inclusion Studies* 4, 1: 131–150.

Mamgain, R.P., and S. Tiwari. 2017. 'Regular Salaried Employment Opportunities in India: Nature, Access and Inclusiveness.' *The Indian Journal of Labour Economics* 60, 3: 415–436.

Mathew, E.T. 1995. 'Unemployed and Self-Employed: Job Preferences and Employment Perspectives.' *Economic and Political Weekly* 30, 44: 2815–2826.

McCormack, W.C. 1966. 'Caste and the British Administration of Hindu Law.' *Journal of Asian and African Studies* 1, 1: 27–34.

Mehrotra, S., and J.K. Parida. 2019. 'India's Employment Crisis: Rising Education levels and Falling Non-agricultural Job Growth', CSE Working Paper #23, Azim Premji University.

Melly, B. 2006. 'Estimation of Counterfactual Distributions Using Quantile Regression.' Discussion Paper, Swiss Institute for International Economics and Applied Economic Research (SIAW), University of St. Gallen, Switzerland.

Miller, P.W., and P.A. Volker. 1985. 'On the Determination of Occupational Attainment and Mobility.' *Journal of Human Resources* 20, 2: 197–213.

Mincer, J. 1974. *Schooling, Experience and Earnings*. New York: National Bureau of Economic Research.

Mitra, A., and S. Verick. 2013. *Youth Employment and Unemployment: An Indian Perspective*. International Labour Organization, Geneva.

Mohan, S.P. 2015. *Modernity of Slavery*. New Delhi: Oxford University Press.

Moll, P.G. 1992. 'Quality of Education and the Rise in Returns to Schooling in South Africa, 1975–1985.' *Economics of Education Review* 11, 1: 1–10.

Moll, P.G. 1996. 'The Collapse of Primary Schooling Returns in South Africa 1960–90.' *Oxford Bulletin of Economics and Statistics* 58, 1: 185–209.

Naylor, R. 1994. 'Pay Discrimination and Imperfect Competition in the Labor Market.' *Journal of Economics* 60, 2: 177–188.

NCEUS. 2009. *The Challenge of Employment in India: An Informal Economy Perspective*. New Delhi: National Commission for Enterprises in the Unorganized Sector, Government of India.

Neff, D.F., K. Sen, and V. Kling. 2012. 'The Puzzling Decline in Rural Women's Labor Force Participation in India: A Re-examination.' GIGA Working Paper 196, Institute of Asian Studies, German Institute of Global and Area Studies, Hamburg: Germany.

Neumark, D. 1988. 'Employers Discriminatory Behaviour and the Estimation of Wage Discrimination.' *Journal of Human Resources* 23, 3: 279–295.

Nielsen H.S. 1998. 'Discrimination and Detailed Decomposition in a Logit Model.' *Economics Letters* 61, 1: 115–120.

Oaxaca, R.L. 1973. 'Male-Female Wage Differentials in Urban Labour Markets.' *International Economic Review* 14, 3: 693–709.

Oaxaca, R.L., and M.R. Ransom. 1994. 'On Discrimination and the Decomposition of Wage Differentials.' *Journal of Econometrics* 61, 1: 5–21.

Omar, A. 2003. 'Origins and Development of the Affirmative Policy in Malaya and Malaysia: A Historical Overview.' *Kajian Malaysia* 21, 1/2: 13–29.

Papola, T.S. 2004. 'Globalisation, Employment and Social Protection: Emerging Perspectives for the Indian Workers.' *The Indian Journal of Labour Economics* 47, 3: 541–550.

Papola, T.S. 2007. 'Social Exclusion and Discrimination in Hiring Practices: The Case of Indian Private Sector.' In *Reservation and Private Sector: Quest for Equal*

Opportunity and Growth, edited by S. Thorat, Aryama, and P. Negi, 101–108. Jaipur: Rawat Publications.

Papola, T.S. 2011. 'Employment in Development: Connection between Indian Strategy and ILO Policy Agenda.' *Economic and Political Weekly* 46, 10: 62–67.

Papola, T.S., and K.P. Kannan. 2017. *Towards an India Wage Report* (994971390602676). International Labour Organization, Geneva.

Phelps, E. 1972. 'The Statistical Theory of Racism and Sexism.' *American Economic Review* 62, 4: 659–661.

Piore, M.J. 1970. 'The Dual Labour Market: Theory and Applications.' In *The State and the Poor*, edited by R. Barringer and S.H. Beer. Cambridge, MA: Winthrop Publications.

Prasad, K.E. 1979. 'Education and Unemployment of Professional Manpower in India.' *Economic and Political Weekly* 14, 20: 881–888.

Psacharopoulos, G. 1982. "The Economics of Higher Education in Developing Countries." *Comparative Education Review* 26, 2: 139–159.

Rama, M. 2003. "The Sri Lankan Unemployment Problem Revisited.' *Review of Development Economics* 7, 3: 510–525.

Randall, R. 2000. *The Debt: What America Owes to Blacks?* New York: Dutton.

Rangarajan, C., P.I. Kaul, and Seema. 2011. 'Where is the Missing Labour Force?' *Economic and Political Weekly* 46, 39: 68–72.

Reimer, C.W. 1983. 'Labour Market Discrimination Against Hispanic and Black Men.' *Review of Economics and Statistics* 65, 4: 570–579.

Reimer, C.W. 1985. 'A Comparative Analysis of the Wages of Hispanic, Blacks and Non-Hispanic Whites.' In *Hispanic in the U.S. Economy*, edited by G.J. Borjas and M. Tienda. New York: Academic Press.

Robinson, J. 1965. *The Economics of Imperfect Competition*. New York: St. Martin's.

Rodgers, G. 1993. 'The Creation of Employment in Segmented Labour Markets: A General Problem and its Implications in India.' *The Indian Journal of Labour Economics* 36, 1: 33–47.

Roemer, J.E. 1979. 'Divide and Conquer: Microfoundations of a Marxian Theory of Wage Discrimination.' *The Bell Journal of Economics* 10, 2: 695–705.

Rudra, A. 1982. *Indian Agricultural Economics: Myths and Realities*. New Delhi: Allied. http://catalog.hathitrust.org/api/volumes/oclc/9575475.html.

Saradamoni, K. 1980. *Emergence of a Slave Caste: Pulayas of Kerala*. New Delhi: People's Publishing House.

Schmidt, P., and R.P. Strauss. 1975. 'The Prediction of Occupation Using Multinomial Logit Models.' *International Economic Review* 16: 471–486.

Scoville, J.G.L. 1991. 'Towards a Model of Caste Economy.' In *Status Influences in Third World Labour Markets: Caste, Gender and Custom*, edited by James G. Scoville, 386–93. New York: Walter de Gruyter.

Scoville, J.G.L. 1996. 'Labour Market Under-pinnings of a Caste Economy Failing the Caste Theorem.' *The American Journal of Economics and Sociology* 55, 4: 385–94.

Sen, A. 2000. 'Social Exclusion: Concept, Application and Scrutiny.' Social Development Paper 1, Bangkok: Asian Development Bank.

Sharma, R. S. 1958. *Sudra in Ancient India*. Delhi: Motilal Banarasidass.

Sheers, D. 1971. 'Matching Employment Opportunities and Expectations: A Program of Action for Ceylon.' Geneva: ILO.

Siddique, Z. 2008. 'Caste based Discrimination: Evidence and Policy.' Institute for the Study of Labour (IZA) Discussion Paper 3737.

Srivastava, R., and A.K. Naik. 2017. 'Growth and Informality in the Indian Economy.' In *Labour and Development—Essays in Honour of Professor TS Papola*, edited by K.P. Kannan, R.P. Mamgain, and P. Rustagi, 357–386. New Delhi: Academic Foundation.

Taubman, P., and M.L. Wachter. 1986. 'Segmented Labor Markets'. In *Handbook of Labor Economics*, edited by O. Ashenfelter and R. Layard, 2: 1183–1217. Amsterdam: Elsevier.

Tendulkar, S.D. 2003. 'Organised Labour Market in India: Pre and Post Reform.' Unpublished paper prepared for the Conference on Anti Poverty and Social Policy at Alwar, India.

Thomas, K.T. 1999. 'Slaves an Integral Part of the Production System in Malabar (19th Century).' In *Proceedings of the Indian History Congress*, 60: 600–610. Indian History Congress.

Thorat, S. 2010. 'Caste, Exclusion, and Marginalised Groups in India: Dalit Deprivation in India.' In *Education for Sustainable Development: Challenges, Strategies, and Practices in a Globalizing World*, edited by A. Nikolopoulou, T. Abraham, and F. Mirbagheri, 3–27. New Delhi: Sage.

Thorat, S., and P. Attewell. 2007. 'The Legacy of Social Exclusion: A Correspondence Study of Job Discrimination in India.' *Economic and Political Weekly* 42, 41: 4141–4145.

Thorat, S., and N. Kumar. 2008. *BR Ambedkar: Perspectives on Social Exclusion and Inclusive Policies*. New Delhi: Oxford University Press.

Thorat, S., and K. Newman. 2010. *Blocked by Caste: Economic Discrimination in Modern India*. New Delhi: Oxford University Press.

Thurow, L.C. 1969. *Poverty and Discrimination*. Washington, DC: Brookings Institution.

Turok, Ben. 2008. *From the Freedom Charter to Polokwane: The Evolution of ANC Economic Policy*. Mill Street: Neq Agenda.

Visaria, P. 1998. 'Unemployment among Youth in India: Level, Nature and Policy Implications.' International Labour Organization, Geneva.

Yamazaki, Genichi. 1997. 'Social Discrimination in Ancient India and its Transition to the Medieval Period.' In *Caste System, Untouchability and the Depressed*, edited by H. Kotani, 3–19. Delhi: Manohar.

Index

For the benefit of digital users, indexed terms that span two pages (e.g., 52–53) may, on occasion, appear on only one of those pages.

Note: Tables and figures are indicated by *t* and *f* following the page number

Ingram Content Group UK Ltd.
Milton Keynes UK
UKHW022032280423
420972UK00003B/31

Bird Head Son

ANTHONY JOSEPH is one of the leading writers of his generation. A poet, novelist, academic and musician, he was born in Trinidad, moving to the UK in 1989. His publications include *Desafinado* (1994), *Teragaton* (1997) and *The African Origins of UFOs* (Salt, 2006). In 2004 he was chosen by the Arts Council as one of 50 black and Asian writers who have made major contributions to contemporary British literature, appearing in the historic 'Great Day' photograph. In 2005 Joseph served as the British Council's first Poet in residence at California State University, Los Angeles. He has performed internationally and also tours with his band The Spasm Band. Joseph lectures in creative writing at Birkbeck College and at Goldsmiths College, University of London where he is a doctoral candidate.

Also by Anthony Joseph

POETRY
   Desafinado (Poison Engine Press, 1994)
   Teragaton (Poison Engine Press, 1997)
   Liquid Textology CD (Poison Engine Press, 2005)

FICTION
   The African Origins of UFOs (Salt, 2006)

MUSIC
Anthony Joseph & The Spasm Band
   Leggo de Lion (Kindred Spirits, 2007)
   Bird Head Son (Naïve/Heavenly Sweetness, 2009)

Bird Head Son

Anthony Joseph

CAMBRIDGE

PUBLISHED BY SALT PUBLISHING
14a High Street, Fulbourn, Cambridge CB21 5DH United Kingdom

© Anthony Joseph, 2009

The right of Anthony Joseph to be identified as the
author of this work has been asserted by him in accordance
with Section 77 of the Copyright, Designs and Patents Act 1988.

First published 2009

Printed by the MPG Books Group in the UK

Typeset in Swift 9.5 / 13

ISBN 978 1 84471 435 3 hardback

Salt Publishing Ltd gratefully acknowledges
the financial assistance of Arts Council England

1 3 5 7 9 8 6 4 2

*For Louise & Meena ïerè
and in memory of my friend
Kemal Mulbocus*

.

Contents

Acknowledgements

Excerpts from this book have been published in *The Caribbean Review of Books*, *New Writing 15*, *The Harlem Studio Museum*, *London Magazine*, *Trespass Magazine*, *Goldfish Magazine* and on *Poetry International Web*. Excerpts from 'Bird Head Son' & 'Carenage' were first broadcast on *The Verb*, BBC3.

Thanks to Louise and to Meena ïerè my hummingbird, Lauri Ramey, Blake Morrison, Stephen Knight, Maura Dooley, my fellow Goldsmiths MA students—2006–07 for their advice and suggestions, Tom Chivers at Penned in the Margins, Brent Edwards at Columbia University, Kamau Brathwaite, Ronnie McGrath, Che Lovelace, Sascha Akhtar, Antoine Rajon and Frank Descollonges at Heavenly Sweetness, Paris, all at Naïve.fr, The Spasm Band: Andrew John, Colin Webster, Paul Zimmerman, Paul Brett, Adrian Owusu, Christian Arcucci and Craig Tamlin, to Melanie Abrahams and renaissance one, Orville 'Kungadread' Jay, Roger Robinson, Martin La Borde, Ursula Thomas, Diane Horsham-Joseph and all my family in Trinidad. Special thanks to Chris and Jen at Salt for their vision.

Bird Head Son

... and I look in the rearview and see a man
exactly like me, and the man was weeping
for the houses, the streets, that whole fucking island.
DEREK WALCOTT — The Schooner *Flight*

Bosch's Vision

It started as I was leaving
    with a dim groan in the afternoon.
I saw my grandmother
    embrace me
        in her hand stitched dress
    and wrench my soulcage open.

I saw vistas of apocalyptic Europe,
    heard obscure tongues.
        Till sudden now the sky become
    peppered with woe.
Slack eyed soldiers were howling
    in the wind.
Botched leper experiments
    and gene mutations
    with veins hung
    like vervain from the neck.

The sun long gone and weeping.

    The oil.

    The Devil.

    No doubt it was.
    The Devil.
    Who chased colour from the earth.
        Who left sulphur where he spoke
        like a jitney carburettor.
    No doubt it was.
    The devil.
    Twisted muscle of night.
    Who crackt
    the sky glass lid.

Maman.
Tell me again why I should leave this island.
Tell me again that those cities exist.
                    All I know of the ocean
                        is that a river
                            starts here.

The day I left Mt Lambert
        the wardrobe doors would gleam.
    It was a day like any other.
                Woodslaves ran and woodslaves waited.
                Lovers lay against the Samaan trees.
                Cattle grazed and bachacs burned
                    in matchbox discoteques.

            But we were going to the airport
        and my brother in the backseat
                        is him I ask: *is me*
                        this happening to?

Kite Season

In the dry heat of February
when the trade winds blew dust across Aranguez savannah
   I pulled
a copybook an cocoyea kite
all round that ragged field an river.

But Mitagau boys from up Calvary Hill
had grind glass paste an razor blade
   on they kite tail.
An they one thrill
is to cut down a young boy kite an bawl—

A'IEU   O

what heavenly light shone at that gap in time
   where the thread met the bow met the compass
      and the sun's pure face?

  And when the line rushed through my hands I ran
behind its brief and flickering tail
as the kite sailed over the Samaan trees,
   beyond the blue hills of Lavantille,
      all down Hell Yard and Lacu Harp
        in the jungles of Port of Spain.

Conductors of his Mystery
for Albert Joseph

The day my father came back from the sea
    broke and handsome
I saw him walking across the savannah
    and knew at once   it was him.
His soulful stride, the grace of his hat,
    the serifs of his name
      ~ fluttering ~
        in my mouth.

In his bachelor's room in El Socorro that year
he played his 8-tracks through a sawed-off speaker box.
    The coil would rattle an the cone would hop
but women from the coconut groves
    still came to hear
    his traveller's tales.

 Shop he say he build by Goose Lane junction.
    But it rough from fabricated timber string.
      Picka foot jook wood
    like what Datsun ship in.

And in this snackette he sold   red mango,
    mints and tamarind.
Its wire mesh grill hid his suffer well tough.
    Till the shop bust,
      and he knock out the boards
      and roam east
      to Enterprise village.

Shack he say he build same cross-cut lumber.
    Wood he say he stitch same carap bush.
Roof he say he throw same galvanize. He got
    ambitious with wood
       in his middle ages.

That night I spent there,
    with the cicadas in that clear village sky,
even though each room was still unfinished
    and each sadness hid. I was with
    my father
    and I would've stayed
    if he had asked.

Brown suede,
    8 eye high
    desert boots.   Beige
gabardine bells with the 2 inch folds.
He was myth.   The legend of him.
Once I touched the nape of his boot
    to see if my father was real.
Beyond the brown edges of photographs
    and the songs we sang
        to sing him back
            from the sweep and sea agonies
                of his distance.

Landslide scars. He sent no letters.

His small hands were for the fine work of his carpentry.
    His fingers to trace the pitch pine's grain.
        And the raised rivers of his veins,
            the thick rings of his charisma,
                the scars—the maps of his palms—
        were the sweet conductors
                of his mystery.

    Aiyé Olokun.

He came back smelling of the sea.

Cutlass

When de cutlass flash
  de cutlass can cleanse
can cutlass can clear bush
  can cutlass clenched

  till sparks grew from stars fallin
    scrapin the road
  on jouvay mornin
Or cut can lash
    a man's bare throat
cut from runnin sideways fastest
      from brutal blade work
    It make him run out of his shadow
make him run out of his skin
    make him run out with a tumblin blade
he pulled   sharp across his throat   till it brittle
    an he gullet spew
      to irrigate the village vinery

was the same cutlass that slit the pig throat
              like a razor
          an the body shook
    Hang it up and let it drip its oil and ambergris umber
      let oil run all down this holy tributary
where the corn stalks keep snakes
      and wildflowers
    Let it run all long the bamboo track
      that leads to the Valencia river
where Sister Phyllis is weepin prayers in glossolalia
      and inscribing a vever for Legba

and an old man is cutting sheaves of sage
scythe ways or Sundays
cleaving coconuts with a three-canal blade
And the nut well bleed
and it humble
cutlass when it flash though
an it cut his achilles

The same cutlass swung from my brother's hip
when we went hunting up Kandahar hill
for sacred reeds and flute wood
naked as we born in this blooming heat
up Five Rivers jungle

Was cut that lash the horsewhip snake in two
against the orange tree
make we strip it twist and pour hot oil
in its living wound

O ma Sylvia
your spirit vest still with me it still with me
your trance of sorrow still
dry and heavy

and the crying bird of your throat
is a hummingbird
for you are loa of birds

Once I was cutting feet for wooden men
shaping their bones on the steel
and somehow snapt the blade's hot handle
and saw the grinning edge rise up

and strike you
        central in the temple
O *ma Sylvia*
            with the hilt

        you was washing white sheets
            in the side house sink

Santa Cruz

In Santa Cruz, the bush, the insect nests and growth
on the branches and the calabash root.
The maldjo ash an sap that oozed
        from the plum tree trunk
            so slack and clear.

I climbed the Chenet, the Sapodilla
and the dudus mango tree
            with white lice on its leaves.
Paraplegic fruit ruined to rot in that epic of mandrake
            behind the pig pen
where the bush was serpent fresh
and the earth stayed wet
under riverless bridges and the talcum fog
            of Pipiol village.

Long grass grew in the gardens of Ignacio and tanty Margaret.
While they sat sippin cocoa tea in their tapia bungalow
reaming through rolls of old photographs
for maps of Orinoco.

Attached to South America
            by the fingertips.

His Hands

Ol' Buckmouth swung a black snake.
      He whippeth me from arse to widow's peak.
    His wicked wrist
            hissed so swift
      it sparked gashes
    like tractor wheels
          through the muddy fields
      of my back
      with his whip
      old nigga grip
      wrapt two time
            around his carpenter's fist.

He maketh me to stand in cold showers
      with the first hair of my manhood
            exposed.
He forceth me
      to eat egg an green banana
      in cow heel soup with
            plenty pepper. He
            maketh me to kneel down on a grater
            and count to one hundred
            and twenty   seven

. . . *o father in heaven* . . .

His hands,
which held my breath to ransom
and learnt me how to hide my stutter
were like brutal knots
of burnt Bajan cedar.

But then those hands
could get gentle on my shoulder
at country weddings and funerals,
in Wallerfield, on Christmas eve.

   And I remember
     that the corn they harvested there that year
      was twisted and dry
        like a dead man's hand.

Jungle

I have an antenna in my beard
and a blood duct that keeps secrets
I have a bone flute that whistles
and an arrow headed temper
that can shave the treetops

    . . . in the jungle . . .

There is a baptist hymn I know
that keeps my amulet shone
     and I know
every shiver of wind in the cane
each gust of rain and hurricane
that trips through this land
this land that knows my dark heart
rivers that know my name

    . . . in the jungle . . .

I have been seeking
between the ditay payee
and the fire plant of my dream
for the river I used to steal fishes from
to put in a jar on the window sill
and feed them wheat and honey
till each one died

those silver-bellied slitherings
were the hourglass
    of rhyme

Mr Buller

Mr Buller seep out sudden
    from deep Cantaro bush
        and it was the talk!
    But how Ma Daisa
        in she seventies
could come jus so
        an marry a man like he
    in these late seventies?
An dance castilian
    in Hilton ballroom
        with this frog face man
who smell like black an white lizard shit
    and spootin spit
an come from cocoa country
        in that baggy brown suit
    an he garrulous mousche
an he bandy two knee
    with he hernia heng low.
        Who spoke drunkwise,
            who could transcribe?
No, his whole head shook when he spoke
and words would roll round his jaw and stay loose
    as if booze
        had them bazodee.

But Buller had a stash of Atlantic 45s
in a broko down cabinet bottom
    —was the pure jump
        rhythm an blues!
But he'd cuss if anyone ever touched his Joe Turner
    an he'd lick down for Ruth Brown.
        He'd bark for Fats Domino—
                no no no!

And if you just as touch he Ray Charles
                      or he Earl Bostic slides
        he lock off the draw
        one time.

Bermudez

for Noel Ramirez

The gold ring blinks on the barber's crooked thumb
as he sharpens his razor, with slapping strokes on leather,
strapt from the drawer in which he keeps his fee
and his brushes in his hairy aviary
behind the tyre shop, near Bermudez biscuit factory
with its cinnamon air, where we pull kites across
the old train tracks, and you
singing high in your heaven with each whip of the tail.
It is here, between the river and the sandbox tree
that I see you most, walking
past the black tongued witch's house,
past the stables through the brittle heat of the savannah,
steep from running sideways fastest,
hunting snakes and strange fruit.

El Socorro

Sweetest thing I ever tasted
was pig gut roast where they split it
in the dirt yard muddy with blood and pepper
when they cut it. Flambeau
and ruddy tungsten
—fire—where they lit it,
that Uncle Ben Grenadian cooked it,
on a three stone fire.

Was hog them drag slit screaming to the slaughter slit
—zwill for dey gullet—
And I heard them cry in that muddy hell.
I saw the glint in the shine-eye blade.
I saw the women pull their skirts up
to cross over blood and rum.
And Uncle Ben bring something there
like pig got gizzard, some gut, eat what?
It dip in lime an black with char
an glow like embers in my mouth.

River Breakin Biche

Lef school and went river breakin biche.
I never look up till a sharp stone trouble my skull.

> *Look im dey!*
> *He peltin stone down de river cliff*

Sharkos duck an it miss Newland Blake
but one hit me right in the centre
an bust my head in two.

> *Look 'e dey!*
> *He run up Pamberi panyard*
> *like he have cutlass blade f' teeth.*
> *Pig foot iron ore upright like a khaki tree —*
> *you cyar ketch he!*

Who tell we rub stinging nettle on Peter Aming seeds
   and hide his clothes up a riverbank?
Who tell we rub stinging nettle all in Aming big eye,
   and throw his clothes to the deep?
And left him crying where the river bend
   with hairy rock for seat.

Up in de panyard rubber knockin steel.
      From this steep see the river twist
   out of Santa Cruz valley,
         through Pipiol an Bourg Malatrese
            —Febeau Village. the Croisee . . .

See it run between the bamboo and the San Juan cemetery,
run where my cutlashed kin sip rum in their solemn holes
   and wait for the river to bust
      —is so they wash
            their feet.

The day I fell into the river my khaki get brown
an stick like magnet to my leg.
I had to walk home via black shack alleys
so no one to notice   the colour   was wet.

Punk

I used to have a ponytail
twisted with beeswax to bud until
it curled like a scorpion's tail.
I uses to twist it and tug it to grow it,
but it grew so slow it got shaved.

I used to have a punk
short front and sides,
the back fat—I used to grease it—
with curl activator —to wave it
but it still sprung tough like spring.

One Saturday (cause Saturday was always
the day for cutting hair)
the barber asked me 'How yuh want it?'
and I said 'High top fade'
cause I was almost grown.

But when I got home the old bull flashed
some serious leather in my waist. He said
'What kinda kiss-me-arse cut is this?'
and took me back same time to the barber
to get my head shaved.

The Cinema

Frizzle-neck chickens pick padlocks under the cinema.
Midday Saturday when it hot in the coop
an that chicken shit start to buzz from the chopping board
    when man watchin Chen Sing kick-up.

In the cinema the ground build tilt, the wall shaky-shaky.
Sound bounce round like few hundred radio
               tumblin down.
The film stock zog-up zog-up
       (like chicken did scratch it)
It jagged and it bruise
      when man watchin Shaolin Temple.
And the soundtrack get contaminate
with San Juan taxi horn and bicycle engine,
  the market shout and the dub wax pump,
      the heifers in the abattoir bawlin!
The pie man's slappin palm. Every coconut head that slash,
    each cuss an cut an planass pass
get mix with the Sheng Fan death grip.
But the seat-back break from balcony to pit,
the screen heng like curtain that twist,
    an kick missin instep
    like chicken missin neck.

Bird Head Son

for Kamau Braithwaite

1

At some dusk burning bush
in the back
yard fowl raking in
the dust dirt an soot
Gripe-green guavas and iguanas
lime tree root
bare naked fruit
of Pomme-cythere an Zaboca

The Sikyé fig and the green plantain
The old man in his Wellingtons
with his cutlass stabbin in
the soft dirt beside the dasheen stream
It's blade glint ** sparks **
colonial iron
colonial black
rubber heel

The leaping tongues of flame
that plead with the darkness to wait
Night is a secret a promise to keep
What burns
in the black pepper soot
of leaf and feather
when he fans the flame?

2

An dat guava tree root dat burn too
De same guava tree dat used to bring out she young—hard an green
Then when de rain come it pulp would glow—it sweet get soft
an it stem get slippery to release the yellow beads of its honey

Well all I could do when I see it that year
was to seek it beating heart
where the fire never reach
A never ask why
When you shivering with sickness in your wicked room
an you motorcar park up an you false teeth rot
an dat same jumbie vine dat you tired kill
still reach in
creep in

Even these trees will die
Even the weaves of beetles and red ant gullies
and the underground streams that trickle will not
Even the sweet Julie mango tree is weeping white lice

Between this spirit bush—a see a Iguana—
sat still in the midday sun with it eye up
an it belly puffin tender

As quick as it is not enough to escape
the stick that breaks its back
Till its spasm is dire
And its mouth becomes a poem   with no words

3

Yuh ever wake up one Sunday mornin
an walk round yuh cassava?
Inspect yuh lime tree
for aphid
yuh dasheen
see how dey growin
An you frizzle neck cock
jus kickin dust back an crowin

You ever ask yuhself
what snake is this lord
dat leave this skin?

You ever walk out in dem Indian garden
an see a aeroplane passin
an imagine
is you in it
dat leavin?

When you never even row boat
an you navel string tie up tie up in dis aloes bush
An' all dem crapaud an lizard that making mischief
know your name

And all dem saga boy still grinning coins on Mt Lambert corner
see you when you pass an asking
        "Ai, you is bird head son?
You mus be bird head son f'true
    cause your father head
        did small too"

Backroads Of The Mythic

Folkways

My grandmother called me into the yard. She'd wrapped sacred seals around her head and was standing under the guava tree staring at the sky. Half the canvas had bled black tar with scattered beads of yellow, green and purple globularity. A hideous wound. Well, death groove my brush broom.

At alternate breaths I remembered the small supermarket where I packed brown paper bags. An old woman with bandaged glasses bought two pounds of birdseed, a soprano saxophone and two tins of fried chicken ice cream. Well, death groove my brush broom and I began to paint: Harmolodic portraits in oxide and oils.

Afraid to climb down now between Bermudez biscuit factory and the old rail line is a gutter. A deep stream of silt to hop over. And under : a bulbous snake. The old man was waiting on the other side with a strap soaked in cat piss an pepper and a bible in the other hand. Perched on a lime tree branch like a parrot; he'd done four weddings that day, all down backroads of the mythic.

Sylvia

Birds and their talons
have sea in their sadness
and sky in the roof of their mouths.

And in old Mt Lambert
the rooms are dishevelled
        and silent

        she left

with her hair tied
wearing a dress of orchids,
looking back
from a photograph I took
        on a sepia avenue.

Blues for Cousin Alvin

Many yards had frizzle-neck fowl
and sheep as white as country cotton.
Baby geese in wire pens   on one side
of the road, bungalows.

My Humber cycle was parked one side,
and on the other side/a forest grew—
of giant hog plum trees, papaya fields
all between: the bungalows.

Hillside of Malick village
        and I am leaning
on a pillar post spitting
                    banana seeds
when cousin Alvin come dancing up from the bottom of the
        bush
to say some thief stook from bike to spoke,
        from chain and wheel tout bagai!

So a run down in de neighbour yard
an a grab dey 3canal cutlass.
        Was go a was goin down de gulley
                in dey mudda arse.
    Till Alvin say 'Better jus
                lower dat blade oui,
                    cause dem boys don't play
                    down in the bungalows.'

    O he lived in the holy mud
    where my real folk blues was.
    O he lived in a plywood house
    with paraffin angles and
            sea cockroach
                    runnin bout.

And as we stand there on the jungle wall
we see a ship pull the horizon

————shut————

Sophocles

The pieta I saw
was where the rain
burst through
a hole in the wall
and my grandfather and four strong men
their black skin splashed
by the water rushing
pressed hard against
the hinge of its gush
and tried to stress it shut
But the water rushed
too strong and they cried
louder
than the storm itself
with the ruthless rain against them
and the glimpse I stole
stayed permanent
like a painting

Barrel

To escape
  she jumpt from a house on stilts
  in to a barrel half filled with water.
  It is as dark then, as she told it—
      hot fear
and then the moment of leaping
and the camera eye that follows
      under
    water in to
the place she leapt to like
     behind her
wooden house. Where the barrel so near
that sharp
  galvanise.

Street side and my position against the angle of a pillar for invisibility.

So high is the wooden veranda she leapt from.

Yet when the old man appears at the banister with his cut-arse hand
     she is there
   telling him where to find me.
If he comes down with black boots—
instead of running I will brace.
But when he comes down in his grey suit he grins like an anchor
and goes walking round the pillar posts
  with his hands shut behind him
 to peer
   in to
the barrel
she leapt

in.

Detritus

Waylaid on this coast
seeking the crayfish from the fisherman's rope.
        I came down to earth
to find trains along the perimeters of your world
and blood among the vapours of your engines.
To arrive at this harbour town
with the cold colonial cobbles,
to ask in shops and snackettes
        for Gillian Street
where you lived with the fishes,
lost in this forgotten place where I can never find you.
But I do see the fishermen bathing naked
under standpipes in the fisheries.
And the Buddha statues
playing peek-a-boo
        between the trees.

The Cat

The cat was a seed encased in a walnut shell.
I dropt it on the pine
   and it crackt like
     beak an egg.

When I saw the emblems of its stress,
I pampered and patcht its broken heart
till the window shone more tender
and cast our shadows to the floor.

I drove north that evening.
Came back on the train like coming back
from New York City.
Insistent I could not leave my engine there
till I saw the bleeding shack
torn up like my mother's breast,
hung up from vines and ligaments.

Its palimpsest revealed a purity of grief.
And I wept
in the wet shed
   with the ducklings.

a dream
of spiders
on the guava tree

one sprung
from a leaf of
fear
to the
ledge where
my grandfather kept
a dusty vial
of lamp oil
with an erudite cork
that sealed
its secret
scent

here the spider leapt
to its hole
in that verge
be/ween
the rim and recesses
of wood along
the edge
out from this
orient world

Blockorama

for Ronnie McGrath

stand leaning dusk
    in bland synthetic night
        pot hounds
        chicken hawks
        red dirt dregs and drains
        with my head hung
        in paraffin yards   tack mud
        gravel pits and dog shit alleys
        between wood shacks for road

I saw her from across the street I saw her in cadmium red
I followed her to the junction
with my hard jazz finger

She stepped out
    —2 seater sports
        her afro took the whole top curve
        to stride—flail of colours—
        to a man stood in a doorway
        stroking his hick an oily beard/red
        green gold dashiki
        pitch oil light
        lamp the hill tracks coming down
        and a crowd start to build and guggle
        in the basketball fields down Goose Lane
        El Socorro
        to rock to real dubroot rockers like
        Louie Lepki and BB Seaton

Roam strolling slick
    in foreign suede
        through rhyming island country
        Through vines of poor folk roads
        rustic in the marigold

My boots are hollow
Her shoes are tallow soled

Seahound of an orchid
    a trumpet
        a mouth like the blues
        and mellow greens of Sunday morning
   evangelical
        soft leatherette
        brass goblets of salvation   Water
        where gusts overtook these humble
chambers
        and how a simple glance of light
        could bruise the island's southern road
        She did always sing
        seen her before
           sing across the black ravine

The Bamboo Saxophone

Bell

This spark arcs a sediment,
   describes a fluent form.
          (her halo broke)
          (her engine froze)
I ply
   shutters loose, make my fist my horn.
     Blow // till my spitty sound rose and tumbled
and my sleeping eye flickered
   in the hologram—dream/
     I blinked to change the scene.
          (Her fever rolled)
          (Her slack wound sewn)

Reed

Once from the spacecraft where we slept on,
   broken bare by our journey,
     and the old wooden engine
went grinding through island countryside.
And I walked behind my father, watching
         the scope of his back.
   In a rigid hand   he holds
   an ox horn trombone.

BARREL

My brother and I, we in jungle now.
We roam through country for sacred bamboo
  —thick/tapered,
brown and wet, the bell end was full up
  with buds of fungus and ringworm.

The other end to blow
  was a soft seam of black crapaud truffle.
I took a stick and said 'Back off this!'
    and lumps of old tar balm and gutty oil,
      bits of wood liver—a little blood came out—
    when I poke it under.
      All these things kept the sound hid,
        sealed
        and holy.

The wind gauge made true scale
  but I preferred a reed,
    a fipple reed, a reed that would rattle and so
      we kept on.

The Duck Coop

A grass grew in the savannah that grew taller at first, the next
taller still. Until it was over seven feet
and covered the entire field
with uncanny lush.
.poison.

That duck coop my grandfather built. The same one I got
bat with white pine to scrub. Same one
I looked around and said
    'Poopa, y'know I could put down
    a nice lil' bachelor pad here,
    put up curtains, terrazzo floor, eh?'

The old man just stood there on the moaning ground
with his truncheon boots and his toothpick scowling,
suffocating love and steady dying.

River Of Masks

The Myst

My brother become the Myst that night. He put his boots on.

He fixed his mask. He slid a brittle edged Gilpin cutlass into the
sheath he pulled from his belt. Nanobyte salt kept the edge well
grim and his under arm grip hid his cow-itch pouch as he ran
through the bush upper Kandahar hill.

He had been planning this arrival since May. And now his bulk
was proper, his gullet root tough. For months I watched, when he
let me, and when he didn't, see me peep, as he assembled his
implements. For the suit, he dyed and synthesized tarpaulin; pure
black with sandbox root. His gloves he proofed with Banga seed
heart, his jackboot steel he sanded off sheen. Bois canon bush did
his dada head: dread. The mask made last with perforated pigskin
leather waxed and moulded on his sleeping head with shallow
holes for hooks and eyes.

I saw him churn old iron on the riverbank. Saw when he swam
under floodgate with a single column of breath, and came back
hours later with handfuls of armoured cascadura, whose scales
he sharpened to blades. He sharpened his toes. With calabash
milk he poisoned the tips.

He drunk duck egg, nog and cowheel porridge, till the muscle
to leap in his legs grew across the width of one of five rivers. His
cryptic grip was wire bent, his speed through jungle elastic. His
cutlass slap would spin heads around, his battle stance was brute
and bad-minded.

Sudden so the sky get dim and snarling when he put his mask on,
and he mount the steep incline
    like a lizard.

The Carnival Suite

1

Snow drives down from the north.
The raindrops before the snow fell
seemed to fall slower
to the ground.
Then a woman in the bakery said
                    'Is that snowing?'
But not yet.
It is Ash Wednesday so I know
                the carnival is over.

2

round de savannah on carnival tuesday
        first go by Garib mas camp
                where dem rich gyal does stay
an bass does rattle all yuh rib an teeth
                    an we sippin
                somethin cold
watchin the DJ slap slide down
        he up in the veranda grinnin
        crab ways sideways when jus so he drop some vincy
            riddum
an people start bawl an dey waist rip roll
        but dat young gyal in she tight-tight jeans
                the one who feel she hoity-toity
        with she barbecue wings and she Carib shandy
        who does dance like she wearing high heel
                we does see she an she sister all bout town
                    like freshwater yankee
                    leave she dey man
        doh even try—unless you name is Jamada
                        you
                        cyar

```
                jam
                dat!
        dem so does only want man with motorcar
            to wine on dey bumsee


                lord a wonder where las-lap go ketch we tonight
        if las lap ketch we here by Cipriani Boulevard
            with all dem ma commère man
            we eh go feel free
            is real jam we need
            leh we go by green corner
                    where dem real yard fowl does be
            leh we go
                up in de harp a de congo
                where Scipio an Gunta does be
            leh we go round by south quay
                    down Mucurapo Road
                    round Roxy roundabout
                    where dem long time jammete does be.
```

3

Beat my brother with a guava wood cane.
Beat him but he will not speak.
Is like
he not
glad to
see me
till I catch rage
and cuss from both sides of my mouth
and hurl tight fists an fingernail his face.
Beat my brother with a guava wood cane.
Cause all he brings are dry words
that quiver to dust

in the chaos parade
of masqueraders
passing us by.

Salt in my eyes.

He does not soothe my love.
His will not meet my gaze.
Beat my brother with a cocoa tree branch.
But when we embrace
     O Den-Den, my nigger
          my brother,
          my blood

:: Night is shaking
feathers shut
behind us ::

4

Jourvert mornin mud mas
in the jungles of Port of Spain
and my brother sips sugarcane brandy
on the East Dry River bridge.
Then we roam a thicket of brimful streets
     through town
in search of
     Saturnalian ointment.

Let us travel dangerous routes
where cut-eyed boys are waiting
to feed us puncheon rum
an learn us how to spit between thick thighs.
Let us follow this spirit procession

past the jetty where fish gut and shrimp stalk
wash up and stinking
in a stagnant black moss
where sequined spears are floating.

Masks

I blew my flute by the river,
    I blew it river side.
I blew blues while he read his poems.
    Wait. I said.
Let me blow this bamboo vine
               hissing in the rivertime
    with the krik krik krak of dusk
       —now—
read my brother, read.

By the time we got to Caura Village
the sun was fading
    the water was cold,
and the ragged eyelets of the mask he wore
       were frowning.
But when he lay   down on that stone
    that splits the river in two
    —river running under—
and the resonance of wood.
I saw my brother close his eyes,
and bare the soft trumpet bone
    of his throat.

Carenage

Just a glimpse
                    of sky

    driving along the coast
        to Carenage.

The surf blinkt between fisherman huts.
        crooked wood. the land tilt
from the steady tug
        of sea beneath.

Magga dog run undulating yards.

        —blue—
        —the blue salt of sky and St Peters fish
            rockin' in the splash.
The nets they've hung
        from palm to sapodilla
are curtains that sway to reveal
            the blushing gust
                    of the sea.

The wet salted scent
    of my brother's back
        at Carenage with its pebble bay.
    Just a poor man's beach that take bus to reach.
  No deep breath
            over lush valleys.
    No grinning bliss of sand.
    No lookout over fables of cocoa.
    No shark an bake shop. No palms.

Bus ride through the fisheries—
              fruit shack an pavement.
Bus ride over precipice—
              rock stone girdle brace.
Bus ride past the bauxite factory—
        army treasury,
              Hart's Cut Bay.

And tonight I call my brother
     from a room of sighs
still missing the sea

          .infinitely

Bougainvillea

We spew ourselves up, but already underneath
laughter can be heard.
— FRANZ FANON, *The Wretched of the Earth*

The road make to walk
on carnival day
— LORD KITCHENER

Bougainvillea: Super 8 Red

KING CARNIVAL
YUH HEADPIECE SO HEAVY
SO SLOW TO WALK
WITH THIS
COSTUME BEHIND
AS IF IT BUILT WITH
YOU IN IT

MIDDAY NEAR MEMORIAL PARK
IN SUCH MERCYLESS HEAT
AND THESE BLUE HILLS
THAT RIM THE CITY
TRUCK BORNE
SOUND
OF ICARIAN TRUMPETS
A REAM OF HORNS
A RHYTHM SECTION
BEATS IRON INTO
SOUND

OX BLOOD AND FIREBRICK

RED

SUCH BLOOD   BEADS OF SERPENT
PURPLE
BEADS AND BELLS AND TEETH
THAT SHIMMER BLAZE
DOWN
FREDERICK
STREET
THRONGS AS THICK AS
WET GRAVEL

SUPER 8 RED

AND BURNT CLAY
BEARDS
   DIFFUSED AND REFRACTED
      INTO LIME GREEN
                        LAMÈ   LUMINOUS
            EYELETS IN
               MAD BULL
   MASKS
               CADMIUM RED OR
         LILAC PALMS
      A SCEPTRE HE HOLDS
         NEMO
      SHONE BLACK AGAINST THIS
         GLITTER
   DIAMANTE AND FRIVOLOUS
      FEATHERS
         GLIMMER
ON HIS FACE
                  WET AND
SUPPLE IS HIS IDIOM
               SWEAT
AND ENDLESS TECHNICOLOR PRAYERS
   O MOTHER OF PEARL WITH
   SCENT OF FRESH PAINT WIRE BENT

WHICH EMBLEMS ARE THESE
            RIVER GODS WITH
SUCH RAMPANT PLUMAGES
      STARTLING IN
THE FIRESKY

THE MOKO JUMBIE
   12 FOOT UP
            STILTS OF WOOD
   PAINTED WHITE/WHITE

PAINTED WOOD
            SLACK
BRUISED WHIP OF HIPS THAT
KEEP TIME
ALL THESE
            COLOURS
            THAT DRIP FROM HIS FACE
            HIS APPOLLIC BUST
                        MONOXYLOUS
      TO REPRESENT WATER
                  OBATALA OR SPIRITUAL
                  BAPTIST

                  THE MUD BAND STRETCHED THERE
      FROM G TO B FLAT
      ON KEATE STREET
OUTSIDE DELUXE CINEMA
            WAITING
FOR CHARLIE'S ROOTS
            TO PASS
            SO MUCH TAR GET JAM
      ON THAT BARBERGREEN
            SO MUCH BLOOD SPUME
                  FROM THEM STEEL WHEEL
      OF STEEL   BAND   PUSHING
      DOWN FROM HILLTOP
                  ROLLING BASS DRUM
                        ACROSS THE DUST AND BIG YARD
      STAGE

      WE USES TO RUN
FROM OIL AND TAR BAND
      LONG TIME
                  BURROKEETS
            AN DEM JAB MOLLASIE

```
            DEVIL MAS
FROM CASABLANCA BADJOHN
       AND HELL'S YARD CATELLI ALL-STARS PAN MAN
FROM DR RAT AND RENEGADES
       AND ALL THESE WARS
       THAT MUSIC MAKE
WHEN TWO BAND CLASH
THROUGH ALL THESE WARS
       WE CARRIED
OUR MOTHERS BASKET
       PLAITED WITH ITALICISED STRAW
               FOR HER RUGGED HARVEST
       OF RED KOOLAID
AND BAKED CHICKEN
       THIGHS
               ELEGIAC
       PRESSED AGAINST
    POEMS IN THIS NERVOUS
           CENTER
       PULLED        SHE
          OUR SMALL HANDS
       AND SPLINTERS
           WHERE THE WEIGHT
       CUT
           HER SHOULDER
               TO FRAGMENTS
WHEN A BOTTLE SMASH
           AND THE BAND GET SLACK
AN SCATTER
          OUR LAUGHTER SWUNG
 FROM DEEP MAGENTA HAZE
              SOME WOUND THERE
      HER BREAST STILL
                     SORE STILL
```

THESE WIRES
    BENT INTO PURPLE TIARAS
AND GUINEA FISHERMAN POLES
    FLAGS AND THEIR EMBLEMS
        WHICH SHOOK ROME
OF ITS SILVER
    WITH DREAD
        BEARDS OF MUD
FROM CREATION
        AND DISSONANCE OF
            MUD
BLACK BENIN TOPSOIL
OF EARTH
        MOIST WORD
    OF THE GRIOT
COME HIS COME
CHANTING
    FROM SOME HOUSE OF DIN
            WE ABSAILED FROM
TO FIND HIM
    IN A DUSTY FIELD
        STUTTERING
            IN RAY MINOR

        — SANS HUMANITÈ —

        CHARLOTTE STREET AND DUKE STREET
    CORNER
SIMPLE SO WE SUCK SUGARCANE
        WATCHING MAS
BUT ALL THIS TEMPORAL TILL
    WEDNESDAYS ASH
        WE THERE
    SATYR TAILED
AT GREEN CORNER

WE WAS
BULLET HOT BY ROXY ROUNDABOUT
WE WAS
CHIPPIN FOOT AN SHUFFLIN
        LIKE PARADIDDLE
RIMSHOT
        LIKE GALVANIZE
                FROM HURRICANE
WE THERE
AT GREEN CORNER
        WHEN MACHETE PELT
                AND THE ROAD GET RED
        FROM ALL THAT
SUPER 8
        SATURATES

        AT ARIAPITA AVENUE
 ADAM SMITH SQUARE
QUEENS PARK WEST AND CIPRIANI BOULEVARD
        WHERE THE ASPHALT BLINKS
        WITH DECALS STREWN FROM
SEQUINED QUEENS
        PIXELATED IN
                THE ST ANNS AIR
UNDER THE
        ALMOND TREES
AT MEMORIAL SQUARE
        WE WERE
                FLESH IN THE SWELTER OF
                        TROPIC FRUIT
                SOAKED
                        BRINEWAYS
                FIRE
                        AND THE LASH OF IT

WAS A HUMMINGBIRD
COAST WE SAILED TO
A MASKED BALL
WE INHERITED
MASKS WE STOLE
MANSIONS WE OVERTURNED IN

SO SHALLOW IS THIS
MEMORY THAT IT PIERCED ME LIKE
CHIRICAHUAN ARROWHEAD
CEREOUS
DROWNED IT IN DOUBLE
BEATEN GOATSKIN DRUMS
FROM GUST AND PLYWOOD
JUNCTIONS
WHERE BLISS THROAT SPARKLES
THERE
EVEN
LIKE SEA SILT AND
JETTY FISH
NEAR PORT AUTHORITY WHERE
CRUSIE SHIPS LANDED LIKE
SPACESHIPS TO THIS
DREAMSCAPE

CONTEMPLATING
THE ROAD

OUR
VERGE OF MEMORY
SPLIT LIKE CANE WITH
CANBOULAY FIRE
WITH GILPIN
TO PLANASS // LEFT MARKS FROM
FLAT SIDE OF THE BLADE

AND MY GRANDMOTHER
        SAID HOW STEELBANDS
            USED TO CLASH
                THERE
IN THAT SACRED PLACE
NEAR BELMONT VALLEY ROAD
        SO DARK WOULD NEVER
            CATCH HER
                IN PORT OF SPAIN

        WE SAW THE WEBBED WINGS OF THE CARNIVAL QUEEN
                ISIS FLUTTERING
            IN HER SECOND SKIN
                PEEP
HER HALO
        AND THE UNDERLUNGS
            OF HER SADNESS
AND THE SEQUINED SPICE OF HER
        PERSPIRING
CAPTURED BY BLUE BOX FLASH TUBE
        TELEFUSION AND DIFFUSE RELAY
            THESE IMAGES
        THE CLACK CALACKA CLACK OF
                THE MIDNIGHT ROBBERS
            COLLECTION BOX
                    AND HIS TALL BLACK
        OVERCOAT WITH STARS AND
            SKULLS AND SMOKE
        BLACK/SKIN
                    GLISTENING WHITE
                        WITH PAINT
AND DEEP SIGNAL
        RED
                FRESH PAINT SCENT
SENT ALONG THE AVENUES

    [62]

WAS WHEN WE KNEW
CARNIVAL WAS COMING
SO POLAROID ON THIS HOT ROAD
WITH TALL
STEMS OF THE JUMBIE
RODE STILTS TO
CROSS   BACK
OVER   OCEANS
AND OVER FROM
SHACK TO STAGE
PERCHED ON
BARBED WIRE
— SPEW AND REVOLUTION —
AND THE COSQUELLE AND
THE DAME LORRAINE
LIFTING HER DRESS
WAS SATURNALIA

WE   CARRIED HIM
THE KING
COLLAPSED UPON
OUR SHOULDERS
HE WORE WINGS
BENT FROM MONGOOSE BONE
HEADPIECE OF GOLD
RADIATING
FROM PERSIAN GOLDMINES
ROAD MAKE TO WALK
SO WE CARRIED HIM
TOWARDS ST JAMES
IN THIS BLUE DEVIL LEAP
NOTHING
IS SACRED
EXCEPT HIS TUNIC OF ABSTRACT
SILK AND MOLLUSC

— MUSCLE IN THE AIR —
TO ABASIA
WAS MILES
WE WALKED
WITHOUT KNOWING
AND EACH STREET THE NEXT
TO SATURATE
THE BLISS OF IT
OPAQUE STEEP
WITH BOUGAINVILLEA
& SUPER 8
RED

The Tropic Of Cancer

The Regal

At Regal cinema by the San Juan abattoir we meet.
In the market square with the pale scent
of cow foot fish and rotting fruit
and the slippery alley black with such blood.
Backroads of the red dusk, terracotta
in its high grim cruciform of tropic Alamo.
And the looming precipice of its heathen spire
smoked with subtitled Corbuccis.
No reels rattled here since my mother used to steal away
to watch westerns on its drapery,
years before this copper sun we meet
when she brings me her sad secret.
How she felt the earth shiver in her bosom,
left side of her breast like an arrow.

The Tropic Of Cancer

Glimpses of her
in insufferable light
from the pitch pine root
of a wooden room
beneath
the tropic of cancer

Up past the bedsprings and coconut coir
and see her walking
past a window
where curtains bloom
in the paraffin night

Glimpses of her
tearing polyps from her heart
by the burnt cedar saw mill on Jogie Road
with the red dust grain
at dusk—her face
pressed against a gate
that would not swing

In Ramkisson Trace with the muddy drains
I saw her once
burn a thorn from her heel
with a candle's blade. In those days.
In those days my mother lived
in a two room apartment beside a mountain
with water-soaked wood stuck in the mountainside
Where she washed her pans and feet
was ochre brown
where the ground
was slippery

At Caura River I see her burn
sugar in a black iron pot

bamboo jungle an creek
   where the river was dark
        beneath
    the tropic of cancer

Yet later I remember her more clearly
detained in airport mystery rooms
   with her bag and soft possessions
      Or among the yellow narcissi
         in Hornsey Rise that winter
       with her lump in tea-cup waiting
     and her wig and beads
   in a hell of hot tears

A Widow's Lament In Guava Season

after William Carlos Williams
for Ursula and Mario Thomas in Malick

Sorrow is her dirt yard,
between the lime bush
and the tamarind,
where vervain creeps beneath
the latrine he left unfinished.
Thirty-five years
she lived with her husband.
Now the ripe mangoes just roll
downhill.
And the orange tree
sighs
as it sings in the sunlight,
its plaintive song of fruit.
And the sugar apple:
force ripe and some green.
But the suffer the love
in her heart blooms wild
like the jungle flowers near her bed.
And this morning as she waters them
she does not sing her morning song.
Today her son tells her,
'Mammy dem pumpkin
in de gully dat daddy did plant
like dey ready to cut', He say,
'The pawpaw like it ripe too.'
And that night as she counts the fireflies
she wonders,
if the river keeps secrets,
will it hide her in its cool beneath?

Hideous Corpus Madre

She picks dry weed off the dead dog's eye
then goes to the dark room of her disease.
In the hospital her big head rolls
and then on the main road
      near the bakery
   she is run down by a ghost boat
and left to pulp on the hot pitch.

What's left
    is all that remains
and I have to brace (of) against a wall
        (her) and wait.
     She may (still) be alive within this
hideous corpus madre.

Look, closer to the risen parts of her
   where the tyre threaded deep and left segments
      of a hip contour,
   a rizzle of skin.   Look closer
for beads of breath
  but none.

And my whole body fills with water
   as her ruined corpse
     is driven away.

Epilogue

*. . . returning home
with the blistering salt of longing
on his lips*
LEROY CLARKE, *Cry*

The Barber

I watched the barber shave a labourer's head
whose Wellingtons were rolled
and his denim whip from bush. A real country man
from La Canoa, with large hands and muddy fingers
and a pointed tonsure ribbed with veins.

I saw the wishbone V of his chin
when he stretched
to let the barber carve his beard
from bone and flesh
with razors and a silverfish.

Was the same barber from Cantaro Village
him self six years since
another man touch my head.
He say 'You eh go get bumps de way I does do it.'
And he shave my skull with a razor blade.
 'This will sting lil bit
        but is to make you know
                you come back home'
An he spray a young boy head
        with spirits.

Jack Spaniard nest
                wrap up under galvanise
                                Cross cut teak appropriate
                to this weather
A horner man beeps—fish man—fish hand
                                with scales
plastic flowers and the pink thick drapes

All these hills are home. All these cliffs and holy
                mountainsides.
Holding on to my people and my people holding onto me and
sudden so the rain came brewing down hard on the hills of mists
of ghosts across the hillsides coming down on these shacks on
these hills my mother suffered in hills of ghosts across the mists
of hillsides coming down and the ocean calling me : away from
the rayo valleys
                and the all night gospel radio

My sister with the sling of love
My sister with banana bread
My sister with the ketch-ass-shack
what breaking down
My sister with the horner man
My sister with the kente cloth
My sister with the tenure track
My sister with the muddy gust of tears

And our mother
        who art in heaven
with the acolytes and wooden crosses
                coming up Jitman Drive
                        in the stinginstinging rain

for Amryl, Avion, Makedia and Martina

Crown Point, Tobago

From the airport to Store Bay
where we swam our last swim
in the blue tides of the Caribbean.
A dip in this nylon pool
so shallow and soft enough to drown in
    yet deep enough to float.

Each footstep notated, each glimpse
recaptured: pirogues and the spray,
green hills in peaks and spurs,
and the sun flash breaking
through the knots of our hair
    to the white coral of our brain.

The steel pan man with his tenor pan
set up under the trinket stand.
He playing pan when the rain start
to bust down like bucket,
sweeping through us, rocking us
    in its slant an slash.

From the ocean to the airport
where we was crossing
when a car pass an—splash—
feathers an a bird falls to the asphalt
as if it been dead since morning
    an only now decide to fall from the sky
    and give up its wings to the earth.

There was a dread mixing mortar in the next yard
who come an calm he hold the bird in his palm
like feathered fruit.
An how he throw the bird on a battle of bush
for its slumber safe from a second death
of crush and gore
on this radical road.

Blues for Brother Curtis

When I see Curtis last August
that yellowbone day after the rain in Five Rivers,
leaning against his blue bottom door
an he show me he sore foot how it ban' up.
An he say how it pain him like hell, an he creak the hinge
so ah peep how the bandage was leaking.
An how foot fly does zoot there so
in his earthen room—linoleum and smoke—
I never did know—that 2 month later I be getting this
        message
            in winter
When breeze have teeth.
An it choke me right here so an a couldn't even bring
one word to speak.

In New Street, Tunapuna, by the ravine
Curtis say 'Fellas, leh we go an get some dead'
Them days 'dead' was in chicken fried
an we walk all up Indian farmland.
But was take Curtis take we to some backyard slaughtery
to buy up a few bag a frozen fowl.
An he laugh like echo chamber.

Wood lice was rot from his room that August day.
An burnt milk was blowing from his pitch oil stove.
An I wondered then, 'But you foot mister man,
        like it weeping black rain?' An when sorefoot bleedin so
        it doh heal.

And when I get the news I put on my winter coat
        and went out into the night   to teach.

Sewe Wangala: A Kalinda

Robber man don't get me
   don't blow me down
         town
         down shantytown
         ravine
whe' they beat silver fish an wabeen
   on the riverbank.

We come like ripe guava
when it season
full it ripe
an sling shot it drop like a 12 gauge shot
that shatter the wings of our mountain gods.

The young blood seep up on the sea an float foam
   from brain coral.
He reel so reel that the paddle broke
   and he tumble down
      cliff an stony crocus bound
   with the snakeskin mask an the kidnap bush
hid in Orinoco navel string.

Robber man.
   Don't lock my neck round Piarco Airport roundabout.
   Don't make mud clog the tracks I cross riverbank.
   Don't sell my eyes for sand puppet teeth.
   Don't seed my seppy for ransom.
   Don't brug my neck with fisherman's twine.
   Don't scope my ruse with jumbie symposium.
   Don't grief my root with rumours of wounds.

hide
the
magic
for
me

comecomecome
leh we pounce on wild Quenk an Agouti,
make we shuffle in the jungles
of Port of Spain.
Leh we roast corn,
roast breadfruit.
Leh we lime
like we used to,
leh we
love.

Who passed on Haymarket, winter night?

Who passed on Haymarket, winter night?
With the bush bug scent that sent me back
to nights in the Lopinot valley?
To the hoot of flying frogs
        on the muddy leaf
—two lungs deep.
To the blue black stains on the cockroach back.
In hurricane light.
To an old woman sewing her slipper—no
        —she swings it—
till rubber splats the gland across the wall.

She also roasts
        scorpions
—that burning insect bone—
with poison rolling round its cryptic spine.
(limb by limb is antidote
        against its sting)

Who passed bearing these tones?
        Haymarket, January.